*Women, Men, and the*
*International Division of Labor*

The SUNY Series in the Anthropology of Work
JUNE NASH, EDITOR

*Edited by* JUNE NASH *and*
MARÍA PATRICIA FERNÁNDEZ-KELLY

# Women, Men, and the International Division of Labor

*State University of New York Press*

*ALBANY*

Published by
State University of New York Press, Albany

© 1983 State University of New York

For information, address State University of New York
Press, State University Plaza, Albany, N.Y., 12246


**Library of Congress Cataloging in Publication Data**
Main entry under title:

Women, men, and the international division of labor.

(The SUNY series in the anthropology of work)
Includes bibliographies and index.
1. Foreign trade and employment—Addresses, essays, lectures. 2. Women—Employment—Addresses, essays, lectures. 3. International division of labor—Addresses, essays, lectures. 4. Labor and laboring classes—Addresses, essays, lectures. I. Nash, June C., 1927- . II. Fernandez-Kelly, María Patricia, 1948- . III. Series.
HD5710.7.W65 1983 306'.36 82-10447
ISBN 0-87395-683-4
ISBN 0-87395-684-2 (pbk.)

# Contents

CONTENTS

# Introduction

Social scientists have abundantly documented inequalities in the exchange of goods and services in the world market with respect to national, regional, and urban-rural differences. This collection of papers focuses on inequalities among different sectors of the labor force, particularly those related to gender, and how these are affected by the changing international division of labor.

The last three decades have witnessed the growing integration of the world system of production on the basis of a new relationship between less developed and highly industrialized countries. In the first two decades, the core industrial countries maintained priority in their position as a source of technological expertise, design, and financial outflows, with the periphery and semiperiphery emerging as the locus for specialized assembly operations. Aided by the consolidation of the multinational corporation since the end of World War II and by the accentuated fluidity of capital investments, this new global division of labor is upsetting previous conceptualizations of politics and economics as core and periphery. Decaying industrial cities of the United States and Europe have in the last decade become characterized by breakdowns of municipal services, marginalization of large segments of the work force, and the atrophy of democratic operations of trade unions and community interest groups. The workforce of these increasingly marginalized "core" economies is shouldering a growing tax burden to support the military hegemony of multinationals that no longer have a base in any nation.

What are some of the distinctive features in this innovative international mosaic?

JUNE NASH

First, the mode of integration of underdeveloped countries into the international economy has shifted from a base relying exclusively on the exploitation of primary resources and labor to one in which manufactures have gained preponderance. This movement has paralleled the proliferation of export-processing zones (EPZs) throughout the world. More than a uniformly defined or geographically delimited concept, the export-processing zone provides a series of incentives and loosened restrictions for multinational corporations by developing countries in their effort to attract foreign investment in export-oriented manufacturing. This has given rise to new ideas about development which often question preexisting notions of national sovereignty.

According to the United Nations Industrial Development Organization, there are at present almost 120 export-processing zones in areas as far distant from one another as the Orient, Latin America, Africa, Western Europe, and the United States. Almost two million people are currently employed in EPZs throughout the world and many more are directly or indirectly affected by their existence. In Asia alone more than three hundred thousand women labor in electronics plants located in EPZs.

While the importance of export-processing zones is still reduced in the international context, they are important for what they suggest will become the norm in the organization of production. Most recently mainland China opened selected areas along its southern coast to foreign investment. Unprecedented privileges have been granted in these "special zones." Thus far Shenzhen, a location adjacent to overcrowded Hong Kong, has attracted one billion dollars in eight hundred separate transactions involving small processing assembly operations owned by Hong Kong-based and other overseas Chinese. This demonstrates the significance of broad economic trends beyond narrow political, ideological, or geographical distinctions.

Second, export-processing zones have flourished, given the capacity of industry to transfer centers of production from core countries to low wage areas. The geographical dispersion of productive stages as part of a wholly integrated manufacturing process has been made possible, in many cases, by the reduction of operations to minute, repetitive, and monotonous manual tasks. By virtue of this fragmentation, training periods for workers have also been curtailed, affording maximum flexibility to industry but increasingly denying workers control over their labor.

Third, footloose industries or runaway shops (as the subsidiaries and subcontracted firms of large multinationals are often labeled) are intimately related to changes occurring in advanced industrial countries. Therefore, the phenomena that this collection of essays discusses have consequences at both ends of the geopolitical spectrum (Katz, this volume).

Recently government officials as well as the media have begun to give attention to what amounts to a veritable epidemic of industrial plant closings in the United States. Several bills pending in Congress, whose purpose is to enact sanctions against firms discontinuing operations in this country, attest to growing concern over the trend towards "deindustrialization." Some economists have advanced figures that give just cause for alarm. For example, Barry Bluestone and Bennett Harrison estimate in their article, "Economic Development, the public sector, and full employment," (in Marcus G. Rashin's anthology *The Federal Budget and Social Reconstruction*, New Brunswick: Transition Books) that there has been a loss of approximately fifteen million jobs between 1968 and 1976 in the United States as a result of plant closures.

Although many of these jobs have simply been eliminated as a result of changes inherent in new productive processes, others have reemerged transformed or intact in the export-processing zones of the Third World. Thus, while there is a decline in blue-collar employment in this country, a new industrial work force is emerging in less developed areas. Paralleling this is the flow of labor from the Third World countries to the declining industrial centers. There they are employed in service jobs or assembly work in electronics and garment industries that occupy vacated factories for brief intervals until the incentives that communities, desperate for employment opportunities, hold out to lure new industries are expended or until federal investigators discover the evasion of taxes or minimal wage laws.

Fourth, the increased fluidity of international investments and the growing mobility of industry portend major political dilemmas in both core and periphery. Corporate representatives view "sourcing" (i.e., the possibility of transferring abroad phases of production that require labor-intensive operations) as an attractive alternative that results in "risk diversification." Indeed, the advantages afforded by large international wage differentials are as important, from the point of view of industry, as the capacity to achieve increased control over workers and to counter demands for higher wages and so-called fringe benefits.

Therefore, with the integration of production on a global scale, manufacturers seek those countries that will guarantee the lowest labor costs and taxes and the fewest restrictions on production. In the move to underdeveloped areas, they leave behind decaying industrial centers no longer able to compete. The wages and benefits won over decades of labor struggle are undermined in the old regions while militarization, which often accompanies industrialization abroad, prevents the mobilization of collective action to win gains on the frontier. The case of Korea and that of the Philippines, described by Cynthia Enloe in this volume, vividly demonstrate the truncation of a development process that would integrate workers in an expanding economy. The redistribution of some profits through government or union action is nullified in both center and periphery.

The fluidity of international capital investments makes it difficult for workers to bring employers to the bargaining table. In the past an employer was a physical being, often part of the same community where workers lived and exposed to a common social and economic fate. At present workers confront an impersonal and faceless corporate hierarchy in headquarters far from the production sites. In the worst of circumstances, people of different nationalities, but hired by a corporation to participate in a similar productive process, appear to be thrust in disloyal competition against one another for low-paying, often hazardous jobs.

Paradoxically, the conditions now exist for the growth of a nascent international work force with a shared position in the world system of production. Yet, the impediments for vindicative action loom large. What may, from the point of view of industry, represent risk diversification may translate, for workers, into political and economic "risk maximization."

Finally, the role of gender in the configuration of this new international arrangement should not be underestimated. The vanguard of industrial investment in the world capitalist system is in the lowest paid segment of those countries paying the lowest wages. Young women in developing countries are the labor force on this frontier just as women and children were in the industrialization of England and Europe in the nineteenth century.

Escaping the patriarchal restrictions of domestic production, young women workers are segregated in the new industrial compounds where they are subject to the patriarchal control of managers (Lim, this volume). But with the loss of domestic production, women have not gained a secure position in industry. The empirical findings in this volume suggest that footloose industries do not generate long lasting employment. Superannuated at twenty-five, women have few options, even when the factories remain. The destruction of subsistence economies, which often follows the inception of new forms of industrialization, eliminates the basis for alternative strategies and increases dependency on factory work (Abraham-Van der Mark, this volume).

The emerging contradictions in the new international division of labor are the subject of contributions to this anthology. They show that the global integration of production has sharpened inequalities between women and men, minorities and dominant racial and ethnic groups. Geographical imbalances have also grown as in the case of the Sunbelt vis-à-vis the Northeast in the United States and of rural versus urban sectors in developing countries.

The rapid shift in investments to take advantage of these sectorial inequalities has often brought about dislocations of families and communities. Manufacturing cycles are not geared to integrated life processes. They are only viable when development is narrowly equated with short-term economic growth. For example, parental planning in the reproduction and socialization of children has not been responsive to labor market demands for some generations. But now even the particular skills and training gained by workers in school or on the job are made obsolete before they are realized by technological change and shifts in production sites.

Social, physical, and psychological disruptions, although varying, are experienced both by the suddenly unemployed head of household who contemplates migration to the Sunbelt after a plant closure, and by the young woman whose diminishing eyesight attests to the peculiarities of a new form of employment in the developing world.

Whereas past migration involved the movement of workers to areas where industry was located, that movement is now outstripped by footloose factories. The infrastructure provided by communities in transportation, energy sources, and training facilities for workers is abandoned as more lucrative fields for investment open. In the early years of their development, corporate enterprises moderated the cycles of economic activity contingent on the fortunes and ability of owner operated factories. Today, corporations provide a network of information and access to developing areas that shortens profit schedules to a decade or less. Electronics enterprises attracted to an abandoned New Hampshire factory on the basis of CETA-subsidized trainees or to Curaçao with tax rebates or even to the Philippines with promises of no unionization leave the moment those advantages run out (Abraham-Van der Mark, Enloe, and Nash in this volume).

Textile, garment, and electrical/electronics industries are in the forefront of this migration to developing areas. However, in the wake of these advances, some sectors of the old centers of production become specialized in services, sales, and research for industries they had gestated. Sassen-Koob analyzes this revitalization process made possible by new migrations of workers who, in accepting low wages and poor working conditions, enable producers to compete with foreign producers. Sassen-Koob clearly shows that the growth of the services sector in old industrial centers such as New York is intimately related to the shift towards production overseas.

The dynamics of global integration exceed the model of development contained in polarized dichotomies. As investments move to developing areas, core countries lose their pivotal position in many respects. However, under these circumstances, industrialization does not provide the generative base for further advances because of the very mobility that brought it to the new sites. Brazil's "miracle" is a case in point. Aguiar shows how multiple coexisting modes of production under state subsidy and linked to the activities of national and multinational enterprises fail to meet the needs of either a developing national economy or a developing family structure. Housing ties workers to the plantation or government project when the firm needs labor; but when these needs change because of seasonal or cyclical downturns in production, families are evicted. The old paternalism of plantation and even slave economies seems benevolent in contrast to the policy of the multinational corporation that opportunistically seizes a government sponsored infrastructure only to close operations when profits sink to less than a third of annual income.

Migrant workers from south of the border move to the tariff-free zones at the United States–Mexican border and into the heartland of Silicon Valley in the San Jose area of California as they try to keep pace with these mobile industries (Fernandez-Kelly, Green, Katz, and Keller in this volume). But even when they keep apace of the physical mobility of the factories, they have little control of the job within industry. Technological change eliminates the production slots of the predominantly female work force, and the new demands for skilled engineers are filled with males.

In the past the family mediated the changing fortunes of wage earners as young and old, male and female, pooled their income. But the very mobility of industry threatens the coalescence of the family as a cooperative network. Young wage earners are separated from parents whom they might otherwise maintain in the homes they support while benefitting from the child care and domestic services the older generation used to provide.

The inflationary effects of a high energy-consuming production system are also borne by labor. Stabilization policies are carried out by international banking institutions to overcome accumulated debts and interests as well as high costs involved in capital intensive ventures. These policies and a sluggish agricultural sector that fails to meet basic consumption needs have the hardest impact on blue-collar families. The problems Jamaican workers faced in making ends meet when confronted with spiraling prices and lower credit facilities in the period 1978–1979, analyzed by Bolles (this volume), are a prelude to what workers in the United States are now experiencing as they try to grapple with the problems brought about by wildly fluctuating supply and demand schedules in the economy. As island economies such as Jamaica and Curaçao lose the characteristics that made them attractive to industrial investment a decade ago, industry moves on to other areas.

In some cases the forefront of industrial change seems to recapitulate the cottage "putting-out" system practiced in seventeenth century England when enterpreneurs brought raw materials to families who produced the yarns and textiles. As capital is absorbed by monopolistic firms, lesser resources are available to maintain even low-overhead garment industries or assembly operations in electronics. Alonso (this volume) examines the Netzahualcoyotl garment workers in Mexico who take over entrepreneurial costs as they exploit their own labor and that of family members in cutting and piecing together garments that were formerly made in small shops. Another development that harks back to the proto-industrial period in the United States when bicycle repair shops became the locus of motorized equipment assembly or grist mills were converted to fulling and dyeing works, is the development in Taiwan of subassembly electronics work in rural villages. Operating in a highly competitive field because of the low capital costs for entry, these Taiwanese entrepreneurs increase the margins of profits in foreign owned industries by absorbing the overhead and operating costs (Hu Tai-Li, this volume).

The theoretical analyses and case studies included in this anthology document the consequences of the movement in garment, textile, and electronic industries in the United States and overseas. We have organized the articles in the following four sections. The first three articles provide an overview of the integration of the global economy, particularly in the electronics industry. Problems concerning reproduction of the social system are raised in the second section. The implications of industrial shifts on migration are discussed in articles included in the third section. We conclude with case studies in the United States and abroad that document the rise and decline of electronics and garment industry in Asia, Latin America and the Caribbean.

The changes in the sectorial composition of labor recorded in these articles are bringing about profound changes in production, the family, and community. Differential employment on the basis of gender has stimulated the movement of women into the border cities and of men across the border into the United States that is analyzed by Maria Patricia Fernández-Kelly and Jorge Bustamante. It has repercussions in declining cities of the northeastern United States, where immigrant labor continues to flow in at the same time that capital moves out, a contradiction that Saskia Sassen-Koob explores.

In the capitalist semiperiphery undocumented workers from Colombia in Venezuelan garment factories described by Magalit Berlin experience some of the same problems that Caribbeans face in New York. Women attempting to escape the restrictions of feudal and domestic household economies find themselves caught in the patriarchal mold of the industrial estates described by Lim and Green. Any attempt to organize the new labor force is discouraged by the massive military machine that, as Enloe shows, is correlated with the advance of industrialization.

Crises in the working class barrios of Rio de Janeiro and the northeast of Brazil are exacerbated by changing demands for the labor of men and women in nationalized and foreign enterprises, as recorded by Aguiar. Families' attempt to mediate the disruptions and dislocations in waning garment industries of the northeastern United States and their advancing counterparts in Brazil are recorded by Safa. In a dependent economy such as Jamaica, this process translates into the losing battle that Lynn Bolles describes.

The very presence of large foreign corporations has brought back into prominence the kind of domestic putting-out industry which José Antonio Alonso studied in Mexico City and Hu Tai-Li observed in Taiwan. We have arrived at the unprecedented stage in the advance of multinational capital accumulation that Abraham–Van der Mark records for Curaçao where the branch of Texas Instruments, opened just over a decade ago, has closed and left behind a trail of unemployment. Having lost the handicrafts and business enterprises that they had developed prior to the entry of industry, women have few options for future employment.

*xiv*

The expansion of the electronics industry in the Salinas Valley of the United States draws upon an ethnically underprivileged labor force for assembly line work at the same time that it tries to attract college educated engineers from elite sectors to the labor force. Thus, the distinction between mental and manual coincides with ethnicity and gender both within and outside of industrial centers as Keller and Katz show.

With the comparative perspective offered by this collection of articles, we are able to grasp some of the mechanisms of control and the developing strategies for resisting them. The crucial questions for policymakers are, as Snow points out, which groups of workers and which parts of the country will suffer with the internationalization of production and what limits will be imposed as internal and external contradictions increase.

In the mid-nineteenth century, Marx hailed the destruction of feudal economy in the advance of capitalist institutions. The progress he recognized no longer characterizes the predatory invasion of the few surviving regions of autonomous subsistence. Today the spread of agroindustry spells the end of "natural economy" among semi-subsistence cultivators in Africa and Asia and hunter-horticulturalists of the South American Amazonian area. The basic cause for the impoverishment of people in the wake of capitalist advance is, in the words of Griffin and Kahn (1976), the "structure of the economy" characterized by "unequal ownership of land and other productive assets, allocative mechanisms which discriminate in favour of ownership of wealth and a pattern of investment and technical change which is biased against labour." The increased investment in labor-saving, capital-intensive technology has contributed to the widening of the gap between rich and poor nations in the decades of the 1950s and 1960s. In the 1970s it has succeeded in reversing the redistributive processes that were the victory of democratic institutions once fostered by capitalist production. The inability of capitalist industry to absorb labor released from the land has brought the system to the level of stagnation once attributed to feudal institutions.

*Part I*

# GLOBAL ACCUMULATION
# AND THE LABOR PROCESS

Papers in this section provide an overview of the themes developed in the volume. The integration of production on a world scale has sharpened sectorial differences within the labor force. The opposition of "First" and "Third" worlds defined in economic terms as capitalist vs. developing economics may still exist, but the terms of that relationship have changed. The workers of First World countries no longer benefit from the accumulation of capital in the periphery. They are in direct competition with low-paid, often unorganized labor in the Third World. June Nash explores the changing relations in industry as they are expressed in union, management, and government strategies and ideologies. Robert Snow analyzes how overseas production has affected the blue-collar work force in the United States. Linda Lim examines the impact of multinational factories on the employment and social status of women in the developing countries.

# CHAPTER 1

# The Impact of the Changing International Division of Labor on Different Sectors of the Labor Force

JUNE NASH

Inequalities in the exchange of goods and services in the world market have been analyzed in terms of national, regional, and urban-rural differences.[1] This collection of papers focuses on inequalities among different sectors of the labor force, particularly those related to gender, and how these are affected by the changing international division of labor.

Three major theoretical positions attempt to analyze and predict the changing relations in the new international division of labor. The first is neoclassical economic theory based on the assumption that the free flow of capital will result in evening the inequalities in exchange. Direct investment in industry should, according to this theory, result in a worldwide leveling of wages as well as price. A second theory is that the global integration of production has resulted in a vertical integration of First and Third World labor force. The division of labor is one in which the bottom of the hierarchy consists of ethnic divisions made up of Third World populations providing the manual labor for world enterprises, and as one moves up the pryamid, nationality becomes increasingly European in the "command centers" controlling research, knowledge and management (Hymer 1973; Palloux 1973). The third major theoretical position is that sectors of the labor force based on gender, ethnicity, age, and education within both industrial core and peripheral nations are differentially rewarded and these differences, along with wage differences between nations, determine the long-run movement of capital.

*3*

Neo-classical market theory fails to encompass political realities in global market exchange. It is even less capable of assessing changes resulting from the global integration of production. Vertical integration theory captures a moment in history when unequal exchange between manufacturing centers and raw materials-producing periphery characterized the global market. But with recent advances in the integration of production on a global scale, it too fails to assess the growing inequalities among sectors of the work force and manufacturing enterprises within core economies as well as between core and periphery. In order to explain these changes, we must turn to a theory that takes into account the international division of labor in the changing process of the accumulation of capital.

Fröbel, Heinrich, and Krëye (1978:124) provide such a focus. In their analysis of the differential labor markets both in advanced industrial countries and the so-called peripheral areas, they draw attention to the dynamics of capital accumulation both within nations and among nations. They analyze the conditions for the present growth and extension of industry as follows. A worldwide reservoir of labor develops at wages 10 to 20 percent of those in developed countries. This is combined with the development of a technology that divides complex production into elementary units that can be easily taught to people anywhere in the world. For the multinationals to survive in the world market, they must maintain the rate of profit for goods produced in competition with low wage workers throughout the world as Hymer (1973:28) and Lorenz (1974:95), who emphasize the vertical integration of labor, recognize. However, because of this process of investing in low wage areas, labor in the former core economies is losing the security developed in earlier stages of industrialization as it competes in an international market. Competition between sectors of the labor force is intensified at the same time that management is centralized internationally, not only at the level of the firm, but also industry-wide as the recognition of common interest becomes shared.

Sectors of the labor force that are not competitive within a developed economy, such as those defined by gender or ethnicity, become competitive at the international level. Whereas trade unions, which grew out of and reflected the imperialist structure of which they were a part, were able to limit entry into preferred occupations in the old industrial countries, they could not affect the allocation of jobs in the newly developing areas (Hechter 1975). The *secondary* labor force—those who are temporarily employed in low skilled and low paid jobs—(Doeringer and Piore 1971) in industrially advanced

*4*

countries is harder hit by international trade than the *primary* labor force—the skilled workers who have better paid, more secure employment—since they are in direct competition. Gerhard Fels (1974) and other participants in a conference on trade in 1973 recognized the need for a regional policy to help workers of "peripheral" regions of Germany and particularly female labor "which is less mobile on an interregional basis than men" and is, therefore, most affected by "adjustment prices" resulting from increased imports from low wage, less developed countries in international competition.

In the decade from the middle of the sixties, a major shift in investment policies took place as developing countries moved from industries that produced goods for internal consumption to industries producing components for export. The shift was provoked by changes in tariff laws encouraging the rapid expansion of industries that produced labor intensive assembly work, especially in garment and electronic manufacturers for reshipment back to industrial centers. These policies, called import substitution and export diversification, are in fact complementary (Donges 1974:354). It may well have been impossible to introduce export diversification unless the earlier stage in import substitution had taken place and provided the infrastructure of managerial skills and a "disciplined" labor force (Donges 1974:346).

The movement abroad was supposed to alleviate the problems of unemployment and decreasing returns to labor which import substitution industrialization had failed to solve. However, far from solving these problems, export industrialization has moved them into an international arena. Business proponents of export industries, such as G.K. Helleiner (1973), support their claims for the future of export industries on the score that the wage gap between rich and poor nations as well as that between unskilled and skilled workers is likely to increase. This claim is borne out in the short run by restrictive labor practices in countries such as Malaysia where the major attraction for investors is a low wage labor force. Moreover, the flexibility and financial power of multinational corporations enabling them to evade labor union or governmental attempts to level wages pose an obstacle to international negotiations in the foreseeable future. Rudolf Scheid (1974:175) comments that Hong Kong, Taiwan, and South Korea have succeeded in giving incentives to direct investment by establishing production conditions "resembling those of early capitalism."

Critics of export industrialization such as W.C. Tyler (1974) and C. L. Salm (1970) point to the increasing unemployment in countries with rapidly developing export industries. In fact, the growth potential for offshore industries is self-limiting since it is predicated on a reserve of labor. As this is absorbed, wages do rise (unless there is an extremely repressive government) but often not at the rate of inflation. Linda Lim (this volume) points to this movement in the migration of the footloose industries from Malaysia to Indonesia and more recently the Philippines following a trend set in Hong Kong in the sixties, when manufacturing exports had a compound rate of growth of 14 percent with 9 percent increase in employment. As unemployment among youthful workers nearly disappeared, there was a rise in wages which discouraged future growth as industries turned to other countries in the Asian periphery. A little noted movement of these industries that I have observed in the declining industrial areas of northeastern United States is that of the electronics assembly companies into abandoned factories. When the tax rebates and CETA training funds used to attract them to the old mill towns are no longer forthcoming, these industries move on to the next high unemployment area, often without advising the employees. With no laws restricting the movement of such operations, workers in one of these plants recalled showing up for work on Monday to find a sign stating "Gone to Jamaica" on the door of the factory. On the basis of such trends in the overseas operations, William C. Tyler (1974:381–2) concludes that, far from providing a long-range solution to the problem of unemployment, accepting offshore industries serves "as a rationale for not undertaking more radical measures to resolve the problems of labor underutilization and marginalization."

Theorists of the vertical integration of the division of labor go beyond strict market analyses to stress political as well as economic forces. They demonstrate how the control over information and decision-making by the multinational corporations leads to the fragmentation of the work force and the defeat of trade union negotiations at an international level.

Their critics point to the inadequacy of the opposition of center and periphery in trying to understand the changing investment scene (Brookfield 1975: Fröbel, Heinrichs and Krëye 1978: Hugon 1978). Loss of autonomy in economic planning is experienced in both central industrial economics and in less developed areas. Stagnation and unemployment are increasingly apparent in mature economies, along with inflation, imbalance in payments in international trade, and regional disparities considered to be the characteristics of less developed countries. Furthermore, there is an increasing tendency for European countries to subsidize marginal industries with low levels of capital investment in response to union pressure (Hugon

1978). At the same time, some governments in the Third World support investments in high technology industries. Hong Kong and Singapore can claim higher investment in technology than that of some European competitors.

In this volume we will compare through case studies the sectorial shifts that are affecting relations in production throughout the world.

## Sectorial Labor Force and the Integration of the World Capitalist System

The integration of the world market reveals the central dynamic of capitalist accumulation and penetration into new areas. In the long run, the accumulation of capital depends on surplus value created by the labor force. Regional differences in the availability and price of the factors of production sometimes obscure the crucial importance of labor theory of value as developed by Ricardo and Marx. Dependency theory stressed the power relations between nations as the basis for unequal exchange. The critique of dependency theory[2] on this score reasserts the importance of productive relations in determining the movement of capital and labor. With the increasing integration of production on a world scale, the importance of labor costs is becoming the principle determinant in allocating production facilities and investments.

In the early stages of the development of industrial capitalism, capital accumulation was made possible by the extreme exploitation of the most vulnerable sector of the working population—at that time women and children. Until 1838 they constituted 62 percent of the labor force. Whereas production increased by 40 percent in the period from 1820 to 1845, wages rose only 5 percent (Hobsbawm 1968). This strategy of accumulation through the employment of defenceless sectors of the work force was repeated in the developing countries of the world in the nineteenth century. In the United States, young unmarried women were the main labor force in the Lowell, Massachusetts, textile mills. In the early days of the mills, these young women enjoyed some advantages from paternalistic labor relations. However, the monotony of the work and the long hours with low wages meant that they often preferred to return to the farm after gaining some savings (Gutman 1977:25–30). Mill owners preferred to employ the newly arriving immigrants, who had no alternative to the sale of their labor.

7

Migration of certain sectors of the labor force, particularly young males, accompanied the movement of capital throughout the nineteenth century. Great Britain supplied not only the capital and technology for the continental railroads, but even the experienced manual labor to actually construct the lines (Hobson 1963:119–20). The migration of people was fraught with contradictions: while promoting free labor policies in Great Britain, English colonists promoted slave labor in the colonies throughout the eighteenth and first half of the ninteenth centuries. As preferred sectors of the English labor force migrated to the colonies, the Irish were brought to England to provide domestic servants. While the rural poor farmhands were pushed out of their homelands and forced overseas by the enclosure acts, those factory workers who had some knowledge and experience with the technology that ensured Great Britain's primacy in industry were prevented from leaving the country. As Sassen-Koob (1981) shows, each movement of labor was a response to a "different surplus-generating process, each with a distinctive role in the international division of labor." International labor migration, as she reviews the process, evolved as an important source of labor during the consolidation of the world capitalist system.

Development in Third World countries replicated some aspects of the process of industrialization in the United States. In Brazil's nascent textile factories, women constituted 91 percent of the labor force in textiles and other secondary industry at the turn of the twentieth century (Saffioti 1978:253). With rising capital-intensive production and unionization of these industries, men were employed in increasing numbers, and women's participation in secondary industries fell to 27.9 percent of the labor force by 1920. Puerto Rico's industrialization was delayed until the twentieth century when World War I interfered with the supply of needlework from Europe. This was carried out in home industries employing women who earned less than a subsistence wage (Pico 1976:206). Tobacco and canning industries provided another outlet for employment of impoverished women workers. Their predominance in industry was so great by the thirties that male dominated unions petitioned the government to intercede. The result was legislation limiting the employment of women by preferential subsidies to industries employing men (Pico n.d.).

The demand for labor in the core industrial countries took priority over the needs for industries located in peripheral regions. Western European countries drew on their immediate peripheries with the Irish going to Britain; Poles, to Germany; Italians and Belgians, to

France (Sassen-Koob 1981). Increasingly, as union organization consolidated the primary work force operating in nationally integrated firms in the twentieth century, migrants moved into service work or industries in the competitive sector.

When there is a shift from males to females in the allocation of jobs, techniques for reinforcing the segmentary market and the ideological distortions are revealed. Such a shift occurred during World War II when there was a sharp increase in the demand for labor at the same time that there was a reduction in the male labor force because of recruitment into the army. As women entered shipyards and factories geared to war production, measures were taken to overcome the cognitive dissonance arising from prior commitments to a male labor force. First, the restriction on women working on the night shift came under scrutiny as production in female segregated jobs expanded. It was discovered that the danger to morality was most prevalent for women aged eighteen to twenty-five, who were classified as "Cinderellas" and prohibited from working the late shift after 11 P.M. when their virtue was most threatened (Nash n.d.). Second, the prohibition against women working in certain jobs considered to be too heavy was reconsidered. With some changes in machine design, women were found to be able to carry out work formerly restricted to men (Baker 1964). Third, there was a radical debasement of jobs. A striking example of this is described by Philip Kraft (1979) for computer programming in defense industries during World War II. Preoccupation with the "hardware" for the ENIAC operational computer proposed to calculate shell trajectories led to management treating the programming aspects of the job as secondary. A group of about a hundred young women just out of college were hired to perform the calculations. Because the work was considered clerical, it was designated as "women's work." However, programming the computer required familiarity with the machine's electrical logic, the physical structure, and the mechanical operation, which the women learned by crawling around the machine. They devised the programs required but in the process changed the engineers' idea of the complexity of the task, which was then reclassified as "men's work." In these experiences we see the resistance to a breakdown of segmented job structure and the strategies to reinstate privileges enjoyed by the primary work force.

In the decades since World War II, we have experienced two periods of expansion of direct investment overseas that have changed the sectorial balances within nations as the integration of the world capitalist system has progressed. The first phase, motivated by es-

*9*

tablishing branches behind tariff branches in the European Economic Community and later in developing countries of Latin America, Africa and Asia, expanded work opportunities for the primary sector of the U.S. labor force and widened the gap between primary and secondary labor force. In the first phase of overseas expansion, the U.S. consumer market was not pirated by foreign branches; in fact, there was a stimulus to production in supplying the machinery and replacements for factories established abroad. The second expansion beginning in the mid-sixties when an amendment to the tariff laws permitted goods shipped abroad for processing to be imported with a duty only on the value added had a negative impact on both primary and secondary labor force. The change came about because article 806.30 of the tariff act permitting the reimportation of processed goods was amended by the passage of article 807.00 in 1963 removing restrictive clauses. Later amendments passed in 1965 and 1966 made it possible for manufacturers to advance and improve items produced overseas and themselves declare the "value added" on which the duty was to be based. These changes in the tariff laws stimulated production in overseas branches of goods destined for the U.S. market. In 1974, a high of $1,928 million dollars worth of goods entered under Title 807.00, coming primarily from the less developed countries—particularly Mexico, Taiwan, Singapore, and Hong Kong (U.S. International Trade Commission 1976).

In the decade of expansion of export-oriented industrialization from 1965 to 1975, the absorption of women in the clothing and electronics manufacturing plants had a direct negative effect on the employment of women in the industrial centers. Fels (1974:193) calls for a reassessment of regional policy to take into account the special burden that female labor and workers in general in the peripheral regions of developed countries must bear in the adjustment process. In the hard-hit northeastern United States where garment and electronic industries were heavily represented, unemployment rose above national average to 8, 10, and even 17 percent in some declining industrialized cities about 1975. The attempted solutions often exacerbated the basic problems; extended unemployment benefits increased the tax burden on surviving industry and hastened its departure to the Sunbelt, and attempts to lure industry with CETA subsidized work force and/or temporary tax abatements encouraged the footloose industries discussed above. The recent reinvigoration of the industrial base with high technology industries is especially vulnerable to international trends.

What these examples suggest is that in the initial phase of capital penetration, there is a strong preference for extremely low-paid, unprotected segments of the population. These may be ethnic or rural migrants without alternative employment, or women. Lacking experience in trade union or political organizations, they are vulnerable to intense exploitation. This trend in intensified as labor is forced to compete internationally. Sectors of the labor force which are noncompetitive in a national setting become competitive as stereotypes about sex or ethnic competency as well as trade union monopolies in the job market are exploded. When a job is exported overseas, cheaper, unorganized female labor can be recruited for work done by experienced workers, often males in the industrial centers. Ethnic groups can enter employment controlled by trade unions or craft guilds in the center economy. The competition between sectors of the labor force is abetted by technological changes contributing to the decomposition of skills as jobs require only the least common denominator of labor force participation. The privileged position of the primary work force is eroded without any gains for the secondary labor force. Furthermore, the expanding tertiary sector of government workers with greater proportions of female and black workers is blocked as tax revenues from industry are lost when firms invest overseas and as individual taxpayers, burdened with the costs of welfare and unemployment caused by private capitalist practices, vote for tax abatement (Sokoloff 1980).

## The Impact of Multinational Practices on the Labor Process

With the expansion of much of their productive activities overseas, there were marked changes in the relationships among business, government and labor in the United States. Foreign investments grew from $158 billion in 1971 to $287 billion in 1976 with total assets of firms with at least one foreign affiliate estimated at $760 billion (United Nations 1978:35). The number of persons directly employed by multinational corporations was ten million in 1976, three to four million of whom were in foreign countries. While the number of U.S. firms included among the largest transnational corporations has declined from ninety-eight out of 156 in 1959 to sixty-seven in 1974, the United States is still the leading country in international operations (Economist 4, Feb. 1978). One-half of U.S. exports are intrafirm transactions, and the production of American

*11*

affiliates abroad is estimated as four times more than American exports (Hugon 1978:113).

What is the effect of these trends? The United Nations report (1978) stresses that there is less response to local needs, whether in subsidiaries in developing economies or in the parent firm. These needs include income-generating employment and social welfare benefits. Sectorial disparities in the labor force are increased with the loss of redistributive mechanisms such as job training for inner-city residents, job training for the hard core unemployed, and child-care centers that enable mothers to work. Given the large increase in women in the wage labor force, these services sponsored or subsidized by the government are necessities, not luxuries.

*Unemployment.* With the spread of multinational corporations, unemployment of the less preferred sectors of the labor force has increased at home and abroad. U.S. based transnationals overseas often employ capital intensive technology that reduces the employment potential of capital investment in countries with high unemployment. As the large foreign corporations absorb local capital and compete for other factors of production, many local enterprises are forced out of business. The average cost of creating each new job in the United States is, according to presidential adviser L. William Seidman (quoted in the *New York Times*, May 7, 1975) forty thousand dollars. The estimate for Latin American countries is twenty-five hundred dollars per job holding (Heillinger and Heillinger 1976:11). As capitalization ratios increase, fewer workers are employed at any given level of development. Moreover, the unaccounted contribution of women and children in rural economies with semisubsistence production is lost when families are forced out by the presence of agribusiness or migrate to the city in search of industrial jobs. The result is the crisis in employment at a worldwide level.

The export diversification industries in "runaway shops" contribute to unemployment in home industry, particularly affecting women and other discriminated groups. Small firms that cannot extend their operations have united with labor groups to object to tariff provisions 806.30 and 807.00 discussed above. A bill to repeal the two articles was introduced in the House of Representatives first in 1970 and later in January 1976. In the first hearing, labor representatives claimed that 112,000 jobs were lost between October 1966 and July 1970, with 25,000 lost in radio and television production alone between July 1969 and July 1975 as a result of the tariff (United Nations Conference on Trade Development 1975). In the second hearing, the AFL-CIO and the International Ladies Garment Workers Union (ILGWU) maintained that the tariff items caused the transfer of U.S. jobs overseas, causing a fall in employment of 32.5 percent in the ten year period 1965–1975 when the Mexican border industrialization program went into effect. The Western Electronics Manufacturing Association and industry representatives from General Electric, countered labor spokespersons on the score that internationalizing of labor-intensive aspects enabled companies to remain competitive by keeping costs down and thereby protected jobs (U.S. International Trade Commission 1976). As yet, very little has been-done to counter the flow of investments and job losses in either industry. Safa's paper in this volume discusses some of these issues in relation to the garment industry.

The argument of industry representatives—that by putting out labor intensive production in offshore industries, skilled jobs are protected—may hold in the short run, but, as experience has shown, the host countries usually make demands on the companies for further investment as the initial labor-intensive phase becomes established. In Latin America auto production that started with assembly of manufactured components ended with 99 percent of each car being produced in Brazil, 95 percent in Argentina, and 85 percent in Mexico. In some cases, local producers have closed plants rather than yield to demands for further local manufacturing content. European plants are more responsive to union protest in the home country than are U.S. firms.

With the entry of China into the field of international production, we can expect more developments in export-oriented investment. Contracts for production by multinational corporations in electronics, textiles, toys, and footwear have required payment for machinery with output that will be shipped to the U.S. market over a period of years. These products, sold under U.S. labels, will compete with domestic production, according to Eugene Therous (*Fortune* March 20, 1979:67).

*Decline of Social Welfare.* Another indication of the failure of multinational corporations to respond to local needs is the threat they pose to social welfare provisions, especially in highly developed economies of Europe and Scandanavia. Hans Günter, in a review of labor relations and the multinational corporations in western Europe (1975:159), notes, that "enterprise corporatism" developed by the multinationals to attend to the social welfare needs of its employees has eroded national welfare policies. These corporate programs are detrimental since much of the population is left out of the agreements and the authority of the central government is weakened.

The loss of a tax base from intrafirm transfers of technology or components affects industrially advanced countries as well as developing nations in their attempts to realize advanced social legislation. Nat Weinberg (1977), formerly of the International Union of Auto, Aerospace and Agricultural Implement Workers of America and now a consultant, scores the "imaginative accounting and the manipulation of transfer prices" that enable the multinational corporations to evade taxes, control foreign exchanges and deceive government and unions as to profits and earnings. The United Nations (1978:2) has recognized the need for uniform accounting practices enforced on an international level.

Far from attempting to overcome the distortions resulting from multinational investments, the U.S. government has fostered them through a tax policy which permits taxes paid to foreign governments to be credited against federal tax payment rather than being deducted as a cost of doing business. A tax deferral credit provides that taxes on profits earned abroad may be deferred until the profits are returned to United States, if ever, Jager (1975:38) figures that the loss to the U.S. treasure was 2.9 billion in 1966 and 4.6 billion in 1970. Sciberas (1977:34–35) emphasizes the importance of intracompany transfers in such tax evasion as these: with U.S. taxes ranging from 5 to 50 percent, the multinational company can reduce its final tax bill by allocating the greatest profit to production in countries with the lowest tax rate. In 1968 the tax bill of multinational corporations was $3 billion worldwide, with $2 billion going to foreign countries. In addition to direct taxes of $1 billion to the U.S. government, the government received only $700 million on royalties and management fees paid by subsidiaries. Tax law loopholes and competition between countries prevent effective state action against the multinationals.

In addition to picking up the tax bill that goes into the developmental stages of technological innovation, U.S. workers and national firms provide the tax base for the Overseas Private Investment Corporation, which insures U.S. based firms against the risks of appropriation, war, and currency inconvertibility. This makes appeals to free enterprise theory, the basic premise of which is profit justification on the basis of risk bearing, somewhat specious.

In summary, the multinational corporations are undermining governmental programs for redistributing profits in their home countries as well as abroad. Municipal and national programs that encouraged class mobility and compensated for the inequality in wealth are losing the tax base as well as the political support needed to provide flexibility and adaptability in the system. As a result, programs for social welfare have been hard hit by declining interest in the government programs designed to remedy the very problems caused by multinational corporation policies. The leading country in the export of capital, the United States, has no national health insurance program, its social security system provides pensions far below those paid in other developed economies, public unemployment compensation is very low in comparison with other nations and disability insurance is lacking except in a few states. There are no national minimum vacation periods and employee participation schemes rarely exist (Weinberg 1977:110). Women are particularly victimized by this process, both as producers and consumers of welfare services. Sokoloff (1980) analyzes the reduction of welfare service employment opportunities for women in the context of a declining patriarchal organiztion of society.

*Decline in Workers' Control over the Work Place.* Along with welfare state policies, attempts to democratize industry through self-management and worker councils are threatened by multinationals. The model of labor-management relations developed in the United States centralizes managerial decision making and limits workers participation in the organization of production. The technological imperative is used to rationalize a situation in which production workers carry out routine tasks requiring minimal training. The export of this model overseas upset the trend toward codetermination in western Europe. The trend was further undermined by the economic crisis with unemployment and inflation in the mid-seventies. Indirectly, the diminishing competitive position of workers in nationalized industries and national firms in central industrial countries has made workers wary of such agreements in a situation of rising unemployment. In the Netherlands, which has, according to Jonathan Kendell (*New York Times* May 5, 1978, D1–3), been in the forefront of European countries in adopting social legislation, unions have not pushed ahead to activate a 1971 law permitting them to enter into coparticipation. The unions agreed to freeze the rate of growth of real wages and go along with government incentives for private investment "to help make Dutch labor and industry more competitive." Unions are "cooled" on the idea of worker councils since they fear that they would encourage sympathetic understanding between workers and management. The Italian unions rejected the

*15*

Christian Democratic government's offer to give labor unions a share in management of state owned companies because, according to Kendell (ibid.), workers were more interested in maintaining jobs and purchasing power as unemployment rose. Unions rejected codetermination as an invitation to "comanaging disaster." Even in countries that espouse an ideal of worker participation, the acceptance of advanced technology from developed countries determines an organization of production antithetical to any meaningful participation in decision making (Leviatan 1976, Bienefeld 1972–3).

Paradoxically the trend toward codetermination in West German industry was fostered by the U.S. occupation legislation following World War II. Three decades later, U.S. multinational corporations acted against codetermination through the Chamber of Commerce. The German Confederation of Workers reminded them that, "This is not a banana republic" (Weinberg 1977:104). In a comparative analysis of the components entering into worker participation in decision making—collective bargaining, decisions on work organization, representation on board or policy council, and partial or complete employee ownership—U.S. companies ranked lowest on all counts except employee decision on organization of work, where Britain was lowest, and employee ownership, where Germany and France had lower involvement. Sweden ranked highest of all European and U.S. companies on all counts and was outstripped only by Yugoslavia in worker representatives on boards and employee ownership (*Fortune* June 15, 1981:68–73). The growing emphasis on "quality of worklife" in American corporations may bring about a cultural revolution in the organization of work that will reverse the trends toward rigid hierarchy and debasement of tasks. However, union leaders in firms that claim to have revolutionized the workplace assert that management has dealt only with relatively superficial aspects of the organization of work.

*Trends in Employment, Wages, and Social Welfare Compared.* In the remarkable trends occurring in the decade of the seventies, overseas operations of multinational corporations supported by government policies in tax and tariff legislation have succeeded in reducing the returns to labor in the United States at the same time that the gap, measured in terms of gross national productivity, between the developed centers and the less developed countries is growing. U.S. wages are now outstripped by German and Swedish wages (Table 1–1) and unemployment is higher than in other industrially advanced countries (Table 1–2). The falling rate of increase in productivity in the United States, which slipped 3.3 percent annually from the fourth quarter of 1977 to the first quarter of 1978 and 4.5 percent the following year (U.S. Department of Labor, *New York Times*, May 5, 1978; May 8, 1979, D1) means that whatever edge U.S. labor had in competition with the world labor market is in decline. In an international comparison of productivity, the change, based in a 1967 index, was 170 for West Germany in 1977 in comparison with 198 for the same period in Japan and only 127 for the United States. In the period 1968 to 1977, wages increased almost fourfold in Japan, while they just doubled in the U.S. (International Labor Office [ILO] 1978). Unemployment went up from 2,817,000 in the United States to 6,855,000 in the same period, while in Japan it went from 590,000 to 1,260,000 (ILO 1978). At the same time, unemployment decreased from 46,000 to 36,900 in Korea and from 492,000 to 406,000 in Puerto Rico (ILO 1978). Slower productivity growth and rising unemployment in the United States cripples the bargaining power of labor. Moreover, a diminishing percentage of U.S. workers are organized. In 1967, 27.9 percent of the labor force of 80,793,000 was organized and in 1977, 26.5 percent of 81,300,000 was organized. This change reflects both the shift from blue-collar to white-collar employment in the United States as well as the loss of blue-collar jobs to overseas offshore production (U.S. Department of Labor 1977).[3] The net result of the worsening of the position of labor in industrial centers is a stimulus to direct investment in low wage countries abroad. This is reflected in the fact that domestic investments remained the same in 1974 as in 1966, at $35.3 billion, while doubling from 13.9 billion to $28.53 billion abroad (Lupo and Freidlin 1975).

The technological lead that enabled U.S. firms to maintain employee productivity at high levels in order to justify wage increases has been lost because of the lack of a government policy regulating the export of technology. As a result, the United States has lost exports and suffers from a high imbalance of payments that contributes to the devaluation of the dollar and rising inflation. Elizabeth R. Jager (1975:31), economist of the AFL-CIO, berates multinational corporations for selling technology at "bargain basement prices" or exporting it directly through production in overseas affiliates (1975:27). A major factor in the U.S. technological lead, as Sciberas (1977:62) points out, is the size of the state market in the developmental stages of technology. This is particularly important in the semiconductor technology where the state market is five times larger than the industrial market (Sciberas 1977:63). Products go from the military,

Table 1-1. Wages in Nonagricultural Sectors

| Country | Hourly Wages (in Special Drawing Rights Equivalents[a]) | | | |
|---|---|---|---|---|
| | 1975 | 1976 | 1977 | 1978 |
| Dominican Republic | 1.33 | 1.08 | 1.20 | |
| France | 2.28 | 2.41 | 2.72 | |
| Germany | 3.39 | 4.05 | 4.40 | 5.44 |
| Japan | 2.62 | 3.08 | 3.68 | |
| Korea | .39 | .53 | .70 | |
| Mexico | 1.33 | 1.05 | 1.20 | |
| Puerto Rico | 2.18 | 2.38 | 2.58 | |
| Sweden | 4.64 | 5.64 | 5.19 | |
| United Kingdom | .81 | 1.07 | 1.12 | |
| United States | 4.11 | 4.47 | 4.81 | |

Source: *Yearbook of Labour Statistics*, Geneva: International Labour Office, 1978.
[a] Special Drawing Rights, based on unconditional international reserve assets, were equivalent to U.S. $1.17 in 1975, U.S. $1.16 in 1976, and U.S. $1.17 in 1977 (International Monetary Fund, *International Financial Statistics* 1978).

which bears the costs of innovation, to the industrial market and finally to the consumer. Although the United States dominates the introduction stage, European and Japanese competitors dominate the "mature stage" when production methods become standardized. The competitive advantage in the world market goes to the imitators who are free of developmental costs and often do not have as high wage costs (Sciberas 1977:23–26).

It is clear that the opposition of center and periphery is inadequate to comprehend the changing scene. Stagnation and unemployment in marginal areas of developed centers rival that found in the Third World since the sixties. The distortion of the economy in the center as well as the periphery has resulted in rampant inflation combined with stagnation, rising corporate profits, and falling real wages. A kind of welfare program for business through tax deferrals, rebates, and even government loans to start plants branch plants in Third World countries supports overseas investments, while social welfare programs within nations are in decline. The gap between rich and poor sectors of the population is widening along with the decline in the redistributive programs. The poorest 10 percent of the world's population account for only 1.6 percent of the world's consumption while the richest 10.4 percent account for 35 percent (Griffin 1974:7). The concentration of resources, technology, and manpower in key firms was reinforced in the seventies as trading on the free market declined. Although large firms recognize their interdependence and

*Table 1–2.* Unemployment

| Year | Country | | | | | | | | | | | |
|---|---|---|---|---|---|---|---|---|---|---|---|---|
| | Germany | | Japan | | Korea | | Puerto Rico | | Singapore | | United States | |
| | (000) | % | (000) | % | (000) | % | (000) | % | (000) | % | (000) | % |
| 1968 | 323.5 | 1.5 | 590.0 | 1.2 | 492.0 | 5.1 | 83.0 | 11.1 | 46.0 | 7.3 | 2,817.0 | 3.6 |
| 1969 | 178.6 | 0.9 | 570.0 | 1.1 | 474.0 | 4.8 | 76.0 | 10.0 | 44.0 | 6.7 | 2,831.0 | 3.5 |
| 1970 | 148.8 | 0.7 | 590.0 | 1.2 | 454.0 | 4.5 | 94.0 | 10.8 | 42.0 | 6.0 | 4,088.0 | 4.9 |
| 1971 | 185.1 | 0.8 | 640.0 | 1.2 | 476.0 | 4.5 | 100.0 | 11.6 | 35.0 | 4.8 | 4,993.0 | 5.9 |
| 1972 | 246.4 | 1.1 | 730.0 | 1.4 | 499.0 | 4.5 | 101.0 | 11.9 | 36.0 | 4.7 | 4,840.0 | 5.6 |
| 1973 | 273.5 | 1.2 | 680.0 | 1.3 | 461.0 | 4.0 | 116.0 | 11.6 | 37.8 | 4.5 | 4,304.0 | 4.9 |
| 1974 | 582.5 | 2.6 | 730.0 | 1.4 | 494.0 | 4.1 | 155.0 | 13.2 | 34.0 | 4.0 | 5,076.0 | 5.6 |
| 1975 | 1,074.2 | 4.7 | 1,000.0 | 1.9 | 510.0 | 4.1 | 177.0 | 18.1 | 39.5 | 4.5 | 7,830.0 | 8.5 |
| 1976 | 1,060.3 | 4.6 | 1,080.0 | 2.0 | 505.0 | 3.9 | 187.0 | 19.5 | 40.5 | 4.5 | 7,288.0 | 7.7 |
| 1977 | 1,030.0 | 4.5 | 1,100.0 | 2.0 | 511.0 | 3.8 | 185.5 | 19.9 | 36.9 | 4.0 | 6,855.0 | 7.0 |
| 1978 | | | 1,260.0 | 2.4 | 406.0 | 2.7 | | 18.6 | | | 6,326.0 | 6.2 |

Note: Numbers in first column under each country should be multiplied by 1,000.

common goals, workers within and outside of the international firms remain fragmented (Hymer 1973:285–90).

## The Emerging Structure of Industrial Relations

The economic imbalance exacerbated by the internationalization of production is bringing about some changes in the outlook and organization of labor-management relations. Although this has not resulted in institutional changes, the changing climate of negotiations is one in which fundamental contradictions are becoming recognized as the international competition of labor is intensified.

The national basis for industry-wide negotiations and contracts established in the thirties and forties is inadequate for management-labor relations at a time when business is conducted in an international arena. Leaders of the French General Confederation of Workers (CGT) expressed the frustration experienced by labor representatives, "The numerous transfers to countries in which wage costs are lower weigh heavily on general wage levels and undermine the many social benefits which have been acquired after many years of struggle by the workers" (ILO 1976:2).

Despite the growing consciousness of the international scope of labor management relations, trade unions have lost power in dealing with multinational corporations. The difficulties they encounter can by analyzed as follows: (1) lack of union recognition, (2) lack of response by multinational corporations to customary restraints operating on national firms, and (3) contradictory polices pursued by different countries in the regulation of foreign corporations within their boundaries and of national companies with overseas branches.

1. *Union recognition.* In most developed economies, unions have been accepted as a given in major industries. This is no longer taken for granted in overseas branches. U.S. firms, which have provided the model for overseas operations in the sixties, trail behind firms of other advanced industrial countries and even their domestic branches in the level of organization. According to the ILO (1976:3) they have acquired a bad reputation among multinational corporations in resisting unionization.[4] Whether this is because of their experience in delaying recognition until legally obliged by the National Labor Relations Board or whether they are taking advantage of the greater flexibility their international operations permit in transferring production is a moot point. Unionization in the United States is declining, with 26.5 percent of the 81.3 million employees

in nonagricultural work enrolled in unions in 1977 compared with 27.9 percent of such workers organized in 1967. This is low in comparision with Sweden, where 90 percent of blue-collar workers are unionized, and with Great Britain, where 45 percent of the labor force is organized (*New York Times*, January 25, 1976). Even Japan exceeds unionization in the United States with 34 percent of the labor force organized. (This compares with only 26.7 of the labor force in foreign industries in Japan being organized [Hanami 1975:178].)

Even when the foreign firms are organized, unions have greater trouble negotiating with the multinational corporations than with national companies, as the following incidents show:

> When the Ford plant is Dagenham, England, was struck in 1971, Henry Ford declared that he would increase production in Asia and threatened Prime Minister Edward Heath that he would move some production to West Germany unless the government would "tame" unions (Sharman 1977:102).
> In the 1973 Chrysler strike in the United Kingdoms, managers warned that there would be no more investments in the United Kingdom until the union could "sort out their differences" (*Economist* June 9, 1973).
> In Belgium a large U.S. electronics firm responded to a strike with a lockout (Gennard and Stauer 1977).
> In Genk, Belgium, Ford managment told striking workers that they would increase production in West Germany; but in a move demonstrating incipient international soldarity, workers there refused to work overtime to make up for lost production.

Less dramatic than such shutdowns, but no less upsetting to negotiating with the international corporations, is information control maintained by the management that makes it impossible for a branch plant union to build its case in a strike. The World Federation of Trade Unions (WFTU) has made the demand for access to information its central target in its campaign with multinational companies. In addition, trade unions are trying to develop a systematic exchange of information on living and working conditions (Gennard and Stauer 1977:75).

*2. Customary restraints ignored.* The restraints operating on national firms to continue production and maintain traditional role allocation in the division of labor are less effective with multinational corporations. Managers of multinational corporations are adamant in rejecting the right of trade unions to enter into decision making regarding production, allocation of investments, and layoffs and have so far rejected unions' attempts to include them as industrial relations questions (Copp 1977:44). The only concession to union participation in such issues was given by N. V. Philips Gloeilampen Fabrieken. In 1969 the company agreed to give the union advance notice of all production plants. Since that time informal discussions between Philips Company and union representatives have been held on economic prospects and planning (Hershfield 1975:25). U.S. companies have been less responsive to such local pressures. When Roberts bought the Arundel Goulhard British firm, the U.S. corporate headquarters closed down four of the five facilities and engaged women as operators in work formerly done by men. Union members were dismissed and replaced by nonunion workers. After a twelve-month strike, the firm was closed in 1969 (Blainpain 1972:122). More recently, in November 1982, the Chrysler Company laid off workers in their United States plants shortly after their Canadian plants struck in an effort to get U.S. workers to put pressure on their Canadian counterparts to settle.

In order to increase managerial flexibility in circumventing local pressures, the automobile industry has designed cars for "regional production." Plants in different countries produce separate components to be assembled behind the protective tariffs of each country. According to Woodcock (Kujawa 1975:199), in deciding on production allocation, managers give priority to cheap labor areas; and when a strike threatens, they can easily shift production to the plant with the least labor trouble.

4. *Contradictory national policies.* Governments pursue contradictory policies with regard to investments of foreign corporations in the country and abroad. Whereas trade unions appeal to national governments to control manpower planning, intracompany exchanges, and financial practices, the government is also responsive to the demands of the unemployed to promote jobs as well as to business interests, so it may curb social legislation and waive guarantees won by labor in the past in the competition for investment.[5] Malaysia introduced legislation stating that a trade union may not be established for three years in a foreign company. The Mexican government has made many concessions to the multinational corporations operating at the border in order to attract investments in an area of high unemployment. In these industries that export products to the U.S. market, the threat of nationalization or other retaliatory action against the U.S. companies is minimized because markets would be lost and tourism, Mexico's main source of foreign exchange of which 86 percent comes from the United States, would decline (Baerresen 1971:108). U.S. companies take advantage of the

Mexican law that permits factories to stop production when they lack supplies—in effect, a lockout. Since the components arrive from twin plants across the border, a parent company can easily control the flow of such material to its plant in Mexico and through this control discipline trade union action (Baerresen (1971:44). The border industrial development program has failed to answer the unemployment problem, particularly of men (Bustamente and Fernandez-Kelly in this volume).

Developing countries often pursue national policies for stimulating investment by underpricing the interest rate on capital (Heillinger and Heillinger 1976:61). In 1969 Brazil cut interest rates from 20 percent to 10 percent. In contrast, Japan allowed interest rates to rise 30 percent at a crucial period in the development of the country after World War II (Heillinger and Heillinger 1976:69). Whereas Brazil's policy stimulated a capital intensive development without meeting the problems of unemployment, Japan's policy contributed to a more autonomous development using manpower effectively.

Differences in regulations of business and standards of social welfare among advanced industrial nations will inhibit the development of a universal code for the multinational corporations. In the United Kingdom, there is an absence of legal restraints. Wage increases are related to employment conditions and productivity. However, health services, pensions, benefits, and severance payments are legislated by the government and hence are not issues for collective bargaining. In Germany the Works Constitution Act of 1952 is the basic law establishing authority, jurisdiction, and structure of the works council. Holidays are established by law and medical benefits are funded by the state. France has a National Social Security plan providing for sickness, accidents, medical, and death benefits as well as unemployment. Law and administrative action are important in negotiating fringe benefits (Kujawa 1975:100). Japanese industrial relations are characterized by paternalistic "enterprise" unions that guarantee lifetime employment and emphasize seniority (Hanami 1975:104). In working out any transnational agreement on a code of conduct, cultural factors and past agreements would have to be weighed in the balance.

## Ideology of Labor Management Relations

Kujawa (1975:115), Blainpain (1972:296) and other analysts of transnational labor relations agree that meaningful bargaining on an international basis is not yet feasible. Rationalizations as to why industrial relations are as they are differ not only between management and labor, but also between different groups representing labor. The only thing consistent with a class perspective in the present structure is that business leaders are content with the way things are and strive for ideological justification of a given situation whereas labor representatives of social democratic, Communist, and "bourgeois" trade unions find it in need of change. According to Kassalow (1977:180). "What keeps unions together is a jointly held concept of the changing power structure of society so that the influence of a wage-earner increases both in the general economy and the companies." Neither unions nor management actively try to change sectorial differences in the labor force. Primary and secondary labor markets exist in both First and Third World areas. Labor migration fostered ethnic segregation, which was often reinforced by trade union activities. The net effect is sharply illustrated by the Colombian migrants in Venezuela (Berlin in this volume).

*Management ideology.* Management's personnel policy is premised on a liassez-faire philosophy that is no longer a guide to real decision making but still serves an ideological function. International bargaining is not yet feasible in the same terms that applied in national negotiations since real wages are a function of market conditions in relation to the supply of other factors of production, technology, the productivity of workers, and the value of the product to consumers.

This laissez-faire approach is buttressed with claims by management, when confronted with inequalities in wages and conditions on a world level, that the firm must adapt to local conditions. It is a kind of cultural relativism that accepts a given condition as inevitable and justifies conformity to retrogressive labor practices in functionalist terms. Management maintains that industrial relations are carried out at the local level, often by a personnel manager who is a national. However, rigorous training in the home country of the firm is standard practice, and the fledgling personnel managers cut their teeth in a branch of the firm located near plant headquarters so that surveillance is close. Furthermore, the degree of centralized control is masked by "harmonization" of operations between branches of the firm, such that what appear to be local decisions are the inevitable result of a series of conditioning factors initiated from the headquarters of the firm.

*Labor Ideology.* The ideology of labor representatives is an explicit factor in recruitment of workers. The existing international trade union operations are primarily institutions growing out of the European Economic Community. The major representatives are the International Confederation of Free Trade Unions (ICFTU), representing 56 percent of organized workers; the World Federation of Trade Unions (WFTU), representing 20 percent; and the World Confederation of Labour (WCL), representing 15 percent. The ICFTU was formed when "democratic" trade unions broke from the WFTU over the issue of cooperating with the economic reconstruction of Europe under the Marshall Plan (Casserini 1972:76). These were primarily drawn from the British Trade Union Federation, the West German Trade Union Federation, the Malaysian Trade Union Congress, and most other "free" trade unions, including the American Federation of Labor. The WFTU, representing labor in six countries, formed after World War II, included the East European countries and socialist oriented unions and federations of western Europe. The CIO of the United States was a member until 1949, when it claimed the Soviet Union was manipulating the organization.

The ICFTU is more integrated in international negotiations than the WFTU at this point in history, although in the early part of the twentieth century the left labor movement had a stronger international bent. This is usually attributed to the fact that the major Communist and Socialist general confederations of workers in Italy and France hold power at the national level and are unwilling to lose their ability to influence government policy.

The ICFTU accents the framework of global production as defined by the business leaders and seeks a place within it in which to negotiate along traditional trade union lines. However, the implications of global business force them into a more militant framework because of the nature of the international competitive labor market. Their demands for a say in production planning, particularly in relation to investment decisions that affect the size of the labor force, is a necessary function in international negotiation and goes beyond what member unions might consider in their own negotiations.

The ICFTU, like management, accepts wage differentials as a necessary aspect of unequal exchange in the world market. Otto Brenner of the International Metal Federation, a trade secretariat many of whose member unions are also members of the ICFTU, expressed this in the following terms (ICFTU 1971:30).

*25*

In my opinion we should draw a very clear distinction between the two concepts [wage differentials and wage "dumping]. Differences in the level of wages—or more specifically, of labour costs—from one country to another are often due to the different stages of development in the various countries. "Stages of development" comprises a lot of factors; a few which play a part are the degree of industrialization, the density of the infrastructure, the standards of vocational training, the availability of raw materials. To put it quite simply, the highly industrialized countries are at a stage of economic development which allows a higher standard of living than in those countries which are only at the start of industrialization. A further important factor, as regards the level of wages, is the strength of trade unions. . . . As a rule, unfortunately, *it is precisely the trade unions in the developing countries which have to operate under conditions of structural unemployment.* [ICFTU 1971:30]

The acceptance of wage differentials between "highly industrialized countries" and "those countries which are at the start of industrialization" implies the need for labor exploitation to bring about the accumulation of capital. Furthermore, Brenner explicitly accepts the fact that the trade unions in developing countries "have to operate under conditions of structural unemployment." The assumption that structural unemployment was a distinctive characteristic of Third World countries changed after 1975 as most developed economies operated with unemployment rates above 4 percent, inflation that surpassed wage gains, and falling rates of unionization.

As yet, international labor organization are not prepared to deal directly with multinational corporations. The ICFTU has called on governments and international organizations to prevent misuse of power by multinationals and formulate a code of conduct. The union challenge to multinational corporations is restricted to publicity campaigns centering on labor disputes in other countries, refusal to work overtime or make shipments to foreign plants, that are being struck and bringing in union officials from foreign branches in a negotiation (Hershfield 1975:3). Beyond that, they can only try to influence governments to revoke legislation illegalizing international solidarity action, to use investment controls to promote freedom of union movements, and to enact legislation forcing a company to avoid manpower dislocations and controlling mergers (Hershfield 1975:3).

Most of the literature on labor in the international setting has concentrated on ideological differences between Communist and "free" trade unions in the European Economic Communities. However, the real dialogue seems to be that between the Third World and developed economies. In the 1971 meeting of the ICFTU, ideological differences became apparent in the discussions although they were not a cause for conflict. Third World spokespersons questioned Brenner's statement that "there are potential benefits to be derived from the activities of multinational companies" (M. Bose, Indian National Trade Union delegate, ICFTU 1971:41). The delegate from the Venezuelan Workers Confederation, pointed to the use of national savings for setting up a Ford assembly plant and the concessions to foreign firms extracting oil. He asserted that these foreign companies, whose operations in Venezuela were subsidized by the government, "created yellow scab trade unions and attempted to impose policies contrary to the trade union movement" (ICFTU 1971:38). V. Kulkarni of India strongly seconded other Third World representatives in pointing to the political power of the multinationals and calling for political action to counter it (ICFTU 1971:39).

In the changing internatinal division of labor, trade unions are losing ground. Locked into a bargaining structure premised on sectorial inequalities in the labor force, both Communist and socialist trade union leaders have failed to take action to overcome a differential wage pattern and segregated job market within or between countries. Organization of favored sectors of the blue-collar worker in core industrialized countries is declining, and unions have not made progress in organizing the women entering the work force. In the United States, for example, only 17 percent of the 40 million women in the work force are in unions (*New York Times* January 25, 1980, A15). Another significant area that has not been organized is migrant labor. Often undocumented, these workers seek employment that is off-the-books—service industries or illegally operating factories. Those who have working papers are oftentimes only able to find work in the most competitive sectors of industry and in service occupations. There is no immediate prospect for organizing labor on an international scale. With trade unions of the left and right in the highly developed countries absorbed in trying to hold on to sectors of the primary labor force, it will probably be left up to the developing countries, which are more conscious of the internatinal thrust of global enterprises and its impact on all sectors of the labor force, to formulate new policies to meet the challenge.

### Transculturation and the International Division of Labor

In this global framework, we must develop an analytical approach that will take into account sectorial differences within countries as well as between countries, since the movement of capital is in response to those changing relations. The acculturation model, commonly used in anthropology to think about cultural exchanges, is inadequate for this task. Over thirty years ago, Bronislaw Malinowski criticized the inadequacy of acculturation theory because of its assumed goal of acquiring Western culture. In the introduction to Fernando Ortiz' book, *Cuban Counterpoint: Tobacco and Sugar* (1947), Malinowski endorses the term "transculturation" chosen by Ortiz because it points to the active exchange that goes on in the contract between people of different cultures as they engage in production.

A theory of transculturation must take into account not only the transfer of culture traits from one society to another, but also the dialectical transformations in social relations within both countries that occur in the process. Whereas the dominance of the multinational corporations determines much of the flow of technology, work organization, and level of production, their very presence abroad changes the character of the corporation in its home base. Relations with the workers in the home country are changed as firm managers take advantage of a competitive international labor force. Workers in the secondary labor force are immediately affected since their jobs are often part of the footloose operations that go overseas. But as unemployment becomes widespread and endemic, even preferred sectors of the labor force in the industrial centers encounter competition in the internatinal arena. The net effect of the transfer of capital abroad has been to reinforce managerial decision-making and weaken the control of organized labor within the plant over hiring and upgrading. At the same time, labor relations in the host country take on some local characteristics in responses to existing rules, regulations, and customary expectations.

I shall focus on transculturation patterns in labor relations that are occurring first in formal negotiations between management and unions and second in the informal relations between manager and workers as well as among the rank and file themselves. These patterns, which are just beginning to be studied, are the best clue to emergent social structures.[6]

*Changes in Formal Negotiations.* The surface structure that multinational corporation representatives present is one of decentralized industrial relations with responsibility for decision making resting on the local representative, usually a national of the host country (Copp 1977:43–46). However, since the multinational corporations exclude local control over decisions about the redevelopment of production facilities or the introduction of new technology—decisions which are accepted by most European, Scandinavian and United Kingdoms corporations—the control by headquarters must be recognized. In the discussion following Copp's (1977) paper at the Cornell meeting on international labor, Ben Sharman contested the claim of decentralization on the basis of the Ford Company's action in Dagenham when management threatened to move production to West Germany when the workers struck. Furthermore, he asserted that since the parent company controls costs, it must set guidelines in industrial relations.

Sharman's comments raise an important point concerning the centralizing tendencies of large companies. These are the result, he states, of the the "harmonization" of a multiplicity of functions rather than the result of central authority. The United Nations (1978:48) report points out that as a result "control can be embedded within the fabric of the firm without being readily apparent to an outsider. . . . The more the national units become conditioned to indirect harmonized control procedures, the more difficult it becomes for them to respond unilaterally to the needs of the local economy."

The term *harmonization* as used in multinational circles is equivalent to what some anthropologists call transculturation. It refers to the process of adjusting the priorities of a powerful productive unit to the particular practices of the environment in which it becomes adapted. What is this process and how does it come about? Copp (1977:46) gives a clue in describing industrial relations practices in his own firm, the Ford Company. Industrial relations professionals from countries where Ford has located branches come to the United States to study and test principles accepted in the corporation at one or more location in the United States before returning to their home country. From then on they turn to the corporate staff only for consultation. The degree of centralization depends upon several factors: the more integrated the production process, the greater the inducement to centralize decision making; membership in employer associations promotes decentralization; the higher the ratio of foreign to home country employment, the greater the tendency to decentralize (Banks and Steiber 1977:4). The very size of the firm introduces a factor of complexity in industrial relations that results in more internally oriented training systems with more explicit and detailed enumeration of carrers, benefits, and evaluations (ILO 1976:40). The adaptablility of the firm will depend on how important the market is to the parent company. The ILO (1976:27) study points out that

Ford and General Motors are less responsive than a company such as Philips because they have a large home market. The amount of capital invested and its relative mobility also influence the degree of response to a local setting. Vaitsos (1974) makes the point that extractive industries made more of a contribution to the host country than recent manufacturing companies that can shift investment.

These centralizing tendencies appear to be opposed to internationalization. They are in fact a product of the movement abroad and reflect the increase in power gained by the multinational corporations. In fact, companies have adopted standards and practices in the host countries, but this is done selectively in terms of advantages to the firm. Whereas wage *levels* are kept in line with local and national labor markets, new wage *systems* are often introduced. The U.S. auto companies pioneered with fixed hourly systems (ILO 1976:28) and wage raises based on productivity. Job evaluations, merit systems, and detailed job descriptions are U.S. innovations that serve as mechanisms of control by the home office.

Among the beneficial practices that multinational corporations have extended abroad are paid vacations, won by steel workers in the United States and extended in Australia, vacation bonuses which originated in West Germany and were included in branch plants, wage increases tied to cost of living; forty-hour work week; and supplementary unemployment benefits extended from United States to Europe (Banks and Steiber 1977:7). The actual transfer of these benefits was not automatic. In order for gains made in the home base to spread, intervention by the ILO, the Organization for Economic Cooperation and Development, the European Economic Community, and visits by the unions were required. But because of the tendency toward diffusion throughout the branches of a corporation, industrial relations managers are extremely cautious about setting precedents and call on corporate headquarters for advice when they are impending.

Union adaptation to the changing relations in production in a global setting has been hampered by the threat of unemployment combined with diminishing resources. Some efforts toward internationalization have been reviewed; as yet, negotiations on a global level are blocked by both corporation and government action. The most significant direction in the immediate future is for workers in the same industry and firm to block efforts to shift production from strike-bound plants to other branches, as was done in the case of Ford in West Germany cited above. In the 1969–70 strike by IUE and UE of General Electric, one union leader attributed the greatest blow to the corporation when the International Longshoremen refused to unload parts shipped from overseas plants to substitute for parts made in the strikebound plant.

In the defensive position into which organized labor has been forced by internationalizing production, unions have not as yet been able to address themselves to the major problem—that of organizing the unorganized workers at home and abroad.

The analytical framework of transculturation takes into account the changes in the industrial centers as well as in the overseas branches. When jobs go overseas, the ethnic and sex segregation that protects preferred segments of the labor force within industrial centers is lost and with it the control of the trade union over allocation of jobs. The deskilling of the work force in these overseas operations involves a program for employing young female workers with high turnover. This limits the organization potential of trade unions, which are now structured along monopolistic lines paralleling that of the corporation.

*Changes in Informal Associations.* Because of the far-reaching effects of formal contract negotiations, industrial relations managers try to keep labor relations at an informal, interpersonal level. This is easier to do in the newly industrializing areas than in old industrial centers where trade unions are alert to the need for legally binding contracts. In the *export estates* of Korea and Singapore, and the "jellybean" operations of Malaysia, the Philippines, and Indonesia, the export industries attract the cream of an incompletely tapped sector of young female workers. Paternalism is promoted in the dormitories, schools, and dining facilities provided by many plants that would rather compete by offering more attractive facilities than by raising wages (Grossman 1978, Lim 1978). In addition, beauty contests, competitive sports, and other recreational activities are provided. A personnel manager in Penang, Malaysia told Rachel Grossman (1978) that the management spent $100,000 a year on recreational programs and thought it a worthwhile investment. It served to reduce worker hostility to management and, as a corollary of this, to lessen solidarity as a class in opposition to management. The company name, emblazoned on smocks in Penang and T-shirts in Ciudad Juárez (Fernandez-Kelly 1980), is a means of promoting identity with the firm rather than with a class.

Personnel policies stressing human relations as a counter to militant unionization (Grossman 1978) are widespread in the offshore industries wherever they are found. The culture of the multinational companies in the newer offshore industries is probably more homogeneous than that of the foreign companies in the United Kingdom and the Continent. This is in part due to their rapid spread in formerly agricultural areas that lacked the defensive organizations of an industrial workforce. It is also related to the nature of the work force. Cut off from traditional careers in marriage and rural agricultural production, young women have less base in the community from which to resist the effects of rapid industrialization. Paternalism, characteristic of the relations between managers, supervisors, and workers in Japanese industries, has diffused rapidly in U.S. firms abroad. In addition, union activities are weak, in part because there is the expectation, both on the part of women workers and management, that they will leave the labor force within a few years. If they defy this and continue working, they are often fired when they reach senior levels in the labor force and would be in a position to gain higher wages and enter into supervisory positions (Yoon n.d.). Whereas the veneer of Western culture that women receive in the factory is superficial, the impact of their entry into production is profound. They often postpone marriage because of fear of losing their jobs and because male unemployment is high (Baerresen 1971:35). When they are laid off, superannuated at the age of twenty-five or over, it is often difficult for them to reenter traditional society. This is particularly true in Asia, where the Westernization of factory culture is more at odds with the society (Yoon n.d.) than in Mexico.

The wider social consequences of an industrialization program such as that of the offshore industries have not as yet been measured. But with two to three hundred thousand young women employed in electronics alone in Southeast Asia (Grossman 1978) and over one hundred thousand in Mexico (Fernandez-Kelly, this volume) we can expect profound changes in reproductive rates, marital patterns, and community life. These are the topics of the papers included in this collection.

## Sectorial Analysis and the Changing Relations in Production

Major shifts in the sectorial composition of labor are bringing about profound changes in production relations. These changes are causing transformations in the family and community analyzed by contributors to this volume. Differential employment of women and men has stimulated the movement of women into the border cities of Mexico as men are being pushed back from the United States, a situation analyzed by Patricia Fernandez-Kelly and Jorgé Bustamente. It has exacerbated the crises in the working class barrios and agriclutural estates of Brazil as changing demands for the labor of men in foreign corporations affects family options for residence, alternative employment for women, and even family size, as analyzed by Neuma Aguiar. The very pressence of large foreign corporations has brought back into prominence the kind of domestic putting-out industry that Jośe Antonio Alonso studies in Mexico City. Comparisons of garment workers in the older industrial centers with those in developing areas, such as those of Helen Safa does in her comparison of United States and Brazilian factory workers, reveal some of the differentials affecting the secondary labor force in various settings. Although women in the declining garment factories of New Jersey opt for smaller families than Brazilian women, both put their domestic responsibilities first in an area of shrinking employment opportunities. The articles by Keller and Katz on electronics workers provide a counterpoint to Linda Lim's analysis of what is happening with those jobs in overseas production sites. The distinction between mental and manual coincides with ethnicity and sex, both within and outside of industrial centers, as Katz and Keller show in their articles on the domestic electronics industry. Van der Mark shows the aftermath of footloose industrialization in Curaçao. Women who had lost the crafts and cottage industries to go into the electronics factories set up by Texas Instruments found themselves without any employment when the firm closed the shop. These growing dependencies increase the vulnerability of a work force to fluctuations in the international market.

These papers provide a comparative basis for analyzing the transculturation occurring throughout the world. If at this stage, the process seems to be "bad" aspects of industrialization driving out the "good"; just as in Gresham's law of currency, the hope is that the new international division of labor will engender consciousness of class interests on an international scale. And with this the structural changes needed to transform relations in production.

### Notes

1. See, for example, studies of regional and national imbalance by Amin (1974); Emmanuel (1974); Cardoso and Faletti (1971); Frank (1967); dos Santos, Vasconi, Kaplan and Jaguaribe (1969); Sunkel (1973).

2. *Latin American Perspectives* devoted its first issue to a critique of dependency theory. The tendency to emphasize relations of exchange rather than of production is noted. Laclau (1971) tries to shift back to the analysis of production by focusing on the changing rates of organic composition of capital and surplus value. This emphasis is more effective in the analysis of offshore industries and their impact on the home base.

3. Whereas organization of the nonagricultural (or industrial) and government labor force has diminished, there has been a slight increase of 1 percent in the decade between 1967 and 1977 for agricultural workers (U.S. Department of Labor 1977).

4. Wide variations in the proportion of unionized workers exist among branches of the same company. For example, Caterpiller has 82 percent unionized workers in the United States, 100 percent in Australia, 20 percent in Brazil, 30 percent in France. Ford plants are 100 percent unionized in Mexico, 80 percent in Venezuela, and 78 percent in the Federal Republic of Germany. General Motors has 100 percent unionization in Mexico, 99 percent in the United States, and 75 percent in Belguim. Among firms that have resisted trade unions are IBM, Kodak, Gillette, Holoprome, Caterpiller, Roberts Arundel,, Continental Oil, Nestle, Goodyear, Firestone, KLM, Air Canada and TWA. Monsanto and Dupont de Nemours have rejected trade unions in their Luxembourg plants. According to the ICFTU (1971:20), Müler Wipperfurth preferred to transfer production to countries like Poland, Czechoslavakia, or Yugoslavia where there were no strikes rather than operate in Italy. These countries have, in addition, promoted multinational corporation investment by providing facilities to stimulate foreign investment.

5. The pressure on developing countries to reduce labor standards as a means of attracting export industries is graphically illustrated by the following excerpt from Lorenz (1974:9):; From the perspective of the export promotion policies of developing countries it follows that, in the interest of the employment effect, the wage level may even be manipulated below the subsistence minimum or the minimum wages determined by the state. The substitutive exports will then be burdened with external costs. In order to prevent "exploitation" of the absolute advantage, the developing countries only have the possibility of slightly reduced surpluses. If the developing countries do not want to be "exploited," they will have to retain a "reserve-army" and thus stay poorer for a longer time. . . . The absolute advantage of low wages may generally be extended by subsidies, devaluation and calculation at marginal costs and the terms of trade may also be changed for the worse.

6. See especially case studies in Zimbalist (1979).

## References

Amin, Samir. 1974. *Accumulation on a World Scale: A Critique of the Theory of Underdevelopment*. New York: Monthly Review Press.

Baerresen, Donald W. 1971. *The Border Industrialization Program of Mexico*. Lexington: D.C. Heath Books.

Baker, Elizabeth. 1964. *Technology and Woman's Work*. New York: Columbia University Press.

Banks, Robert F. and Steiber Jack, eds. 1977. *Multinational Unions and Labor Relations in Industrialized Countries.* Cornell International Industry and Labor Relations Report No. 9. Ithaca: New York State School of Industry and Labor Relations, Cornell University.

Bienefeld, M. A. 1972–73. "Planning People." *Development and Change* 4:51–87.

Blainpain, Roger. 1972. "Efforts to Bring about Community Level Collective Bargaining in the Coal and Steel Community and the European Economic Community." In *Transnational Industrial Relations: The Impact of Multinational Corporations and Economic Reginalization on Industrial Relations.* (Symposium at Geneva), ed. Hans Günther. London: Macmillan, St. Martin's Press, pp. 120–34.

Brenner, Otto. 1971. "Introductory Remarks," International Confederation of Free Trade Unions (ICFTU), Geneva.

Brookfield, Harold. 1975. *International Dependence and Development.* London: Methuen.

Cardoso, Fernando H. and Faletti, Enoz. 1971. *Dependencia y desarrollo en América Latina.* Mexico: Siglo XXI.

Casserini, Karl. 1972. "The Challenge of Multinational Corporations and Regional Economic Integration to the Trade Unions, Their Structure and Their International Activities." In *Transnational Industrial Relations, The Impact of Multinational Corporations and Economic Regionalization on Industrial Relations* (Symposium at Geneva), ed. Hans Günther. London: Macmillan, St. Martin's Press. pp. 70–83.

Copp, Robert. 1977. "Locus of Industrial Relations Decision Making in Multinational Corporations." In Banks and Steiber 1977:43–8.

Doeringer, P. B. and Piore, M.J. 1971. *International Labor Market and Manpower Analysis.* Lexington: Heath and Lexington Books.

Donges, Jürgen B. 1974. "Conditions for Successful Substitution and Export Diversification in Less Developed Countries: A Summary Approach," In Giersch 1974:336–60.

dos Santos, Teotonio; Vasconi, Tomas A; Kaplan, Marcos; and Jaguaribe, Helio. 1969. *La crisis del desarrolismo y la nueva dependencia.* Lima: Instituto de Estudios Peruanos.

*Economist,* June 9, 1973; Feb. 1978.

Edwards, Richard C., Reich, Michael, and Gordon, David M., eds. 1975. *Labor Market Segmentation.* Lexington: Heath Lexington Books.

Emmanuel, Arghiri. 1974. *Unequal Exchange: A Study of Imperialism of Trade.* New York: Monthly Review Press.

Fels, Gerhard. 1974. "The Export Needs of Developing Countries and the Adjustment Process in Industrial Countries." In Giersch 1974:76–95.

Fernández Kelly, María Patricia. 1980. "*Chavalas de Maquiladora*; A Study of the Female Labor Force of Ciudad Juárez Offshore Production Plants." Ph.D. thesis, Department of Anthropology, Rutgers University, New Brunswick, N.J.

*Fortune,* March 20, 1979; June 15, 1981.

Frank, Andrew G. 1967. *Capitalism and Undervelopment in Latin America: Historical Studies of Chile and Brazil.* New York: Monthly Review Press.

Fröbel, Folker; Heinrichs, Jürgen; and Kreye, Otto. 1978. "The New International Division of Labour." *Social Science Information* 17, no. 1; pp. 123–142.

Gennard, John and Stauer, M.D. 1977. "The Industrial Relations of Foreign Owned Subsidiaries in the U.S.," In Banks and Steiber 1977:301–17.

Giersch, Herbert, ed. 1974. *The International Division of Labour: Problems and Perspectives.* Tübingen: Mohr.

Griffin, Keith. 1974. "The International Transmission of Inequality." *World Development* 7:3–16.

Grossman, Rachel. 1978. "Women's Place in the Integrated Circuits," *Southeast Asia Chronicle,* and *Pacific Research,* Issue, 9, nos. 5–6 (July–October).

Günter, Hans. 1975. "Labor and Multinational Corporations in Western Europe: Some Problems and Prospects." In Kujawa 1975.

Gutman, Herbert J. 1977. *Work, Culture, and Society in Industrializing America: Essays in American Working-Class and Social History.* New York: Knopf.

Hanami, Tadashi. 1975. "The Multinational Corporations and Japanese Industrial Relations." In Kujawa 1975.

Hechter, Michael. 1975. *Internal Colonialism: The Celtic Fringe in British National Development 1536–1966.* Berkeley: University of California Press.

Helleiner, G.K. 1973. "Manufacturing Exports from Less Developed Countries and Multinational Firms." *Economic Journal* 83:21–47.

Heillinger, Stephen H. and Heillinger, Douglas A. 1976. *Unemployment and the Multinationals: A Strategy for Technological Change in Latin America.* Port Washington: Kenniat Press.

Hershfield, David C. 1975. *The Multinational Union Challenges the Multinational Company.* New York: The Conference Board.

Hobsbawm, Eric. 1968. *Industry and Empire: the Making of Modern English Society, 1750 to the Present Day.* New York: Pantheon Press.

Hobson, J.A. 1963 *The Export of Capital.* London: C.K. Constable

Hone, A. 1974. "Multinational Corporations and Multinational Buying Groups." *World Development* 2 (Feb.): 148–9.

Hugon, Felipe. 1978. "Les firmes multinationals et la division internationales du travail." *Buletin du Centre de Documentation d'Etudes Juridiques, Economiques, et Sociales,* 7, no. 8 (December).

Hymer, Stephen. 1973. "The Internationalization of Capital." In *International Business and Ecomony* ed. D.S. Henley, East Lansing: Michigan State University. pp. 278–98.

International Confederation of Free Trade Union (ICFTU). 1971. *The Multinational Challenge.* Report of Conference, June 24–6. Geneva.

International Labor Office. 1976. *The Impact of Multinational Enterprises on Employment and Training.* Geneva.

———.1977. *Social and Labour Practices of Some U.S. Based Multinationals in the Metal Trades.* Geneva.

———.1978. *Yearbook of Labour Statistics.* Geneva.

International Monetary Fund. 1978. *International Financial Statistics.*

Jager, Elizabeth, R. 1975. "U.S. Labor and Multinationals." In Kujawa 1975:22–46.

Jedel, Michael J. and Kujawa, Duane. 1975. "Industrial Relations Profiles of Foreign-owned Manufacturers in the U.S." In Banks and Steiber 1977:54–79.

Kassalow, Everett. 1975. "The International Metalworkers' Federation and the Latin American and Asian Automotive Industry." In Kujawa 1975:187–213.

————.1977. "Locus of Industrial Relations Decision-Making in Multinational Corporations." In Banks and Steiber 1977:167–181.

Kraft, Philip. 1975. "Transnational Industrial Relations: A Collective Bargaining Prospect." In Kujawa 1975:94–137.

————.1979. "The Industrialization of Computer Programming: From Programming to 'Software Production.'" In Zimbalist 1979.

Kujawa, Duane, ed. 1975. *International Labor and the Multinational Enterprises*. New York: Praeger.

Laclau H., Ernesto. 1971. "Feudalism and Capitalism in Latin America." *New Left Review* 1 (May–June):19–38.

Leviatan, Uri. 1976. "The Process of Industrialization in the Israeli Kibbutzim." In *Popular Participation in Social Change*, eds. J. Nash, J. Dandler, and N. Hopkins, pp. 549–58. The Hague: Mouton.

Lim, Linda. 1978. *Women Workers in Multinational Corporations: The Case of the Electronics Industry in Malaysia and Singapore*. Michigan Occasional Papers, no. 9. Ann Arbor: University of Michigan.

Lorenz, Detlef. 1974. "Explanatory Hypotheses on Trade Flows Between Industrial and Developing Countries." In Giersch 1974:83–121.

Lupo, L.A. and Freidlin, J.N. 1975. "U.S. Direct Investment Abroad 1971–1974." In *Survey of Current Business*. Washington, D.C.

Murphy, Robert F. 1971. *The Dialectics of Social Life*. New York: Basic Books.

Nash, June. 1980. "Structural Change and Strikes in the Electrical Machinery Industry." Paper delivered at the New York Academy of Science, December.

————.n.d. "Field Notes, Research in Progress, Pittsfield, MA." MS.

*New York Times*, May 7, 1975; Jan. 25, 1976; May 5, 1978; May 8, 1979.

Ortiz, Fernando. 1947. *Cuban Counterpoint: Coffee, and Sugar*. New York: Alfred A. Knopf.

Palloux, Christian. 1973. *Les firmes multinationales et la proces d'internationalisation*. Paris: François Maspero.

Pico Vidal, Isabel. 1976. "The History of Women's Struggle for Equality." In *Sex and Class in Latin America*, eds. J. Nash and Helen Safa. New York: Praeger. Reprinted by J.F. Bergin Press, 1980.

————.n.d. "The Quest for Race, Sex, and Ethnic Equality in Puerto Rico." Paper read at the Latin American Studies Association, San Francisco, November 14–16, 1974.

Saffioti, Heleieth. B. 1978. *Women in Capitalist Production*. New York: Monthly Review Press.

Salm, C.L. 1970. "Desemprego e subemprego en Brasil." *Revista Brasileira de Economic* 24, no. 4, p. 110.

Sassen-Koob, Saskia. 1981. "Towards a Conceptualization of Immigrant Labor." *Social Problems,* 29 (October), pp. 65–85.

Scheid, Rudolf. 1974. "The Export Needs of Developing Countries and the Need for Adjustment in Industrial Countries." In Giersch 1974:151–75.

Sciberas, Edmond. 1977. *Multinational Companies and National Economic Policies.* Greenwich, Conn.: Jai Press.

Sharman, Ben. 1977. "Comments." In Banks and Steiber 1977.

Sokoloff, Natalie. 1980. Between Love and Money. New York: Praeger.

Sunkel, Oswaldo. 1973. "Transnational Capitalism and National Disintegration in Latin America," *Social and Economic Studies* 22, no. 1, pp. 132–71.

Tyler, William C. 1974. "Employment Generation and the Promotion of Manufactured Exports in Less Developed Countries: Some Suggestions." In Giersch 1974:363–98.

United Nations Committee on Transnational Corporations. 1978. *Transnational Corporations in World Development: A Reexamination. New York* (78–05492).

United Nations Conference of Trade and Development (UNCTAD). 1975. *Subcontracting Arrangements in Electronics between Developed Market Economy Countries and Developing Countries.* New York.

US. Department of Labor. 1977. *Handbook of Labor Statistics.* Washington, D.C.: Government Printing Office.

U.S. International Trade Commission. 1976. *Background Information and Compilation of Materials on Items 807.00 and 806.30 of the Tariff Schedules of the U.S. Subcommittee on Trade of the Committee on Ways and Means, U.S. House of Representatives, 95th Congress, 2nd session, July 25, 1976.* Washington, D.C.: U.S. Government Printing Office.

Vaitsos, Constantine V. 1974. "Efectos de las inversiones extranjeras directas sobre la ocupació en los paises en vias de desarrollo." *Economía* 41, no. 2 (April, June):377–401.

Wallerstein, Immanuel. 1977. "Rural Economy in Modern World Society." *Studies in Comparative International Development* 12 no. 1 (Spring):29–36.

Weinberg, Nat. 1977. "The Impact of Multinational Corporations and Unions on the Industrial Relations." In Banks and Steiber 1977:97–119.

Yoon, Soon Young. n.d. "The Role of Young Women in the Development Process, Especially in Industries of South Korea." Report submitted to United Nations, Division of Population and Social Affairs, December 15, 1977.

Zimbalist, Andrew. 1979. *Case Studies on the Labor Process.* New York: Monthly Review Press.

# CHAPTER 2

# The New International Division of Labor and the U.S. Work force: The Case of the Electronics Industry*

ROBERT SNOW

Since the mid-1960s, industrial production has been internationalized at an increasingly rapid pace. Through direct investment and subcontract arrangements, corporations from the United States and other industrialized nations have shifted many of their labor-intensive operations to low wage Third World countries. Components or materials are shipped from the home country for assembly, and finished products are returned to the home country for sale. Corporations have adopted this strategy in the face of mounting domestic and international competition as a way of reducing labor costs. They have also been drawn by the prospect of readily available and relatively docile workers. *Offshore sourcing*, as this type of internationalized production is known, has been particularly apparent in the electronics and garment industries, although the model is now spreading to other U.S industries, notably automobile production, in the face of competition from foreign imports. The rapid rise of offshore sourcing has changed the world economy with consequences for the work forces in both the United States and the Third World. These consequences are still inadequately explored.

For labor unions, industrialists, government officials, and social scientists in the United States, the debate over offshore sourcing has revolved around one central question, often very baldly posed: does offshore sourcing destroy or create jobs for workers in the United States? As will be seen below, in this simplistic form, the question has generated a battle with no clear victor.

The convener of a recent U.S. Department of Labor conference on the impact of international trade and investment on employment introduced the volume of proceedings with this statement:

> An area of almost unrelieved ignorance has involved the relationship between U.S. investments abroad and U.S. employment. . . . It is probably no accident that in the past, estimates of the employment impact of U.S. foreign investment have ranged from a job loss of over a million to a job gain of over half a million, and sometimes in the same study. [U.S. Department of Labor 1978:5]

The issue has been a heated political controversy in the United States because spokespersons for the various interest groups cannot agree on either the facts or their consequences. Writings by protectionist unions and corporations on one side and free-trade groups on the other have tended to be polemical, convincing only those who chose to be convinced. Economists writing on the subject have relied heavily upon econometric models to project future employment trends. Both polemical and econometric writings are unsatisfying because they deal with the impact of offshore sourcing on the structure of the U.S. work force in highly aggregated and hypothetical terms.

To grasp the impact of offshore sourcing on the work force and on society, the question must be posed much more specifically: who are the workers who have gained or lost jobs as a result of corporate decisions to move production overseas? In a given industry, has there been a loss of jobs for unskilled versus skilled workers? for women versus men? for minorities versus whites? for all parts of the country or for a few geographic areas where the industry is concentrated? These types of differences in the structure of the work force are more important in social terms than a crude tally of jobs gained or lost. Moving away from generalizations based on aggregated statistics produces a clearer picture of the social consequences of the internationalization of production, and looking at what has occurred in the recent past rather than framing scenarios of what might occur in the future further grounds the argument in social reality.

This article examines the impact of offshore sourcing by the electronics industry on the U.S. work force over the past twenty years. As will be shown, the electronics industry has been one of the prime examples of offshore sourcing since the mid-1960s. Despite the very rapid growth in the reliance of the U.S. electronics industry on workers in the Third World, particularly in Asia and Latin America, for low skill, low wage production processes, the total number of jobs for electronics workers in the United States has increased by 64 percent since offshore sourcing began in 1964—from a work force of 264,800 in 1964 to 434,200 in 1978 (U.S. Department of Labor 1979c:333). While these statistics disprove the simplistic argument that offshore sourcing has reduced U.S. electronics employment, they mask important shifts in the composition of the electronics work force. At the national level, two trends appear. First, both the percentage of production workers in the electronics work force and their absolute number have decreased. The increases in employment opportunities in the electronics industry have come in white-collar categories. Second, the percentage and absolute number of women in the electronics work force have declined since the mid-1960s. This is significant because the electronics work force has always been characterized by a very high percentage of women. The bulk of the new jobs in electronics are being created in traditionally male technical, white-collar sectors where women remain underrepresented. (Obviously a high percentage of electronics production workers are women, and therefore the categories *production workers* and *women workers* overlap to a large degree. Statistics available at the national level, however, do not disaggregate production workers by sex nor women workers by job category.)

Changes in the structure of the electronics work force, however, are not felt by all parts of the country equally. The electronics industry is geographically concentrated in seven states, and California and Massachusetts alone account for over a quarter of U.S. electronics employment. Within these two states, electronics production has been concentrated in two metropolitan areas, San Jose and Boston. The electronics industry in both of these centers has shown strong growth, particularly since the 1975 recession. As a result, these centers of the electronics industry have not been the regions adversely affected by the declining importance of production workers and women. In fact, both Massachusetts and California have witnessed substantial increases in overall electronics employment; and at least in the San Jose area where detailed statistics are available, the absolute number of both blue-collar workers and women has increased. However, this overall growth masks an important shift in the structure of the work force. The percentage of blue-collar workers in the San Jose electronics industry has dropped considerably since the mid-1960s, indicating that the increase in the number of blue-collar workers is the result of the rapid growth of the electronics industry in the area, despite the declining proportion of production worker positions created. Opportunities for women considered as a group in the San Jose

*41*

electronics work force have not been adversely affected. In contrast to the national-level trend noted above, the number of women workers in the San Jose electronic work force has increased and their percentage has remained relatively constant; however, women are increasingly likely to be in clerical jobs, not production work.

These facts suggest that the loss of electronics industry jobs for production workers and women that is revealed in the national-level statistics has occurred not in the growth centers of the industry but in other parts of the United States. This is not surprising because, at least since the mid-1960s, the electronics industry in both San Jose and Boston has been characterized by a higher percentage of white-collar employees than the nation as a whole. These core areas have been the sites of research and development and corporate management whereas many production-worker tasks have been carried out in other parts of the United States or overseas. It appears that reliance on offshore sourcing has affected the U.S. growth centers of the electronics industry less than the peripheral areas in the United States where routine production processes have been carried out. Indeed, in the late 1970s, both the San Jose and Boston area reported labor shortages, including shortages of applicants for traditionally female blue-collar positions.

Finally, the available figures indicate that the most serious impact of offshore sourcing on the structure of the U.S. electronics work force occurred during the late 1960s and early 1970s when many corporations first opted to move some of their labor-intensive production processes overseas. At the national level, the percentage of blue-collar workers and women in the U.S. electronics work force appeared to have stabilized by the late 1970s. Even if offshore sourcing continues, it is unlikely that the proportion of these types of workers will drop still further unless the organization of production is dramatically altered again. This remains a possibility with the introduction of new forms of automation, increased competition from Japanese producers of electronics goods, and the generally uncertain future of an economy plagued by recession and high inflation.

Wages paid by the U.S. electronics industry have not kept pace with increases in the wage rate for U.S. industrial workers as a whole. Perhaps because of the low wages received by electronics production workers, the percentage of ethnic minorities in the blue-collar electronics work force has increased considerably. In San Jose the percentage of minority workers in the blue-collar work force has doubled since 1966, and case studies indicate that immigrant workers make up a large proportion of the electronics work force in both San Jose and Boston. These changes are, of course, also partly explained by changing trends in migration. Whatever the reason, during the past fifteen years, electronics production work has increasingly been carried out in the Third World; it has also increasingly been carried out by Third World workers, usually women, in the United States.

Although no definite causal connection can be proved, the internationalization of production in the electronics industry has occurred during a period that has witnessed the national level decline in opportunities for production workers and women in the industry, the strengthening of the industry centers in the United States, and the increasing reliance upon minority workers in blue-collar jobs. Taken as a whole, this suggests that offshore sourcing may contribute to and exacerbate the existing inequalities and imbalances in U.S. society: production workers and women, already less privileged then white-collar workers and men, have lost further ground; the affluent and developed centers of the electronics industry have grown and become even more heavily white-collar than before; production-worker jobs in the industry centers have become less attractive to native born Caucasian workers with better paying options, leading to a much heavier reliance on minority and immigrant workers.

This article examines the available evidence for these conclusions. It focuses first on the literature that discusses the relationship between offshore sourcing and U.S employment. It then looks in some detail at the recent history of employment trends in the U.S. electronics industry at the national level, in California and Massachusetts, and in the San Jose area where much of the industry is headquartered. The impact of offshore sourcing on production workers, women, and minorities is emphasized. Finally, some speculations are advanced regarding future employment trends in the U.S. electronics industry and in other U.S. labor-intensive industries facing a growth in offshore sourcing or large-scale importing.

## Review of Literature

Debates regarding the impact of offshore investments and imports on U.S. employment have generated a voluminous and highly polarized literature. U.S. labor unions have charged that decisions by U.S. corporations to establish production facilities overseas have resulted in the loss of a large number of actual or potential U.S.

jobs. They point out that such corporate policies are encouraged by tariff laws that facilitate imports from foreign subsidiaries of U.S. corporations—notably Articles 806 and 807 of the U.S. Tariff Schedule (see, for example, Kirkland 1974, Jager 1978, Sheinkman 1978). Corporations in industries adversely affected by imports have also advocated the adoption of more protectionist policies.

On the other side of the debate, spokespersons for corporations that rely upon offshore sourcing and free-trade lobby groups hold that offshore factory investments, in fact, create jobs in the United States by keeping American corporations efficient and competitive (See Gerstacker 1974; *Journal of the Flagstaff Institute* 1978.) If U.S. firms remain competitive in the world market, those who espouse this position argue, they will expand and develop new products, employing more U.S. workers.

As mentioned above, most of the available social science literature dealing with the relationship between overseas investment and domestic employment has been written by economists. Their findings are commonly based upon econometric models that, in turn, rest upon a variety of assumptions about the workings of the economy. They tend to discuss future trends, not those that have actually transpired. Many of the studies that are cited in the debate over the impact of foreign investment on domestic employment deal primarily with the broader issue of the potential effects of cheap imports, encouraged by the reduction of tariffs and other trade barriers, on the U.S. labor force. Some of the recent research regarding the impact of imports and/or investments on U.S. employment supports the conclusion that a significant number of U.S. jobs are lost because of imports and investment (e.g., Frank and Freeman 1978). Other researchers conclude that, whether or not overseas investment causes actual job loss, it is detrimental to labor because it restructures the domestic economy, increasing the share of wealth going to capital while decreasing the share going to labor (Musgrave 1975:xvi) and/or lowers wages of workers in affected industries (Frank and Freeman 1978:165). Musgrave's research and statements by the AFL-CIO note that offshore investments also tend to weaken the bargaining power of organized labor in the United States (Kirkland 1974:94; Musgrave 1975:xvii). Still other studies find that the creation of U.S. jobs is stimulated by investments and imports or that aggregated job loss is minimal and of relatively short duration (Baldwin 1976, Baldwin and Lewis 1978, Bale 1976, Hawkins and Walter 1972, Jacobson 1978, Monson 1978). And a sprinkling of researchers remain agnostic (Horst 1976, Horst 1978, Vernon 1977).

For a sociologist, the literature is unsatisfying first because much of it deals with the question of the relationship between employment and imports or investments at a very high level of statistical aggregation, and second because it speculates about hypothetical future differences in labor force patterns that might arise from changing one or another parameter in the econometric models, while virtually ignoring the historical record.

There are several problems with the high level of aggregation. It tends to conceal the different dynamics at work in various industries. As John Dunning points out, the impact of investments or imports on declining industries is substantially different from their impact on industries that are rapidly expanding (n.d.:35). Horst stresses the rather obvious, but often overlooked, fact that different types of offshore investments have different impacts in the home country: investments in overseas factories are different from investments in sales offices or other nonproduction facilities (Horst 1978:150). Furthermore, for a variety of historical, geographical, economic, and political reasons, a given industry is apt to be centered in one or several regions of the home country, not evenly distributed across the nation. This means that a loss or gain in employment in a given industry is apt to be felt in specific locales. It is also clear that a given industry tends to be characterized by a specific type of work force: it will rely upon a certain proportion of highly skilled white-collar workers and low skill blue-collars; of male and female workers; of white and non-white workers; of U.S. born and foreign-born workers. A change in the import or investment practices of corporations in a given sector may, therefore, have serious employment consequences for specific segments of the labor force in certain parts of the country, a fact to which the unions have paid much more attention than the social scientists (see Sheinkman 1978).

Some of the social science studies cited above have factored in the differences between types of industries (Baldwin 1976, Baldwin and Lewis 1978, Dunning n.d., Hawkins 1972, Horst 1976, 1978, Jacobson 1978, *Journal of the Flagstaff Institute* 1978); between workers of different skill levels (Baldwin 1976, Baldwin and Lewis 1978, Bale 1976, Dunning n.d., Frank and Freeman 1978, Hawkins and Walter 1972, Hufbauer 1978, Jacobson 1978); and between different regions or states (Baldwin 1976, Baldwin and Lewis 1978, Dunning n.d., *Journal of the Flagstaff Institute* 1978). Although several statements by unions and others critical of overseas investment mention the impact on women, minority, and older workers

*45*

in particular (e.g., Sheinkman 1978, Axelrad 1979), few of the social science studies mention these specific groups of workers.

The work of Baldwin and Lewis (1978) is the most comprehensive examination of disaggregated worker characteristics—excepting sex and ethnicity—currently available. Their overall conclusion is that substantial multilateral tariff cutting could be attempted without causing "significant adverse aggregated trade and employment effects in the U.S. economy" (242). With regard to workers of different skill levels, Baldwin and Lewis's model predicts that a 50 percent across the board tariff cut would result in a slight increase in demand for highly educated technical workers and farmers while producing a slightly lowered demand for low skill workers, especially semiskilled operatives—0.14 percent decline (252). In terms of geographical distribution, the model suggests that a 50 percent tariff cut would mean a net job loss of more than one thousand workers in only five states while three states would gain a few hundred workers each (253–254). As the authors conclude, the magnitude of their projected changes in employment level are all extremely small. Baldwin and Lewis also examine the results of the hypothetical tariff cut upon 367 specific industries. Again, they find relatively small negative employment consequences for all but a very few sectors. In nineteen industries out of the 367, the authors predict that a 50 percent tariff cut would actually stimulate a 0.5 percent or greater increase over the industry's 1967 labor force level.

The Baldwin and Lewis material is the most thorough currently available; however, despite the apparent detail of their model, their data do not give a clear picture of the impact of tariff shifts on specific types of workers in particular states in a given industry. The level of aggregation remains too high. An examination of the social impact of the consequences of changing investment or import policy demands this greater degree of specificity.

This paper focuses on changes in the labor force in one of the U.S. industries most heavily affected by U.S. investment in offshore factories, electronics. A number of studies have examined the impact of overseas investment on the electronics industry. Some of the unions that have organized electronics workers, notably the International Brotherhood of Electrical Workers (IBEW), have claimed that these "runaway shops" and imports have destroyed U.S. jobs. "American manufacturing industries, especially those involving significant labor content—jobs for American workers—have been virtually destroyed by imports." (*IBEW Journal* 1977:36) cited in NACLA 1977. Studies by the North American Congress on Latin America

(NACLA) (1977) and the Pacific Studies Center (1978) found that, whereas offshore sourcing by U.S. electronics firms has not reduced the number of actual U.S. jobs, the creation of new jobs in the United States has not kept pace with industry expansion or with the number of jobs created overseas. Other studies find a rapid rate of U.S. job creation in electronics (Baldwin 1976:147; Dunning n.d.:35–36; *Journal of the Flagstaff Institute* 1978:6).

### The U.S. Electronics Industry

The U.S. electronics industry has relied heavily upon overseas subsidiaries for labor-intensive assembly work since the mid-1960s, and U.S. firms continue to seek foreign sites where cheap and well-disciplined labor is available. Although accurate statistics on the amount of direct foreign investment by electronics corporations is difficult or impossible to obtain, an examination of the U.S. Customs Office statistics on the value of imports brought into the U.S. under Articles 806/807 of the Tariff Schedule gives an approximation of the rate of expansion of U.S. owned production facilities oveseas.[1] A 1978 Flagstaff Institute Study found that, between 1970 and 1976, the 806/807 share of the total U.S. electrical industry (Standard Industrial Code 36), which includes electronics (SIC 367) grew at a faster rate than for any other U.S. industry (*Journal of the Flagstaff Institute* 1978:29). This means that the dependence of the electrical industry on foreign workers, as measured by 806/807 statistics, was growing faster than for any other U.S. industry. Statistics for the dutiable value (that is, the value added overseas, largely wages to foreign workers) of 806/807 imports of electronic tubes, transistors, and semiconductors, which have been the fastest growing segment of the electronics industry, show a rapid and steady increase from 1972 (when 806/807 statistics for the category begin) to 1978 with a slight dip during the recession of 1975 (see Table 2–1). The U.S. electronics industry is both rapidly growing and rapidly expanding overseas.

The U.S. electronics industry was originally centered in the Northeast; but California now has the largest number of electronics workers of any state, and the majority of electronics manufacturing workers are in seven states: California, New York, Illinois, New Jersey, Pennsylvania, Massachusetts, and Indiana (Electronics Industry Association 1979:128). The San Jose area in California and the Boston

Table 2-1. Dutiable Value of Electronic Tubes, Transistors, and Semiconductors Imported into the United States under Articles 806.30 and 807 of the U.S. Tariff Schedule

| | |
|---|---|
| 1972 | $129,336,000 |
| 1973 | 235,702,000 |
| 1974 | 384,478,000 |
| 1975 | 339,546,000 |
| 1976 | 501,623,000 |
| 1977 | 524,607,000 |
| 1978 | 625,724,000 |

Source: Journal of the Flagstaff Institute 1979 (July):53–54.

area in Massachusetts are two of the most important centers for electronics in the United States.

Electronics manufacturing has relied heavily upon a semiskilled work force which is heavily female. In 1978, 52 percent of all electronics (SIC 367) employees were women (U.S. Department of Labor 1979c:333). During the most recent year for which comprehensive national data are available, 1973, 73.0 percent of all operatives and 67.5 percent of all laborers in electronics were women; 89.7 percent of all women in the electronics industry were in three occupational categories: 57.8 percent were operatives and 13.1 percent were laborers and another 18.8 percent were office and clerical workers (U.S. Equal Employment Opportunity Commission [EEOC] 1975:103). Therefore, any substantial change in demand for semiskilled electronics employees—operatives and laborers—would have a great impact on women workers.

In examining the impact of offshore sourcing by U.S. electronics corporations on employment and specifically employment for production workers and women, it is useful to examine national, state, and county or metropolitan statistics over time. One must keep in mind, of course, that many other events occurring during the same time period—notably wars, business booms and recessions, inflation, the development of new products and production techniques, and automation—have affected employment levels and that these factors may well have had a more important effect on employment than offshore sourcing. However, given the rather bald way in which the debate has been posed—whether offshore soucing creates or destroys U.S. jobs—it is useful to examine the historical record of electronics, the U.S. industry most highly dependent on overseas production.

## Electronics Employment—The National Level

Before attemptong to examine the changes in labor force patterns for specific subcategories of electronics workers, it is necessary to document the changes occurring in overall electronics employment over time at the national level. The most complete source of information for labor patterns in the United States as a whole is the U.S. Department of Labor's Bureau of Labor Statistics (BLS). Unlike data from most other agencies, statistics in the BLS volume *Employment and Earnings, 1909–1978* (1979c) have been standardized to make them comparable over time, despite changes in the Standard Industrial Code (SIC). The changes in the SIC hamper the usefulness of reports from other agencies.

As Table 2–2 shows, overall employment in Electronics Components and Accessories (SIC 367) has increased considerably during the twenty year period from 1958 to 1978, with dips during 1963–1967, 1970–1971, and 1975. The highest all-time level of employment is also the most recently entry, December 1978 (462,100 employees). This figure represents a 40 percent growth in the number of U.S. jobs in electronics since the bottom of the 1975 recession (August 1975—328,800 employees). For the semiconductor industry (SIC 3674), which constitutes the fastest growing segment within the electronics industry and one of the segments most heavily reliant upon offshore sourcing, there has been a 49 percent growth in employment since the bottom on the recession (April 1975, 118,600 employees to December 1978, 177,100 employees).

For comparison it may be helpful to examine the experience of two other industries that have been seriously affected by imports and subcontracting offshore: textiles (SIC 22) and garments (SIC 23). Unlike electronics, both of these industries have declined in the United States for some time (see Table 2–3). Their histories and economic dynamics are very different from electronics; however, like electronics, both are heavily reliant upon a labor-intensive, semi-skilled work force, much of which has traditionally been female. (In 1978, 47.2 percent of all textile employees and 81.1 percent of all apparel workers were women [U.S. Department of Labor, 1979c:504–504, 547] compared with 52.5 percent of all electronics workers.) Employment in Textile and Mill Products reached its highest level in March 1948, and the December 1978 level is 33.4 percent below this peak. Almost the same number of persons were employed in textiles in December 1978 (914,400) as in June 1958

*Table 2-2.* Production Workers and Women Workers as a Percentage of Total Employment in Electronics (SIC 367) (in thousands)

| Year | All Employees | Production Workers | Production Workers/All Employees (percentage) | Women Employees | Women Employees/All Employees (percentage) |
|---|---|---|---|---|---|
| 1958 | 178.9 | 133.9 | 74.8 | – | – |
| 1959 | 213.3 | 160.9 | 75.4 | 123.1 | 57.7 |
| 1960 | 233.5 | 170.0 | 72.8 | 131.3 | 56.2 |
| 1961 | 243.0 | 176.7 | 72.7 | 136.8 | 56.3 |
| 1962 | 266.1 | 198.2 | 74.5 | 153.9 | 57.8 |
| 1963 | 262.5 | 192.0 | 73.1 | 149.6 | 57.0 |
| 1964 | 264.8 | 194.0 | 73.3 | 151.5 | 57.2 |
| 1965 | 307.1 | 232.6 | 75.7 | 181.0 | 58.9 |
| 1966 | 388.6 | 297.9 | 76.6 | 233.6 | 60.1 |
| 1967 | 384.9 | 280.1 | 72.8 | 222.9 | 57.9 |
| 1968 | 381.4 | 270.1 | 70.8 | 215.5 | 56.5 |
| 1969 | 394.0 | 276.0 | 70.0 | 222.1 | 56.4 |
| 1970 | 366.7 | 244.1 | 66.6 | 195.0 | 53.2 |
| 1971 | 329.4 | 213.1 | 64.7 | 171.1 | 52.0 |
| 1972 | 354.8 | 230.9 | 65.1 | 188.8 | 53.2 |
| 1973 | 410.7 | 272.7 | 66.4 | 224.0 | 54.5 |
| 1974 | 421.0 | 275.4 | 65.4 | 227.7 | 54.1 |
| 1975 | 338.2 | 207.1 | 61.2 | 170.7 | 50.5 |
| 1976 | 366.0 | 229.5 | 62.7 | 190.2 | 52.0 |
| 1977 | 398.3 | 248.8 | 62.5 | 207.5 | 52.1 |
| 1978 | 434.2 | 272.5 | 62.8 | 227.8 | 52.5 |

*Source:* U.S. Department of Labor, Bureau of Labor Statistics, *Employment and Earnings, U.S., 1909–1978* (Washington, D.C.: Department of Labor 1979), pp. 333–334.

Table 2-3. Employment Patterns

| | All-Time High Level of Employment | | December 1978 Level of Employment | Percent Increase Since Lowest Point of 1975 Recession | Percent Increase January 1958 to December 1978 |
|---|---|---|---|---|---|
| | Date | Number of Employees | | | |
| Total U.S. Private Non-agricultural Establishments | Dec. 1978 (Time Frame, 1919–1978) | 72,367,000 | 72,367,000 | 19.0% | 66.2% |
| Electronic Components and Accessories (SIC 367) | Dec. 1978 (Time Frame, Jan. 1958–1978) | 462,100 | 462,100 | 40.5% | 163.4% |
| Semiconductors (SIC 3674) | Dec. 1978 (Time Frame, Jan. 1972–1978) | 177,100 | 177,100 | 49.3% | —[a] |
| Textile and Mill Products (SIC 22) | Mar. 1948 (Time Frame, Jan. 1939–1978) | 1,368,000 | 910,400 | 11.9% | -1.9% |
| Apparel and Other Textile Products (SIC 23) | Oct. 1973 (Time Frame, Jan. 1939–1978) | 1,461,000 | 1,305,300 | 10.0% | 9.8% |

Source: U.S. Department of Labor, Bureau of Labor Statistics, 1979c.
[a] Data on employment in the semiconductor industry only extend back to 1972.

(928,400). Since the lowest point of the 1975 recession (March 1975), employment has increased by only 11.9 percent.

For the apparel industry, employment reached its all time peak in 1973, and the December 1978 level is 10.6 percent below this figure. Recovery from the 1975 recession has been even less vigorous than in textiles.

These employment figures show that, despite the heavy reliance of the electronics industry on offshore factory investments for labor-intensive production, the rate of increase in the total number of jobs in the U.S. electronics industry has been greater than the rate for all private U.S. nonagricultural employment and much greater than for two other industries affected by imports and offshore investment: textiles and garments. This means that, at least in its crudest form, the argument that offshore investment has destroyed U.S. electronics jobs must be discarded.

### Electronics Employment—Skill Levels

These aggregated employment statistics support industry statements that the electronics industry is growing so fast that, even with considerable offshore sourcing jobs for members of the U.S. work force have increased in number. What the aggregated statistics mask, however, is a change in the composition of the work force. Such a change has serious implications for social structure, even if overall employment continues to increase. In the words of Raymond Vernon (1977:116), writing of the impact of internationalized production on the makeup of the U.S. work force: "More certain than the change in the total number of U.S. jobs is the change in the mix: the number of jobs available for the unskilled has been reduced, while the number available to the skilled has increased. . . ." Cast in this light, the question of the impact of internationalized production shifts from that of aggregated employment gain or loss to a concern with changes in the level of job skills required by the electronics industry; and, with this, to a concern with changes in the demographic makeup of the U.S. electronics work force. Is there a loss of jobs for unskilled versus skilled workers? for women versus men? for minorities versus whites?

The highest number of production workers[2] employed in electronics (313,500) was recorded in November and December 1966 (see Table 2–4). The December 1978 level (293,200), although representing a rise compared with recent years, remains 6.5 percent below the 1966

*Table 2–4.* Production Workers

| | All-time High Level of Production Worker Employment | | Dec. 1978 Level of Production Workers | Percent Increase Since Lowest Point of 1975 Recession | Percent Increase 1958– 1978 |
|---|---|---|---|---|---|
| | Date | No. of Prod. Workers | | | |
| Total U.S. Private Nonagricultural Employment | Dec. 1978 (Time Frame, 1947–1978) | 59,323,000 | 59,323,000 | 19.6% | 62.0% |
| Electronic Components and Accessories (SIC 367) | Nov.– Dec. 1966 (Time Frame, 1958–1978) | 313,500 | 293,200 | 47.9 | 119.0 |
| Semiconductors (SIC 3674) | Dec. 1978 (Time Frame, 1972–1978) | 85,700 | 85,700 | 59.6 | – |

*Source:* U.S. Department of Labor, Bureau of Labor Statistics, 1979c.

peak. Statistics for the semiconductor industry (SIC 3674) compiled by the U.S. Department of Commerce[3] show that between 1954 and 1977 the highest level of employment for production workers was reached in 1974 (81,600). More recent statistics from the Bureau of Labor Statistics show an increase to 85,700 production workers by December 1978.

Although the decrease in the absolute number of electronics production workers since 1966 is significant, an examination of the changes in the percentage of production workers in the total electronics work force is even more revealing (see Table 2–2 and Table 2–5).

During the late 1950s and early 1960s, before offshore sourcing began, over 70 percent of all employees in electronics were production workers, reaching a peak of 76.6 percent in 1966, the same year in which the absolute number of production workers peaked. Thereafter, the percentage of production workers declined almost steadily to 61.2 percent in 1975, a significant shift in the composition of the work force during precisely the years when the practice of offshore sourcing was growing rapidly among U.S. electronics corporations (see Lim 1978, Moxon 1974, Reynis 1976). Since 1975 the percentage of production workers, based on annual averages, has hovered between 62.5 and 62.8 percent.

*Table 2-5.* Number of Production Workers Compared to Total Employment in the Semiconductor Industry (SIC 3674)

| Year | All employees | Production workers | Percentage of Employees that are Production Workers |
|------|---------------|--------------------|-----------------------------------------------------|
| 1954 | 4,300 | 2,500 | 58 |
| 1956 | 11,200 | n.a. | n.a. |
| 1958 | 23,400 | 17,600 | 75 |
| 1959 | 36,500 | 28,100 | 77 |
| 1960 | 52,600 | 37,200 | 68 |
| 1961 | 53,200 | 35,100 | 66 |
| 1962 | 53,100 | 34,000 | 64 |
| 1963 | 56,300 | 37,500 | 67 |
| 1964 | 55,300 | 37,900 | 69 |
| 1965 | 67,400 | 48,700 | 72 |
| 1966 | 82,200 | 59,100 | 72 |
| 1967 | 85,400 | 57,900 | 68 |
| 1968 | 87,400 | 60,500 | 69 |
| 1969 | 98,800 | 69,300 | 70 |
| 1970 | 88,500 | 60,300 | 68 |
| 1971 | 74,700 | 45,500 | 61 |
| 1972 | 97,600 | 58,400 | 60 |
| 1973 | 120,000 | 74,700 | 62 |
| 1974 | 133,100 | 81,600 | 61 |
| 1975 | 96,700 | 52,400 | 54 |
| 1976 | 102,500 | 57,900 | 56 |
| 1977 | 112,900 | 62,400 | 55 |

*Source:* U.S. Department of Commerce, 1979:28.
*Note:* n.a. = not available

Statistics on the semiconductor industry (Table 2-5) show that the proportion of production workers are relatively steady between 1964 and 1970, varying between 66 percent and 72 percent of all employees. Between 1970 and 1977, however, the figure fell from 70 percent to 55 percent. Using the more recent Bureau of Labor Statistics data mentioned above, one finds a further decline in the share of production workers in the work force to 46.9 percent (76,000 out of 162,000 total employment).

In short, during the years since offshore sourcing was adopted by the electronics corporations, both the absolute number of production workers and the percentage of production workers in the total electronics work force have dropped.

### Electronics Employment—Women Workers

Women make up a substantial percentage of the electronics work force. They are concentrated in operative and laborer jobs on the factory floor and in clerical jobs in the white-collar sector. Studies in Asia have shown that a high percentage of the jobs created by electronics corporations investing there are for semiskilled females. Hence, it is logical to look at changes in female participation in the U.S. electronic work force during the years since offshore sourcing began, to see if fewer U.S. women are employed in this industry.

The peak of U.S. female employment in electronics was reached in November 1966 (249,700), the same year that the number and percentage of production workers peaked (see Table 2-2). The December 1978 level (242,000), is 3.1 percent below the 1966 peak. As with production workers, even more important than the actual number of women employees is the decline in the percentage of women in the electrical components and accessories work force (SIC 367:) from 1958 to 1966, the percentage of women fluctuated between 56.2 to a high of 60.1 percent of the electronics work force; since the 60.1 percent peak in 1966, the proportion of women to men has declined almost steadily to a level of 50.5 to 52.5 percent (1975-1978).

For the years 1972-1978, the only years for which national data broken down by sex on the semiconductor industry are available, the peak in the number of women workers is December 1978 (84,700). The percentage of female workers has remained relatively steady during the seven year period, fluctuating between a high of 50 percent in 1973 and a low of 46 percent in 1975. The 1978 level was 48 percent; however, for the comparable years in the SIC 367 category as a whole, the same trend holds true. (Peak in numbers, December 1978; percentage fluctuates between a high of 54 in 1973 and a low of 50 in 1975.)

To summarize, during the years when offshore sourcing was initially adopted by U.S. electronics corporations, namely 1964-1975, job opportunities in electronics for U.S. production workers and women were significantly reduced.

### Electronics Employment—The Regional Impact

The U.S. electronics industry is not randomly distributed across the nation but, as mentioned above, is heavily concentrated in seven states. Two of these states, California and Massachusetts, have been selected for close scrutiny here because electronics constitutes an important part of these two states' economies—see Tables 2-6 and 2-7 (although only 1.7 percent of all U.S. production workers are employed in electronics, 4.6 percent of all California production workers and 3.5 percent of all Massachusetts production workers are employed in electronics), and because jobs in these two states employ over 27 percent of all U.S. workers in the electronics industry (based on statistics compiled from the U.S. Department of Commerce 1976 Annual Survey of Manufacturers).

Furthermore, within these two states, electronics employment is concentrated in two areas: the San Jose Standard Metropolitan Statistical Area (SMSA) in California (which is coterminus with Santa Clara County) and the Boston SMSA in Massachusetts. Just over half of all California electronics workers in December 1978 were employed in the San Jose SMSA (50,400 out of a total of 96,000) based on the *California Labor Market Bulletin*; the Boston SMSA dominates Massachusetts electronics employment to a comparable degree (19,542 out of 38,000) based on data from the Massachusetts Department of Employment Security. Given the heavy concentration

*Table 2-6.* Electronics Workers in California and Massachusetts, 1976 (SIC 367)

|  | Number of All Electronics Employees | Number of Production Workers Only | Percentage of All U.S. Electronics Employees | Percentage of U.S. Electronics Production Workers |
|---|---|---|---|---|
| Total U.S. | 323,000 | 218,800 | 100% | 100% |
| California | 70,100 | 45,800 | 21.7 | 20.9 |
| Massachusetts | 19,200 | 13,600 | 6.0 | 6.2 |

*Source:* U.S. Dept. of Commerce, *1976 Annual Survey of Manufacturers.*

*Table 2-7.* Electronics Workers (SIC 367) as a Percentage of Total Labor Force, 1976

|  | Total Employment | Total Production Workers | Percent of U.S. Total Employment | Percent of Total Prod. Workers | Percent of State Employment | Percent of State Production Workers |
|---|---|---|---|---|---|---|
| U.S.—All industries | 18,753,000 | 13,052,000 | 100% | 100% | – | – |
| U.S.—SIC 367 | 323,000 | 218,800 | 1.7 | 1.7 | – | – |
| California—All industries | 1,540,500 | 993,400 | 8.2 | 7.6 | 100% | 100% |
| California—SIC 367 | 70,100 | 45,800 | 0.4 | 0.4 | 4.6 | 4.6 |
| Massachusetts—All industries | 590,900 | 387,500 | 3.2 | 3.0 | 100% | 100% |
| Massachusetts—SIC 367 | 19,200 | 13,600 | 0.1 | 0.1 | 3.2 | 3.5 |

*Source:* U.S. Dept. of Commerce, *1976 Annual Survey of Manufacturers.*

of electronics production in these relatively compact geographic areas, one would expect that any shift in the number of electronics workers or in the skill level or sex composition of the electronics work force would be felt most acutely in these areas. However, in practice, few of the conclusions derived above from national-level data actually apply to the growth centers of the electronics industry in San Jose and Boston.

Because of changes in the Standard Industrial Code that occurred in 1972, it is difficult to obtain comparable statistics for the state and metropolitan areas that cover the period to 1972. Keeping these limitations on the data in mind, available information does show that both California and Massachusetts have witnessed rapid growth in the number of persons employed in electronics since 1972, with the exception of the 1975 recession (see Table 2–8). Focusing on the years for which comparable information is available for both states, these figures show a 41 percent increase in overall electronics employment from 1973 to 1978 in California and a 136 percent increase from 1973 to 1978 in Massachusetts.

In the San Jose and Boston SMSAs, the same trend is apparent, although San Jose has grown much more rapidly than Boston (see Table 2–9). Again, taking the years for which data are available from both areas, 1973–1978, San Jose saw a 47 percent increase while in Boston the gain was much more modest: 9 percent. However, these figures should be considered in light of the rapid acceleration in the rate of electronics employment creation in both Boston and San Jose

*Table 2–8.* Electronics Employment Figures (SIC 367), California and Massachusetts, 1972–1979 (in thousands)

| California | | | | | | | |
|---|---|---|---|---|---|---|---|
| 1972 | 1973 | 1974 | 1975 | 1976 | 1977 | 1978 | 1979 |
| 52.0 | 68.9 | 78.5 | 65.7 | 74.8 | 82.3 | 97.1 | n.a. |

| Massachusetts | | | | | | | |
|---|---|---|---|---|---|---|---|
| n.a. | 27.4 | 29.3 | 27.6 | 29.9 | 34.4 | 37.2 | 38.8[a] |

n.a. = not available
[a] Based on preliminary statistics, January–June, 1979
*Sources:* California Employment Development Department, *Wage and Salary Employment, by Industry, 1972–1978* (Sacramento: California Employment Development Department, 1979). Massachusetts Division of Employment Security, *Employment Review,* various issues, 1974–1979 (calculations based upon their statistics).

*Table 2-9.* Electronics Employment (SIC 367) Figures, San Jose SMSA*, Boston SMSA*, and United States

| San Jose Standard Metropolitan Statistical Area (figures in thousands) | | | | | | | | |
|------|------|------|------|------|------|------|------|------|
| 1970 | 1971 | 1972 | 1973 | 1974 | 1975 | 1976 | 1977 | 1978 |
| n.a. | n.a. | 23.8 | 33.7 | 38.9 | 33.0 | 38.8 | 42.4 | 49.6 |

Boston Standard Metropolitan Statistical Area
(actual figures)
(Note: 1970–1974 data based on 1967 SIC code; 1974–1978 data based on 1972 SIC Code.)

| 15,389 | 12,450 | 14,317 | 17,056 | 16,485 | 14,594 | 15,661 | 17,725 | 18,802 |
|------|------|------|------|------|------|------|------|------|

United States, Total
(figures in thousands)

| 366.7 | 329.4 | 354.8 | 410.7 | 421.0 | 338.2 | 366.0 | 398.3 | 434.2 |
|------|------|------|------|------|------|------|------|------|

* Standard Metropolitan Statistical Area.
*Sources:* California Employment Development Department, *Wage and Salary Employment by Industry, San Jose Metropolitan Area, 1972–1978* (Sacramento: California Employment Development Department, 1979). Massachusetts Division of Employment Security, *New Labor Areas, Employment and Wages by New Labor Areas, Then by Industry* (computer printout). U.S. Department of Labor, Bureau of Labor Statistics, *Employment and Earnings, U.S., 1909–1978.* Washington, D.C. 1979c.

since 1977. Both areas have witnessed a sudden boom in electronics employment.

Although detailed statistics on the composition of the Boston electronics work force are not publicly available,[4] U.S. Equal Employment Opportunity Commission (EEOC) Reports on the San Jose Standard Metropolitan Statistical Area reveal several important trends (see Table 2–10). First, in contrast to the national-level data, the number of blue-collar workers has almost doubled between 1966 and 1978; however, concurrent with this increase in number, the percentage of blue-collar workers has decreased from 49 percent to 35 percent. Second, again in contrast to national-level trends, the number of women in the San Jose electronics work force has increased almost two and a half times. Their percentage has fluctuated considerably over the twelve year period but in 1978 was at almost exactly the same level as it had been in 1966 (45 percent in 1966 and 44.5 percent in 1978). Finally, the number of minority workers in the blue-collar electronics work force has increased almost fourfold and their percentage has almost doubled from 23 percent to 45 percent since 1966.

The San Jose area is the core of the U.S. electronics industry. The changes in employment trends described above indicate that the rapid growth of the San Jose industry has witnessed a greater expansion of the white-collar work force than of the blue-collar. The proportion of blue-collar workers in the San Jose electronics industry was 49 percent in 1966. This was already substantially below the national level of production workers, 77 percent in 1966. The changes in San Jose's electronics industry since 1966 have shifted an already

*Table 2-10.* Trends in Electronics (SIC 367) Employment in the San Jose SMSA*, 1966–1978

|  | All Employees | Blue-Collar[a] Employees | Blue-Collar Employees as Percentage of all Employees | Women Employees | Women Employees as Percentage of All Employees |
|---|---|---|---|---|---|
| 1966 | 15,317 | 7,495 | 48.9 | 6,900 | 45.0 |
| 1969 | 19,758 | 6,232 | 31.5 | 6,594 | 33.4 |
| 1970 | 25,610 | 7,960 | 31.1 | 9,406 | 36.7 |
| 1971 | 24,504 | 7,493 | 30.6 | 9,077 | 37.0 |
| 1972 | 24,601 | 8,015 | 32.6 | 9,740 | 39.6 |
| 1973 | 33,420 | 12,813 | 38.3 | 14,849 | 44.4 |
| 1974 | 38,122 | 16,175 | 42.4 | 18,708 | 49.1 |
| 1975 | 39,852 | 13,072 | 32.8 | 16,103 | 40.4 |
| 1978 | 41,088 | 14,391 | 35.0 | 18,288 | 44.5 |

* Standard Metropolitan Statistical Area
*Source:* U.S. Equal Employment Opportunity Commission Reports, 1966–1978.
*Note:* EEOC Reports are only filed for companies with 100 or more employees and have certain other limitations on their generalizability.
[a] For definition of blue-collar employees, see Appendix.

heavily white-collar employment structure further in that direction, to the point where the San Jose electronics industry is almost twice as heavily white-collar as the nation's as a whole—San Jose's electronics work force is now 35 percent blue collar whereas the national electronics work force is 63 percent production workers (U.S. Department of Labor 1979c:333–334 and various U.S. EEOC Reports). The extremely rapid overall employment growth in the San Jose electronics industry has increased the number of jobs for blue-collar workers, but their relative share of employment opportunities has slipped.

*59*

If San Jose is typical of other growth centers of the U.S. electronics industry, namely Boston, Dallas, and Phoenix, the absolute numbers of production workers in these areas can be presumed to have risen because of rapid industry growth. The corollary of this, however, given the nationwide decline in the number of electronics production workers, particularly during the late 1960s and early 1970s, is that the noncore areas that were already more heavily blue-collar were the losers during the years when offshore sourcing grew in importance: the number of white- and blue-collar jobs in the research and development centers of the industry have increased, but blue-collar jobs in towns in other parts of the United States where routine production tasks were carried out presumably decreased as this work was transferred to overseas plants. This trend may now be changing again as electronic corporations seek new U.S. sites for production.

The number of women workers in the San Jose electronics industry increased from 6,900 in 1966 to 18,288 in 1978 according to EEOC Reports based on factories with 100 or more employees. During the same years, the number of women in electronics nationwide decreased from 233,600 to 227,800 (U.S. Department of Labor 1979c:333). As with the production worker figures cited above, the implications of these differing trends is that jobs for women in electronics were not lost in the industry centers, but in other parts of the United States. The overall percentage of women in the San Jose electronics industry was roughly the same in 1978 as in 1966; however, a marked change in the types of jobs filled by women occurred between 1966 and 1969 (Table 2–11). In 1966, more than three-quarters of San Jose women electronics employees were in blue-collar jobs; in 1969, only 56 percent were in these jobs. That proportion has remained relatively stable since then. This basic shift occurred during the years when offshore sourcing was restructuring the industry. Although the absolute number of women in blue-collar electronics jobs has doubled, the proportion of low-skilled blue-collar jobs being created for women by the rapid growth of the San Jose electronics industry has decreased. As offshore sourcing and plant relocations to other parts of the United States have increased, women employed in the industry center are increasingly likely to be employed in white-collar, particularly clerical and office, jobs.

During the years since offshore sourcing was introduced, the ethnic composition of the blue-collar work force in the San Jose electronics industry has changed dramatically (Table 2–12). The percentage of minority workers, notably those of Hispanic and Asian ancestry, almost doubled from 23 percent in 1966 to 45 percent in 1978. Perhaps partly as a result of offshore sourcing, wages for production work in the electronics industry have not kept pace with the national average. U.S. Department of Labor (1979c) data for all private nonagricultural establishments show $5.69 as the average production or nonsupervisory worker hourly earnings in 1978 compared to $4.91 for production workers in electronics. What appears to have happened in the San Jose center of the industry is an increasing abandonment of low-wage blue-collar electronics jobs to minority workers by whites. (For case study confirmation of this, see Keller 1979.) Although publicly available U.S. EEOC data at the national level is only available for two years, these reports show that minority workers increased from 17.2 percent (31,243) of the blue-collar work force in 1971 to 20.2 percent (46,701) in 1973. If, as appears likely, this rapid increase over a two year period has continued on a national level, it would indicate that, parallel to the trends in San Jose, the

*Table 2-11.* Women Employees in the Elecronics (SIC 367) Work Force, San Jose SMSA*, 1966–1978

|  | Women Employees | Women In Office and Clerical Work | Women in Office & Clerical Work As A Percentage of All Women Employees | Women In Blue-Collar Work | Women in Blue-Collar Work As A Percentage of All Women Employees |
|---|---|---|---|---|---|
| 1966 | 6,900 | 1,383 | 20.0 | 5,272 | 76.4 |
| 1969 | 6,594 | 2,325 | 35.2 | 3,701 | 56.1 |
| 1970 | 9,406 | 2,979 | 31.7 | 5,498 | 58.4 |
| 1971 | 9,077 | 2,828 | 31.2 | 5,216 | 57.5 |
| 1972 | 9,740 | 2,746 | 28.2 | 5,925 | 60.8 |
| 1973 | 14,849 | 3,655 | 24.6 | 9,640 | 64.9 |
| 1974 | 18,708 | 3,975 | 21.2 | 12,488 | 66.8 |
| 1975 | 16,103 | 4,232 | 26.3 | 9,520 | 59.1 |
| 1978 | 18,288 | 4,889 | 26.7 | 10,221 | 55.9 |

* Standard Metropolitan Statistical Area
*Source:* U.S. Equal Employment Opportunity Commission Reports, 1966–1978

low-wage blue-collar jobs that continue to exist in the U.S. electronics industry are more and more heavily occupied by nonwhites.

In San Jose, the years since offshore sourcing began have seen rapid growth in the numbers of jobs for virtually all categories of employees. These increases imply that other parts of the United States where routine electronics production had been carried out had

*61*

to absorb the losses that occurred in job opportunities for production workers and women, particularly during the late 1960s and early 1970s. In this way the restructuring of the industry that has occurred since the mid-1960s appears to have contributed to the uneven development of the United States itself: industry centers in the United States have grown more important whereas some peripheral areas have lost out. The restructuring has also witnessed a rapid increase in the number and percentage of minority workers in blue-collar jobs. As more and more routine electronics jobs have been relocated to the Third World, more and more Third World workers have been hired to fill comparable jobs in the United States.

## Conclusion

Industrial production is increasingly being internationalized. This process is creating a new international division of labor, with consequences for workers in both industrialized and Third World nations. The U.S. electronics industry has established a large number

*Table 2-12.* Blue-Collar Minority Workers in Electronics (SIC 367). San Jose SMSA*, 1966–1978

|      | Blue-Collar Employees | Minority Blue-Collar Employees | Minority Employees As Percentage of Blue-Collar Employees |
|------|-----------------------|--------------------------------|-----------------------------------------------------------|
| 1966 | 7,495                 | 1,731                          | 23.1                                                      |
| 1969 | 6,232                 | 2,516                          | 24.3                                                      |
| 1970 | 7,960                 | 2,533                          | 31.8                                                      |
| 1971 | 7,493                 | 2,142                          | 28.6                                                      |
| 1972 | 8,015                 | 2,487                          | 31.0                                                      |
| 1973 | 12,813                | 4,326                          | 33.8                                                      |
| 1974 | 16,175                | 5,523                          | 34.1                                                      |
| 1975 | 13,072                | 4,552                          | 34.8                                                      |
| 1978 | 14,391                | 6,444                          | 44.8                                                      |

* Standard Metropolitan Statistical Area
*Source:* U.S. Equal Employment Opportunity Commission Reports, 1966–1978.

of factory subsidiaries, notably in Asia, since the early to mid-1960s. These factories employ large numbers of young Asians, particularly women, for semiskilled, labor-intensive tasks.

During the years since offshore sourcing began, overall employment in the electronics industry in the United States has increased; however, both the absolute number and the percentage of production workers and women in the U.S. electronics work force have dropped substantially.

The number and percentage of minority workers in the electronics work force has increased, especially in blue-collar jobs, and there is evidence from both San Jose and Boston (Keller 1979, Bookman 1977) to indicate that a very high percentage of the blue-collar work force is made up of recent immigrants. In short, production jobs in the U.S. electronics industry are being increasingly relegated to those groups with few employment alternatives.

The electronics industry has been largely concentrated in seven states. California and Massachusetts together have a large percentage of all U.S. electronics workers; and within these two states, the San Jose and Boston areas are the two most important centers for the industry. Data for San Jose show great employment growth, particularly of white-collar positions, although the percentage of blue-collar jobs has declined and blue-collar positions have been increasingly filled by minority people. Other sections of the United States that are more peripheral to the electronics industry absorbed the loss of production worker jobs and jobs for women during the late 1960s and early 1970s.

The post-1975 recession boom in the electronics industry may be changing the composition of the work force yet again. Journalistic (e.g., *Electronic Business* 1979c:109–110) and interview evidence indicate a current labor shortage in electronics in both California and Massachusetts, including a shortage of women operatives. Corporations are actively seeking new sites in the United States for production work. Trends in the electronics industry change rapidly, and the 1980s may see a very different type of work force in the U.S. electronics industry.

It is important to note that the major change in the composition of the U.S. electronics work force occurred during the late 1960s and early 1970s. The rapid growth of offshore sourcing since then, as documented by Article 806/807 figures, has not produced a commensurate decrease in the level of production workers and women employed in the United States. This tends to argue that the industry restructuring carried out at the beginning of the offshore boom altered the demand for these types of workers in the United States. The current employment mix in the electronics work force has stabilized, at least since the 1975 recession. Despite the attractions of offshore sourcing, a considerable portion of electronics manufacturing remains in the United States because the rapid rate of change in products and production techniques requires close contact between engineers and the production line and because a high percentage of electronics products are purchased by the U.S. military. By law these products cannot be produced outside the United States. To continue electronics manufacturing in the United States under the present arrangement, a certain percentage of production workers and women appears to be necessary even if much of the new labor-intensive production continues to go offshore. This balance could be upset by a new, and now evident, recession, further automation of production, or new competition from Japanese or other producers of semiconductors (see e.g., *Business Week* 1979:66–86).

Having briefly examined the employment record of the U.S. electronics industry, it is possible to speculate about the future impact of offshore sourcing on the U.S. work force with somewhat greater specificity. If other U.S. industries were to internationalize production along lines similar to those adopted by the electronics industry, the principal result would be the reduction of industrial employment for those who have traditionally filled jobs in labor-intensive industries, namely women and workers with few skills. The remaining blue-collar jobs, particularly if wage rates remained low as they have in electronics, would increasingly become the domain of immigrant and nonwhite workers, further underlining the polarization of white-collar versus blue-collar sectors. The workers displaced by these changes in the structure of the work force would, if current trends continue, be absorbed in the service sector. Unions and other critics have pointed to the limited capacity of the service sector to absorb the large number of workers who would be displaced if industry restructuring continues to reduce production jobs.

However, if the experience of the U.S. electronics industry is any indication, these employment trends are not continuous, even in a case where an industry relies increasingly upon offshore sourcing. A certain relatively stable percentage of electronics manufacturing jobs have continued to be necessary in the United States. As mentioned above, even the textile and garment industries, which have been hard pressed by imports and offshore subcontracting agreements, have employed a fairly constant number of workers since the mid-1960s, and have actually shown some employment growth since the 1975 recession. In short, the expansion of offshore sourcing in other industries may have a serious negative impact on the position of unskilled workers during the period of industry restructuring. Unskilled production worker jobs and jobs for women will be lost and the wages for those jobs that remain may not rise as quickly as the national average. This could make these jobs the domain of minorities and immigrants with few other options.

But industrial work is not likely to disappear from the American scene. The internationalization of production in an unstable world system has limits imposed by a variety of factors, from political risk to rising shipping costs. The crucial question remains which groups of U.S. workers in which parts of the country will suffer until these limits are reached.

## *Appendix*

U.S. Department of Labor, Bureau of Labor Statistics definition of production and related workers:

> Production and related workers include working supervisors and all nonsupervisory workers (including group leaders and trainees) engaged in fabricating, processing, assembling, inspection, receiving, storage, handling, packing, warehousing, shipping, maintenance, repair, janitorial and guard services, product development, auxiliary production for a plant's own use (e.g. power plant), and recordkeeping and other services closely associated with the above production operations. [U.S. Department of Labor 1979c:943]

U.S. Equal Employment Opportunity Commission definition of blue-collar workers, made up of three subcategories, craftsmen, operatives, and laborers.

> *Craftsmen (skilled).*—Manual workers of relatively high skill level having a thorough and comprehensive knowledge of the processes involved in their work. Exercise considerable independent judgment and usually receive an extensive period of training. Includes: the building trades, hourly paid foremen and leadmen who are not members of management, mechanics and repairmen, skilled machining occupation, compositors, and typesetters, electricians, engravers, job setters (metal), motion picture projectionists, pattern and model makers, stationary engineers, tailors and tailoresses, and kindred workers.
> *Operatives (semiskilled).*—Workers who operate machine or processing equipment or perform other factory-type duties of intermediate skill level which can be mastered in a few weeks and require only limited

training. Includes: apprentices (auto mechanics, plumbers, bricklayers, carpenters, electricians, machinists, mechanics, plumbers, building trades, metalworking trades, printing trades, etc.), operatives, attendants (auto service and parking), blasters, chauffeurs, deliverymen and routemen, dressmakers and seamstresses (except factory), dryers, furnacemen, heaters (metal), laundry and dry cleaning operatives, milliners, mine operators and laborers, motormen, oilers and greasers (except auto), painters (except construction and maintenance), photographic process workers, stationary firemen, truck and tractor drivers, weavers (textile), welders, and flamecutters, and kindred workers.

*Laborers (unskilled).*—Workers in manual occupations which generally require no special training. Perform elementary duties that may be learned in a few days and require the application of little or no independent judgment. Includes: garage laborers, car washers and greasers, gardeners (except farm) and groundskeepers, longshoremen and stevedores, lumbermen, raftsmen and wood choppers, laborers performing lifting, digging, mixing, loading and pulling operations, and kindred workers. (U.S. Equal Employment Opportunity Commission 1966–1978).

## Notes

* I am grateful for the critical comments and assistance of many people who read an earlier draft of this paper, especially Su Green, Rachael Grossman, Mark Lester, Kevin Clements, Cynthia Enloe, Lenny Siegel, Alice Cook, Fred Deyo, and Anno Saxenian. Many of these readers continue to disagree with my conclusions, but their comments were invaluable in helping me reach them. This paper was finished in 1980 as part of the impact of Transnation Interactions Project of the Culture Learning Institute at the East-West Center in Honolulu.

1. Article 806.30 and Article 807 permit U.S. corporations to ship unfinished articles or components to subsidiaries overseas, have them assembled, and ship them back to the United States where they pay customs only on the value added overseas, i.e., the wages, production expenses, profits, and assists incurred outside the United States.

2. The Bureau of Labor Statistics uses the category *production worker* and the Equal Employment Opportunity Commission uses the category *blue-collar worker*. The definitions are found in the Appendix. Although the categories are comparable, in referring to statistics in this article, I have used *production worker* only to refer to BLS data and *blue-collar* only to refer to EEOC data.

3. The BLS has only compiled statistics on the semiconductor industry since 1972; therefore, Department of Commerce statistics derived from several sources are used here.

4. I am indebted to Su Green who obtained the U.S. Equal Employment Opportunity Commission statistics for the San Jose SMSA under the Freedom of Information Act.

## References

Axelrod, Marcie and the PHASE Staff. 1979. "Profile of the Electronics Industry Workforce in the Santa Clara Valley." Mountain View, California: Project on Health and Safety in Electronics (PHASE).

Baldwin, Robert E. 1976. "Trade and Employment Effects in the United States of Multilateral Tariff Reductions." *American Economic Review* 66:142–148.

Baldwin, Robert E. and Lewis, Wayne E. 1978. "U.S. Tariff Effects on Trade and Employment in Detailed SIC Industries." In *The Impact of International Trade and Investment on Employment*, edited by U.S. Dept. of Labor, pp. 241–249. Washington, D.C.: U.S. Dept. of Labor.

Bale, Malcolm D. 1976. "Estimates of Trade-Displacement Costs for U.S. Workers." *Journal of International Economics* 6:245–250.

Bookman, Ann. 1977. "The Process of Political Socialization among Women and Immigrant Workers: A Case Study of Unionization in the Electronics Industry." Ph.D. thesis, Harvard University.

Business Week, 1979. "Can Semiconductors Survive Big Business?" *Business Week* (December 3): 66–86.

California Employment Development Department. 1979. *Wage and Salary Employment by Industry*, 1972–1978. Sacramento, California.

Dunning, John H. n.d. "The Consequences of International Transfer to Technology by TNCs: Some Home Country Implications." ms.

*Electronic Business.* 1979a. "Companies Set Sights on Oversea Sites." (May):90–103.

———. 1979b. "How Electronics Companies Repudiate Unions." (July):30–34.

———. 1979c. "People Crunch Drives Firms to New Methods of Recruitment." (July):109–110.

Electronics Industry Association, 1979. *EIA Yearbook, 1979*. Washington, D.C.: Electronics Industry Association.

Frank, Robert H. and Freeman, Richard T. 1978. "The Distributional Consequences of Direct Foreign Investment." In *The Impact of International Trade and Investment on Employment*, edited by U.S. Dept. of Labor, pp. 153–170. Washington, D.C.: Dept. of Labor.

Freeman, Richard, 1978. "Comment." In *The Impact of International Trade and Investment on Employment*, edited by U.S. Dept. of Labor, pp. 99. Washington, D.C.: Dept. of Labor.

Gerstacker, Carl A. 1974. "Worldcorps: Job makers or Job Takers?" *Business and Society Review* 11:88–94.

Hawkins, Robert G. and Walter, Ingo. 1972. *The United States and International Markets*: Lexington, Mass.: Lexington Books.

Horst, Thomas. 1976. "American Multinationals and the U.S. Economy." *American Economic Review* 66:149–154.

———. 1978. "The Impact of American Investments Abroad on U.S. Exports, Imports, and Employment." In *The Impact of International Trade and Investment on Employment*, edited by U.S. Dept. of Labor, pp. 134–154. Washington, D.C.: U.S. Dept. of Labor.

Hufbauer, Gary C. 1978. "Introduction: Foreign Investment and Technology Transfer." In *The Impact of International Trade and Investment on Employment*, edited by U.S. Dept. of Labor, pp. 136–137. Washington, D.C.: U.S. Dept. of Labor.

Jacobson, Louis S. 1978. "Earnings Losses of Workers Displaced from Manufacturing Industries." In *The Impact of International Trade and Investment on Employment*, edited by U.S. Dept. of Labor, pp. 87–98. Washington, D.C.: U.S. Dept. of Labor.

Jager, Elizabeth. 1978. "Comments from the Floor." In *The Impact of International Trade and Investment on Employment*, edited by U.S. Dept. of Labor. p. 313. Washington, D.C.: U.S. Dept. of Labor.

*Journal of the Flagstaff Institute*. 1978. "Research Report: Data Pertaining to the Impact of 806:30 and 807 on Employment in the United States and Abroad." 2, no. 2, pp.1–29.

Keller, John F. 1979. "Employment Patterns of Women in California's Electronics Industry." Paper presented at American Anthropological Association, Cincinatti, Ohio.

Kirkland, Lane. 1974. "Worldcorps: Job Makers or Job Takers?" *Business and Society Review* 11:88–94.

Lim, Linda Y.C. 1978. *Women Workers in Multinational Corporations: The Case of Electronics Industry in Malaysia and Singapore*. University of Michigan. Ann Arbor: Michigan Occasional Papers no. 9.

Massachusetts Division of Employment Security, 1974–1979. *Employment Review*. Various issues.

Meier, Richard L. 1977. "Multinationals as Agents of Social Development." *Bulletin of the Atomic Scientists* (November):31–35.

Monson, Terry D. 1978. "An Extension of Bale's Labor Displacement Cost Estimates." *Journal of International Economics* 8:131–133.

Moxon, Richard. 1974. "Offshore Production in the Less Developed Countries—A Case Study of Multinationality in the Electronics Industry." *New York University* Bulletin, 98–99:1–80.

Musgrave, Peggy B. 1975. *Direct Investment Abroad and the Multinationals: Effects on the United States Economy*. Prepared for the use of the Subcommittee on Multinational Corporations of the Committee on Foreign Relations, United States Senate. Washington, D.C.: U.S. Government Printing Office

Neumann, George R. 1978. "The Direct Labor Market Effects of the Trade Adjustment Assistance Program: The Evidence from the TAA Survey." In *The Impact of International Trade and Investment on Employment*, edited by U.S. Dept. of Labor, pp. 107–126. Washington, D.C.: U.S. Dept. of Labor.

North American Congress on Latin America (NACLA). 1977. "Electronics: The Global Industry." *Latin America and Empire Report* 9, no. 4, pp. 1–25.

Pacific Studies Center. 1977. *Silicon Valley: Paradise or Paradox? The Impact of High Technology Industry on Santa Clara County*. Mountain View, California: Pacific Studies Center.

Reynis, Lee Ann. 1976. "The Proliferation of U.S. Firm Third World Offshore Sourcing in the Mid-to-late 1960s: An Historical and Empirical Study of Factors Which Occasioned the Location of Production for the U.S. Market Abroad." Ph.D. Dissertation, Dept. of Economics, University of Michigan.

Segall, Joel. 1978. "Introduction to the Conference." In *The Impact of International Trade and Investment on Employment: A Conference on The Dept. of Labor Research Results*, pp. 5–9. Washington, D.C.: U.S. Dept. of Labor, Bureau of International Labor Affairs.

Sheinkman, Jacob. 1978. "Letter to the Editor." *Consumer Reports* (May):251.

Snow, Robert T. 1977. *Dependent Development and the New Industrial Worker: The Case of the Export Processing Zone in the Philippines.* Dissertation. Dept. of Sociology, Harvard University.

U.S. Department of Commerce, 1976. 1976 Annual Survey of Manufacturers. Washington, D.C.

U.S. Department of Commerce. 1979. A Report on the U.S. Semiconductor Industry. Washington, D.C.: Dept. of Commerce, Industry and Trade Association.

U.S. Department of Labor. 1978. *The Impact of International Trade and Investment on Employment: A Conference on the Dept. of Labor Research Results.* Washington, D.C.: U.S. Dept. of Labor, Bureau of International Labor Affairs.

———. 1979a. *Industry Wage Survey. Semiconductors, September 1977.* Washington, D.C.: U.S. Dept. of Labor, Bureau of Labor Statistics.

———. 1979b. *Employment and Earnings.* Washington, D.C.: U.S. Dept. of Labor, Bureau of Labor Statistics (April).

———. 1979c. *Employment and Earnings, United States, 1909–1978.* Washington, D.C.: U.S. Dept. of Labor, Bureau of Labor Statistics.

U.S. Equal Employment Opportunity Commission. 1966–1978. Reports for San Jose Standard Metropolitan Statistical Area.

———. 1973. *Equal Employment Opportunity Report—1971: Job Patterns for Minorities and Women in Private Industry.* Washington, D.C.: U.S. Equal Employment Opportunity Commission.

———. *Equal Employment Opportunity Report—1973: Job Patterns for Minorities and Women in Private Industry.* Washington, D.C.: U.S. Equal Employment Opportunity Commission.

Vernon, Raymon. 1977. *Storm Over the Multinationals: The Real Issues.* Cambridge: Harvard University Press.

# CHAPTER 3

# Capitalism, Imperialism, and Patriarchy: The Dilemma of Third-World Women Workers in Multinational Factories

LINDA Y. C. LIM

## Introduction

Female employment in multinational factories in developing countries has recently become the subject of much academic and political interest. Studies have been done analyzing the growth and spread of such employment and its impact on women in particular countries and industries.[1] The findings generally point to a central theoretical and political question that as yet remains unanswered: Is the employment of women factory workers by multinational corporations in developing countries primarily an experience of *liberation*, as development economists and governments maintain or one of *exploitation*, as feminists assert, for the women concerned? Does it present a problem or a solution to the task of integrating women into the development of their countries?

This paper examines the theoretical issues raised by the available case study material, in an attempt to resolve this question. It emphasizes economic analysis, and suggests that the interactions between capitalist, imperialist, and patriarchal relations of production are responsible both for the phenomenon of female employment by multinationals and for the dilemma it poses for women workers and for progressive feminist analysis and political action.

## Capitalism and the Relocation of Manufacturing Industry to Developing Countries

Capitalism is the economic system prevailing in the parent countries of multinational corporations and in the world market which they dominate. It is a mode of production based on private ownership of capital (the "means of production"), employment of wage labor, and production for exchange on a free market to earn private profit that is accumulated and reinvested for growth and further profit. Whereas the Western nations and Japan are developed economies in a mature or advanced stage of capitalism, many developing countries are embarking on economic programs aimed at further developing the capitalist relations of production first introduced in them by colonialism and world market forces. This colonial heritage, combined with the dominance of the world capitalist system, forces even those new nations that have embraced socialist ideologies of development to tolerate some degree of private enterprise and foreign investment producing for exchange on the world market.

The relocation of manufacturing industry from developed to developing countries by multinational corporations engaged in "offshore sourcing" is part of a new international division of labor and pattern of trade in manufactures.[2] From plants in the Third World, multinational subsidiaries export manufactures to their home countries. From their home countries they import capital and technology in exchange. This is the direct result of two developments in the world capitalist economy which began in the 1960s. First, growth in international trade intensified inter-capitalist competition among the developed nations. In particular, the ascendancy of Japan as a major industrial power and its rapid and highly successful penetration of Western consumer markets led American and European manufacturers to invest in developing countries as a means of reducing costs in competition with the Japanese (Reynis 1976). In the 1970s, the slowing down of growth in Western and world markets further intensified these competitive pressures.

Second, the accelerating development of capitalist relations of production in a number of developing countries resulted in some of their indigenous entrepreneurs manufacturing for export to Western markets, beginning in the 1960s. This placed them in direct competition with Western manufacturers, who were forced to relocate to these same countries in order to be cost competitive in their own home markets. This trend continued through the 1970s on an ever larger and wider scale, particularly in Asian countries like Hong

Kong, Taiwan, South Korea, and Singapore, whose larger local firms have themselves become multinationals operating offshore manufacturing plants in other developing countries.

Thus, Western manufacturers in several industries located plants in developing countries in response to the competitive challenge from other mature capitalist countries, especially Japan, and from newly industrializing developing capitalist countries, mainly in Asia. The crucial factor in the competition was and is the cost of production, which differs between mature and developing capitalist economies according to their stage of development. In the 1960s and early 1970s, the mature Western economies experienced tight domestic labor markets—low unemployment rates, high wages, and chronic labor shortages in many industries. Labor-intensive manufacturing industries—those which employ large numbers of workers in generally unskilled or low-skilled jobs—were the most affected, and these countries began to lose their international comparative advantage in industries such as garments, shoes, plastic toys, and electronics assembly. The developing countries, on the other hand, had relatively abundant supplies of labor, reflected in the rural-urban migration of surplus labor off the farms; high urban unemployment rates; and low wages. Cheap labor, combined in many cases with government-subsidized capital costs, including tax holidays and low interest loans from government banks (Lim 1978), gave these countries a comparative advantage in world trade in labor-intensive products.

It is labor-intensive industries, then, that tend to relocate manufacturing plants to developing countries, thereby becoming multinational in their operations. This is a rational competitive response to changing international comparative cost advantages. In a free world market, factors of production like capital and labor will tend to move to locations where they are most scarce and can therefore command the highest returns from their employment in production. Through the nineteenth and early twentieth centuries, this was reflected in fairly free international migration of labor, but subsequent restrictive national immigration policies together with transportation costs and imperfect market information have increasingly inhibited the mobility of labor across international boundaries, except for the legal and/or illegal immigration of "guest workers." Capital, however, remains internationally mobile, especially from the developed to developing countries, a flow encouraged by policies of the latter's governments that offer profit tax holidays, duty free imports and exports, unrestricted remittance of profits, repatriation of capital, and so forth.

The relocation of manufacturing industry from mature to developing capitalist economies is an outcome of the expansion of capitalism on a world scale, reflecting the different rate and degree of development of capitalist relations of production, particularly the wage-labor market, in different nations. It is aided by state policies in both developed and developing countries, but remains largely a market phenomenon.

### Imperialism, Nationalism and the Multinational Corporation

Imperialism—the system of military, political, economic, and cultural domination of the Third World by its former colonial masters—was historically the outgrowth of capitalist development in the West. In the economic sphere, it is characterized by the exploitation of natural and human resources in the Third World by Western capitalist enterprises. Although *bourgeois* economists were in agreement with classical Marxists—including Lenin, Luxemburg, and Marx—that imperialism, or Western investment in developing countries, would be an agent of capitalist development in the Third World, modern-day theorists of imperialism—including dependency theorists and "world-system" analysts following André Gundee Frank and Immanuel Wallerstein—argue that it retards such development.

Most of the latter analysis has been applied to the sectors of primary production for export and import-substituting industrialization in developing countries. But manufacturing for export by multinational subsidiaries also has its critics.[3] It is pointed out that workers' wages are much lower and their working conditions worse than in the multinationals' home countries; that few transferable skills or industrial linkages are generated; that there is heavy dependence on foreign capital, technology, skills, inputs, and markets; that few taxes are paid in the host country and high profits that accrue only to foreigners are mostly remitted overseas.

Although the above are true in most situations, it should be noted that manufacturing for export in developing countries is not the sole preserve of multinationals. Many local firms are also involved, and in some countries—such as Hong Kong, Taiwan, and South Korea—and industries, such as garments, they may outnumber the multinationals. In general, Third World enterprises engaged in manufacturing for export to Western markets are smaller, less capital intensive, and more labor intensive than multinational subsidiaries and are concentrated in simple-technology industries with competitive markets and relatively low profit margins. Wages are usually lower and working conditions worse, sometimes much worse, than in the multinational sector. Skills are low, and there is dependence not only on foreign markets, to which access is less easy than for the multinationals, but also on foreign technology and inputs purchased on the world market. Tax payments and reinvestment rates may be higher than for multinational subsidiaries; but since earnings are less, absolute contributions may be lower.

Comparisons between multinational subsidiaries and local firms in export manufacturing in developing countries suggest that the former may contribute more to the host economy in terms of market access, output growth, total wage-bill, and skill and technology acquisition. Local firms may, however, contribute more to the national development of capitalist relations of production in the long run, in developing a class of indigenous entrepreneurs in the manufacturing sector. They may reinvest more, since they do not remit profits overseas and are less likely to transfer operations. But competition with multinational subsidiaries in factor, input and output markets may inhibit the development of independent indigenous enterprises and entrepreneurs (Lim 1978b; Pang and Lim 1977). A complementary relationship is possible, but it tends to maintain local firms in the dependent position of subcontractors and suppliers to foreign firms and markets.

Despite the validity of many of the criticisms against it, manufacturing for export does enhance the development of capitalist relations of production in developing countries, mainly by spurring the growth of industrial wage labor and an indigenous industrial capitalist class. Multinationals and local firms make somewhat different contributions to this process. Two more questions remain. First, what are the long-run prospects for a multinational-led, export manufacturing sector in a developing country? Second, is it likely to lead to the development of an independent national capitalism in the developing country?

One of the criticisms commonly levelled at manufacturing for export by multinational corporations is that it is likely to be only a temporary phenomenon in developing host countries. Multinationals that relocate manufacturing capacity in these countries are "footloose" because they are not bound to any particular location by a need for local markets or local input sources other than labor, which is abundantly available everywhere. Therefore, it is argued, they will tend to move away from a location if labor market conditions or government policies change to make it less competitive—that is, if wages rise more in one location than in others or tax holidays expire in one location but are offered in other "newer" locations. Although this has happened in individual firm cases, it has not yet threatened the viability of an entire export–manufacturing sector in any country.

On the contrary, in the less developed countries where most of the export oriented multinational subsidiaries are concentrated—Hong Kong, Taiwan, and Singapore—changing comparative costs, particularly the appearance of tight labor markets, have resulted in an upgrading of the industries producing for export. Multinationals, encouraged by host government policies, have begun relocating more capital-intensive, technology-intensive industrial products and processes from their home countries to these location. Labor-intensive processes are replaced or shifted to more labor-abundant locations as comparative advantages continue to change between developed and developing countries and among developing countries themselves.

This suggests that, at least in some developing countries, the multinational-led export manufacturing sector does mature over time, further developing capitalist relations of production. Wages rise, working conditions improve, more skills are imparted, more local linkages generated, more taxes paid, and more profits reinvested locally. Although the countries where this is happening are still a minority in the Third World, they are the ones that have had the longest experience with multinational subsidiaries in manufacturing for export.

But what about local firms and the development of an independent national capitalism? As previously noted, competition with multinationals may inhibit the growth of indigenous enterprises. But as the multinational subsidiaries continue to grow and to upgrade and diversify their products, they generate more local linkages, make more input purchases from local suppliers, and subcontract some of their simpler products and processes to local manufacturers. This may stimulate the growth of indigenous enterprises, though they remain in a dependent position vis-à-vis the multinationals. But from the point of view of enhancing capitalist development, dependence may not be a problem if it results in accelerated growth and the emergence of an indigenous industrial capitalist class. A nationalist industrial policy that excludes multinationals may result in more independence but less growth and thus a smaller indigenous capitalist class since the advantages multinationals possess in stimulating supply sources and in providing technical and managerial training would be lost.

Although dependency theorists and others who argue that multinationals retard the development of capitalism in developing countries are right with respect to their criticisms of the early stages of labor-intensive manufacturing for export, the experience of some important developing countries suggests that bourgeois economists and classical Marxists alike might be right in the longer run. That is, multinationals do foster the development of capitalist relations of production and are often more successful in this than indigenous firms. The relocation of industry between countries continues if firms behave rationally in response to changing comparative advantages. Although multinationals may shift labor-intensive industries out of some developing countries as comparative costs change, so do national firms in these countries, (as in the case of Singapore firms that shifted their labor-intensive processes and products to cheaper-labor countries like Malaysia, Indonesia, Sri Lanka, and Bangladesh); so long as new industries and processes are moved in, capitalist relations of production continue to develop and mature.

### Patriarchy and the Female Labor Market

Patriarchy is the system of male domination and female subordination in economy, society, and culture that has characterized much of human history to the present day. In the economic sphere, it is reflected first in the sexual division of labor within the family, which makes domestic labor the sole preserve of women. Their involvement in production activities outside the home varies with different societies and different stages of development, but is, particularly in those countries where capitalist development has penetrated (Boserup 1970), often accorded inferior status and reward compared to the activities of men.

In the pure capitalist model of "bourgeois" economists, conditions of perfect competition prevail in the labor market, where workers are hired solely on the basis of their marginal productivity.[4] Although productivity differences may be correlated with the sex of a worker, sex itself, like race, religion and other *ascriptive* characteristics, is irrelevant in the hiring process. Where there are no productivity differences between the sexes, discrimination cannot exist in a free labor market. The employer who discriminates on the basis of sex will be less profitable than the one who does not because productivity of the worker is the only relevant criterion (Becker 1957).[5] Thus, competition and the progress of capitalist relations of production should eventually eliminate any differences between the sexes in the labor market.

This model is clearly invalid in the real-world capitalist labor market, where sex differences obviously exist. Not only is participation in the wage-labor force lower for women than for men, but they are also concentrated in a narrow range of occupations characterized by low wages, low productivity, low skill levels, high turnover, insecurity of tenure, and limited upward mobility. One of the most distinctive and persistent features of the capitalist labor market is the segmentation of the labor market and occupational segregation by sex (Blaxall and Reagan, 1976). Productivity differences between male and female workers is one explanation for this phenomenon, but they themselves reflect differential access to the determinants of productivity, such as education and skill training and different levels of technology in the jobs to which they are assigned. In addition, there is an element of pure discrimination by employers, that is, discrimination unrelated to any productivity differences between male and female workers.

Patriarchal institutions and social relations are responsible for the inferior or secondary status of women in the capitalist wage-labor market. The primacy of the sexual division of labor within the family—man as breadwinner and woman as housekeeper and child raiser—has several consequences for the woman who seeks wage employment. Socialized to accept this sex role in life, she has little motivation to acquire marketable skills; is often prevented by discrimination from acquiring such skills; and, even after she has acquired them, may be prevented by discrimination from achieving the employment or remuneration that those skills would command for a man.

Discrimination itself is based on the patriarchal assumption that woman's natural role is a domestic one and that she is therefore unsuited to many kinds of wage employment, either because her productivity will "naturally" be lower than a man's in the same employment or because it will be adversely affected by her domestic responsibilities. Family duties do often reduce a woman's mobility, stability, and efficiency as a worker and most women who participate in the capitalist wage-labor market do so because of the inadequacy of the family income earned by their menfolk in wage employment. Attitudes of families, employers, and the women themselves, domestic responsibilities, and their own lack of skills limit their employment opportunities and weaken their bargaining position in the labor market.

It is this *comparative disadvantage* of women in the wage-labor market that gives them a comparative advantage vis-à-vis men in the occupations and industries where they are concentrated—so-called female ghettoes of employment. In the manufacturing sector of mature capitalist economies, women are concentrated in labor-intensive industries where the wages earned are often insufficient to support an entire family. It is assumed by employers and society in general that women work only for "pocket money" for luxuries or to make a secondary income contribution to families where the principal breadwinner is a male. In addition, it is believed that women do not have the need or the inclination to be career-minded and upwardly mobile in the job hierarchy and so do not mind dead-end jobs with no prospects of advancement. They also have certain feminine social and cultural attributes that make them suitable to certain kinds of detailed and routine work, such as sewing garments and assembling electronic gadgets. That is, they are careful and conscientious workers, patient enough to endure long hours of repetitive work (Lim 1978b).

Thus, both the demand for and supply of female labor are determined by the culture of patriarchy, which assumes woman's role in the family as natural and consigns her to a secondary and inferior position in the capitalist wage-labor market. Occupational segregation and differential remuneration by sex is explained by an assumed productivity differential between men and women, based in part on this sex role differentiation. Even where women are acknowledged to be more productive than men, they are often paid less; and prevailing wages are always lower in female-intensive than male-intensive industries and occupations even at equivalent skill levels. This is contrary to the prediction of neoclassical economic theory that higher productivity means higher, not lower, wages.

The labor-intensive industries in which women manufacturing workers are concentrated in mature capitalistic economies are the very industries that are losing their comparative cost advantage to newly industrializing countries. It is likely that these labor-intensive industries maintained their comparative advantage as long as they did because they employed the lowest-paid workers in those countries—women, often women of minority races. Thus it is female-intensive industries that have the greatest propensity to "run away" from the developed countries and relocate manufacturing facilities in the Third World, where wages are even lower than those of women in the developed countries. In the developing countries as well, traditional patriarchal social relations ensure that women occupy a similarly secondary and inferior position in the wage-labor market and so are the preferred employees of multinational and local employers in labor-intensive export industries.

Although the relocation of manufacturing industry from mature to developing capitalist countries reflects changes in world capitalism, the employment of women in these industries reflects the influence of patriarchy on the female labor market in both mature and developing countries. Women's comparative disadvantage in the capitalist wage-labor market enhances the comparative advantage of firms that employ them in labor-intensive industries producing for the world market. This disadvantage—reflected in low wages—is greatest for women in countries where capitalist relations of production are least developed, since there they have the fewest opportunities for wage employment and the weakest bargaining power in the labor market. Patriarchal social relations are also strongest and most restrictive of female wage employment where precapitalist modes of production, like various forms of feudalism, persist. Thus, female employment in export manufacturing industries is most prevalent in those developing countries where capitalist relations of production are developing most rapidly, but traditional patriarchy is sufficiently strong to maintain women in an inferior labor market position.

## Imperialism, Patriarchy and Exploitation

Studies of Third World women workers in multinational export factories tend to focus, explicitly or implicitly, on the exploitation of these women by their multinational employers. Absolutely low wages and poor working and living conditions are often cited as evidence of such exploitation. In an earlier work, I pointed out that the concept of exploitation is an established one in all schools of economics, from the bourgeois to the Marxist, though the particular definition of it may vary. All, however, agree that

> exploitation . . . is a *relative* concept, bearing no direct relation to the *absolute* level of wages paid: so long as the worker does not receive the full value of her product, however defined, she is exploited. A higher wage may also entail a higher rate of exploitation if greater intensity

of work, longer working hours, better equipment and organization of
production, etc. mean that labor productivity, and hence the value of
the worker's output, is proportionally greater in the higher-wage than
lower-wage situation. [Lim 1978b]

Thus, focussing on absolute conditions faced by workers does not
lend itself to useful theoretical or political analysis.

In the economic sense defined above, all workers employed in
capitalist enterprises are exploited to produce profits for their employers. But the degree of exploitation differs among different groups
of workers. In addition to being paid less than the value of the
output they contribute, Third World women workers in multinational
export factories are paid less than women workers in the multinationals' home countries and less than men workers in these countries
and in their own countries as well, despite the fact that in relocated
labor-intensive industries their productivity is frequently acknowledged to be higher than that of either of these other groups. Thus,
Third World women workers are the most heavily exploited group
of workers, both relative to their output contribution and relative
to other groups. Although all are subject to capitalist exploitation,
Third World women workers are additionally subject to what might
be called imperialist exploitation and patriarchal exploitation.

Imperialist exploitation—the differential in wages paid to workers
in developed and developing countries for the same work and output—
arises from the ability of multinationals to take advantage of different
labor market conditions in different parts of the world—a perfectly
rational practice in the context of world capitalism. In the developing
countries,

> high unemployment, poor bargaining power vis-a-vis the foreign investor,
> lack of worker organization and representation and even the repression
> of workers' movements, all combine to depress wage levels, while the
> lack of industrial experience, ignorance and naivete of workers with
> respect to the labor practices in modern factory employment enable
> multinational employers to extract higher output from them in certain
> unskilled operations. [Lim 1978b:11–12]

Patriarchal exploitation—the differential in wages paid to male and
female workers for similar work and output—derives from women's
inferior position in the labor market, discussed in the previous section
of this paper.

Although multinational employers of women factory workers in
developing countries do practice all of the above forms of exploi-

*80*

tation, they do so only in response to labor market forces, specifically the international and sexual segmentation of labor markets. Differences in the degree of development of capitalist relations of production and natural restrictions on the international mobility of labor are responsible for differential wage rates between countries whereas patriarchal institutions and attitudes limiting the employment opportunities open to women are responsible for differential wage rates between the sexes. Multinationals may, consciously, attempt to preserve these differentials from which they benefit; but in general they merely take advantage of them since they exist.

In fact, it may be argued that the activities of multinationals in labor-intensive export manufacturing in developing countries might in the long run contribute to a reduction of national and sex wage differentials—in other words, a reduction of the imperialist and patriarchal components of capitalist exploitation of Third World women workers. To the extent that these multinationals contribute to the development of capitalist relations of production, particularly to the growth of demand for wage labor and to the upgrading of skills, wages will rise in the developing countries. If at the same time the relocation of industry from the developed countries reduces demand for labor in those countries, wage increases there will decline. Both factors will reduce over time the wage differential between the developed and developing countries—that is, the degree of imperialist exploitation.

Because multinationals engaged in export manufacturing in the developing countries employ mostly women workers, they increase the demand for female labor more than the demand for male labor. Female wages will then rise relative to male wages, and female unemployment rates will fall. Sex wage differentials, reflecting the degree of patriarchal exploitation of women workers, will narrow. In some countries governments have already expressed concern about the lack of employment creation for men—whom they consider to be the principal breadwinners—in multinational export firms.

So far, the narrowing of national and sex wage differentials has been imperceptible in most cases. In most developing host countries, multinationals manufacturing for export constitute too small a sector of the economy to have a significant impact on the national labor market. Even where, as in a handful of Asian countries, they are an important sector of the economy and have contributed to rising wages, wages have increased just as rapidly in the developed countries with generalized inflation. Furthermore, the relocation of industry has not reduced the overall demand for labor in the developed countries, where capitalist development continues in different sectors. With respect to sex wage differentials, although female wages have risen, high turnover of labor and the short average working life of women factory workers keeps their average wages low. The countries in which female wages have risen most rapidly are also those where male employment creation has been proceeding apace, and male wages have often increased even more rapidly in other sectors of the economy.

Continued imperialist and patriarchal exploitation in multinational factories in developing countries does not, however, imply that the women employed in these factories are worse off than they would have been without such employment. On the contrary, the vast majority are clearly better off, at least but not only in a narrow economic sense, for being subject to such exploitation. For one thing, wages and working conditions are usually better in multinational factories than in alternative employment for women in indigenous capitalist enterprises. Although in the relative economic sense defined previously they may be more exploited in the multinationals, in terms of producing a greater surplus or marginal product over and above the wage they receive, than in indigenous enterprises, in an absolute sense their incomes tend to be higher and they are better off. This is true also when compared with women's traditional economic roles as housewives and unpaid family labor in farms and shops.

### Capitalist Development and Liberation from Patriarchy

In developing as in mature industrial economies, the state of development of capitalist relations of production defines the employment opportunities available to wage labor. Patriarchal social structures and cultures divide these opportunities by sex, typically limiting female wage labor to a narrow range of inferior jobs. In this situation the entry of labor-intensive export manufacturing industries and of multinational corporations in particular into sex segregated local labor markets has two somewhat contradictory effects. On the one hand, multinational *and* local employers can take advantage of women's inferior position in the labor market to employ them at lower wages and poorer working conditions than exist for men in the same country and for women in developed countries. This is what I have termed patriarchal and imperialist exploitation. Both local firms and multinationals benefit from the gap between workers' wages in the developing country and final product prices in markets of developed countries.

On the other hand, the expansion of employment opportunities for women in these industries does improve conditions for women in the labor market. In however limited a way, the availability of jobs in multinational and local export factories does allow women to leave the confines of the home, delay marriage and childbearing, increase their incomes and consumption levels, improve mobility, expand individual choice, and exercise personal independence. Working for a local or foreign factory is for many women at least marginally preferable to the alternatives of staying at home, early marriage and childbearing, farm or construction labor, domestic service, prostitution, or unemployment, to which they were previously restricted. Factory work, despite the social, economic, and physical costs it often entails, provides women in developing countries with one of the very few channels they have of at least partial liberation from the confines and dictates of traditional patriarchal social relations.

Given their lack of access to better jobs, women workers usually prefer multinationals as employers over local firms since they offer higher wages and better working conditions and often have more "progressive" labor practices and social relations within the firm [Lim 1978b]. Indeed, the more multinationals there are in any one country and the longer they have been established, the stronger becomes the workers' bargaining position. Exclusive employment of female production workers in labor-intensive export industries creates occasional labor shortages, resulting over time in rising wages, greater job security, and improved working conditions for women in indigenous as well as multinational enterprises.[6] Greater competition for female laborers will tend to reduce the degree of exploitation found in women's work.

Whether or not market forces alone will expand women's employment alternatives beyond the traditional "female ghettoes" of low wage, low skill, dead end jobs depends on the state and rate of development of capitalist relations of production in the economy as a whole. In an economy that is rapidly growing, diversifying, and upgrading itself in all sectors, high demand for labor might eventually propel women into skilled industrial and nonindustrial jobs from which they have previously been excluded by custom, education, or employment discrimination. This will improve the wages and working conditions of women who remain in factory employment as production workers, given the reduction in the numbers of women available for work.

So far, such a situation is an exceptional one among the many developing countries that host multinational corporations in female-intensive industries. Even where rapid growth occurs, employers may escape the tightening labor market by importing migrant labor, by automation, and by shifting labor-intensive processes to other countries, as they have done in the home countries of the multinationals and are now doing in rapidly developing countries like Singapore. In this latter country, growth in other industries and sectors has prevented these actions from having a depressing effect on wages, and the government's high wage policy has furthermore forced firms to shed or shift their labor-intensive activities. Also, when women ascend the job hierarchy, it is usually to take jobs vacated by male workers who have since advanced even higher in the hierarchy of skills and incomes. That is to say, although rapid growth may enable women to improve their position in the labor market in absolute terms, relative to men they remain in an inferior position.

Employment of women in modern capitalist industrial enterprises in developing countries does contribute to an expansion of employment opportunities and thus to some economic and social liberation for women in patriarchal societies that customarily restrict them to a domestic role in the family. But such wage employment on its own or combined with generally rapid capitalist development throughout an economy cannot significantly undermine the patriarchal social relations responsible for women's inferior labor market position on which their very employment is predicated. In other words, capitalism cannot wipe out patriarchy, though exploitation in capitalist enterprises can provide some women with an at least temporary escape from traditional patriarchal social relations.

### Exploitation and Liberation: A Dilemma for Political Action

The above analysis has identified the relocation of manufacturing industry from mature to developing capitalist countries as the outcome of the expansion of capitalism on a world scale,, reflecting differences in the development of capitalist relations of production between nations, particularly of the wage labor market. The relocation is carried out by multinational corporations, whose export manufacturing activities in developing host countries can and do enhance the development of capitalist relations of production. The almost exclusive employment of female labor in many relocated industries is based on women's inferior position in the wage labor market, resulting from patriarchal social relations. Although women workers in these multinational factories are exploited relative to their output, to male workers in the same country, and to female workers in developed countries, their position is often better than in indigenous factories and in traditional forms of employment for women. The limited economic and social liberation that women workers derive from their employment in multinational factories is predicated on their subjection to capitalist, imperialist, and patriarchal exploitation in the labor market and the labor process. This presents a dilemma for feminist policy towards such employment: because exploitation and liberation go hand in hand, it cannot be readily condemned or extolled.

Many of the studies of female employment in multinational export factories in developing countries focus their criticism on the multinational corporation as chief perpetrator of all the forms of exploitation that these women workers are subject to in their employment. But although the multinational does take advantage of national and sexual wage differentials and sometimes reinforces them, it is not responsible for creating them and cannot by its own actions eliminate them. National wage differentials are the result of differences in the development of capitalist relations of production between nations, whereas sex wage differentials originate in indigenous patriarchy.

Removing the multinational—the logical if extreme conclusion of an antiimperialist political stand—will, in the absence of a credible alternative form of development, drastically reduce employment opportunities for women in developing countries. This will weaken their labor market position and subject them to even greater exploitation by indigenous capitalists and continued subordination to traditional patriarchy. This is clearly undesirable for the economic and social liberation of women. A less radical solution—attempting to reduce imperialist exploitation by imposing reforms on the multinational or local employer—is unlikely to succeed even if host governments were willing, which is doubtful. Export manufacturers operate in highly competitive international markets with generally elastic supply and, in important industries like garments and shoes, inelastic demand. Host governments and workers can neither demand nor enforce better wages and working conditions in profit-oriented multinationals that are mobile between countries. Local firms are often less competitive than multinationals in the world market and, with their lower profits, are unlikely to be able to absorb the costs of such reforms.

Another possibility for reducing imperialist exploitation is through international action to restrict multinationals from exploiting market wage differentials between nations—for example, by standardizing certain terms and conditions of work in particular industries or occupations. This is clearly unrealistic, given the different stages of development of capitalism and different labor market conditions in different countries. Furthermore, workers in developed and developing countries tend to have opposing interests vis-à-vis the relocation of manufacturing industry. National interests inhibit the development of international labor solidarity. For example, protectionist groups of employers and labor unions in the multinationals' home countries have furthered their own self interest by citing exploitation of women workers overseas as a reason why goods made by these workers should be prevented from reaching their destined markets by means of tariffs, quotas, and other restrictive trade practices. This has the effect of pitting workers in mature and developing capitalist countries against each other.

Because patriarchal social relations are at the bottom of women's subjection to imperialist exploitation, it is logical to turn to an attack on traditional patriarchy as a means of improving the position of women. The successful elimination of patriarchal institutions and attitudes, discrimination, differential socialization by sex, and the sexual division of labor within the family would equalize male and female employment opportunities and incomes, ending the sex segregation of the capitalist labor market. This is also difficult to envisage, given the deep cultural and psychological as well as economic and social foundations of patriarchy, which is found in advanced as well as developing capitalist countries and in socialist countries as well. Furthermore, in developing countries, national identity is very much bound up with a traditional, often feudal, patriarchal culture. An attack on traditional patriarchy may be construed as an attack on national identity and thus arouse the forces of a reactionary nationalism against the liberation of women. Indeed, one of the dangers of multinational exploitation of Third World women workers is that it arouses local antiimperialist sentiment that becomes identified—as in fundamentalist Islamic ideology in Iran—with traditionalism and opposition to wage employment by women.

Even if traditional patriarchy is successfully undermined and equality in the capitalist labor market achieved for women workers, they will remain subject, together with male workers, to capitalist exploitation in a capitalist economy. Capitalist employers themselves are unlikely to be indifferent to the elimination of sex differences in the labor market. Although employers of predominantly female workers may be expected to oppose sex equalization because it would reduce the supply and thus raise the wages of women workers in low skill, labor-intensive and dead end jobs, employers in male-intensive industries where labor is scarce may welcome the entry of female labor as a means of increasing the labor supply and reducing wages. The balance between these opposing interests and the attitude of male workers themselves, depends on the state and rate of development of capitalist relations of production. A nation that is rapidly growing and upgrading into high skill, high wage industries and occupations and experiences rising demand relative to supply of labor is likely to have greater sex equalization in the labor market than one which is only slowly growing or stagnating, with high unemployment and a dependence on low wage, labor-intensive industries. In other words, rapid capitalist development is more conducive to sex equalization in the labor market but by itself cannot be expected to bring about such equalization.

Elimination of worker exploitation altogether can only occur if capitalism itself is eliminated. This presents enormous difficulties for the small developing country in a world dominated by capitalism and imperialism. Domestically, a necessary precondition is the unity of the working class, which is hampered by sex, race, regional, and other differences within the labor force. So long as patriarchal relations of production persist, male and female workers remain divided by occupational segregation and by the tendency for male workers to assume the position of a labor aristocracy. If development is slow and mainly in low skill industries, male unemployment and low wages will limit this aristocracy to a small segment of the male work force, rather than creating a male elite that opposes female workers. Thus, the elimination of patriarchy would facilitate the elimination of capitalism itself. However, the elimination of capitalist exploitation does not necessarily facilitate the elimination of patriarchal exploitation, as the experience of present-day postcapitalist societies indicates. In all the "socialist" countries, including the USSR, China and eastern Europe, women occupy an inferior position in the labor force and in social and political life relative to men (though the difference may be less than in mature capitalist countries). Indeed, in some cases, the struggle against a capitalism identified with imperialist exploitation can lend itself to a reinforcement of traditional patriarchy and opposition to women's participation in the labor force. Finally, to the extent that socialist societies are likely to be less materially successful than capitalist societies—at least in the short and medium run—the elimination of all forms of exploitation may be achieved at the cost of lower absolute wages and standards of living and working for both men and women.

## Conclusion

This paper has sought to spell out the complexities involved in an analysis of female employment in multinational export factories in developing capitalist countries and in any attempt to formulate policy or political action on behalf of these women workers. The interplay of capitalist, imperialist, and patriarchal relations of production and the simultaneously exploitative and liberating consequences of this form of wage employment for women, point out the inadequacy of simplistic anti-capitalist, anti-imperialist or anti-patriarchal analyses and strategies to relieve exploitation.

Within the existing structure of economy and society, pro-capitalist and pro-imperialist strategies—for example, encouraging maximum investment by labor-intensive multinational factories—may serve an antipatriarchal aim—by increasing the demand for female labor and raising female wages absolutely and relative to male wages where, as in many developing countries, male wage employment is growing more slowly. Multinationals generally offer a better employment alternative to women than local enterprises in modern and traditional sectors of the economy and also provide a limited escape from the domestic roles imposed by traditional patriarchy. But there are limitations to the success of this strategy in raising women's wages permanently. Because female employment creation in multinational factories is based on patriarchal exploitation—low absolute and relative wages for women workers—the elimination of these conditions may well bring about an elimination of the jobs themselves, given the international mobility of multinational capital and the availability of exploitable female labor in other countries. A similar limitation faces attempts to impose reforms on the multinationals through government policy actions or worker organization and labor union activity on an enterprise, national, or international scale.

In the larger national context, a pro-capitalist, pro-imperialist strategy on behalf of women workers can generate a "backlash" response from traditional patriarchy, making a general and genuine liberation for women more difficult. It also weakens worker solidarity where anti-imperialist and anti-capitalist struggles exist. On the other hand, these struggles are unlikely to succeed so long as the labor force and labor market remain divided by sex, and so these struggles would be strengthened by the undermining of patriarchal relations of production.

Ultimately, it is the existing structure of the economy and society that has to be changed if the exploitation of women in the labor force is to be eliminated. Capitalist market forces and employment based on imperialist exploitation cannot liberate women from patriarchal exploitation that is the very condition for their entry into wage labor in multinational factories producing for the world market. In the long run, capitalism and imperialism only perpetuate and may even reinforce patriarchal relations of production, which in turn reinforce capitalist and imperialist relations of production. Although the liberation of women workers as women and as workers can only come about through some combined struggle against capitalist, imperialist, and patriarchal exploitation, the specific strategies to be undertaken depend on the particular historical, social, economic and political circumstances of each national unit in the context of an international capitalism.

*Notes*

1. For a few examples of relevant case studies, see Snow 1977, Lim 1978b, Paglaban 1978, Grossman 1979, Fernández Kelly 1980, United Nations Industrial Development Organization (UNIDO) 1980.
2. See, for example, Leontiades 1971, Adam 1975, Moxon 1974, UNIDO 1979, Fröbel, Heinrichs, and Kreye 1980.
3. See, for example, Nayyar 1978, Fröbel, Heinrichs, and Kreye 1978, Takeo 1978; Landsberg 1979, Sivanandan 1980.
4. Marginal productivity is a theoretical concept central to neoclassical economic doctrine: it is the addition to a firm's total output value resulting from the employment of one additional worker or unit of labor.
5. In neoclassical economic theory, this is true in all but the pure and unattainable case of perfect competition in both product and labor markets, where labor is paid exactly the value of its marginal product. In Marxist economic theory, even the "normal profit" or "zero economic profit" earned by perfectly competitive firms—the return just necessary to maintain them in their line of production, which includes a return to capital—represents "surplus value" exploited off labor.
6. Indigenous firms have to compete with multinationals in the labor market; multinationals are the leaders in setting wages and working conditions. In Singapore, the improvement of wages and working conditions in the female labor market are illustrated by the following facts: Starting wages have more than doubled in five years (ahead of inflation); fringe benefits have improved (for example, the extension of paid holiday time to

two weeks in the year); part-time shifts have been instituted to suit housewives; the desired age of workers has risen from sixteen to twenty-three years to up to fifty years; there has been a dramatic reduction in rotating shifts and microscope work in electronics factories; and a five-day week is typical. Singapore workers have become a "labor aristocrary" in the Southeast Asian region.

## References

Adam, Gyorgy. 1975. "Multinational Corporations and Worldwide Sourcing." In *International Firms and Modern Imperialism*, ed. Hugo Radice. Hamondsworth, England: Penguin.

Becker, Gary Stanley. 1957. *The Economics of Discrimination.* Chicago: University of Chicago Press.

Blaxall, Martha and Barbara Reagan, ed., 1976. *Women and the Workplace: The Implications of Occupational Segregation.* Chicago: University of Chicago Press.

Boserup, Ester. 1970. *Woman's Role in Economic Development.* London: Allen and Unwin.

Fernández-Kelly, María Patricia. 1982. "Mexican Border Industrialization, Female Labour Force Participation and Migration." Working Paper. Center for the Study, Education and Advancement of Women. University of California, Berkeley.

Fröbel, Folker; Heinrichs, Jürgen; and Kreye, Otto. 1978. "Export-Oriented Industrialization of Underdeveloped Countries." *Monthly Review* 30, no. 6, pp. 22–27.

.1980. *The New International Division of Labour: Structural Unemployment in Industrialised Countries and Industrialisation in Developing Countries.* Cambridge and New York: Cambridge University Press.

Grossman, Rachel. 1979. "Women's Place in the Integrated Circuit." *Southeast Asia Chronicle, Pacific Research,* Issue, 9 nos. 5–6.

Landsberg, Martin. 1979. "Export-led Industrialization in the Third World: Manufacturing Imperialism." *Review of Radical Political Economics* 11, no. 4, pp. 50–63.

Leontiades, James. 1971. "International Sourcing in the Less-developed Countries." *Columbia Journal of World Business* 6, no. 6, pp. 19–26.

Lim, Linda Y. C. 1978a. "Multinational Firms and Manufacturing for Export in Less-developed Countries: The Case of the Electronics Industry in Malaysia and Singapore." Ph.D. Dissertation, University of Michigan, Ann Arbor.

. 1978b. *Women Workers in Multinational Corporations: The Case of the Electronics Industry in Malaysia and Singapore.* Michigan Occasional Papers, no. 9. Ann Arbor, Michigan: University of Michigan, Women's Studies Program.

Moxon, Richard W. 1974. "Offshore Production in Less-developed Countries—A Case Study of Multinationality in the Electronics Industry." *Bulletin,* nos. 98–99 (July). New York University: Graduate School of Business Administration, Institute of Finance.

Nayyar, Deepak. 1978. "Transnational Corporations and Manufactured Exports from Poor Countries." *Economic Journal* 88:58–84.

Paglaban, E. 1978. "Philippines: Workers in the Export Industry." *Pacific Research* 9, Nos. 3–4.

Pang Eng Fong and Lim, Linda Y. C. 1977. *The Electronics Industry in Singapore: Structure, Technology and Linkages.* Economic Research Centre, University of Singapore, Research Monograph Series, no. 7.

Reynis, Lee Ann. 1976. "The Proliferation of U.S. Firm Third World Sourcing in the Mid-to-Late 1960's: An Historical and Empirical Study of the Factors Which Occasioned the Location of Production for the U.S. Market Abroad." Ph.D. dissertation, University of Michigan, Ann Arbor.

Sivanandan, A. 1980. "Imperialism in the Silicon Age." *Monthly Review* 32, no. 3, pp. 24–42.

Snow, Robert. 1977. "Dependent Development and the New Industrial Worker: The Export Processing Zone in the Philippines." Ph.D. dissertation, Harvard Universilty.

Takeo, Tsuchiya. 1978. "Free Trade Zones in Southeast Asia." *Monthly Review* 29 no. 9, pp. 29–39.

United Nations Industrial Development Organization (UNIDO). 1979. "Redeployment of Industries from Developed to Developing Countries." Industrial Development Conference. 419 (October 3).

———. 1980. "Women in the Redeployment of Manufacturing Industry to Developing Countries." UNIDO Working Papers on Structural Change, no. 18, UNIDO/ICIS. (July 8).

*Part II*

# PRODUCTION, REPRODUCTION, AND THE HOUSEHOLD ECONOMY

Throughout the development of industrial capitalism, the household has borne the burden of adjustment to changes in employment levels, inflation, and wage fluctuations. From the early years of the Industrial Revolution in England to the present in developing countries, the household unit has resisted dependency on factory employment by clinging to a semisubsistence strategy. Helen Safa compares the production and reproduction strategies of Brazilian and U.S. factory workers. Neuma Aguiar shows how the different kinds of economic enterprises, including plantation, government sponsored cooperative, and multinational corporations, relate workers to contrasting, coexisting modes of production. Lynn Bolles, who carried out her research in Jamaica when the International Monetary Fund imposed strictures on government programs in the interest of a stable environment for investing, is able to demonstrate how the world system impinges on the domestic economy. José Antonio Alonso has studied the backwash effect of the penetration of multinational investment in the Mexican economy as marginal, labor-intensive industry such as garment manufacturing reverts to a cottage "putting-out" system. These studies show the contradictions in an uneven development process.

# CHAPTER 4

# Women, Production, and Reproduction in Industrial Capitalsim: A Comparison of Brazilian and U.S. Factory Workers

HELEN I. SAFA

Women have always constituted a source of cheap labor for industrial capitalism (Saffioti 1971). But the way in which women are incorporated into the paid labor force differs for women of different cultures, classes, and stages of capitalist developmment. With the development of industrial capitalism and the movement of production outside the home into the factory, the family ceased to function as a productive unit and became dependent on wages earned outside the home. Although production became increasingly public, reproduction remained within the private sphere of the family, though clearly also affected by the larger economic changes occuring in society. As Bridenthal (1976:5) has pointed out, "For women, the experience has become one of pulls between opposing forces, work and family" and the constant attempt to reconcile the dialectic between the two.

It is through the allocation of labor at the household level that we can see how larger economic forces impinge on women's productive and reproductive role. This paper will examine the way in which women combine their productive role in paid labor with their reproductive role as wives and mothers in two societies at very different stages of development: Brazil and the United States. Although more industrialized than most Latin American countries, Brazil is still heavily dependent on foreign sources of capital and technology for much of her industrialization and economic growth. Partly as a result of this dependence and the rapid shift into capital-intensive industrialization, Brazil is also characterized by a labor surplus and high rates of unemployment and underemployment, much greater than ever existed in the United States. Under these conditions of labor surplus, clearly only the most productive members of the potential labor force can find employment, excluding large numbers of women, particularly older, married women with children (cf. São Paulo 1978:74). Thus, the percentage of women employed in Brazil is less than half of that in the United States, and only 9.93 percent of married women in Brazil are employed compared to 41 percent in the United States (Vasquez de Miranda 1977:270).

This study focuses on women factory workers in these two societies because factory work represents entry level jobs into the formal labor market in both countries for workers with relatively low educational and skill levels. In Brazil and most Third World countries, due again to the large labor surplus, there exists an extensive informal labor market in which women play a predominant role, working as domestic servants, street vendors, and in other forms of casual labor (cf. Arizpe 1977). Factory work then often represents the first stable form of employment open to Third World women and is generally reserved for young single women who were born in the city or have lived there since childhood and thereby been able to acquire more education than most migrant women, who are largely confined to the informal labor market.

The data analyzed here consists of one hundred interviews with young, mostly single women employed in a textile and a garment plant in São Paulo, Brazil, and eighty interviews with older, mostly married women employed in a garment plant in New Jersey. Data were collected between 1979 and 1980.[1] São Paulo was chosen for comparative purposes because it is the most highly industrialized city in Brazil if not in Latin America and the center of capital accumulation and economic growth, the showplace of the "Brazilian miracle." In São Paulo, the percentage of women employed is 35.3, almost double the national average of 18 percent, but the number of women employed drops off sharply after the age of twenty-four, when most women marry (São Paulo 1978:75). Thus, in São Paulo and Brazil generally, single women still constitute the primary source of cheap female labor, much as in the early stages of industrialization in western Europe and the United States (Tilly and Scott 1978). At a more advanced level of industrial capitalism as in the United States, however, young women remain in school longer and are primarily employed in clerical and other white-collar jobs. Therefore, marginal industries, such as the garment industry examined here, are forced to turn to a supplementary labor reserve, namely older, married women for these low-paying, unskilled jobs. Thus, it would appear that in advanced capitalist countries, married women generally constitute a secondary labor reserve, at least in blue-collar jobs, and are employed only when the supply of young single women is not sufficient. Even in São Paulo, the women employed in the garment plant (who constitute 20 percent of the sample) are older and more likely to be married than the women employed in the textile factory. Therefore, the nature of the industry as well as the nation's stage of development help determine labor recruitment patterns.

How do these different recruitment patterns for women in paid productive labor at different levels of capitalist development affect the allocation of labor at the household level? A look at the household composition of these two samples appears to indicate a very different allocation of labor in Brazilian and U.S. working-class families. Whereas the Brazilian women are generally members of large households with multiple wage earners, the New Jersey families are small, with one or two wage earners. These differences in household composition and number of wage earners within Brazilian and U.S. working class families can be explained, I think, by different survival strategies[2] of working-class families within an industrial capitalist mode of production at two different stages of development. In Brazil, where married women are generally denied access to formal paid employment in factory jobs because of the abundance of young single women for these jobs, other family members are forced to become wage earners at an early age since multiple wage earning is critical for the family's survival. In the United States, however, where married women may continue to be employed, it is not as necessary for other family members, particularly children, to contribute to the family income. Both Brazilian and U.S. working-class families often rely on more than one wage earner. In New Jersey it is generally husband and wife who are employed. In São Paulo, with lower wages and higher costs of living, several members of the household, including children, are forced to work.

Through a study of the allocation of labor at the household level, we can see how Brazilian and U.S. working-class families employ different strategies to maximize their family's well-being. Both groups of working-class families have lost control over the means of production through the process of proletarianization and have to survive through the sale of their labor. They have entered what Tilly and Scott (1978:105), referring to early industrialization in western Europe, term a "family wage economy," in which "the composition of

97

the household no longer was dictated by a need for household laborers, as in the family economy, but by a need for cash. The balance between wage earners and consumers in the household determined family fortunes."

In order to maximize the number of wage earners per family, São Paulo working-class families incorporate other adult kin into the household and send as many members into paid labor as early as possible. In contrast, New Jersey working-class families are much smaller, with only one or two wage earners per household. Among married couples the principal breadwinner is usually the man, but women often continue to work after marriage and childbirth to supplement family income and to support their children's prolonged education. Women may also reduce the number of children they have in order to invest in the upward mobility of a few rather than in the labor of many. In short, whereas in the São Paulo family wage economy, the emphasis is on the maximization of the number of wage earners per household, in New Jersey the reduction in the number of wage earners is balanced by the reduction in the number of consumers, particularly children. In both São Paulo and New Jersey families, however, the household and not the individual remains the basic unit of decision making, allocating the labor of household members to paid wage or domestic responsibilities so as to maximize the family's chances for survival or upward mobility.

### Brazilian Factory Women

While the United States may be characterized as an advanced capitalist economy, where the vast bulk of the population depends on wages, Brazil is a dependent capitalist society still incorporating many precapitalist features. Brazilian industrialization, particularly in the postwar years, has been largely financed and directed from abroad, particularly in the São Paulo area, where this study was conducted. The textile industry was one of the first industries in São Paulo and has remained technologically quite mixed, with very modern, capital-intensive plants, especially in synthetics, and some older, more labor-intensive plants, particularly in natural fibers such as the cotton textile factory studied here. The proportion of women workers is generally much lower in capital-intensive, highly automated plants, which favor a reduced number of male workers at higher wage and skill levels (cf. Blay 1978:144–5).

Economic development and industrialization has apparently not led to higher labor force participation rates for Brazilian women, at least in industry. In the São Paulo area, despite very rapid rates of industrialization since 1940, the percentage of women employed in the secondary sector[3] increased from only 14 percent in 1940 to 17 percent in 1970 (Vasquez de Miranda 1977:266). This is due to the fact that industrialization in São Paulo in recent decades has been primarily capital-intensive in such industries as metallurgy, machinery, chemical, pharmaceuticals and electronics. Although bureaucratic and clerical activities for women have increased in these larger establishments, these occupations have been limited predominantly to younger single women who have completed high school, and some have even started college (Blay 1978:213). Thus, although the overall activity rate for women has not changed much since 1940, there has been a marked shift of women out of agriculture and into services with industry remaining fairly stable (Population Council 1978:9; Blay 1978:142).

The labor force for industrialization in the São Paulo area was drawn largely from foreign immigrants (especially Italians) and rural migrants expelled from their peasant and artisan activities in the countryside. In our sample 57 percent of the women factory workers are born outside the greater São Paulo area, chiefly from the surrounding state of São Paulo and the Northeast. However, as was pointed out earlier, factory workers in Latin America generally are not recent migrants, and our sample is no exception. Over 60 percent of the migrants in our sample have been living in the city for over ten years, while over half said they came as children with their parents. The educational level is also higher than that found among recent migrants, who are generally employed in the informal economy as domestic servants, petty vendors, and so forth. Among the factory women interviewed, 65 percent have completed primary school (signifying four years of education), and 23 percent have gone on to secondary school. In short, a factory job in Brazil and Latin America generally, represents a considerable advancement over jobs in the informal sector. Although wages are very low by U.S. standards (48 percent earn between two and three minimum salary units monthly)[4], they are still higher and much more stable than what can be earned in the informal sector, especially by women.

However, most women work in factories only for a short period, from the time they finish primary school until they marry. Thus, in our sample 49 percent have worked in this factory less than four years and all but three of these women are under twenty-four. Among these factory women 64 percent are under twenty-four (24 percent under eighteen) and only 13 percent are married and 5 percent formerly married.[5] The most apparent reason behind the small number of married women employed at the factory is the reluctance of the owners to pay the rather liberal maternity benefits to which permanently employed pregnant women in Brazil are entitled. Cultural attitudes also work against the employment of married women (cf. Blay 1978:273), and 51 percent of our sample of single women indicated that they planned to work only until marriage or pregnancy. Although cultural attitudes undoubtedly favor married women staying home, it would appear to be primarily the abundance of a cheap, unskilled supply of young unmarried women that mitigates against the employment of married women.

Hence, Brazilian factory women are forced to make a real choice between their productive and reproductive roles; if they marry and have children, they will probably be forced to give up working, at least in factory jobs. Undoubtedly, many married women continue to work in the informal economy, in self-employed activities that are deemed more compatible with their domestic role.

Employed single women living at home are expected to contribute to the family income. Only 23 percent of our sample (and not one married woman) indicated that they spend their salary only on themselves, the rest contributing all or most of their salary to family and household expenses. Asked what would happen if they were not working, 42 percent noted that their families could not afford to buy the same things. It would seem then, that the meager wages of these women makes a substantial contribution to the family's welfare.

In fact, Brazilian working-class families appear to be surviving by following a policy of multiple wage earning, which drives both men and women into the labor force at an early age (São Paulo 1978:65). In our sample, 89 percent of the women started working under the age of eighteen, mostly in factory work.[6] Those currently living with their parents almost always started working under eighteen, suggesting it is parental pressure that forces them to find a job. Households tend to be large and to include large numbers of young adults who can work and contribute to the family income. Thus, 28 percent of our sample consist of households numbering seven or more members, with 40 percent of the families having four or more working members each. (In the large families with seven or more members, 85 percent have four or more working members.) In most cases our respondents live with their parents (sometimes only the mother), siblings, and occasionally other related young adults of the same generation such as cousins.

Where neither parent is present, the woman may be living with siblings or other relatives and friends. However, young married couples generally live alone or with their children and seldom with other relatives. Only two women live alone. The point is to maximize the number of working members of the household, all of whom are expected to contribute to the family income.

The relationship of family income to the number of persons working in the household is shown by the fact that the highest incomes are found in households with the largest number of workers. Thus, 52.6 percent of families in our sample with monthly incomes of 6,000–10,000 cruzieros or more have from four to seven working members, compared to 25 percent of those with one to three working members (Table 4–1). Many of these working members are brothers and sisters of the respondent. Most of these siblings are also employed in factory or service jobs. Among 68 percent of respondents, from one to three additional siblings are employed in the household; and in more than three-fourths of these families, incomes range between 4,000 and 6,000 cruzeiros monthly. This is still low considering the large size of these families; but at this stage at least, older children seem to make a substantial contribution to family income.

Table 4–1. São Paulo: Number of Workers in Household by Family Income in Cruzeiros

| Number of Workers in Household | Family Income in Cruzeiros | | | | |
|---|---|---|---|---|---|
| | Less than 3,000 Cr. | 3001 to 4,000 Cr. | 4,001 to 6,000 Cr. | 6,000–10,000 Cr. and more | Row Total |
| 1 to 3 Workers | 8 13.3 66.7 | 14 23.3 77.8 | 23 38.3 67.6 | 15 25.0 42.9 | 60 60.6 |
| 4 to 7 Workers | 4 10.5 33.3 | 4 10.5 22.2 | 10 26.3 29.4 | 20 52.6 57.1 | 38 38.4 |
| 7 to 10 Workers | 0 0.0 0.0 | 0 0.0 0.0 | 1 100.0 2.9 | 0 0.0 0.0 | 1 1.0 |
| Column Total | 12 12.1 | 18 18.2 | 34 34.3 | 35 35.4 | 99 100.0 |

Note: Figures in cells represent number of respondents, row percentage, and column percentage respectively.

It is difficult to know how these families survive when children are small and unable to work particularly since it is difficult for mothers to make up for their children's lack of earning capacity. It is significant that in our sample, married women have lower family incomes than single women (see Table 4–2), most of whom live in households with various wage earners. Married women with children may continue to earn some income through the informal economy by doing piecework at home or petty vending, but this is generally not the equivalent of a paid factory or other formal job.[7] This hardship undoubtedly helps account for the high rate of infant mortality in São Paulo today, which increased 40 percent in the 1960–70 decade along with the decline in purchasing power.[8] (Wood 1977:57). At the same time, high infant mortality rates induce families to have large numbers of children in the hope that some will survive to adulthood.

Rapid inflation and lagging wage rates have accelerated the decline in purchasing power of working-class families in recent years, resulting in a decrease in the real minimum wage in São Paulo from one hundred U.S. dollars in 1960 to seventy U.S. dollars in 1970 (ibid.:58). Minimum wage rates have been tightly controlled to keep labor costs low and have not kept up with the rapid rise in prices. As a result, from 1958 to 1969 the purchasing power of the wage

*Table 4–2.* São Paulo: Income in Cruzeiros by Marital Status

| Income in Cruzeiros | Married | Single | Formerly Married | Row Total |
|---|---|---|---|---|
| Less than 3,000 Cr. | 3 | 9 | 0 | 12 |
| | 25.0 | 75.0 | 0.0 | 12.1 |
| | 20.0 | 11.1 | 0.0 | |
| 3,001 to 4,000 Cr. | 4 | 14 | 0 | 18 |
| | 22.2 | 77.8 | 0.0 | 18.2 |
| | 26.7 | 17.3 | 0.0 | |
| 4,001 to 6,000 Cr. | 5 | 27 | 2 | 34 |
| | 14.7 | 79.4 | 5.9 | 34.3 |
| | 33.3 | 33.3 | 66.7 | |
| More than 6,001 Cr. | 3 | 31 | 1 | 35 |
| | 8.6 | 88.6 | 2.9 | 35.4 |
| | 20.0 | 38.3 | 33.3 | |
| Column Total | 15 | 81 | 3 | 99 |
| | 15.2 | 81.8 | 3.0 | 100.0 |

*Note:* Figures in cells represent number of respondents, row percentage, and column percentage respectively.

of the head of the average family fell by 36.5 percent; and even with more members working, the family's real income still fell by 9.4 percent (São Paulo 1978:64). The value of minimum wage fell from one hundred U.S. dollars in 1970 to eighty-two U.S. dollars in 1974 (ibid.:46). Workers have responded by extending the number of hours worked and by increasing the number of workers per family. The number of members employed in the average working-class family in São Paulo from 1958 to 1969 increased from one to two (ibid.:63), with many more probably working at nonregulated and unreported jobs in the informal economy. Women also try to stretch an insufficient wage by substituting domestic labor inputs (such as kitchen gardens and chickens) for market purchases (Schmink 1979:9). Consumption patterns have also changed, with a decreasing percentage of income spent on such basic items as food and clothing and an increase in transport, education, and recreation (São Paulo 1978:68).

The necessity for a multiple wage-earning strategy in Brazil has therefore been made particularly acute by a government policy that has allowed prices to rise while keeping wages tightly controlled to keep labor costs low. This was the price the poor of Brazil paid for the "economic miracle" initiated by the military government in 1964, which slowed considerably in the early 1970s in the wake of the worldwide recession. During this period income inequality in Brazil, already among the highest in Latin America, grew markedly; a recent study found that from 1960 to 1970 the share of total income among the richest 5 percent of the population increased 72 percent while nearly 75 percent of the population experienced no change during this ten year period (Population Council 1978:11). The top 5 percent of the population took home 36.3 percent of total income, a share virtually the same (36.2 percent) as that of the poorest 80 percent (São Paulo 1978:60). The Population Council (ibid.:11) citing studies by J. Kocher (1973) and R. G. Repetto (1974) notes:

Studies of the relationship between fertility and economic development indicate that, for countries at similar aggregate income levels, the less skewed the social and economic distribution, the lower the overall fertility level and the more rapid the fertility decline. . . . In other words, the more the benefits of economic growth accrue to a small minority of the population, the greater would be the tendency for low-income groups to maintain high fertility.

The data presented here offer one possible explanation for these findings. That is, poor families continue to have large families under conditions of extreme income inequality because there is no advantage in reducing the number of wage earners in the family. High fertility levels of course mean increased numbers of workers, which can keep wages down by increasing competition for jobs, not only between men and women but among men as well. Thus, high fertility levels may be contradictory to the long-range aggregate interests of the working class as a whole; but, I would argue, it still appears functional to the individual working-class family, which has only its labor to sell. As long as men as the principal breadwinners are not being paid the equivalent of a family wage that is enough to support themselves and their dependents, then other members of the family are forced to contribute. In Brazil today minimum salaries do not even cover the maintenance of the worker during his/her working years, much less the long-term consumption needs of the household (Schmink 1979:8)

### Factory Women in New Jersey

In the early days of industrialization in the United States, the textile industry also employed only young unmarried women. In New England, where the textile industry began, these women were primarily the daughters of farm and artisan families and lived in boarding houses furnished by the factory and under close surveillance by the management. However, as the industry burgeoned, the cost of these relatively good living conditions for a resident female labor force grew too expensive for textile owners, and they turned increasingly by the middle of the nineteenth century to immigrant labor from abroad (Kessler-Harris 1975:220–1). Immigration thus proved another fruitful way of reproducing a cheap labor supply, particularly because immigrant women tended to work all their lives, married or not. Married women often worked at home taking in boarders and sewing at exploitative piecework rates on the putting-out system.

With the entry of immigrant women into the labor force, working conditions in the textile factories deteriorated rapidly, as did real wages. The cost of labor decreased since immigrant women were paid less and did not have to be accommodated in relatively expensive boarding houses, which were designed primarily to protect the chastity and reputation of native-born American women. The proportion of gainfully employed immigrant women or their daughters increased steadily until 1910, when reform movements designed not only to improve factory conditions but to "Americanize" these women began to take effect (ibid.:228). Immigrant women, especially mothers, were encouraged to stay at home to take care of their children and to regard retirement from paid labor rather than job advancement as a sign of upward mobility (ibid.:223). Special concern was voiced over the health of these women, probably reflecting, as in Britain, a concern over the poor quality of future generations.

One of the chief outcomes of the reform movement was the initiation of protective legislation for women.[9] Nothing so symbolized women's dual productive and reproductive role. As Kessler-Harris (1975:229) notes, protective legislation "recognized that women had two jobs, one of which had to be limited if the other were to be performed adequately. Yet legislation institutionalized the primary role of social reproduction by denying that women were full-fledged members of the working class. . . . Protective legislation thus provided a device for dividing workers along gender lines and stratifying the work force in a period when homogeneity in levels of skill threatened to lead to developing class consciousness and to give rise to class conflict."

As in Brazil, protective legislation for women reduced competition with men by reducing the economic desirability of female employees (ibid.:230). Reduced competition from women and children was accompanied and probably contributed to rising wages for men, which made it financially easier for many married women to remain home. Unions also contributed to the establishment of a family wage, though some unions were often antagonistic to women (ibid.:224). Humphries (1977:251–2) has documented the way in which both protective legislation and a family wage were championed by the English working class as a way of reducing the labor supply, particularly of married women. As in the United States, this was also one of the few issues on which the working class could seek middle-class support.

Despite these obstacles the percentage of married women in the U.S. labor force has increased dramatically, especially since World War II, and as of March 1974, represented 58 percent of all working women (U.S. Dept. of Labor 1975:16). However, the increase has not been uniform in all sectors or for all age and ethnic groups. The tremendous growth in clerical jobs in the postwar period attracted primarily young and childless white women initially, but the demand gradually absorbed married women with children as well (ibid.:13–14).

Black women shifted out of the domestic service category into other types of service jobs (ibid.:105). Older married women without clerical skills were relegated to marginal industrial jobs like the garment industry. They face less competition in these poorly paid, marginal industries from younger women, who prefer cleaner, more well paid clerical jobs. Older women also possess the sewing skills necessary to compete at the piecework rates on which most garment plants operate. Because of its marginality, the garment industry has always provided a haven for newly arrived immigrants, most recently Hispanics, who do not possess the language and other educational skills needed in clerical and other types of service employment.

Although the median age of operatives and particularly sewers is higher nationally than either clerical or service workers (1970 Census of Population, vol. 1, Part 1, Table 226), in the garment plant we studied in New Jersey, certain special factors contributed to the older age of their female labor force. The most important factor is that the plant basically has been following a slow process of attrition, not hiring many workers in production since the 1950s. However, many female workers who were hired in the 1940s and 1950s have stayed on, so that 71 percent have been working in the same plant twenty years and more. Eighty percent of these women are over forty and over half are married. The remainder are almost equally divided between single and formerly married (usually widowed) women, the majority of whom are over fifty. Most of these women live in the local working-class neighborhood or nearby, the daughters of Italian, Polish, and other east European workers who were attracted to the job possibilities in manual labor in this area earlier in the century. Their husbands are also predominantly factory workers as are their brothers and sisters. They live in a blue-collar world.

The reason this plant has not hired many workers since the 1950s is that production has been moving to other areas, first cheaper labor areas within the United States (e.g., West Virginia), then to Puerto Rico in the 1950s, and now to newer foreign areas like the Dominican Republic. This has become a prevalent trend in the garment industry in the Northeast, which suffered a 40 percent decline in jobs in the 1960–70 decade, a loss which continued at the rate of 12,000 jobs per year through 1973 (Bureau of Labor Statistics 1975:104–5). The decline is brought on primarily by the desire to cut labor costs by moving to areas of lower wages and nonunionized labor, both in the United States and abroad. The "runaway shop" thus represents a new strategy for supplying a cheap labor force in advanced capitalist societies where unions and other factors have helped to drive up labor costs and is particularly attractive to labor-intensive industries such as garment. Rather than importing immigrant labor, the runaway shop "exports jobs."

The women at the New Jersey plant are aware that jobs are being lost and fear for the security of their own employment even though the plant is unionized. One of the chief complaints is that workers are constantly being switched from one job to another (to replace lost personnel), which slows down their piecework rate and hence their wage. One of the branches of the factory often closes one day a week for lack of work, and of course the women are not paid a full wage.

Wages in the garment industry are the lowest of any major industrial group in the United States, about three dollars an hour in 1974 (North American Congress for Latin America, 1976:8). Though wages can be increased substantially through piecework, almost 40 percent of the women sampled earn between $100 and $139 a week, while the highest weekly salaries run to $160 and over. Though much higher than those of Brazilian women factory workers, wages are still insufficient to support a family and barely enough for a single person to live on. Over half the families sampled have a total annual income of less than $10,000. Significantly, the lowest incomes are found among the single and formerly married (mostly widowed) women in our sample, 40 percent of whom depend solely on their own wages. In 68 percent of these families with a single wage earner, annual incomes are under $8,000 (Table 4–3). Single women live alone or with a relative (usually a sister) and often in a home that they have inherited from their parents and thus have considerably reduced housing costs. Widows and other formerly married women either live alone (45 percent) or with their children (45 percent), most of whom contribute to the family income. The highest incomes in this sample are found in families with two or more wage earners, most of whom are husband and wife. All but five of the forty married women in our sample have households with two or more wage earners.

However, although both husband and wife may work, there is a clear difference from the Brazilian multiple wage-earning family, particularly in the dependence on their children. In New Jersey, grown children do not make a major contribution to family income because (1) the number of children per family is quite small and (2) children receive a much higher education and require longer years of support. Once they leave school, they tend to marry and have their own families to support.

Table 4–3. New Jersey: Number of Wage Earners in Household by Total Annual Income

| Total Annual Income | One | Two | Three or More | Row Total |
|---|---|---|---|---|
| Under $5,000 | 3<br>30.0<br>12.5 | 4<br>40.0<br>13.8 | 3<br>30.0<br>23.1 | 10<br>15.2 |
| $5,000 to $7,999 | 13<br>65.0<br>54.2 | 4<br>20.0<br>13.8 | 3<br>15.0<br>23.1 | 20<br>30.3 |
| $8,000 to $9,999 | 5<br>41.7<br>20.8 | 5<br>41.7<br>17.2 | 2<br>16.7<br>15.4 | 12<br>18.2 |
| $10,000 to $15,999 | 2<br>14.3<br>8.3 | 10<br>71.4<br>34.5 | 2<br>14.3<br>15.4 | 14<br>21.2 |
| $16,000 and over | 1<br>10.0<br>4.2 | 6<br>60.0<br>20.7 | 3<br>30.0<br>23.1 | 10<br>15.2 |
| Column Total | 24<br>36.4 | 29<br>43.9 | 13<br>19.7 | 66<br>100.0 |

Note: Figures in cells represent number of respondents, row percentage, and column percentage respectively.

The families of these New Jersey women factory workers are much smaller than in São Paulo. Median household size in New Jersey is approximately 2.5 compared to 5.06 in São Paulo; 53 percent of these New Jersey households consist of one or two persons. Although it must be recognized that most of these families are at a different stage of the life cycle, with most children grown and living outside the household, the total number of children they have had is also much smaller; over half of the New Jersey women had only one or two children. In São Paulo, 43.3 percent of our respondents had over five siblings.[10]

This small number of children is all the more striking when compared to the families in which these women were raised, which were much larger: 20 percent of these New Jersey women had seven or more siblings, whereas another 20 percent had five to six. In short, when we compare total number of siblings among older women factory workers in New Jersey with the size of families in the younger generation in São Paulo, they begin to look very similar. Clearly there has been a sharp decline in family size from their parents to their own generation among our New Jersey respondents, although in both cases we are dealing with a predominantly Catholic population: two-thirds of the New Jersey women as compared to 80 percent of the São Paulo women are Roman Catholic.

There appear to be several factors that help explain this drastic reduction in family size in New Jersey. First, many of these women were bearing children during the Great Depression, which induced low fertility levels in the United States generally. Second, the economic value of American children during this period was reduced by legislation such as child labor laws and compulsory education (which are also law in Brazil but often not implemented).[11] Third, contraceptive technology might have been more widespread in the United States during the period these women were having children (1940–50) than in Brazil today, where income as well as lack of information serves as a real barrier (Population Council 1978:16).

In addition, however, changes in labor demand and the consequent cost of children in the United States may have induced these families to have fewer children. As increased opportunities for both sexes open up in the United States in white-collar jobs requiring higher levels of education, working-class families may have been induced to reduce their number of children in order to give them more education. There was no longer a need for a large labor pool, as is still prevalent in Brazil, but for a smaller number of more highly skilled workers prepared to meet the growing demand for administrative as well as skilled industrial jobs. At the same time, the cessation of large-scale immigration and the movement of younger women into white-collar jobs opened up marginal jobs in the garment industry for older, married women who previously might have been denied employment (cf. Wool 1976:24). The additional income provided by the women's employment, while small, may have helped these families to give their children a higher education. It is doubtful if they could have managed solely with the husband's salary, since most men, like their wives, were employed in relatively low-paying factory jobs.

The movement out of blue-collar into white-collar jobs among New Jersey working-class families can be seen by comparing the employment of the father and the son (Table 4–4). Whereas most fathers (husbands of our respondents) were or are employed in blue-collar jobs, in families with sons, 55 percent of the sons are employed in white-collar jobs compared to 40 percent in blue-collar or service work. While the sample here is very small and therefore should be interpreted with a great deal of caution, the trend toward white-collar employment is unmistakable. The percentage of daughters in

*109*

white-collar work is even higher (70 percent) probably reflecting the surge in clerical employment among women. In addition, the degree to which white-collar employment is dependent on a higher education is shown by the fact that most of the oldest sons and daughters of these New Jersey working-class families who now hold white-collar jobs have been to college and sometimes graduate school (Tables 4–5 and 4–6).[12] Although it is difficult with the data collected here to establish a relationship between the mother's employment and the children's education, it is worth noting that in all but a few cases, among the children who went to college or graduate school, the mothers have been working twenty years and more.

Clearly we are dealing with a very different survival strategy from that observed among Brazilian working-class women. Families are quite small, but both husband and wife work to promote their children's mobility from blue-collar into white-collar work. This reflects the decreasing demand for blue-collar workers in the United States, particularly among women, and the tremendous increase in white-collar and particularly clerical employment. It also reflects increasing educational opportunities in the United States, made possible through mass public education, though not without considerable

*Table 4–4.* New Jersey: Occupation of Father and First Son

| Father's Occupation | Son's Occupation | | | |
|---|---|---|---|---|
| | White-Collar | Blue-Collar | Unemployed Ed. | Row Total |
| Blue-Collar | 4 50.0 36.4 | 3 37.5 37.5 | 1 12.5 100.0 | |
| White-Collar | 1 100.0 9.1 | 0 0.0 0.0 | 0 0.0 0.0 | 1 5.0 |
| Service Worker | 1 50.0 9.1 | 1 50.0 12.5 | 0 0.0 0.0 | 2 10.0 |
| Not Working | 5 55.6 45.5 | 4 44.4 50.0 | 0 0.0 0.0 | 9 45.0 |
| Column Total | 11 55.0 | 8 40.0 | 1 5.0 | 20 100.0 |

*Note:* Figures in cells represent number of respondents, row percentage, and column percentage respectively.

*110*

financial support and sacrifice from parents. As Gimenez (1977:19) points out:

> Only under exceptional circumstances will the capitalist classes make direct investments to upgrade the quality of specific sectors of the labor force. . . Ordinarily that upgrading is financed by the workers themselves who, by investing in their own "human capital" or by reproducing labor power of quality higher than their own, through the training and/or education of their offspring, give rise to the phenomenon of "social mobility." It is through the process of self-upgrading, into which the working classes and salary earners are forced, that differences in reproductive behavior emerge.

## Conclusion

Self upgrading among workers involves a dual burden on the household: not only must they bear the direct costs of education (some of which may be absorbed by the state), but they must also suffer the loss of their children's earnings that would otherwise have been allocated to the family. Minge-Kalman (1978) documents this very well in the case of European peasant families that are in a transition toward wage labor. As the children cease to work on the

*Table 4-5.* New Jersey: Occupation and Education of First Son

| Education of First Son | Occupation of First Son | | | |
|---|---|---|---|---|
| | White-Collar | Blue-Collar | Unemployed Ed. | Row Total |
| High School or less | 3<br>27.3<br>23.1 | 7<br>63.6<br>63.6 | 1<br>9.1<br>100.0 | 11<br>44.0 |
| College | 4<br>50.0<br>30.8 | 4<br>50.0<br>36.4 | 0<br>0.0<br>0.0 | 8<br>32.8 |
| Graduate Work | 6<br>100.0<br>46.2 | 0<br>0.0<br>0.0 | 0<br>0.0<br>0.0 | 6<br>24.0 |
| Column Total | 13<br>52.0 | 11<br>44.0 | 1<br>4.0 | 25<br>100.0 |

*Note:* Figures in cells represent number of respondents, row percentage, and column percentage respectively.

*111*

Table 4-6. Occupation and Education of First Daughter

| Education of First Daughter | Daughter's Occupation | | | |
|---|---|---|---|---|
| | White-Collar | Blue-Collar | Unemployed Ed. | Row Total |
| High School or less | 5 50.0 31.3 | 5 50.0 83.3 | 0 0.0 0.0 | 10 43.5 |
| College | 9 81.8 56.3 | 1 9.1 16.7 | 1 9.1 100.0 | 11 47.8 |
| Graduate Work | 2 100.0 12.5 | 0 0.0 0.0 | 0 0.0 0.0 | 2 8.7 |
| Column Total | 16 69.6 | 6 26.1 | 4 4.3 | 23 100.0 |

Note: Figures in cells represent number of respondents, row percentage, and column percentage respectively.

family farm and require more years of education for skilled wage labor, their foregone labor is made up by the parents, chiefly by the mother. She writes:

> Since much of the foregone labor of children is labor that would have been allocated to the family farm—which is continued by mothers when fathers take wage labor—on the average, the mother's labor hours increase more than the father's as children's education level increases. [Minge-Kalman 1978:18]

I think a similar argument for a reallocation of labor at the household level can be made for urban working-class families. In the case of São Paulo we are dealing with older children and young adults, aged 15–25, whose labor is not appropriated directly by the family but contributed in the form of wages to the family income. If these young people require and have the opportunity to obtain a higher education and cannot work and contribute to the family income, then the family must compensate for this loss of wages in some way. The data from New Jersey factory families suggests that they may compensate by having women continue to work past the age of marriage and childbearing, which in turn may induce the woman to have fewer children. This would then help explain why the industrial female labor force in São Paulo (and Brazil generally) consists largely of young unmarried women whereas in the United States there is a much higher percentage of older married women employed in factory work. The work of married women in the United States helps compensate for the loss of their children's wages. The change in the composition of the family wage economy also helps explain why Brazilian urban working-class families continue to have large families while New Jersey working-class families have only a small number of children. To put it simply, there are no incentives for Brazilian urban working-class people to reduce family size in ways similar to those favored by New Jersey workers.

The limited growth of the modern industrial sector in a dependent capitalist society such as Brazil, where growth is heavily dependent on foreign technology, capital and markets, inhibits the development of a mass, skilled labor market such as occurred in the United States or western Europe during the height of industrial growth (Safa 1977). In 1972–73, for example, of São Paulo's 735,000 employees in the industrial sector only 18 percent were skilled (São Paulo 1978:74), despite the fact that the city represents the height of Brazilian industrial growth. Thus, São Paulo workers have not the incentive to educate their children for a more skilled labor market that our New Jersey families had. The continued existence of a labor surplus also prevents the formal employment of more marginal sectors of the labor force, such as married women with children, who only entered the labor force in large numbers in the postindustrial or monopoly capitalist phase of most advanced industrial societies. Older married women were only recruited for and retained in these marginal jobs when the tremendous surge in clerical employment and prolonged education exhausted the supply of younger single women.[13] Thus, it would appear to be only at a later stage of industrialization, when there is a sharp reduction in the demand for unskilled workers and an increasing demand for skilled workers (in administrative and clerical tasks as well as production) and when there are educational opportunities readily available to working-class families to enable them to acquire these skills, that there may be a reduction in family size to enable working class families to invest more in a few children than in the labor of many. Preparing children for these more skilled jobs requires more family expenditure and a prolonged period of dependence that in itself may require married women to work.

Although the problem of labor power in Brazil may be similar to other dependent capitalist economies, it has undoubtedly been made more acute by the antilabor policies of the Brazilian military gov-

*113*

ernment, which took power in 1964. Though they did succeed in promoting growth rates of nearly 10 percent between 1968 and 1972, few of the benefits of this boom went to the working class. On the contrary, in São Paulo itself, the center of the boom, they paid for it in terms of declining real wages, high infant mortality, malnutrition, lowered life expectancy, and other indicators of worsening social conditions (Wood 1978:60–61; São Paulo 1978). As we have shown, despite the increasing numbers of household members in the labor force brought on by the decline in purchasing power, real family income in São Paulo continued to drop between 1958 and 1969 (ibid.:59). Though the families studied here are by no means the worst off in terms of income and other indicators of living standards, their "success" appears to depend largely on the maintenance of a multiple wage-earning strategy (cf. Schmink 1979:9).

## Notes

1. Because of its small size, the sample does not pretend to be representative of factory women in either locale. We are more interested in the relationship between work and other variables in the two cultures.

2. Tilly (1978a:3) defines the analysis of family strategies as "the principles which lead to observable regularities or patterns of behavior among households. It asks who participates in making decisions, what concerns and constraints impinge on them. It asks who bears the cost or benefits from strategies in which individual interests or needs are often subordinated." Tilly (ibid.) adds that "these strategies have different effects on individuals, depending on their position and activities in the family. All household members' imperatives and choices are shaped by their position in the family, by the economic and social structures in which the households is located, and by the processes of change which these structures are undergoing."

3. The perspective adopted here defines economic sectors in the following way: the primary sector includes agricultural and mining activities; the secondary sector contains transformations such as manufacturing and processing and the tertiary sector refers to services.

4. In 1976–77 the minimum salary in Brazil was equivalent to 71 U.S. dollars monthly (Population Council 1978:15). It is adjusted annually based on a complicated formula combining productivity and cost of living measures.

5. Most of the married women have been married only a short time (less than five years) and only ten have children.

6. Minimum wages are lower (or nonexistent) for minors, which makes them all the more attractive for unskilled factory jobs. In 1972 in São Paulo, 70 percent of the boys and 49.5 percent of the girls aged fifteen to nineteen were in the labor force (São Paulo 1978:75).

7. The percentage of women working at home in São Paulo in 1972 increased from 38 percent at ages twenty-five to twenty-nine, to 63.4 percent

at ages thirty to thirty-nine, and continues to increase through age sixty-nine. (São Paulo 1978:75).

8. In São Paulo in 1961, 62.9 infants died per one thousand live births compared to 89.5 in 1970 and 95 in 1973. Much of this is attributed to the decline in the real minimum wage, lack of public services such as water and sewers, and malnutrition.

9. Protective legislation in the United States initially included regulation of hours of work (e.g. no night shifts, limited number of hours), minimum wages, and sanitary working conditions. It is interesting that minimum wages for women were established earlier than for men.

10. Because of the wide age differences in our sample and since so few of our Brazilian respondents are married, we compared the size of the family in which Brazilian factory workers were raised with the total number of children borne by New Jersey factory women.

11. The Population Council reports that "among children aged 7–10, the proportion enrolled in school in 1970 was 66.3%, although the first eight years of schooling are free and "compulsory" (p. 13).

12. Miriam Cohen (1977) documents the way in which the changing employment structure in New York City during the depression induced Italian working class families to orient their daughters toward white-collar work because the future looked better there than in factory (largely garment) labor. This, in turn, resulted in a marked increase in educational levels. For example, by 1950, although only 8 percent of the first generation of Italian female workers were employed in clerical labor, 40 percent of the second generation were in those occupations. Cohen attributes this not to *embourgeoisement*, but as a shift in working-class strategies made necessary by the city's employment structure (ibid.:135).

13. Although many of the women in our New Jersey sample were hired at an early age, I would argue they would not have been retained had their been an ample supply of younger, single women to replace them. In fact, when production reached its peak in the early 1950s and labor was in scarce supply, the factory was very lenient with married women, allowing them unpaid maternity leaves, time off during summer vacations or when their children became ill, and so forth.

## References

Arizpe, Lourdes. 1977. "Women in the Informal Labor Sector: The Case of Mexico City." In *Women and National Development: The Complexities of Change*. Chicago: University of Chicago Press.

Blay, Eva Alterman. 1978. *Trabalho demesticado: A mulher na industria Paulista*. São Paulo: Editora Atica.

Bridenthal, Renate. 1976. "The Dialectices of Production and Reproduction in History." *Radical America* 10, no. 2, pp. 3–11.

Bureau of Labor Statistics. 1975. *A Socio-economic Profile of Puerto Rican New Yorkers*. U.S. Dept. of Labor, Middle Atlantic Regional Office, New York, N.Y. Regional Report 46.

Cohen, Miriam. 1977. "Italian-American Women in New York City, 1900–1950: Work and School." In *Class, Sex, and the Woman Worker*,

Milton Cantor and Bruce Laurie, eds. Westport, Connecticut: Greenwood Press.

Gimenez, Martha. 1977. "Population and Capitalism," *Latin American Perspectives*, no. 4, pp. 5–41.

Humphries, Jane. 1977. "Class Struggle and the Persistence of the Working Class Family." *Cambridge Journal of Economics* 1:241–258.

Kessler-Harris, Alice. 1975. "Stratifying by Sex: Understanding the History of Working Women." In Labor Market Segmentation, Richard C. Edwards, Michael Reich, David M. Gordon, eds. Lexington, Mass.: D. C. Heath.

Kocher, J. 1973. Rural Development, Income Distribution and Fertility Decline. New York: Population Council.

Minge-Kalman, Wanda. 1978. "A Theory of the European Household Economy during the Peasant to Worker Transition: With an Empirical Test from a Swiss Alpine Village." *Ethnology*. Vol. XIV, No. 4,, pp. 340–366.

NACLA. (North American Congress for Latin America) 1975. *Capital's Flight: The Apparel Industry Moves South*. Vol. XI, no. 3, New York.

Population Council. 1978. *Brazil: Country Profiles*. Prepared by Mello Moreira, Lea Melo da Silva and Robert McLaughlin.

Repetto, R. G. 1974. "The Relationship of the Size Distribution of Income to Fertility, and the Implications for Development Policies and Economic Development, Annex A, Washington, D.C.: International Bank for Reconstruction and Development.

Safa, Helen Icken. 1977. "The Changing Class Composition of the Female Labor Force in Latin America." *Latin American Perspectives.*, no. 4, pp. 126–136.

Saffioti, Heleieth. 1971. A mulher na sociedade de classes. São Paulo: Quatro Artes.

São Paulo Justice and Peace Commission. 1978. *São Paulo: Growth and Poverty*. London: Bowderdean Press.

Schmink, Marianne. 1979. "Women, Men and the Brazilian Model of Development." Paper presented at Latin American Studies Association. Mimeographed.

Tilly, Louise A. and Scott, Joan W. 1978. *Women, Work and Family*. New York: Holt, Rinehart and Winston.

———. 1978a. *Women and Family Strategies in French Proletarian Families*. Michigan Occasional Papers, No. 4, Ann Arbor, Mich.

U.S. Department of Labor. 1975. *1975 Handbook on Women Workers*. Women's Bureau, Bulletin 197.

Vasquez de Miranda, Glaura. 1977. "Women's Labor Force Participation in a Developing Society: The Case of Brazil." *Signs: Journal of Women in Culture and Society* 3, no. 1.

Wood, Charles H. 1977. "Infant Mortality Trends and Capitalist Development in Brazil: The Case of São Paulo and Belo Morizonte." *Latin American Perspectives* 4, no. 4, pp. 56–65.

Wood, Harold. 1976. "Future Labor Supply for Lower Level Occupations." *Monthly Labor Review* 99, no. 3 (March): 22–31.

# CHAPTER 5

# Household, Community, National, and Multinational Industrial Development

### Neuma Aguiar

Working-class communities may occupy different structural positions related to distinct modes of production. The analysis of a plantation, a governmental irrigation project, and a multinational corporation illustrate three variations in the way housing relates to work opportunities. In the first two cases, housing facilities are tied to jobs, although in the third case, if workers lose their jobs, they may keep their residences if they or their families have alternative working opportunities in the area. In all these cases, there are different patterns of interaction between the management of the industrial plant and workers in residential communities.

Working class housing analysed within a Marxist frame of reference may be considered as part of the means of workers' subsistence. As shelter for the workers and their families, housing contributes to the reproduction and subsistence of the working force. As part of the work contract, housing is also the site for work.

Marx (1971:469) proposed that, with the development of capitalism, workers become dispossessed of land, raw materials, instruments of production, means of subsistence (such as housing), and money. The workers, having lost the means of subsistence, are forced into the labor market where they must exchange their labor power for money. They must then purchase the means for their subsistence, including the purchase or rental of a house.

Capitalists buy the working capacity of workers by paying them with money for a number of hours of work. Part of what the workers earn in the production of goods for the capitalist is allocated to the

*117*

maintenance and reproduction of the work force. This includes not only biological reproduction, but also the nourishment, socialization and education of the future labor force as well as the cost of maintaining their labor capacity. These costs, underwritten by wages, are conceptually distinct from the value contributed by labor to the product (Marx 1906:342–343). The proceeds from the daily expenditure of labor which exceed the cost of its reproduction as translated into wages are appropriated by the capitalist as surplus value. When this surplus value is not expropriated, workers may work only that time required to earn their subsistence (Marx 1906:207; 1971:478).

Although capitalism is characterized by the existence of a labor market of free workers, anomalies to this form of social organization of production had already been distinguished by Marx who pointed to two such departures from private industrial capitalism: the plantation and the Asiatic mode of production. I shall examine each of these in relation to access to housing provided in the labor contract. I shall distinguish housing as a site of work, as work payment, and as shelter. As such, it is a constituent element of many modes of production in addition to the domestic mode of production.

*1. The Plantation System.* Marx indicated that in the free market world of capitalism, the plantation was a form of social organization that made use of forced labor. Even after slavery was abolished, plantations maintained their work force by manipulating workers' subsistence through payments in kind such as housing or other more direct forms of labor extraction such as the extension of credit. For example, the plantation owner may advance cash or goods required for the workers' subsistence; and when he pays them he may discount the amounts he advanced. He charges high interest rates in both transactions (Palmeira 1979).

Buying the production (e.g., piecework) is distinct from buying the workers' labor time. By distinguishing workers' obligation for housing or other subsistence needs advanced by the employer from the payment for production, the workers may be held in debt. Good crops may improve the workers' standing. However, during bad crops the risks are generally borne by the workers.

The development and growth of the plantation throughout the world is a form of social organization of production stimulated by the development of industrial capitalism in Europe. The Brazilian cotton putting-out industries were developed to underwrite the introduction of textile machinery (Marx 1906:406–552). Stimulated by the British textile industries, plantations introduced machinery. This capital investment was not sufficient to alter the social organization of production, as had occurred in the European Industrial Revolution with the transition from manual to machine production. (The tendency was sharpened with the American Secession War.) This may be considered as a mercantile mode of capitalism developed under the influence of industrial capitalism (Kay 1975:96–156).

Brazilian cotton plantations also proved to be quite adequate in supplying British capitalist industries with the raw materials necessary to maintain their rate of growth. In order to understand the dynamics of plantation development, we must go beyond the nation-state to the international division of labor in a world perspective.

Just as they were linked to European capitalist industries, plantations were also connected with capitalist industries within national boundaries. The stimulus to the introduction of machinery in agricultural production was twofold. First, In order to meet the accelerated capacity of mechanized industries that transformed agricultural products, factory managers needed large supplies of raw materials. Second, In order to overcome the gaps resulting from irregular production of agricultural goods resulting from high seasonal vulnerability, the new industries sought continuous, assured supplies throughout the year. Labor in processing industries is underutilized if raw materials are supplied discontinuously and the company has limited storage capacity. Productivity in the supply of raw materials in a small plot, peasant, agrarian structure is limited. The resulting losses are, for the most part, transferred to the workers who are paid for their production and not for their labor time.

*2. Government Irrigation Projects.* In order to analyze a governmental irrigation project using housing and other subsistence items as forms of payment for labor, I shall utilize as a paradigm the Asiatic mode of production (Marx 1971:433–437). In this mode of production, the individual utilizes a tract of land but without ownership, which is vested in the collectivity, in this case the state. Tracts of land are cultivated by families, which constitute the community. This collectivity is in possession of the social conditions of work comprising both agricultural and manufacturing activities. Housing also belongs to the collectivity, and individual units are used by the families in accord with community norms. The corporate base for the community is the organization of irrigation channels which provide the conditions for agriculture. The whole is administered by state functionaries, who extract surplus work from the collectivity.

*119*

The coexistence of this form of social organization of work with industrial capitalism constitutes a major difference from the development of capitalism described by Marx (1971:433–437). Moreover, this present form does not constitute a survival from a preexisting mode of production because its planning and implementation are rather recent. Although transactions in kind are common within the irrigation project, dealings with the outer world are made in money, as will be shown in the discussion of the case study.

*3. Industrial Capitalism.* In Brazil industrial capitalism has been a widespread form of social organization of production. In its forms of payment for labor, the workers' subsistence needs are met by a salary. Brazilian private industries as well as multinational companies use this form of payment. However, wage payments are not the only form of compensation found in Brazil today.

Industrial capitalism is combined with mercantile capitalism and the Asiatic mode of production in the Brazilian social formation. The specification of articulated modes of production is used here as an analytic device that I consider to be more fruitful than that of polar types—capitalism and its negation. As an example of this type of analysis, some authors have used the concept of the informal labor market to analyze the social group not included in the capitalist sector of developing countries (PREALC 1976). Others have preferred the notion of a reserve army in referring to the same social group (Lewin 1977). The use of either of these two concepts gives priority to the category of capitalist production, dumping whatever does not fit in this category into a vast residue. This residue has become so big that it is difficult to take it seriously as an analytical category. For example, in Brazil the level of capitalization varies from one part of the country to another. In this paper, the place of housing is considered central to the analysis of any mode of production. This approach brings women's several work roles into focus. Marx (1971:473) mentioned that with the development of capitalism, the accumulated patrimony in the mercantile form was invested in the acquisition of the conditions of production of industrial capitalism. Workers who were removed from their places of origin became united through a place of work. This disassociated them from their means of subsistence, not only from the point of view that their working capacity had to be exchanged for their means of subsistence, but from a physical point of view since their location of work had become spatially differentiated from their housing. Weber (1961:97–98) addressed himself to this question when he discussed labor in industry and housing. Men appeared as the commanders of production and heads of households, whereas women had the heaviest share in production, being responsible for both agricultural and domestic production. This suggests that greater proximity between domestic and extradomestic tasks is associated with sharper sexual hierarchy separating male and female work roles. The three cases presented—a plantation, a governmental irrigation project, and a multinational corporation—may be used to analyze the relation between housing, industry, and the sexual division of labor in the distinct modes of production. All three types of enterprises, taken here as case studies, were originally related to cotton production and manufacture. The composite production apparatus involves multinational, national, private, and state enterprises in Brazil.

## Plantation Work, Housing, and Community

In 1975 a northeastern Brazilian cashew plantation of 3,750 hectares had 2,853.2 hectares on which there were 285,320 trees in 9 fields. There was a poor harvest that year due to a drought. The workers collected a total of 634,460 kilograms of cashew fruits and 34,994 kilograms of cashew nuts, according to plantation records. In the previous year, 1974, there had been a much better crop, 2,014,570 kilograms of fruit and 155,399 kilograms of nuts. The cashew harvest lasts for four months, from September to December, and the figures correspond to the crop obtained during those months. The plantation had 186 families living and working on its premises with a total of 1,225 family members (see Table 5-1). Of these, one-sixth were less than five years old and, according to plantation work patterns, were the only ones not of work age. Of the total number of family workers, 640 were men and 585 were women. During 1975, 67 families worked gathering cashew fruits and nuts. In addition, 434 workers were employed in the processing phase of production. Of the 247 collectors of fruit and nuts, 118 were children of twelve or less; 104 of the total number of collectors were women and 143 were men. Work teams were commonly made up of family members such as a mother and her children (36 percent of the teams), children (37 percent), or the father with his children (10 percent). (The remaining teams were of varied composition.)

The work day would start at dawn or around 4:00 A.M., when the plantation truck picked up workers and transported them from their homes to the fields. The work day ended around 4:00 P.M. Work

*121*

Table 5-1. Work Situation on a Brazilian Plantation by Sex, Age, and Conjugal Status

### Men

| Work Situation | Single | | | | | | | | Married | | | | | | | Total |
|---|---|---|---|---|---|---|---|---|---|---|---|---|---|---|---|---|
| | Before 1920 | 1920–1929 | 1930–1939 | 1940–1949 | 1950–1959 | 1960–1969 | 1970–1976 | Total | Before 1920 | 1920–1929 | 1930–1939 | 1940–1949 | 1950–1959 | 1960–1969 | Total | |
| Working | – | 100% (1) | 66% (2) | 66% (8) | 88% (111) | 62% (126) | 2% (2) | 55% (250) | 100% (17) | 100% (44) | 93% (37) | 98% (52) | 90% (28) | 100% (1) | 96% (179) | 67% (429) |
| Not Working | 100% (1) | – | 33% (1) | 33% (4) | 12% (15) | 38% (76) | 98% (107) | 45% (204) | – | – | 7% (3) | 2% (1) | 10% (3) | – | 4% (7) | 33% (211) |
| Sub Total | (1) | (1) | (3) | (12) | (126) | (202) | (109) | (454) | (17) | (44) | (49) | (53) | (31) | (1) | (186) | (640) |

### Women

| Work Situation | Single | | | | | | | | Married | | | | | | | Total |
|---|---|---|---|---|---|---|---|---|---|---|---|---|---|---|---|---|
| | Before 1920 | 1920–1929 | 1930–1939 | 1940–1949 | 1950–1959 | 1960–1969 | 1970–1976 | Total | Before 1920 | 1920–1929 | 1930–1939 | 1940–1949 | 1950–1959 | 1960–1969 | Total | |
| Working | – | – | 57% (4) | 77% (10) | 82% (80) | 46% (78) | 1% (1) | 43% (173) | – | 18% (6) | 24% (17) | 27% (12) | 36% (20) | – | 30% (55) | 39% (228) |
| Not Working | 100% (1) | – | 43% (3) | 23% (3) | 19% (18) | 54% (92) | 99% (110) | 57% (226) | 100% (8) | 82% (28) | 76% (21) | 73% (32) | 64% (35) | 100% (7) | 70% (131) | 61% (357) |
| Sub Total | (1) | | (7) | (13) | (98) | (170) | (111) | (399) | (8) | (34) | (38) | (44) | (55) | (7) | (186) | (585) |
| Total | (1) | (1) | (10) | (25) | (224) | (372) | (220) | (853) | (25) | (74) | (78) | (97) | (86) | (8) | (372) | (1225) |

consisted in filling eighteen-kilogram tins with cashew nuts and ten-kilogram boxes with cashew fruits. Previously mothers would quit working when their children became hungry and go home to feed them. As the houses were separated from the fields, mothers did not return to work with their children after lunch. In order to keep the families in the field, the plantation management instituted a lunch hour during which a tent was set up and rice, beans, manioc flour, and eggs were served daily. At the end of the month, the meals were discounted from the money owed to the worker for what she or he had produced.

The level of productivity varied a great deal from person to person. According to the workers, a collector of high ability was able to fill three tins of nuts a day. An average sized family was able to fill between ten and twelve tins a day. (The process of cheating workers through the use of nonscale measurements of weight in plantation work has been described by Palmeira [1979].)

The work was paid on a production basis.[2] During the height of the season when there were a lot of cashews to be collected, the plantation paid Cr(Cruzeiro)$.40 per box. (It bought a similar box obtained outside the plantation boundaries for Cr$2.50, of which Cr$.50 was paid to a middleman as a commission for obtaining the fruit.) The amount of money the workers earned for working on a production basis was then diminished by the advances that had been made to them by the plantation owners. This type of work remuneration can be classified as usury because of its nonsalaried and exploitative character.

This organization of production differs from capitalist social relations of production in that the plantation does not buy laboring time from the majority of its workers but only from a small part of them. It buys the production from which it discounts what it had advanced for worker subsistence. It discounts the advanced money from the production achieved. Workers' subsistence is not incorporated into salaries but is given to them in the form of loans, credit, or in kind.

The piecework done on the plantation is not the same as that done in an industrial capitalist factory. In the latter, piecework is paid in addition to a salary. The plantation's use of this mercantile device of per-piece remuneration of labor would not be considered irrational from a capitalist standpoint. Under this mode of production characterized by high seasonality in the production of raw materials, piecework prevents a loss in accumulation from both fixed (machinery) and variable (labor) capital in industry. The form of work remuneration used by plantations guarantees them the necessary work without their becoming committed to the maintenance of the labor force during periods when there is no longer raw material to collect or process.

The organization of production of the cashew nut plantation is closer to the capitalist mode of production than to other modes because some workers were in fact remunerated on a time basis, even though they may have been hired as journeymen rather than as permanent workers. By employing only people who had residential ties to the plantation, the owner was able to advance housing and subsistences to workers on usurious terms.

The cashew plantation contained two main units for processing fruit and nuts as well as a primitive unit for processing manioc. In the processing sector of the plantation during 1976, 467 workers worked between the first half of October and the first half of January with only 277 workers or 48 percent who had a stable contract with the factory remaining to the end. The rest were seasonal workers. Fifty-four percent of the permanent workers were male. Most of the factory workers worked on a temporary basis, under contract patterns quite similar to the organization of work in the agricultural sector of the plantation. Most people were employed in removing the cashew nut from the fruit, which was done with the help of machines. From 48 to 50 percent of the seasonal workers worked in this sector. No permanent workers were employed in this type of job. The work consisted in standing beside a production line, picking up the fruit, cutting off the nut, and dropping it into a receptacle below the cutting table. The receptacle served to measure how much each worker produced. The plantation paid Cr$.70 for a full receptacle. The plantation did not buy the time of these workers but paid them for the amount produced. Older workers and children often did this type of job.

The cashew-processing unit originally operated in the state capital. It was moved to the farm in order to take advantage of the labor supply available when the fruit collecting and processing had finished. Also it permitted shifting the 434 workers it had when it moved from one production unit to another. For example, workers could be shifted from processing nuts, which can wait, to processing cashew fruits, which cannot wait. The processing of nuts also operated on a putting-out system. Seventy percent of its workers worked on a production basis and eighty percent of these production workers were women. Ninety-two percent of all the cashew nut production workers were women.

124

On the plantation, the work that was not paid on a production or per-piece basis was paid at an hourly rate. Adult males were remunerated at a rate of Cr$1.57 per hour of work. Adult females were remunerated at a rate of Cr$1.23 for the same work time. To obtain the same wage as a working man, a woman had to perform supervising functions; but when men became supervisors they earned Cr$1.66 per hour of work. There were three working shifts of eight hours a day. Workers worked sixteen hours and rested eight by alternating shifts.

Plantation housing was given only to the male head of the family. The granting of a house guaranteed the plantation a monopoly on employment of the head of the family, even if the plantation had no work to offer to the housekeeper.[3] The plantation had eleven clusters of houses, a set of apartment houses, and isolated houses to grant to the workers. The housing clusters were sharply stratified according to the types of workers. Houses had from one bedroom, one living room and one toilet to three bedrooms, two living rooms, kitchen with utensils, bathroom, garden and backyard. The latter type was assigned to plantation administrators. In order to be entitled to a house, a couple had to be legally married and there must have been at least four members in the family who were considered potential workers.

The plantation moved the worker up the housing ladder according to advances in his work career. There was a high rate of turnover in the housing clusters, and it was the permanent workers rather than the seasonal workers who had more of an opportunity to build community ties. However, all workers were bound together by family ties. New family ties developed on the plantation as marriages were contracted and ritual godparenthood was established. There was a high rate of weekend visiting, as we discovered through interviews on Sundays. It was a time for family members, both those living within the plantation and those living outside, to gather. The strength of family ties was a basis for a great solidarity among many workers, but this did not constitute a basis for the development of a working-class awareness of their common social condition.

Almost every evening, workers, primarily young people who lived close to the administration center, would congregate in the main square of the plantation where a television set was put. There were rigid curfews for entertainment, and a strong moral code was enforced that regulated courtship that developed. In the case of young people who decided to be married, the plantation would celebrate a whole group of weddings together on a particular date in the plantation's church. The young husband was then entitled to put in a claim for a dwelling for his newly constituted family. Divorces were highly discouraged because the family unit is essential in this form of social organization. Divorced people were forbidden to visit the plantation; and, even if this was not always enforced formally, the local moral code resulted in its de facto compliance. If the husband died, the widow would be expelled no matter how much she used to work unless there was a young male adult to whom the plantation would delegate household responsibility.

The plantation also dismissed the workers it could not keep working throughout the whole year. For instance, between 1974 and 1975, 800 workers were dismissed at the end of the harvest season. The administration predicted it would dismiss at least 300 workers between 1975 and 1976. Besides this, they estimated that at least 150 female workers would be dismissed who worked in the plant that was being moved to the plantation.

The plantation administration regularly dismissed workers when their work was not needed. However, they prevented workers from quitting of their own volition. This situation was in part a result of the debt system. As there was no steady work guaranteed, families inevitably incurred debts. Families became so indebted to the company store that they were threatened if they thought of leaving the farm without first paying what they owed. Families also had no means to move elsewhere. When the management needed workers, it would send trucks into the dry lands to help workers move with their belongings to the plantation premises. However, there was no transportation available for the families who wanted to quit. Because they had no way to carry back their furniture, workers who wanted to move had a problem in returning to their places of origin. Only those who were already too poor to have any possessions when they arrived at the plantation had freedom of movement. This situation, in combination with buying the workers' production in advance with loans in the form of subsistence and housing, prevented the workers from leaving the plantation premises.

Rental for housing was discounted from the paycheck of the male head of the family every other week. There was no fixed amount of payment for the house. A variable proportion of earnings were discounted; at the time of the research it was 20 percent of the check. When the worker was very productive that week, he would pay a higher sum than in the weeks he did not do as well. This was not the only discounting for housing made from family earnings.

Because workers were paid on a production basis, payment due had to be calculated individually. The plantation was always short of petty cash to pay for the broken amounts. To eliminate the problem of making change, it discounted all salary fractions from the paychecks under the title of housing rent. The amounts charged per house were arbitrary and variable. This form of patrimonial rent charged by the plantation can also be classified as usury.

The workers usually bought their food at the company's store. They could buy it on credit and have the amounts they owed discounted from their paychecks. On holidays there was no work and therefore no payment. Thus, during the periods of time when there was less work because of holidays, it was very common for workers to increase their debts with the company's store.

The plantation rhythm of work greatly affected household responsibilities. For example, although both men and women worked on the plantation, men had the more stable and better-paid jobs; as a result, women were required to provide the major input into domestic work. The tight schedule of factory work meant that members of the family who remained at home spent a good part of the day preparing the meals to be delivered to factory workers at the proper time. Because this work was in rigid shifts, the families had to correctly calculate the time for preparing and delivering the meals. At certain hours of the day, young members of families would walk together from their homes to the plants carrying the meals for their relatives who were working in the factories. Industrial machinery thus imposed a diurnal rhythm of work on household production. The schedule for field workers, being on the basis of piecework, imposed a slightly less rigid structure on the household as a working unit in that there was no fixed time of work and the plantation had to furnish lunch for the field workers. On a year-round basis, however, factory work was regulated by the rural sector of production. The amount of fruit obtained regulated the number of days the daily workers could work in the processing plants.

The housing contracts of those who moved with the factory to the plantation location were greatly affected by the administration's attempt to extract more work from the workers. Whereas in the previous location workers were dismissed seasonally, the factory owner in the new plantation-based factory required a continuous labor supply and therefore resorted to residential ties. Thus, on the plantation, being dismissed meant losing both house and work.

*127*

## Work, Housing, and Community in a Governmental Irrigation Project.

The Brazilian Government, at the suggestion of the Superintendency for the Brazilian Northeast (SUDENE), offered incentives to regional development through direct intervention in the economy. This project was operated through another agency, the Brazilian Office for Works against the Droughts or DNOCS. This agency, previously known for its clientele politics, started a new program that was directed toward supporting landless farmers. Government projects in the past had given priority to property owners, particularly in irrigation projects. This form of interference in the economy may be compared with other regional development practices. Although the cashew plantation described above is a private enterprise, it received governmental subsidies through SUDENE. One of its loans, obtained from Articles 34 and 18 of the SUDENE law, underwrote the construction of the cashew juice processing plant.

The Brazilian government expropriated 1,985 small properties and regrouped them in 407 new plots, dividing them among families specially selected to take part in the program. By expropriating the land, not from large but from small landowners, the government hoped to minimize the political costs of the program. The agency made substantive investments in the area, such as controlling the water available for cultivation through dam construction. It regulated the water flow of local rivers and built irrigation channels that made available a year-round supply of water to the newly constituted plots in the development program.

The case study described in this paper is one of the eight irrigation projects being implemented in the Northeast and one of the twelve planned for the area. Its total area comprised 75,000 hectares, but only 1,375 hectares were under cultivation. The project directors planned to triple the cultivation area in a short time.

Most of the land was planted with cotton, although rice, beans, bananas, oranges, and grass were also cultivated. In 1975 there were 275 families living and working in the experiment and recruitment was being expanded. Families comprised approximately 1,700 residents with equal proportions of men and women. One-fifth of the residents were less than five years old. However, children in the irrigation project received much more schooling than those of other working-class families because there was a heavy emphasis on education. This made fewer children available for work, in contrast to the cashew plantation. There was a consensus that the school year should be programmed so as to allow children to help with the harvest. The project had more families working in a smaller area than the cashew plantation. Crops yielded 1,600 tons of cotton, 220 tons of beans, 800 tons of rice, 650 tons of corn, 21 tons of oranges, 363 tons of bananas, and 31 tons of milk annually. The irrigation project had four times the productivity of local cotton plantations that operated under sharecropping arrangements. The project also doubled the average local productivity levels for rice and tripled the productivity levels for beans.

The project directors defined the following criteria for the selection of families to live and work on the project. The head of the family had to be a landless male nineteen to fifty years of age with a wife and children. They were interviewed by the technical personnel and bureaucrats related to the project. If selected, they were given cultivation and residential plots on the project. Cultivation plots measured from four to five hectares. The residential plot included an eighty square meter house with one living room, two bedrooms, one kitchen, one bathroom, a yard, a storage bin in which the harvest and tools were kept, and a corral for keeping animals.

The houses and cultivation plots were granted to the families at no charge. Neither were they charged for the energy that was consumed (although this was a provisional situation because there were plans to put in meters for that purpose). As the definition of ownership of the plots was still under discussion by governmental authorities, no charges were being made although there was talk of charging the workers for the water channeled to their plots.

The first governmental plan was to transfer ownership of the housing and cultivation plots to the workers. However, after the end of the five year experimental term, the managers of DNOCS were persuaded that an irrigation law should be issued by the state granting, not the property, but the possession of land to the workers. According to this law, workers would have the right to use the land and their children would inherit the same right. It was predicted that if actual ownership of the property were transferred to the workers, the project might turn into a commercial failure because most workers would not show interest in producing more than their consumption needs.

The social organization of this project can be compared to the Asiatic mode of production in spite of the fact that it coexists with capitalism. The government irrigated the land and distributed the plots among families who did not have property rights to the land but merely the possession of it. Ownership of the land was held by the government whereas the right to use it was held by the family.

The workers cultivated the plots with the technical guidance of 298 government officials. Disobedience of technical instructions was severely punished. The product resulting from the collective effort was allocated to the cooperative and independent sales of crops were forbidden. Violation of this clause would lead to expulsion from the project. The cooperative weighed, stored, and sold the collective produce, dividing the result of the sales according to each family's input. Part of the earnings was retained by the cooperative as a compulsory deposit to capitalize the cooperative. This amount was increased every year by two percent of the earnings but the amount was soon to be raised to ten percent. The proceeds from the sales were deposited at once in the workers' accounts after the deduction of loans made to them for the purchase or rental of tools and other implements for plot cultivation. Because workers received cash only once a year, low-interest loans granted by government officials and guaranteed by the state enabled workers to invest in their land.

Before allocating their produce to the cooperative, the families withdrew part of it for family consumption. Experimental ponds for aquaculture were being introduced in the project to supplement the families' diet with additional protein.

In the first irrigation model the SUDENE officials conceived, the property and capital investment in the project would be transferred to the workers. This would have made them into small landowners managing the irrigation project through the cooperative. Under the actual DNOCS administration of the project, however, property rights were not granted to the workers, nor did they become governmental workers because they did not work for a salary. Their produce was sold and redistributed, but they were not small businessmen because free market principles did not operate in the project. The workers could grow only those crops which they were told to grow. This differs from the original plan in which people would have produced whatever they wanted. In experimentation with the somewhat freer enterprise format of the original model, however, an atomistic type of production resulted that was hard to sell in the regional market and also very hard to administer. The cooperative was indebted and the project appeared to be a commercial failure. As a result, freedom of choice was curtailed under the threat of loss of residential rights. The workers were not free to live where they wanted; but in order to live on the project, they had to grow food as they were told to do. An authoritarian style of management was introduced. Matters were decided by the technicians without consulting the workers through the cooperative network.

Every head of a household was a member of the cooperative with the right to one vote. Generally, the men attended meetings and women did not participate. Only once did a woman attend the meetings when her husband was sick. At first she encountered some resistance to her participation, but this soon disappeared.

The social workers hired by the State had social values dictating that women should do work related to the home. They tried to impede women from joining their husbands in agricultural work. Their participation in cultivation was further hindered by their responsibilities in tending the cattle that were kept in the residential plots. Governmental policies ordinarily limited the hiring of itinerant laborers that would tend to push women who were wives of residential workers into the agricultural work in periods of peak activity. At the time of the study, women's involvement in plot cultivation was low and temporary workers with no residential ties to the project tended to be hired. This introduction of nonmembers into the cooperative project generated a sharp stratification. Thus although the standard of living of the families residing on this irrigation project was much higher than that of the plantation workers, the project was not successful in introducing a totally new organization of production in that seasonal exploitation of the work force through temporary hiring of workers remained.

The irrigation project also put heavy emphasis on industrialization, with the aim of local processing of all products. The rice, for example, was locally processed. Cotton production, however, was industrialized in the central cooperative to which the irrigation project cooperative was affiliated. At the same time, the project's officials were searching actively for contracts with private industries which would buy the project's products. One production contract had been negotiated for the sale of a tomato crop to the cashew plantation. The industrial workers on the project were all male public servants. The irrigation workers paid them for the extra hours of work they had to put in during the harvest season. They also paid them with a share of the production that was allocated to family consumption.

The irrigation project workers formed a community with frequent visiting among families. Their capacity for uniting in terms of common interests, however, was controlled by the government officials who managed to curb dissent and who expelled those who threatened their authority. Clearly, the practice of threatening workers with the loss of their houses resembled the authoritarianism of the private plantation. Information gained from interviews indicated that government officials in key positions in the project were also private proprietors of their own plantations.

Sex roles were greatly differentiated on the irrigation project. Women did not work in industry and were discouraged by the social workers from engaging in agricultural production. They did not represent the family within the cooperative; nor did they manage the family's credit. In contrast, women on the plantation joined their families in both agricultural and industrial work, although they received smaller payments for equal work. As on the plantation, however, housing was entrusted to the men and not to the women. Likewise, on the irrigation project, if a man was separated from his family or if the male head of the household died and the family did not have a male adult to substitute for him, the woman had to quit the enterprise. In contrast to the plantation where, if women did not work outside the house, they managed the family's joint income, women in the irrigation project could not perform this role. This was due to the management of the project's credit operations being vested in the male head of the household. Paradoxically, the greater participation of women in credit matters occurred in the plantation concurrently with the more sharply differentiated and stratified system of social relations.

## Multinational Enterprise, Housing, and Community

A multinational industry for textile production—whose head-quarters was located in New York with branches in Argentina, Uruguay, Colombia, and Venezuela—bought its first plant in Brazil in 1956 during the initial phase of the recent industrial boom. The company expanded its operations in 1964 when it bought its second factory. The major plant was located in Rio de Janeiro and the smaller plant in Grand Rio.

The expansion of the company occurred during the growth of multinational investment in the textile sector in Brazil. Due to the stimulus to foreign investment initiated by the central government, new industrial investments were directed to this sector. Incentives produced both the renewal of the Brazilian industries and the entrance of multinational investments into a previously Brazilian-only sector. The entrance into this particular enterprise was made by the ac-quisition of a Brazilian national textile industry.

After a first period of expansion, the consumer goods sector, which had undergone high growth, began to encounter obstacles. Several industries reduced their investment considerably, and production levels declined (Façanha 1978:11-12). One such industry was the United States-based textile factory that constitutes the third case study in this paper. In Brazil, the enterprise was listed as one of the thirteen key industries in the textile sector and as one of the two hundred largest in the whole country. An initial investment of 17 million dollars in Brazil had been recovered in three years of operation, and it had shown profits of 7 billion cruzeiros (approximately 400 million dollars) in the previous year. The factories produced fifty tons of polyester and 1.2 million meters of cotton monthly. The decision to close down their two plants was made at a moment when their credit had been cut down as a result of the home plant having gone bankrupt. When the firm threatened to close down its two plants, which maintained 2,000 employees, the government objected because of subsidies it had granted to the industry.

The United States firm responded by trying to obtain other subsidies for its branches. At the same time, it was looking for another location for its polyester plant because the raw material produced in Brazil cost 50 to 60 percent more than its price on the world market. As a result, the corporation wanted to move the polyester plant to Venezuela where the raw material was being produced at a more competitive price. This would cut down production costs for the manufacture of polyester textiles and result in a more competitive price on the world market. Moreover, the Brazilian plant was located in an upper middle-class residential area in the southern part of Rio de Janeiro where high land value increased production costs. In addition to providing an important source of employment in the two cities, it was one of the major sources of revenue in the smaller city. The State government bargained for the maintenance of the plants due to the fiscal incentives it had given them. The State claimed an indemnification for the incentives it had given. The industry settled for maintaining the smaller branch only. It began by dismissing 400 of its 1,050 workers in the larger branch. The branch that was maintained had 600 workers, 80 percent of whom were female. The larger factory had a greater male contingent.

In previous years, workers used to live in a residential sector next to the factory. This was removed by road construction and replaced by high-rise apartment buildings, to which few workers had access.

The old workers were doubtful they would find equivalent jobs and feared not being hired by another factory due to their age. The overall impact of the closedown on the larger urban area was less

*133*

than in the smaller city where the effects were more visible. The threat of closing down caused panic in the smaller city. The factory offered good salaries relative to other work opportunities in the area and it was unlikely workers could have their jobs replaced. The plant that was closing, however, had only six unionized workers, and a union speaker revealed it had been difficult to organize the factory due to management control.

The workers in these plants were wage workers, paid on a monthly basis, in contrast to the plantation and to the irrigation project workers. Housing was not granted to the workers by the employer. Families did not necessarily work together in the same plant, although familial ties between workers were common. When large families have distinct jobs in different factories and family members of both sexes work, they are better able to withstand difficulties one of their members may go through due to job dismissal. However, when a single or major bread earner, male or female, loses employment, the maintenance of the household can be threatened. The disassociation of household and work in combination with repression of union participation result in a low sense of community among workers and a hesitation to demand compensation for their job losses.

Discontinuity in the supply of raw materials could not be solved by cutting down the wages through industrial relocation and housing contracts for work as in the case of the plantation. The solution found by the corporation was to close down the industry. Loss of work was not concomitant with loss of housing, although changes in housing arrangements could be a consequence of the loss of work.

## Conclusions

These case studies make possible a comparative analysis of the position of housing in the social organization of production.

In the case of the multinational textile corporation, workers use their salary for housing. This form of social organization is part of the industrial capitalist mode of production. Workers are threatened not with the loss of their housing, but with the loss of their work.

Scarcity or oscillating prices of raw materials enter into industrial decision making related to plant location. Decisions to move cause dismissal of many laborers affecting them to a greater or lesser extent depending on the position of the dismissed female or male worker in the family and the proportion of the total family earnings that wage supplies.

The cashew plantation operates more as a putting-out manufacture than as an industry proper, hiring workers as in a mercantile mode of production. Housing is granted separately from the payments for labor, which are made on a production basis (Nash 1979:181). Scarcity or oscillating prices of raw materials are solved by periodic dismissals of workers. A layoff of workers may have critical effects on the whole family, but the consequences are harsher to women, as when they become widows or are separated from their husbands, because they lose both work and housing. Whereas residence grants are used to maintain an available labor force for times when their work is needed, no provision is made for the needs of workers who are laid off. Payments on a production basis generate ties to the industry through a debt system. Decisions to move plant sites may be taken to change the organization of production, cutting down on labor costs. With this change, women cannot be directly hired by the factory, unless their husbands have a housing contract with the enterprise.

The irrigation project is analogous to the Asiatic mode of production, conceived not as a precapitalist formation but as a form of production articulated with industrial capitalism and with the mercantile form of which the plantation is a part. Families have a key role in the possession of land cultivated for collective benefit in this form of social organization of production. Land ownership belongs to the state and the control of the productive apparatus is maintained by governmental functionaries who are charged with making decisions on the types of production that should be developed and its location in the market. Scarcity is handled through technical devices to control nature. This type of enterprise also uses housing as a device to manipulate working-class needs. The threat of dismissal generates conformity to governmental policies enforced by state bureaucrats. Also, housing is granted to the male heads of households, and the bureaucratic requirements of the social organization inhibits the women from taking part in the decision making that affects the families' and the communities' destinies.

A sharper sexual division of labor originates in this form of social organization of production. The families are wealthier, but women are less involved in the decision-making process because key decisions are either made by the governmental officials or else, and to a lesser extent, by the male heads of households. Women in this social organization may also lose both the household and work if their husbands die or separate from them.

## Notes

I want to thank June Nash for encouraging me to think in terms of the relationship between community and multinational corporation. I thank Louise Lamphere and Juarez Bahia for the materials they made available to me on this multinational corporation case. I thank Lauretta Copello Mendes and Maria d'Ajuda Almeida e Silva for their assistance in the gathering of data for the cashew plantation and to Paola Cappelin and Maria Júlia Natividade Cruz for the same in relation to the irrigation project.

1. The concept of mode of production is used here to mean a system of articulated forms of production, constituting a certain pattern combining disparate elements, which may be taken as an object of analysis for a given social process (Balibar 1967:204). The specificity of this concept may be used to include housing in the forms of production, thus providing for a better accounting of women's work. Stated in this manner, the concept is not tied to the historical succession which characterized its original formulation (Marx 1971:433–479), and it allows for alternative historical developments. An example of this is offered by Hobsbawm (1971) who shows that certain types of manufactures characterizing the mercantile mode of production, as developed in countries such as Holland and Italy, were never revolutionized industrially as in England. The manufacturing activities existing in those countries which he denominates "feudal factories" were very successful in producing a limited amount of merchandise for a selected clientele. Their success limited their possibility of turning into another mode of production.

2. "On a production basis" is used here to indicate payment on a piecework basis—that is, amount produced rather than time invested. Payment is thus nonsalaried and the amount will vary from worker to worker, from day to day, and from container to container used to measure the amount of goods produced.

3. Other household codes in the plantation were studied by Palmeira (1977).

## References

Balibar, Étienne. 1967. "Sur les concepts fondamentaux du matérialisme historique." In Lire "le Capital," by Louis Althusser and Étienne Balibar, pp. 79–89. Paris: François Maspero.

Façanha, Luiz Otávio. 1978. "A industrialização dos mercados industriais Brasileiros." IUPERJ and PECLA: Seminar on Brazil and the New International Order, Friburgo, December.

Hobsbawm, Eric. 1971. En torno de los origenes de la Revolución Industrial. Buenos Aires: Siglo XXI.

Kay, Geoffrey. 1975. Development and Underdevelopment: A Marxist Analysis. London: Affiliated Publishers.

Lewin, Helena et. al. 1977. Mað de obra no Brasil: Um inventário crítico. Rio de Janeiro: Vozes.

Marx, Karl. 1906. Capital. Vol. 1. New York: Modern Library.

————. 1971. *Elementos fundamentales para la crítica de la economía política.* Buenos Aires: Siglo XXI.

Nash, June. 1979. "Anthropology of the Multinational Corporation," in G. Huizer and B. Manheim, eds. *The Politics of Anthropology.* The Hague: Mouton

Palmeira, Moacir. 1977. "Casa e trabalho: Nota sobre as relações sociais na 'plantation" tradicional." *Contraponto* 2: 103–114.

————. 1979. "The Aftermath of Peasant Mobilization." In *The Structure of Brazilian Development*, ed. Neuma Aguiar. New Jersey: Transaction Books.

PREALC. 1976. *El mercado informal de trabajo.* Santiago: OIT.

Weber, Max. 1961. *General Economic History.* New York: Collier Books.

# CHAPTER 6

# Kitchens Hit by Priorities: Employed Working-Class Jamaican Women Confront the IMF

A. LYNN BOLLES

In May 1978 the Government of Jamaica, headed by moderate socialist Michael Manley from 1972 to 1980, accepted the stringent fiscal controls set by the International Monetary Fund (IMF) in order to receive a loan of U.S.$240 million.[1] In keeping with its parliamentary role as opposition party, the right-wing faction voiced criticisms of the agreement, as did the centrists, for similar reasons. However, those groups politically affiliated with the left spoke adamantly in opposition to the program, particularly the Workers' Liberation League, which became the Communist Workers' Party of Jamaica (WPJ) six months later. The premise of the WPJ's argument was that the IMF's requirements could be reduced to a simple formula: lower wages for Jamaican workers and higher profits for multinationals. Nevertheless, the IMF plan was implemented and effectively locked the Jamaican economy into the international capitalist system, and the assessments of the left proved all too true as the working class struggled against the effects of the plan at the workplace and at home.

This article will examine some of the specific effects which the IMF program had on the productive and reproductive activities of working-class women in Kingston, from the inception of the plan in May 1978 to March 1979.[2] The case study characterizes the manner in which reproduction, in a broad sense, adapts to shifts in Jamaica's position in the international market. We will focus on the social, cultural, and economic responses of urban female industrial workers and their households to the program and note its effects on the manufacturing sector in Kingston, the place where the women work. Our purpose is to provide an insight into how working-class women and their households in Kingston dealt with these externally linked policies at home and at the workplace. Such analysis will underscore the interaction between the operations of the international capitalist system and the functioning of a peripheral economy such as Jamaica and the direct effect of that relationship on household-level activities (Deere 1978:58–66).

A number of scholars have analyzed the effects that economic development programs (i.e., expansion of capitalism) have had on the productive and reproductive activities of Latin American working-class women (see Nash and Safa 1976; Schmink 1979; Fernández Kelly 1980).[3] Those functions that generate income in cash or kind are considered productive. Reproductive functions, on the other hand, are those that in a broad sense encompass a whole set of domestic chores and household activities; for example, childbearing, child rearing, cooking, and other restorative processes. How these two functions operate under deteriorating transitional economic conditions predicated by Jamaica's shift of position in the global marketplace is the central concern here.

A cursory review of employment figures shows that with the growth of capitalism in Jamaica, working-class women have been channeled predominantly into service occupations; this tendency was heightened by the expansion of the tourist sector in the 1950s.[4] Second to the service sector, the largest employer of working-class women in areas of heavy capital investment has been offshore "screwdriver" manufacturing.[5] The crucial significance of these economic factors for Jamaica is indicated by the fact that over a third of the households islandwide are headed by women. Taking another perspective, we find that in 1978 among women listed as labor force participants approximately 31.6 percent (445,000, primarily working-class women) were head of household (Jamaica, Department of Statistics 1979a:10). Clearly, the functioning of the national economy and fluctuating levels of capital penetration have tremendous effect not only on working class women, but also on their household members, including especially children.

The present discussion is divided into three major sections. Section one describes Jamaica's economic situation during the research period, focusing on the manufacturing sector and the intrusion of the IMF. Section two is a profile of the respondents of the research, 127 working-class women and households. Section three analyzes several

*139*

ways in which these women, key figures in their households, have responded to conditions generated by IMF policies.

### Manufacturing, the Economy and the IMF

In 1949 the Jamaican Parliament passed the Pioneer Industrial (Encouragement) Law, which provided income tax concessions and import duty relief to any industry not already in operation in Jamaica on a "substantial scale." The Pioneer Law was modeled after Operation Bootstrap, which was then directing the economy of Puerto Rico. "Industrialization by invitation" in Jamaica was explicitly designed to attract international capital investment, at almost any price.

By 1952 when the Jamaica Industrial Development Corporation was established as a government agency designed to stimulate, facilitate, and undertake the development of industry on the island, "industrialization by invitation" was already changing the Jamaican economy. In a few short years, the Jamaican industrial sector was providing for both domestic and export markets. Growth rates in 1950 and 1970 (at an annual rate of 8 percent) were based on expansion of the mining, construction, tourist and manufacturing sectors (Jefferson 1967:12). However, the expansion of these activities was made possible only with heavy capital inflows, mainly from North America, generally in the form of direct investment.

The economic conditions which Jefferson (1972), Girvan (1971), and other critics of the model described as problematic, did prove ultimately to cause Jamaica's inability to sustain growth. Dependence on external financing and lack of ability to generate internal financing eventually led to the country's present balance-of-payments crisis.

After 1972 the Manley government took some steps to rectify many of the economic and social blocks noted by progressive Caribbean social scientists. However, the 1973 world "oil" crisis further aggravated the economy. Also at that time, the world demand for bauxite—Jamaica's highest earner of foreign exchange—dropped; and the price of sugar, Jamaica's other major export, declined simultaneously. In addition, the tourist trade decreased. As a result, the country's economic growth came virtually to a halt. This nascent economic crisis was complicated by international politics, in that many foreign investors viewed Jamaica's renewed friendship with Cuba as a step leading the country to Communism. Many abandoned production and left the island.

*140*

In 1974 the Manley government outlined a policy called *Democratic Socialism*, which was based on the concept of a mixed economy. This policy reaffirmed the critical role of the private sector and rewarded it through material incentives. But, at the same time, it called for a redistribution of wealth and privilege and created many social programs, such as an expanded adult literacy program, free university tuition, more health clinics, nutrition programs in schools, sugar cooperatives, and agrarian reform programs to redistribute land so it could be better utilized amongst farmers and rural workers. Tax revenues partly supported all of these efforts. Also, the Jamaican government initially placed a 7.5 percent levy on the export of bauxite, increased the royalties paid to the government by international bauxite companies, and gained 51 percent ownership in the production process.

The additional source of revenue from the bauxite levy afforded the government an increase of approximately 152 million Jamaican dollars (J$) in the first year (Jamaica Bauxite Institute 1976:32). However, the levy by itself could not be expected to make the economy more stable. This was indicated by the decline in growth of the GNP to a low of -6.7 percent in 1976 and 4.0 percent in 1977 (National Planning Agency of Jamaica [NPA] 1978:21).

The reduction of international market demands for Jamaica's products and services, the higher cost of petroleum and its by-products, the structural crises in the national economy generated by its industrialization-by-invitation development model, and the high cost of government programs resulted in a balance-of-payments problem for Jamaica. At the same time, the United States government had grown totally disenchanted with Jamaica's pursuit of Democratic Socialism, its friendship with Cuba,and its activism for the New International Economic Order (NIEO). In 1976 Henry Kissinger visited the island for a "holiday." Kissinger shortened his vacation when he failed to convince Prime Minister Manley that U.S. intervention was better for the country's economy than Jamaica's alternative path towards greater self-reliance. Strangely coincidental was the Export-Import Bank's lowering of Jamaica's credit rating from a top to a bottom category shortly after Kissinger's visit. In addition, according to numerous sources in Jamaica and *Covert Action* (August–September 1980), there began a systematic destabilization program, set against the Manley government by the U.S. Central Intelligence Agency. The United States also decreased its foreign aid, a vital source of funds for Jamaica's economy. The pressures against Manley's alternative path of development were being carefully or-

chestrated in the United States in a fashion analogous to its programming the overthrow of Allende's Chile.

To make ends meet, the Jamaican government had to find other
sources of monies to assist local private enterprise and its own
programs. Loans were obtained from the European Economic Community and the World Bank. At the end of the fiscal year 1977–78,
31.8 percent of the approximately J$1,900 million gross national
debt was owed to international lending agencies and agencies of
foreign governments (e.g., World Bank, the U.S. Agency for International Development, and Canadian banks). The remaining outstanding debts were owed to internal sources (e.g., National Development Bank). Also during that fiscal year, the percentage of debt
servicing in the national budget rose from 8.0 percent to 15.9 percent
(NPA 1978:39).

*Implementation of the IMF Program.* This balance-of-payments
problem culminated in the Government of Jamaica's turning to the
International Monetary Fund for loans.[6] As mentioned at the outset
of this article, Jamaica accepted stringent fiscal controls to obtain a
U.S.$240 million loan. Terms negotiated for the three-year IMF
agreement included a one-year "crawling peg" 15 percent devaluation
(1.5 percent per month from J$1.25 = U.S.$1.00 to J$1.87 =
U.S.$1.00). Also included as a part of the IMF stabilization or
anti-inflation program were strict controls on lines of credit given by
commercial banks, requirements for the Bank of Jamaica to maintain
a certain level of foreign exchange, liberalization of import controls,
control of wage increases, weakening of consumer price controls,
and greater hospitality to foreign investment.

The major principle behind the design of the IMF program was
to force Jamaica to remain in the international capitalist system by
controlling the flow of its international trade. The IMF dictated that
the total value of Jamaica's imported goods—already in excess of
its exports—had to be increased even further in proportion to exports,
the IMF maintaining all the while that this policy would be the one
most beneficial for the Jamaican economy. This aspect of the program
was to be facilitated by infusing additional foreign exchange into the
country's economy, thus allowing it to continue to import. By requiring maintenance of a set level of foreign exchange in the central
bank and by controlling commercial bank credit, the program determined how this source of capital could be utilized. The government
had to severely scrutinize its expenditures abroad. Simultaneously,
by devaluation of local currency and frozen wages, the country's

own exports would become cheaper on the international market. Theoretically, production and earnings would therefore eventually increase due to this lower export price. Greater export earnings would make the country a better risk for foreign investors. However, the burden of this program was placed on the shoulders of the person on the street, via higher prices for consumer goods and services coupled with higher taxes and wage controls (see Payer 1975). In order for the Fund's stabilization to function, both the controlled foreign exchange and domestic policies had to operate together. If either one did not work, then the fund applied more severe stipulations through government budgeting.

In order to maintain control over the functions of the Jamaican economy, the IMF surveyed the situation on a monthly basis. "Passing the IMF test" became the major criterion for credit rating. On the basis of the credit rating achieved, Jamaica procured other loans and lines of credit, increasing its indebtedness and continuing in a cycle which Payer (1975) called "the debt trap." The following examination of the manufacturing sector illustrates just how trapped Jamaica's economy became.

*Screwdriver Manufacturing.* The IMF's program had particular implications for Jamaica's manufacturing sector. The depression cut deeply into domestic sales because of higher consumer prices. Devaluation raised costs (in local currency) of imported components— the essence of the screwdriver type operation. Paying for and buying imported materials became more and more difficult and high interest rates raised bank loans beyond the reach of most manufacturers. In addition, increases in the cost of petroleum on the international market acted as another drain on the finances of industry.

The existence of these industries depended on the availability of foreign exchange on almost every level of production. The problems of business in turn affected the wider population by putting many people out of work and setting limits on pay increases for wage earners. Furthermore, increases in the costs of production were passed on to the consumer. This situation was exacerbated by the already high rate of national unemployment, which stood at 26.0 islandwide in 1978, and in some areas hovered between 60 and 80 percent. (Jamaica, Department of Statistics 1979:3). By gender, unemployment was 15.7 percent for men and 37.7 percent for women (ibid.). In the manufacturing sector, the unemployment rate was 16.0 percent for men compared with 33.5 percent for women (Jamaica, Department of Statistics, 1979:83). Possibly this disparity by sex in em-

*143*

ployment resulted from the fact that the Jamaican development program invited types of industry that often did not provide employment for women. (In the case of capital-intensive industry, employment opportunities for Jamaicans were extremely few, regardless of gender [see Table 6-1]). According to an officer of the Jamaican Industrial Development Corporation (JIDC), one of the major causes for the high numbers of unemployed women in the manufacturing sector was the exodus of garment firms to other areas of the Caribbean where labor costs were lower and labor unions and labor legislation less effective.

Most closings of garment and textile concerns in Jamaica had occurred prior to the stabilization program and were blamed on the political uncertainties raised by the Manley election in 1972. However, the economic trend aggravated the situation for those remaining. In 1979, the JIDC courted South Korean garment firms to invest in the sector. In a speech to local manufacturers, Prime Minister Manley's key phrase was "export or perish." However, given the total economic picture, maintaining exports proved a hard task to accomplish.

*The Female Working Class.* One of the effects of postwar capitalist development in Jamaica is that it has provided the conditions necessary for the formation of a working class, particularly for women. Conditions for membership in the working class include the selling of labor power and a degree of class consciousness that can be identified through factors such as social origins, education, level of income, and, in the Jamaican context, color of skin.[7]

The actual size of the Jamaican working class has been a subject to controversy among left-wing groups, but usual estimates are about 35 percent of the total labor force or about 45 percent of the employed labor force (see Gonsalves 1977:90). Gonsalves attributes the low percentage of working class membership in Jamaica to the relatively

*Table 6-1.* Employment in Manufacturing, Selected Years

| Year | Females | Males | Total | % Total Labor Force |
|------|---------|-------|-------|---------------------|
| 1960 | 43,865 | 45,658 | 89,523 | 24.6 |
| 1969 | 30,000 | 52,600 | 82,600 | 11.6 |
| 1972 | 28,871 | 64,258 | 93,129 | 12.6 |
| 1977 | 18,200 | 54,400 | 72,600 | 10.3 |

*Source:* Department of Statistics, Jamaica, Statistical Yearbook, 1977: *The Labour Force*, 1978.

underdeveloped nature of capitalism on the island in comparison with that found in advanced capitalist countries (Gonsalves 1977:90). This contention seems to be supported by 1978 figures which show 40 percent of the entire labor force as self-employed and/or independent workers (see Table 6-2).

With regard to working-class women, if the combined occupational groups classified as service, craftsmen and so forth, and unskilled manual labor are considered to constitute the working class, then 37 percent (94,300) of the total employed female labor force can be designated working class. Upon further analysis, examining just the manufacturing sector, women in that sector alone and again occupying service, craftsmen and so forth, and unskilled manual jobs represent 13 percent (12,400) of the employed female working class. Finally, taking the broader view again, these 12,400 women represent approximately 5 percent of the total employed female labor force (277,100), which means that 5 percent of the total employed female labor force is occupied in working-class jobs in the manufacturing sector.[8] Another large employer of working class women is agriculture, which shows 8.9 percent (24,800) participation. (It should be noted here that agriculture is also the sector of production in which the majority of all Jamaicans are occupied, though most often as self-employed persons, therefore not included in these calculations.)

Another crucial point in understanding the female working class in Jamaica is to examine the high overall level of female participation in the labor force. In 1978, 62.3 percent of all women on the island were employed. Boserup (1970:176) and a number of other authors have commented on the high rate of participation by women in the work force in comparison with that of other women, both in Third World and advanced capitalist countries. One factor in this high level of labor force participation is the fact that poor working-class women in Jamaica have traditionally played an important role as economic providers for their households (see Mair 1974, Powell 1976). Table 6-3 documents the employed labor force by industry group and gender. Clearly, women have been active in the labor

*Table 6-2.* Categories of Household Types

| Nuclear Based | | Visiting | | Mothers without mates | |
| N | % | N | % | N | % |
| --- | --- | --- | --- | --- | --- |
| 44 | 34.6 | 63 | 51.9 | 12 | 15.2 |

*Source:* notes of the author

force, but their participation has been largely confined to the service sector.

In terms of female employment in the sectors of heavy capitalist investment, women show a definitely lower rate of participation than do men. Table 6-3 affords an additional perspective on the situation, since it incorporates selected years, inclusive of the impact of the industrialization-by-invitation model in the economy. It is not surprising to note that by the late 1960s when it was becoming clear that the national economy was entering a period of crisis, the employment rate for women in the manufacturing sector began its rapid decline. This sector had developed as a resultant feature of heavy North American capitalist investment and had been the largest employer of working-class women outside the agricultural sector. Hence, as capitalists retreated from the Jamaican manufacturing sector, the rate of unemployment for female industrial workers rose, furthering the marginalization of working-class women in the productive process.

In summary, capitalist development in Jamaica created the necessary conditions for greater female membership in the working class by providing employment in the manufacturing sector, which became the largest employer of working women in productive areas of heavy capitalist investment. It also established an atmosphere conducive to heightened female working-class consciousness due to the tremendous rate of female unemployment in manufacturing beginning

*Table 6-3.* Household Composition

| Nuclear Relation | N | % | Visiting | | Mothers without mates | |
|---|---|---|---|---|---|---|
| | | | N | % | N | % |
| Mo | 44 | 100. | 63 | 100. | 12 | 100. |
| Fa | 44* | 100. | 63** | 100. | – | – |
| Child | 255 | 5.8 | 130 | 2.1 | 24 | 2.0 |
| MoSis | 4 | 1.7 | 4 | 2.5 | 10 | 12.6 |
| MoBro | 3 | 1.3 | 12 | 7.5 | 8 | 9.6 |
| MoMo | 2 | .88 | 5 | 3.1 | 5 | 6.0 |
| Niece | 4 | 1.7 | 3 | 1.8 | 1 | 1.2 |
| Others | 4 | 1.7 | 2 | 1.2 | 3 | 3.6 |
| DaBabyFa | 3 | 1.3 | – | – | 1 | 1.2 |
| MoDaChild | 2 | .88 | – | – | 2 | 2.4 |

*deceased
**5 abroad
*Source:* notes of author

in the late 1960s. All of these events were underscored by the high rate of female labor force participation in the society and a traditional ideology that acknowledged the importance of women as economic providers for their households. The manner in which working class women reacted to economic conditions can be seen in the following case study of female industrial workers.

## A Case Study

The 127 working-class women in this study represent some of the more fortunate persons in Jamaica, as they were employed full time. Case histories were collected and observations were made of their daily lives at their places of work and in some instances also at their homes. After a degree of mutual trust was established, about a dozen women extended invitations for home visitations. Initial contact with these women was made through their trade union affiliations. Hence, all of the women represented belonged to labor organizations and were employed in factories located in Kingston.

Industrial types represented include various food and paper processing businesses, health aid items concerns, and garment and printing shops. These concerns were owned and operated by joint venture (local and foreign capital) local private enterprise, the Government of Jamaica, and multinational corporations. The majority of these women had been employed in their present jobs for an average of seven years, although some had as much as twenty years of service. Job categories include operators, assembly line workers, folders, checkers, packers, and others. Only twenty-three women (18 percent) were performing a different kind of job than their first job at their present place of work. Although they had been employed on a fairly stable basis, it is clear also that there had been little occupational mobility.

For seven out of ten women, their present job was their first steady work. Previous employment had included domestic service, catering, work in garment and electronics, food processing, and postal service. Occasional work for the rest of the sample had included higglering (street vending), baby sitting, and casual factory work. In terms of wage scales, the women in this sample received from J\$48 to J\$117 per week. The average wage was J\$68, which was higher than nearly three-quarters of the Jamaican female labor force at the time of the study.

147

The average age of these employed female factory workers was thirty-five years. Very few of the women had more than a primary school education. Most had migrated from the rural areas to Kingston at approximately age fifteen after finishing their school days. These women held financial responsibility for the viability of their domestic units, and this was the important factor in their need for employment.

In the present research, the degree of the worker's financial responsibility and the functioning of other economic activities for household survival have been ascertained by analyzing the composition of the domestic units. Household structural types include fifty-two in stable coresidential units; (nineteen legally maried; thirty-three common-law unions, combined due to many similar responses based on coresidency); fifty-two in visiting relationships (in which the parents of the children reside separately but visit each other on a regular basis); and a composite group of twenty-three single women who are the sole supporters of their households. The single-woman group includes widows, separated married, separated consensual-union women, and all others not currently involved in a relationship with a man.

By examining household structural types, two organizational features become apparent: (1) variation in number of kin in residence; and (2) variation in the structure of reproductive functions. In stable-union households, units are organized around the nuclear familial structure, with perhaps a few extended kin (e.g., cousins) also in residence. Usually there are two wage earners per household, the woman worker and her husband/partner. In contrast, in visiting-union and single-woman households, there are many more sisters, brothers, cousins, nieces, and nephews in residence. And, for the most part, the female industrial worker is the only wage earner in both those types of households. However, a number of kin participate in various types of informal economic activities in these households, such as petty vending, casual manual labor, and so forth. Therefore, for the visiting-union and single-woman households, economic participation for household survival encompasses a wide range of activities.

Another distinctive feature contrasting the stable-union households on one hand and the visiting-union and single-woman composite on the other is the organization of household domestic labor (reproductive functions). In the stable-union category, the woman worker performs the bulk of domestic chores alone (such as food shopping, housework, cooking, etc.) as well as being employed full-time in a factory job. In the visiting-union and single-woman households, however, in addition to her full-time employment the woman worker shares domestic chores with other relatives in residence (usually female). Often the worker performs one or two domestic tasks alone, and the rest are carried out by other household members. For example, the worker may do the shopping, but the laundry is done by a sister with whom she shares the house. The principal activity for most women in visiting-union and single-woman households is to provide income derived from a wage for the upkeep of the household as a viable unit.

These observations of household structure and function show a strong correlation to our earlier discussion of the high unemployment rate resulting from the development and sudden reduction of screwdriver manufacturing. Particularly among visiting union and single-woman working-class households, those who cannot be accommodated in long-term, formal-sector economic activities have been incorporated in these households headed by women who do wage work. These extended household members contribute to household maintenance by assuming responsibility for the bulk of reproductive activities and by engaging in informal-sector activities.

When we look at the figure presented in the previous section, citing 5 percent participation in the industrial sector by the employed female labor force, we can appreciate the added significance this figure takes on. This is especially true because a sizeable percentage of these women are the heads of extended households. The present case study is an indication of the vital significance of these few jobs in the lives of a much greater number of people.

In sum, the working-class women and households under discussion denote the variation in familial social structure that has been prominent in the literature on Caribbean household organization (e.g., Clarke 1966). Variation in structure also implies that the domestic units' division of labor is dependent upon household composition and that it involves more than the presence or absence of men as husbands or partners. The economic functions of these households will be illustrated in greater detail in the following section.

### "The Poor Can't Tek Nuh More"

When wages are held down but the price of utilities and government services and taxes are raised, this seems like a very curious attack oninflation, since all the measures depress the real income of the ordinary citizen. [Payer 1975:36]

The main problem of this economic recovery program, if one accepts the rationale of why a country has to negotiate with the International Monetary Fund in the first place, is that it depressed the standard of living of the majority of the nation. In order to overcome the economic obstacles presented by the structural crisis of the national economy and IMF policies, the members of these urban working-class households participated in a number of economic activities, in addition to wage labor. The manner in which a domestic unit utilized various economic resources depended upon its membership. That is, the way in which the household benefited from such a relationship depended on which resident had access to a particular resource or group.

One economic activity that incorporated the participation of the entire household, regardless of composition, was the operation of domestic networks of exchange. The households of the female industrial workers did not limit their kin networks to the confines of the physical residential unit. Instead, the domestic network encompassed family and close friends who lived near by and even those living some distance away. Relatives and friends who lived close by were regular visitors, and calls were reciprocated. Along with the social aspect of the visitations was a constant flow of goods, services, and cash when available. Often the goods exchanged were items from the work place. In a number of factories where these women were employed, goods could be bought at wholesale price or special employee price. One multinational operated a commissary for its workers, and products could be bought without exchange of cash. The purchases were deducted from the worker's pay. One subsidiary of a multinational was a dairy products plant. When butter and cheese were absent from the grocers' shelves, workers could still obtain them at their commissary. The products could then be exchanged for services within a domestic network. For example, one woman in a visiting-union household supplied her neighbors and friends with cheese that she had bought at the commissary. In return her neighbor often provided child care on short notice, and her boyfriend's sister performed small personal errands during the day while the woman was at work.

Another type of reciprocal interaction involved the exchange of goods for other kinds of commodities. One married woman, employed in a health aids firm, supplied her cousin with much needed baby-care products. Those items were available to the worker in the company store, which featured its own goods, produced in Jamaica or by other subsidiaries. As a reciprocal measure, the cousin, who was employed in a bakery, gave her relative several loaves of bread, which she purchased at the worker discount.

Relatives who reside in the rural areas of Jamaica often provide important additions to the operation of urban domestic networks. To illustrate, two women workers have sisters who are higglers and sell in the market place in Kingston. Every weekend when the higglers travel from St. Ann's parish to Kingston to sell their produce, they also visit their relatives. In addition to an exchange of local news and information, the higglers provide their urban kin with fresh vegetables and receive in return items that are in short supply in rural shops. In one instance, the brother-in-law of the urban worker met a man selling flashlight batteries (then in very short supply islandwide). The brother-in-law purchased some batteries and gave six to the woman industrial worker, who in turn shared half of her portion with her sister, the higgler, upon her next visit.

Thus the reciprocal exchanges that take place in the domestic networks of these urban working-class households provide mechanisms to compensate for the shortcomings of the wider economic system. The women industrial workers in these households take advantage of benefits available at their places of work to make their contribution to the exchange network. Those household members not employed in the formal economic sector focus even more energy on exchange network activities to obtain for their households goods and services that would not be otherwise available to them, due to the lack of cash (caused by lack of employment) to obtain them. These informal patterns of distribution and consumption have evolved in greater complexity as a response to provide increased access to the society's limited resources.

Two other points should be kept in mind in analyzing the domestic network as a fundamental informal economic device in Jamaica. First, these networks have always operated within the society, because of Jamaica's history as a peripheral economy and the social inequalities inherent in such a system. (It may be noted that upper-class Jamaicans also participate in domestic networks to some extent, but the elite do not depend on this system to subsist, as is the case for many working-class households.) With the additional prob-lems created by the national economic crisis, working-class domestic networks have become even more crucial for household survival. Second, domestic networks involve reciprocal arrangements between individuals entailing the exchange of goods and/or services and require very little, if any, cash basis for transactions to take place. This type of economic interaction is a key function in Jamaica where for the majority, cash is a scarce commodity, becoming even less available with the passage of time. The limited amount of cash available for these domestic units is closely budgeted, and expended with diligence, as will be discussed next.

*Kitchens and Priorities.* As mentioned earlier, one of the results of the IMF antiinflationary program has been a soaring cost-of-living index. Government institutions designed to subsidize basic food commodities in Jamaica have been made more ineffective than ever. This is due to the fact that food subsidies were not essentials of the IMF package. Distributors and retailers also added a markup of 22 to 66 percent to the cost of goods, which was hidden by the general increase in price. Between May 1978 and March 1979, the cost of living rose approximately 30 percent (*The Struggle* 1979). This sit-uation presented an incredible problem for mothers raising children, and much juggling and hustling was necessary just to survive.

Table 6-4 represents the financial priorities of six groups of women workers who were asked by trade union personnel to prepare weekly budgets for a family of four. This exercise was done during rank and file family-life seminars, sponsored by the trade unions. Three groups prepared a budget in August 1978 using J$40 per week, and three groups used J$45 per week in March 1979. Despite the changing of classifications (their own modifications), there was a definite trend as to what was being supplemented or changed in weekly budgets. There were two items which remained constant, rent and pocket money. Rent, these workers said, could still be found that was relatively cheap, according to the needs of the individual's family. As for pocket money, one woman summed it up, "What is life worth if we don't have some little money in we pocket?" Pocket money was not really a luxury, but actually served to pay for everything not included elsewhere in the budget—church tithes, baby sitters, and so forth. Items that were decreased in allocations were clothing and hire purchase (installment plan buying).

At the same time, items which were increased serve as significant indicators of the serious impact of the financial crisis on the house-

*Table 6-4.* Weekly Budget Listed in Jamaican dollars

| Items | August 1978 | | | March 1979 | | |
|-------|---------|---------|---------|---------|---------|---------|
|       | Group 1 | Group 2 | Group 3 | Group 4 | Group 5 | Group 6 |
| Rent | 4.00 | 5.00 | 8.00 | 2.00 | 5.00 | 8.00 |
| Food | 10.00 | 10.00 | 5.00 | 15.00 | 15.00 | 12.00 |
| Pocket Money | 4.20 | 4.00 | NA | 4.50 | NA | 5.00 |
| School lunch | 5.00 | 3.00 | 4.00 | 6.00 | 4.40 | 6.00 |
| Savings | 4.00 | 3.00 | 3.00 | 6.00 | 4.00 | 2.00 |
| Transport | 10.00* | 2.50 | 5.00 | 3.00 | 7.00 | 3.00 |
| Hire Purchase | NA | 4.00 | 6.00 | 3.00 | 3.00 | 3.00 |
| Medical | NA | 2.50 | 3.00 | NA | NA | 2.00 |
| Clothing | NA | 3.00 | 6.00 | NA | 4.00 | 5.00 |
| Health Insurance | 2.80 | NA | NA | 8.50 | 2.60 | NA |
| Life Insurance | NA | 3.00 | NA | NA | NA | NA |
| Total | 40.00 | 40.00 | 40.00 | 45.00 | 45.00 | 45.00 |

*includes lunch

hold and individual level. Transportation expenditures had to be increased due to the fact that gasoline had increased to J\$3.50 (U.S.\$1.97) per imperial gallon by March 1979. These women relied on independently owned (illegal) minibuses called *robots* and also conventional bus transportation. Increased gasoline prices were passed on to them in higher fares. School children still had to be given money daily for bus fare and lunches; and although children's bus fares had not increased, lunch prices had.

Food showed the most dramatic increment in price. For example, in the ten month period, the price of margarine rose from J\$.50 per tub to J\$1.29; corned beef rose from J\$.79 per tin to J\$2.00; and a large loaf of bread increased from 80 cents to more than a dollar. Other staples, such as sardines, counter flour, chicken necks and backs, salt fish, and rice, at least doubled in price. Not only were there extreme increases in the price of food itself, but also there were increases in the prices of gas and kerosene fuel for stoves, which further increased the cost of feeding a household. The scarcity of imported raw materials made matters even worse, and at times some necessary commodities were simply not available at any price. In March 1979 no bar soap or detergent powder could be found on supermarket shelves. Quantities of these items that had been hoarded were resold on street corners in the downtown market area for outrageous prices.

Clearly, the viability of a working-class household was dependent on the ability of someone to budget carefully. Household finances were usually controlled by the woman factory worker. Moreover, these women workers were directly responsible for the major household expenditures in 84 percent of the visiting-union households, 81 percent of the single-woman households, and 63 percent of the stable-union households.

Women did receive substantial financial aid from other household members for the payment of rent and utilities, particularly from husbands/partners (stable unions) and boyfriends (visiting unions) and older children (single-woman households). Payment of such bills confirmed a person's right to be a resident and showed his or her commitment to the domestic unit. In addition, as indicated by Whitehead (1976), when a man provides shelter for a household, it establishes his right over that domestic unit, with added emphasis on the expectation of fidelity from the woman. Due to the high rate of unemployment, however, many men who would have assumed the financial responsibility of paying rent and perhaps child support were unable to do so. Less than a quarter of the women in visiting unions received regular support from their boyfriends, and slightly over half were given cash on an infrequent basis. None of those in the single-woman category received steady financial support from the fathers of their children, and only five (22 percent) received cash even on an occasional basis.

Hence, the single woman group represented working-class women who were primary supporters of their domestic units. In comparison to the other two household structural types, the single woman group was the poorest, and women in this group tended to be very critical of the national economic scene. This was evidenced in their political consciousness, which was derived from two sources: the workplace, and trade union affiliation.

Because of the structure of production in screwdriver manufacturing, workers become very aware of economic dependency of Jamaica on the world economic system. All raw materials and components must be imported. When the necessary foreign exchange to procure these essesntial resources is lacking, then production slows down or ceases, and workers suffer accordingly. One single woman with a primary school education explained the essence of Jamaica's role in international trade:

> The tin line has been down two weeks now. Mr. James (the manager) did not fill out the forms properly for to get the foreign exchange to buy the material. It come from Canada. The IMF man control the thing now, you know, so things have to be just so. And we workers suffer 'cause production shut down 'cause we need those things. And Mr. James, he a fool to play with it. We ask him where the material, and he say it's coming. We know he mess it up. Jamaica don't have the money no more. Each factory must wait a turn to get the money. I hear the tin is on the dock in Toronto, waiting to be shipped to us here.

Trade union affiliation and political party membership usually indicate a certain sentiment and understanding of the functions of the international capitalist system. The woman quoted above belonged to a proManley government trade union and had voted Peoples National Party (PNP) for all of her voting experiences.

Viewing the problem from another political orientation, other women workers attributed the causes for the economic crisis and Jamaica's disadvantaged position in the international capitalist system directly to the local situation. The mismanagement of the Peoples National Party (Manley's), the "invasion" by Cuba (sponsored by Manley), the evils of socialism (purportedly being instituted by the PNP), the Prime Minister himself, or a combination of these factors were blamed for the economic structural crisis. As is characteristic of much of the political activity in the Caribbean, directives coming from the government were received with a very personal feeling. As one woman, who had recently separated from her consensual partner because he had been unemployed for two years, stated, "Mi hava man—Michael; him a burden enuf fe we!"

During the ten month period (May 1978 to March 1979), some of the strongest forces, numerically, for political action were women's groups. Women's collective action was not a new phenomenon in Jamaica, but women's political actions in general had gained much international credibility since the "success" of the March of the Pots and Pans in Chile. Women as a collective political force were utilized by all factions—government, opposition, and the left. Two demonstrations held in January and February 1979 were part of the effort to destabilize the Manley government. Poor women, organized by a faction of the conservative element, marched through Kingston and in various other locations on the island, under a banner denouncing the Manley government for the rising cost of living. Another group of women, proManley and anticonservative, held a counter demonstration, calling for greater self-reliance to overcome an inherited set of problems. Finally, a third group of women, led by the progressive forces, demonstrated, calling for an end to U.S. imperialism and decrying the IMF, in solidarity with international progressive movements.

The number of participants in these demonstrations varied according to region. Although the outcry against inflation was universal, different groups attributed the problem to different sources, and proposals to correct the situation varied according to which faction was making the recommendation. As emphasized above, all the political groups utilized the working-class women's distressful political and economic consciousness to dramatize their various points of view. The fact that these women so effectively conveyed the message of the various factions is an indication that their incorporation in these political movements is a subject that merits further analysis by social scientists.

## Conclusion

The Kingston women factory workers represented here are members of a particular sector of the Jamaican population that has the advantage of steady, full-time employment in unionized shops. However, much of the job security they enjoyed in the past has been diminished by international financial and political events. These international occurrences are felt on two levels: in the factory and at home.

The women in this sample were employed in screwdriver manufacturing concerns, which were totally dependent on access to foreign exchange in order to produce, assemble, repackage, or process. When there was no foreign exchange for factories to import materials, work slowed down or ceased altogether. The externally oriented antiinflationary package of the International Monetary Fund that is responsible for controlling foreign exchange shortages, has not provided any significant relief for the general population of Jamaica. On the contrary, the IMF program has been responsible for a soaring cost-of-living index and creating a scarcity of items essential for industry and consumers. The manufacturing sector's dependence on foreign resources has made its female production workers also vulnerable to events of international trade and finance. Moreover, as has been illustrated, these female industrial workers are quite aware of these circumstances. Many of them were able to relate how production had slowed down or halted because management did not get the necessary foreign exchange from the Bank of Jamaica to import materials.

Lately, a number of scholars have dealt with the impact of expanding multinational corporations, which seek cheap female labor in the developing world (see articles in this volume). Female industrial employment in these areas has created situations that directly affect women's roles by incorporating them in wage labor (a situation in direct contrast with their former roles in household production). Case studies on this topic offer many opportunities for comparative study of social and economic change.

The case of Jamaica, however, differs from the cases in the above mentioned regions because Jamaica's situation represents a later stage in the process of international movement of capital to surplus-labor regions of the world. In studying the case of Jamaica, we are dealing with the question What happens when these corporations move to other areas? In Jamaica, a once booming, export-oriented garment industry departed, leaving thousands of women without jobs. The garment industry had been a major component in the industrial development of Jamaica, particularly for women. When this industry left, these women were again forced to make social and cultural adjustments, this time due to the paucity of wage labor available to them. The least fortunate had to try to maintain themselves and families with no formal-sector income. The more fortunate (those represented by the present sample of union women workers) had to try to maintain their families (which included many persons who might themselves have been employed in the formal sector, were work still available) with insufficient formal-sector incomes. Both groups were hurt by the soaring consumer prices caused by IMF policies. Those who had wage jobs were hurt in addition by frozen wages and by work stoppages and slowdowns due to the foreign exchange crisis, also caused by IMF policy. The departure of international capital followed by the devastating impact of the IMF plan escalated the economic crisis for Jamaica, especially for working women.

The urban workers and their households in this study exemplify a situation in which households alter their productive and reproductive functions in response to changes in the role their country (in this case Jamaica) plays in a global context. Two principle examples of these changes have been given. First, we have seen that in many instances the inclusion of extended family members as household residents made it possible for the bulk of reproductive functions to be taken care of by someone other than the woman workers (particularly in the cases of visiting-union and single-woman households). Second, household members (including women workers but most often other members) engaged in extensive networks of exchange to supplement the productive function of the working women (e.g., by obtaining goods for the household) and to some extent to provide for reproductive functions (e.g., by obtaining child care).

In addition to making adjustments in the productive and reproductive functions of their households, women were cognizant of the global market and Jamaica's position in that context; and they were aware of its effect on their own lives. Therefore, they sought to make their difficult situation known by means of public demonstration. Thus, by employing a combination of sociocultural strategies, they hoped to insure the survival of their households.

## Notes

The author wishes to thank Noma Petroff for her editorial assistance and comments.

1. Background of the events leading up the IMF involvement can be found in *Socialism*, vols. 5 and 6 and Beckford and Witter (1980).

2. Research was carried out from June 1978 to November 1979 in Kingston, Jamaica. The exchange rate noted is Jamaican $1.77 = U.S.$1.00.

3. Research has been carried out on rural and peasant women.

4. Between 1953 and 1978, no less than 40 percent of the employed female labor force was concentrated in the service sector.

5. The term *screwdriver* when locally applied to industry in Jamaica, refers to the type of industrial development that took place with little investment in the physical plant in Jamaica. Because of the minimal capital commitment of these light industries, they were comparatively free to leave when labor conditions and so forth in other parts of the world seemed more favorable. Thus, they also earned the local appellation "footloose industry," an indication of minimal integration and commitment to the generation of growth in the economy.

6. In July 1977, Jamaica received a standby agreement for U.S.$75 million. The loan was to be made in four installments, providing that Jamaica would meet certain fiscal requirements. In January 1978, the IMF refused to make the second payment because Jamaica had failed the Net Domestic Assets Test.

7. A number of scholars have thoroughly examined the social stratification system in the Caribbean that links class to color.

8. By comparison 18.6 percent of working-class U.S. black women were employed in similar occupations, excluding the service sector, in 1978.

## References

Arizpe, Lourdes. 1975. "Women in the Informal Labor Sector: The Case of Mexico City." *Signs* 3, no. 1, pp. 25–32.

Beckford, George, and Witter, Michael. 1980. *Small Garden—Bitter Weed.* University of the West Indies, Mona: Maroon Publishers.

Boserup, Ester. 1970. *Women's Role in Economic Development.* New York: St. Martin's.

Clarke, Edith. 1966. *My Mother Who Fathered Me.* 2nd ed. London: Allen and Unwin.

*Covert Action.* 1980. (August–September), no. 10.

Deere, Carmen Diana. 1978. "The Differentiation of the Peasantry and Family Structure: A Peruvian Case Study," *Journal of Family History,* winter.

Fernández-Kelly, María Patricia. 1980. "'Maquiladoras' and Women in Ciudad Juárez: The Paradoxes of Industrialization Under Global Capitalism." Unpublished manuscript.

Girvan, Norman. 1971. *Foreign Capital and Economic Underdevelopment in Jamaica.* Kingston, Jamaica: Institute of Social and Economic Research, University of the West Indies.

Gonsalves, Ralph. 1977. "The Trade Union Movement in Jamaica: Its Growth and Some Resultant Problems." In *Essays on Power and Change in Jamaica,* eds. Stone and Brown, pp. 89–105. Kingston, Jamaica: Jamaica Publishing House.

Jamaica, The Government. Department of Statistics. 1979. *The Labour Force.*

Jamaica Bauxite Institute. 1976. "Bauxite Alumina and Aluminum in 1975," Kingston. Mimeographed.

Jefferson, Owen. 1972. "Jamaica's Post War Economic Development," *New World Quarterly* 3, no. 3, pp. 1–12.

Mair, Lucille. 1974. "A Historical Study of Women in Jamaica from 1655 to 1844," Ph.D. dissertation in history, University of the West Indies, Mona.

Nash, June and Safa, Helen, eds. 1976. *Sex and Class in Latin America.* New York: Praeger.

National Planning Agency of Jamaica. 1978. *Social and Economic Survey,* Kingston: Government Printing Office.

Payer, Cheryl. 1975. *The Debt Trap: The IMF and the Third World.* New York: Monthly Review Press.

Powell, Dorian. 1976. "Female Labor Force Participation and Fertility: An Exploratory Study of Jamaican Women." *Social and Economic Studies* 25, no. 3, pp. 234–258.

Safa, Helen I. 1980. "Export Processing and Female Employment: The Search for Cheap Labor." Paper presented to the Burg Wartenstein Symposium, no. 85, Wenner Gren Foundation for Anthropological Research.

Schmink, Marianne. 1979. "Women, Men and the Brazilian Model of Development." Paper presented at the Latin American Studies Association meetings, Pittsburgh, Pennsylvania.

*Socialism.* The Theoretical Organ of the Workers Party of Jamaica, Kingston.

U.S. Department of Commerce, Bureau of the Census. 1980. *A Statistical Portrait of Women in the United States.* Washington: Government Printing Office.

Whitehead, Tony L. 1976. *Men, Family and Family Planning: Male Role Perception and Performance in a Jamaican Sugartown.* Ph.D. dissertation in anthropology, University of Pittsburgh.

# CHAPTER 7

# The Domestic Clothing Workers in the Mexican Metropolis and Their Relation to Dependent Capitalism

José A. Alonso

## Historical and Theoretical Antecedents

Since the decade of the sixties a number of social scientists from the Third World have been seeking an adequate explanation of the contradictory processes of social change that their countries are experiencing. Samir Amin (1973), for example, has formulated the thesis that a new type of international cooperation has emerged between the developed and underdeveloped nations of the world. The novelty of this international division of labor stems from the new role played by the peripheral capitalist countries. Unlike the situation in the past, when the unindustrialized countries were almost exclusively exporters of raw materials, the new role of the periphery is now primarily that of a source of cheap labor.

In the case of Mexico, this asymmetric international collaboration presents two specific characteristics. The first characteristic was accentuated in 1955 (Cordero 1977) when the Mexican government opened the door to direct foreign investments, chiefly from the United States. Since then U. S. capital has been accumulating on an ever growing scale in the manufacturing sector. The second characteristic, originating in the decade of the sixties, consists of the runaway shops located on Mexican territory along the U. S. border. Both phenomena have been carefully analyzed by Mexican and other social scientists. Underlying the process of industrialization in Mexico are two tendencies found in capitalist countries: (1) the growing need of monopoly capital, mainly U.S. capital, to find new areas of investment in order to cover the increasing costs of labor in the United States and other central capitalist countries; and (2) the growing structural unemployment and underemployment generated in the peripheral capitalist countries such as Mexico.

Nevertheless, there are other structural manifestations of the unequal "collaboration" between Mexico and the industrialized countries (primarily the United States). One of these manifestations is the uncontrolled appearance of thousands of domestic seamstresses in the metropolitan area of Mexico City. These workers constitute an important and massive sector of the female work force, a sector that has been skillfully manipulated by a handful of garment manufacturers located in the downtown area of Mexico City.

Although this phenomenon is not exclusive to the Mexico City metropolitan area, there has been, as far as this author can tell, no published investigation of such domestic industries in other Latin American countries. The lack of scientific research can be explained, however, by the clandestine nature of the phenomenon, a clandestinity imposed by the structural organization of the garment industry itself. In Mexico there have been brief explicit references to this type of domestic industry (Durand and Tunón 1977) and, in a broader context, other Latin American researchers (Jelín 1974) have analyzed industrial processes similar to the domestic industries of Netzahualcoyotl (Neza), a marginal area on the outskirts of Mexico City.

## The Domestic Garment Industry of Neza

A brief review of the functioning of the domestic garment industry of Neza is necessary in order to understand the importance of this industrialization process as a structural symptom of the dependent development experienced by Mexico in the past four decades. This brief outline is based exclusively on the interviews the author conducted with over two hundred domestic seamstresses from January 1976 to May 1977.

The clothing industry is probably the most important industry in Neza, at least in terms of the number of workers who make their living by participating in this industry and the number of factories. There is a great variety of clothing workshops and factories—in size, in number of employees and sewing machines, in type of garments produced, and so forth. In the downtown area of Neza, as is usual in the clothing industry, there is a growing number of clothing factories whose owners do not reside in the city. These factories are "runaway shops." In the 1960s competition from the monopolistic clothing firms forced many labor-intensive, nonmonopolistic clothing factories to flee from Mexico City in search of cheaper labor. Nearby in the metropolitan area, Neza was singled out as a prime site for these runaway factories for reasons which will be explained below.

The subject of this reaearch consists of Neza's clothing workshops where the sewing machines are installed in the household of the head seamstress; and, in most cases, all the workers belong to the same family. In Neza, these domestic workshops are called *maquila* workshops. The Spanish word *maquilar* means in this context that the domestic seamstresses neither design nor cut the raw material; they simply assemble and sew the previously cut material, which usually comes from the downtown area of Mexico City.

## Types of Workshops and the Work Process

The *maquila* workshops can be divided into several types:

1. Unipersonal workshops: the head seamstress is usually the mother of the family, who may be helped occasionally by her children or other relatives. She picks up the cut material in Mexico City, sews it by herself at home, and brings it back to Mexico City by a certain date. In these workshops there are usually one or two sewing machines, generally not even standard industrial types.

2. Multipersonal workshops: besides the head seamstress, other members of the family (usually daughters) work on a regular basis. These shops are larger than the unipersonal ones. There are several sewing machines; and, besides the standard industrial sewing machine, they frequently have other types of machines such as the zigzag. Weekly productivity, therefore, is larger and more diversified. Because of that, the industrialist of Mexico City sometimes takes the responsibility of carrying the material back and forth.

3. Multipersonal workshops with some employees who do not belong to the family. Here the head seamstress, usually a woman with experience in the needle trade, hires several young girls in order to maintain a constant level of production. The girls are paid very low salaries because they lack experience and are learning the trade, as the head seamstress puts it. Very few girls remain for over a year in the same workshop, because they soon get married or go to Mexico City to look for a job as seamstresses in the clothing factories.

*163*

4. Multipersonal workshops in which the head seamstress becomes a full-time manager of her shop. The sewing machines are more numerous and diversified, and in many cases the machines are moved to a special room to avoid interference with family life. These domestic workshops are beginning to look like small clothing factories: the employees have a regular schedule (time to check in, out, a lunch hour, etc.).

The industrial activity of these workshops follows to a great extent the same basic procedure. The following steps seem to be the most relevant:

1. The material is always previously cut. The seamstresses assemble and sew the garments, and in the larger workshops they also press and pack the finished material.

2. The cut material comes from the clothing industries that are located in the downtown area of Mexico City.

3. A very high proportion of these domestic seamstresses pick up the cut material and bring it back to the jobber-merchant when it is finished.

4. The seamstresses have many other expenditures: the sewing machines, electricity, oil and spare parts, thread.

5. Articles 311 to 330 of the Mexican Labor Law deal with domestic industries. According to the author's observation, none of them is applied in Neza. The domestic seamstresses do not even know the existence of such regulations.

6. Before handing the cut material to the seamstresses, the industrialists or jobber-merchant of Mexico City demand some guarantees. They like to keep the original bill of sale received by the seamstresses when they bought their sewing machines.

7. Most of the seamstresses have two full-time jobs: housewife and seamstress. Due to the seasonal character of the clothing industry, the daily hours of work varies almost every month. Because of their double load of work, however, the seamstresses very seldom work less than twelve hours a day.

8. Once their sewing work is finished, the seamstress must bring it back to Mexico City by a set date. The industrialists are very demanding when it comes to reviewing the work of the seamstresses. If some pieces are missing, the women must pay for the material that they received and for the work they did; in other words, they pay for the whole garment even though they did the sewing.

9. The salaries are among the lowest paid in the Mexican industry and do not include any sort of social benefits. Needless to say, the

industrialists are less punctual in paying the salaries than in demanding the clothes.

10. At least 80 percent of these domestic workshops are "underground." Since the piecework wages are so low, the seamstresses cannot afford to pay taxes. Their only way out of this situation is to remain clandestine.

11. Because of this underground situation and of the competition that exists among the seamstresses, most of the women workers carry out their industrial activity as isolated workers. They do not trust one another. They are not even willing to reveal the location of other domestic seamstresses because they are afraid of reprisals. Inspectors take advantage of this situation by creating on informal network of bribes that the seamstresses have to pay if they want to survive.

12. A fundamental aspect of Neza's domestic clothing industry is the "contracting system." Besides the many seamstresses working directly for some firm located in downtown Mexico City, others have such a low level of productivity that their only possibility for work is to sew for a contractor, most of whom live in Neza. The contractors pick up large amounts of cut material in Mexico City and distribute it to ten, twenty, or even more domestic seamstresses in Neza. The piecework system is instrumental in creating a long chain of contractors.

## Neza's Domestic Clothing Workshop: A Result of Mexico's Uneven Industrial Growth

Mexican investigators (Solis, Navarrete, Aguilar, etc.) and foreign researchers (Hansen) recognize that the industrialization process in Mexico has generated a remarkable sustained economic growth for more than three decades, along with acute structural contradictions. This author's thesis is that the superexploitation of the domestic seamstresses of Neza is the logical result of the interaction of three historic processes:

1. The uneven growth of the Mexican industry.

2. The uncontrolled appearance of urban *marginality* in the metropolitan area of Mexico City.

3. The intradomestic role played by the seamstresses as housewives.

Although detailed commentaries on each of these three aspects must be omitted here for lack of time and space, it can be said, however, that since 1940 the basic contradiction in a peripheral capitalist country such as Mexico may be summarized as follows: Starting in 1955, U.S. capital began to take over Mexican industries that produced durable consumer goods (Alvarez and Sandoval 1975; Cinta 1974). This process of denationalization of Mexican industry was accompanied by the constant reduction of the domestic market due to, among other things, the growing inflationary rate and, since 1976, the devaluation of the Mexican peso by almost 100 percent. However, the constant reduction of the purchasing power of the working population does not significantly affect the big industrial companies because they do not depend on the domestic market. The sector most affected is the small industries controlled by national capital. Thus, the main result of the development model chosen by the Mexican elites is the increasingly uneven distribution of profits within industrial sectors. Because of the interests manifested by foreign—mainly U.S.—investors, it is much easier for industrial sectors with capital-intensive factories to grow at a steady rate, whereas the older labor-intensive industries find it more and more difficult to survive.

Clothing industries are a good example of this trend. It is worth taking a closer look at them to put Neza's domestic workshops in perspective. The census data of 1965 reveal the critical situation of the private manufacturing industries usually controlled by national investors. Out of 135,000 factories, 64 percent are light industries that concentrate only 21.9 percent of the capital and 58 percent of the labor force. Furthermore, a typical feature of this manufacturing sector is the artisan-like character of production: 114,366 establishments (84 percent) give employment to 227,778 workers (16 percent) and their share in the invested capital amounts only to 1.8 percent, while the value of their output is only 3.9 percent of the total production. The salaries, wages, and social benefits paid by these small factories represent less than 3 percent of the total amount paid by the manufacturing industries. Against these artisanlike shops (properly speaking, because they seldom have more than five employees), the modern factories, which amount to no more than 5.7 percent of the total number of industries, concentrate 91.8 percent of the invested capital, and their share in the total output is as high as 88.5 percent; they give employment to 72.4 percent of the labor force and their expenses in salaries, wages, and social benefits amount to 89.6 percent of the total in this sector (González-Salazar, Gloria, *Subocupación y Estructura de Clases Sociales en México*, 1972).

This statistical information helps us to understand the most important consequence of foreign investments in the Mexican manufacturing industry, i.e., the increasingly disparate development experienced by the two types of industries: those with enough capital to renovate their technological equipment in order to increase their productivity and those that receive less investments or none at all and, consequently, experience a technological lag. This latter type of industry is typically a consumer goods industry such as the clothing factory.

The steady decline of the Mexican clothing industry is closely related to the failure of the import substitute industrialization model, that is, the attempts to substitute exports for internally produced goods. This model makes traditional industries more dependent on the national market. As a result, the decline in traditional industries (including the clothing industry) is more serious than one would have expected at first, because the very same model of economic development, which has produced such an uneven income distribution in Mexico, is also responsible for the slow growth of the industries that produce non-durable goods for the domestic popular market, due to the limited expansion of demand (Ibarra 1974).

As far as the clothing industry is concerned, technological renovation is becoming more and more difficult for most national industrialists because of the recent introduction of foreign capital in this sector of Mexican industry. When a few foreign investors take over some of the leading clothing factories, one can predict that only the owners of these factories will be able to keep up with the pace of technological change typical in the clothing industry. This is exactly what has been happening in Mexico since the 1960s. Huge foreign investments are concentrated in a few clothing industries; and, as a result, the split of the Mexican clothing industries is growing deeper every year. There is a selected group of clothing factories with modern technology and capital monopolizing a market of small dimensions but with powerful economic resources. On the other hand, there is the vast majority of the Mexican clothing industries remaining at the same technological level and producing for the popular market, which has less economic potential. Therefore, the industrialists are not interested in the technological renovations of their factories. Instead, their answer to the problems created by industrial competition relies on finding and superexploiting the unorganized labor force.

Compared with their American colleagues, these Mexican clothing industrialists are at a disadvantage because Mexico has no economic control over other peripheral capitalist countries. The only possibility open for these Mexican entrepreneurs to find cheap labor lies in the new marginal cities located on the outskirts of Mexico City.

Within the metropolitan area of the capital, Neza contains the labor force that is most easily exploited for the following reasons:

1. Neza is the biggest marginal city of Mexico and Latin America. Since the 1950s the population has grown at a vertiginous rate: sometimes by ten thousand new immigrants per month (Unikel 1971).

2. More than half of these new immigrants come from the capital. The high rate of unemployment and the low level of wages force the working population of Mexico City to seek inexpensive housing in the peripheral zones of the metropolitan areas. Since 1945 Neza has appeared to the poor residents of Mexico City as the best answer to the housing problems they have been facing. Neza has offered them the best opportunity to buy a few square meters of real estate (from two to five pesos per square meter) (Alba Muñiz María 1976).

3. This population, therefore, did not settle in Neza because of job opportunities. As late as 1972 there were only ninety-six industrial establishments in Neza, including factories, small industries, and workshops. Their declared total capital was only 13,360,825 Mexican pesos. Twenty-five of these enterprises declared capital assets of between 200 and 900 pesos. Only two had capital assets exceeding one million pesos, another two possessed over 500,000 pesos in capital assets (Ferras 1974). Up until 1976 the only significant industry in Neza was the garment industry. This "declared" industry employs mostly women who work in small sweatshops owned largely by residents of Mexico City. These sweatshops account for 47 percent of the legal or declared (registered) industries of Neza; however, the declared capital of these workshops was only 290,000 Mexican pesos in 1972; that is, approximately 2.17 percent of the total industrial capital. The uneven capital distribution of Neza's industry becomes apparent when one considers that the 13 largest industries accounted for 94 percent of the total capital.

Neza's inability to generate employment was confirmed by the national survey of dwellings (1976), which showed that Neza employed only 17 percent of the labor force living in Neza. Other cities in the metropolitan area, such as Naucalpan and Tlanepantla, much more industrialized than Neza, give employment to 50 percent and 32 percent, respectively, of the labor force living in each of those cities.

The same difference between these three cities appear in regard to the percentage of women economically active. Although in Naucalpan the percentage is 24.5 percent, in Neza it is only 16.2 percent. On the other hand, open female unemployment in Naucalpan is 6 percent, while in Neza it is 14 percent Mexico, (*IX Censo Nacional de Poblacion,* 1970).

Although this investigation of the domestic clothing industry in Neza shows that these official figures are very deficient, almost 80 percent of Neza's domestic workshops are not registered, which means that at least three thousand domestic seamstresses, fully integrated into Mexico's economic life as full-time workers, do not appear included in the official census. Based on these data, we can make the following revealing observation: according to the official 1970 census, Neza had twenty-six thousand economically active women. If we add the three thousand clandestine domestic seamstresses, the female labor force ascends to at least twenty-nine thousand. In brief, it can be said that at least 10 percent of Neza's economically active female population is not included in the official censuses and documents.

The decisive question, therefore, is the following: How is it possible to provide employment and, at the same time, maintain such a large clandestine sector of the female labor force? The answer, in this author's opinion, is that the workers are not integrated into the Mexican garment industry as proletarians in the classic sense of the word. Neza's demostic clothing workshops are a structural manifestation of the "petty industrial mode of production."

### Neza's Domestic Workshops and the Petty Industry Mode of Production

It would be impossible to summarize here the discussion centering on the different modes of production that have been put forth by many Latin American social scientists, such as Ruy M. Marini (1973), Augustín Cueva (1975), Ernesto Laclau (1973), Roger Bartra (1976), and Sergio de la Peña (1975)

This author's thesis is that the domestic seamstresses of Neza are superexploited by Mexican monopoly capital because of their twofold insertion in the Mexican clothing industry. First, as domestic workers who receive none of the social benefits explicitly enumerated in the New Labor Law of Mexico (Trueba and Trueba 1973). Thus, their salaries are lower than the minimum legal wage; they are always piece wages; they work normally more than eight hours a day; they do not receive any social benefits; and aside from the seasonal character of the clothing industry, their work is highly unstable.

Second, these domestic seamstresses work as semiindependent producers, albeit in a situation of profound structural ambiguity. On one hand, they receive all the raw material—already cut—from the jobber-merchants located in the Federal District; but on the other hand, and given the characteristics that shall be mentioned shortly, these seamstresses may be regarded as autonomous producers whose products are acquired by monopsonic purchasers who control the clothing market for the working masses of the Mexican metropolis.

This character of being semiindependent producers has been affirmed by the findings of the investigation in Neza. The principal features are:

1. All the domestic seamstresses are owners of *the means of production*. They own and directly purchase their sewing machines—up to several of them. *They also own the installations*, since like the other residents of Neza, they moved there with the objective of purchasing their own small property.

2. Ownership of the means of production implies a *series of expenses fully borne by the seamstresses* themselves (oil, thread, repairs, etc.).

3. Because they own the means of production, the seamstresses of Neza *must pay taxes* to the municipal authorities just as any other industrial producer. The Mexican Clothing Chamber constantly tries to force seamstresses to pay monthly fees like the other garment manufacturers.

4. In view of these pressures, the seamstresses of Neza resort to *clandestinity* as the best way to evade payment of taxes. The seamstresses who subcontract workers must use clandestine connections with certain lawyers to avoid paying the wage increases called for by Mexican authorities due to the devaluation of the Mexican peso.

5. As genuine representatives of the petty industry mode of production, the industrial operations carried out by these seamstresses tend to be *simple and without the technical complications* usual in the modern garment industry. The machines they use are almost exclusively the standard industrial sewing machine and the overlocking model. This in keeping with the Marxist assertion (Marx 1932) that the main characteristic of the petty industry mode of production is that it includes the concentration of the means of production but at the same time excludes the free development of

the social productive powers as well as the division of labor within each separate process of production.

6. Finally, the seamstresses of Neza *do not look upon themselves as simple proletarians*. They dream of having their own workshop, their own small business that will grow with the years. Therefore, none of them belong to any Mexican labor organization, not even the government-controlled unions.

## Conclusions

Mexican clothing industrialists themselves have publicly described as "pirates" the entrepreneurs who utilize clandestine domestic workshops.

Unlike the domestic industry of Europe in the seventeenth century, the superexploitation of the Neza seamstresses does not contribute to the accumulation of capital in the hands of the industrial elite engaged in the development and technological advance of Mexico. On the contrary, because of this superexploitation, many clothing industrialists become jobber-merchants. The participation of the domestic seamstresses of Neza contributes to the stagnation of the Mexican clothing industry and not to its development and modernization

### References

Aguilar, Alonso. 1976. "Capitalismo monopolista de estado: subdesarrollo y crisis." *Estrategia* 2 (July). pp. 30–52.

Alba, Muñiz María Eugenia de. September 1976. "Control político de los migrantes urbanos: Un caso de estudio: Ciudad Nezahualcoyotl." Unpublished thesis submitted to the "Centro de Estudios Internacionales," El Colegio de México, for the degree of Master of Political Science, Mexico City.

Alvarez, Alejandro and Sandoval, Elena. April–June, 1975. "Desarrollo industrial y Clase obrera en México," *Cuadernos políticos* 4. pp. 70–83.

Amin, Samir. 1973. *Le developpement inégal. Paris: Le Éditions de Minuit. The third chapter translated by Gerardo Davila and published as Desarrollo desigual,* Mexico: Editorial Nuestro Tiempo, 1974.

Bartra, Roger. 1976. *Estructura agraria y clases sociales en México.* 2nd. ed. Mexico City: Ediciones ERA.

———. 1976. *Caciquismo y poder político en el México rural.* 2nd ed. Mexico City: Siglo XXI.

Censo Nacional de población. Mexico, 1970.

Cinta, Ricardo. 1974. "Burguesía nacional y desarrollo," In *El Perfil de México en 1980*, vol. 3. Mexico City: Siglo XXI.

*171*

Cordero, Salvador. 1977. "Concentración industrial y poder económico en México, Mexico City.

Cueva, Augustín. 1974. "Problemas y perspectivas de la teoría de la dependencia," *Historia y Sociedad* 3 (fall). pp. 564–577.

———. 1975. "El uso del concepto de modo de producción en America Latina." *Historia y Sociedad* 5. (Spring). pp. 201–217.

Durand, Carmen and Tuñon, Esperanza. 1977. "El trabajo femenino en la industria de la confección," *Economía Infoma* 4 (March).

Ferras, R. 1974. "Immigration et croissance urbaine, l'exemple de Nezahualcoyotl." Cuadernos del CES, El Colegio de Mexico, No. 20, 1977.

González Salazar, Gloria. 1971. *Problemas de la mano de obra en México.* Mexico City: UNAM.

———. 1975. "La participación de la mujer en las actividades laborales de México,;; *La mujer en America Latina*, SepSetentas, no. 211, Mexico City.

Hansen, Roger. 1974. *La política del desarrollo Mexicano.* 5th. ed. Mexico City: Siglo XXI.

Ibarra, Davis. 1974. "Mercados, desarrollo y política económica: Perspectivas de la economia de México." In *El Perfil de México en 1980*, vol. 1, 5th ed. Mexico City: Siglo XXI.

Jelin, Elizabeth. 1974. "Formas de organización de la actividad económica y estructura ocupacional: El caso de Salvador, Brasil," *Desarrollo económico* 53 (April).

Laclau, Ernesto. 1973. "Feudalismo y capitalismo en América Latina." In *Tres ensayos sobre América Latina.* Cuadernos Anagrama, vol. 63. Barcelona.

Marini, Ruy Mauro. 1973. *Dialéctica de la dependencia*, Mexico City: Ediciones ERA.

Marx, Karl. 1932. *El capital.* Translated by S. Moore and E. Aveling, vol. 1. Chicago.

Peña, Sergio de la. 1974. "Comentario." In *El Perfil de México en 1980*, vol. 3. Mexico City: Siglo XXI.

Solís, Leopoldo. 1973. *La realidad económica Mexicana: Retrovisión y perspectivas*, 4th. ed. Mexico City: Siglo XXI.

Trueba U., Alberto and Trueba B., Jorge. 1973. *Nueva ley federal del trabajo reformada*, 19th printing, Mexico City: Editorial Porrua.

Unikel, Luis. 1971. "La dinámica del crecimiento de la Ciudad de México," *Comercio exterior* 21 (June).

# Part III

# LABOR FLOW AND
# CAPITAL EXPANSION

Disjunctures brought about between employment opportunities and the labor supply have brought about massive migrations among regions and nations as investment patterns change in response to the new dynamics of capital accumulation. Saskia Sassen-Koob explores the paradoxical case of New York City where a declining manufacturing base in light industry expells workers at the same time that there is a new demand for immigrant labor in service occupations responding to the multinational corporations based in the city. María Patricia Fernández Kelly and Jorge A. Bustamante analyze the burgeoning electronics industry on the Mexican–U.S. border and its impact on the different sectors of the work force. Magalit Berlin reveals the plight of Colombian garment workers in Venezuela as the women try to find a niche in the urban slums to which they migrate using networks based on national identity.

# CHAPTER 8

# Labor Migrations and the New International Division of Labor

SASKIA SASSEN-KOOB

The use of foreign labor, whether slaves or immigrants, has been a basic tendency in the development of the world capitalist system. It has taken many forms depending on a formation's place in the international division of labor and the particular mode of specialization prevalent at a given time. Generalizing, we can identify several dominant patterns. In a first phase, that of capitalist penetration, the use of foreign labor consisted mostly in the forced migration of labor from one area in the periphery to another. In a second stage, that of the consolidation of the world economic system, international labor migrations emerged as the main system for the supply of foreign labor. The labor flow was directed from periphery to core areas. The composition of the labor-supplying periphery varied over time, initially consisting primarily of the less industrialized European countries and eventually encompassing countries of Latin America, the Mediterranean basin and Asia.

Since the middle of the 1960s, two major new migratory flows have developed indicative of a new pattern in the relationship between world accumulation and labor migrations. One of these flows is the intraperiphery migration to areas of high economic growth: to countries with large oil-exports and to areas with new industrial zones, notably Export Processing Zones and world market factories. The other major new flow is the migration from Southeast Asia and the Caribbean Basin directed largely to a few old centers of the world economy experiencing severe economic decline in traditional components of their economies: first London and, more recently, New York City.

The new intraperiphery migrations can be seen as yet another instance of the typical pattern according to which migrants go to areas of economic growth. Yet, insofar as growth in this case is rooted in the recomposition of world capital and insofar as labor migrations are conceptualized as a dependent variable, it may be useful to distinguish these new intraperiphery flows from other flows directed to areas of economic growth, for example, Western Europe after World War II.

The new migrations to the core from Southeast Asia and the Caribbean Basin are both historically and analytically unusual as a pattern because they are directed to areas with pronounced job losses, especially in sectors likely to employ immigrants. Since "capital emigration"[1] from the old capitalist centers is a basic tendency in the last fifteen years, analyzing the place of this new immigration may throw light on the characteristics of economic decline and the possibility of a transformed role of such centers in the new international division of labor.

Here I will analyze what is distinctive about the current labor migrations, with a particular emphasis on the new periphery migrations to declining core areas. This requires placing the current phase in a broader historical and theoretical context. The first section discusses the use of foreign labor as a basic tendency in capitalist development, and the second, the specificity of labor migrations as one of several modes of supplying foreign labor. The third section uses the case of New York City from 1960 to 1980 for the empirical and theoretical elaboration of the argument.

The argument is the following. The shift in the location of rapid industrial growth from the old industrial centers to peripheral areas, notably the new zones in Southeast Asia, the Caribbean Basin and the Mexico-United States border, as well as the vast industrialization programs in OPEC members, has a) been a central factor in the decline of traditional components in the economies of old industrial centers, and b) together with the transnationalization of capital generally, generated a pronounced expansion in the international demand for advanced specialized services. The production of these services is disproportionately concentrated in a few old centers at the core, such as London and New York City. The same processes that generate decline in old industrial centers, also generate an economic recomposition to the advantage of a few major urban

*176*

centers and to the advantage of a high-income professional workforce in those centers. The new migrations to the core are primarily associated with this recomposition rather than with the decline of traditional economic sectors as is usually argued in the migration literature. And the new intraperiphery migrations are associated with that decline which re-emerges as rapid industrialization in select peripheral areas.

### The Use of Foreign Labor

An adequate labor supply system is essential to realize the surplus-generating possibilities of an area. In general, the development of labor supply systems has been an integral part of the broader process of incorporation into the world capitalist system. Characteristics of the labor supply system in a given area—e.g., slavery, peonage, wage labor—can be accounted for by that area's role in the world economy (Wallerstein 1974:86–94). These labor supply systems have historically incorporated a variety of mechanisms through which workers from foreign areas, both capitalist and non-capitalist, were drawn or forced into the capitalist world economy.

Labor scarcity has historically been a central problem capitalists have had to solve in order to realize an area's potential to generate surplus—a fact easily forgotten today in core countries with high unemployment. Any situation in which the characteristics of the labor supply threaten existing or foreseeable levels of accumulation can be defined as one of labor scarcity (Portes 1978:471–482; Sassen-Koob 1978:516–518). Included in this definition are absolute shortages such as those experienced by the Arab oil-exporting countries today and relative scarcities such as those in many advanced industrialized countries where successful working-class organization and the welfare state have strained the supply of cheap and powerless labor. Specific tendencies within the capitalist system have generated specific types of labor scarcities. For example, rapid industrialization creates a need for a direct, quantitative increase in the labor supply which is only partly offset by labor-saving technologies. On the other hand, declining profits generate a need for cheap labor in core countries to offset the victories of organized labor.

The use of foreign labor, under conditions of labor scarcity, has taken many forms depending on a country's place in the international division of labor and the particular mode of specialization prevalent at the time in the world system. For example, the use of Chinese contract labor on Caribbean plantations in the nineteenth century differs significantly from the use of Irish immigrant labor in England at the same time. These were different labor supply systems resulting from different surplus-generating processes, each of which played a distinctive role in the international division of labor. In the Caribbean the basic mechanism for world accumulation was the transfer to the center of value produced in the periphery through the development of export-oriented production, e.g., plantations (Amin 1974; Beckford 1972). In England, on the other hand, the surplus generated was not exported but transformed into additional labor power, thus creating a process of expanded reproduction (Marx 1970).

Furthermore, the use of foreign labor in surplus-generating processes with similar characteristics (e.g., industrialization) may have a different politico-economic role depending on the mode of international specialization prevalent at the time. For example, the rapid industrialization of both the United States at the turn of the century and the Arab oil-exporting countries today generated a pronounced need for foreign labor. But industrialization and labor immigration in the United States occurred at a time when the world economy was still in the process of articulation and the struggle for hegemony at the core was leading into a new phase of the international division of labor. Industrialization in the oil-exporting countries today is taking place under conditions of technological dependence and an unusually high incidence of imports. International specialization today incorporates a certain level of industrialization in most of the world. Industrialization is no longer a base for core status.

Using location in the international division of labor as a criterion, I have tentatively identified four types of instances in the development of world capitalism that have historically generated significant levels of labor imports. Each of these instances subsumes a variety of concrete historical moments or stages in the development of the international division of labor. Hence, periodization is, to a degree, subordinated for the sake of a more analytic conception of the international division of labor. To classify migrations belonging to different historical stages into one category clearly has shortcomings. On the other hand, in light of the prevalence of accounts of single migration streams in the literature on immigration, it seems useful at this point to identify common roots among apparently highly divergent processes. Elsewhere (Sassen-Koob 1981) I have discussed the relation between concrete historical stages and analytic categories in the study of immigrant labor. The purpose here is merely to provide a general background for the detailed discussion of labor migrations that follows.

The first instance can be characterized by the association of labor imports with the expansion of the capitalist mode of production into the periphery. The basic mechanism of accumulation in this case is the international transfer to the center of value that is produced at the periphery (Emmanuel 1972; Amin 1974:133f.). One way of accomplishing this is the development of export-oriented production at the periphery, most typically mines and plantations and, today, highly labor-intensive manufacture. Mines and plantations entailed the *sudden* introduction of large-scale production in areas where noncapitalist modes of production had been prevalent or exclusive. Mobilization of the necessary labor force thus required an equally sudden transformation of subsistence producers into wage laborers, slaves, or peons (Schapera 1947). This accounts, in part, for the violence of the process of capital penetration into the periphery. In areas where the surplus-generating possibilities exceeded the local labor supply and where economic or technological constraints to the substitution of labor by capital existed, the new enterprises imported workers. Let me cite some examples, since I will not return to this case in the paper.

In Ceylon (Now Sri Lanka), the labor force required for coffee and, later, tea production was formed through the import of hundreds of thousands of South Indians. Nearly one million were imported in the 1840s and 1850s alone (Halliday 1975:156–7). The labor supply needed for sugar production in the Caribbean was first formed through the import of slaves. When slavery became inefficient, the slaves were freed and transformed into wage laborers. The additional needs for labor were satisfied through the import of at least one-half million workers from India, who typically came on five-year contracts with free transportation both ways (Williams 1970:348). Similarly, in Brazil, slave labor was imported to work the mines and plantations and was later replaced by wage labor; Europeans, particularly from Southern Italy, were offered free transportation and a subsistence plot if they agreed to be wage laborers on coffee plantations (Furtado 1963:chapters 20–24). African plantations and mines frequently resorted to seasonal migrant workers recruited from distant tribes, a precursor of today's widespread international migrations of workers within Africa (Lasserre-Bigorry 1975; Amin 1974a; Arrighi and Saul 1973; Wolpe 1975; Wilson 1976).

In the second instance, labor imports are associated with capital expansion and, unlike the first case, a significant level of capital accumulation at the periphery. The large migrations to the United States in the late 1800s and early 1900s can be seen as a process called forth by accumulation rather than simply as expansion aimed at value transfers to the core (Thomas 1973). The association between labor imports and capital expansion is even clearer in the case of the oil-producing countries today. The construction and operation of a production apparatus financed by oil revenues could not be taking place without large scale labor imports covering the whole occupational range. However, the association between labor imports and accumulation, hence a changed role in the international division of labor for these peripheral areas today, is more difficult to establish in this case than in that of the United States at the turn of the century. The decision to launch an accelerated industrialization program has entailed the reinjection of oil revenues extracted from the advanced industrialized countries back into the world accumulation process, which reproduces the dominance of the center over the periphery.[2] Unlike the mines and plantations described in the first instance, value transfers to the center are here mediated by a program of national construction involving basic industry. On the basis of this changed role in the accumulation process, I have tentatively included the case of the oil-exporting countries in this second instance, characterized by the association of labor imports with accumulation at the periphery.

In the third instance, labor imports are associated with intense capital accumulation at the center.[3] Examples of this include the large migrations of Irish workers into the industrialized cities of Britain—estimated to have reached 700,000 by 1850 (Jackson 1963:11)—and the migrations of Southern and Eastern Europeans into Switzerland, old Germany, and France throughout the 1800s and early 1900s (see, e.g., Cinanni 1968:29).[4] After World War II, reconstruction generated a large demand for labor which, in most of the Western European countries, could only be satisfied through labor imports. However, even in the cases of acute labor shortages, such as those of Switzerland, Luxembourg, and the German Federal Republic, an important factor determining the desirability of labor imports as a solution to labor shortages was its profitability due to cost-lowering and anticyclical effects.

In the fourth instance, labor imports are associated more directly with the reproduction of capital's dominance over labor at the center. In this category, we can place the labor imports by Western European countries after World War II as well as several aspects of immigration policy and practice in the United States during the last few decades.[5]

Such imports increase the level of profits of certain firms and, more generally, of capital as a whole by lowering the cost of labor and the cost of the reproduction of the labor force. Furthermore labor imports operate as an anti-cyclical mechanism by facilitating the export of unemployment and by exercising a downward pressure on the demand for foods and services due to the fact that there are few dependents for each breadwinner.[6]

These, then, are the four types of instances in which labor imports have historically played a significant role in the constitution of the labor supply needed for the world accumulation process. As I indicated earlier, these are not historical stages. At a given time, different types of foreign-labor supply systems were prevalent in different locations of the world economy. For example, slavery became an important labor supply system in Brazil at a time when it was being replaced by other types of labor in the United States. On the other hand, the same type of foreign labor supply system may be prevalent in different locations of the world economy at different times, for example, the use of Indian contract labor in the Caribbean last century and the use of Caribbean contract labor in the United States and Venezuela today.

Both the patterns described above and the more historical analysis of labor migrations in the next section underscore the unusual coexistence of capital emigration and labor immigration in one location such as New York City today. Additional variables need to be specified in order to explain this case, the subject of the last section.

### Migration as a Global Labor Supply System

International labor migrations did not evolve as an important labor supply system until the phase of consolidation of the world capitalist economy (Portes 1978; Zolberg 1979). The earlier phases of capitalist penetration and incorporation into a single world economy under the hegemony of Europe had generated different types of systems for the supply of labor. The most important ones relied on 1) forced movements of people from one area of the periphery to another, and 2) the subjugation of indigenous and hitherto autonomous populations and their forced transformation into laborers through such means as slavery, *mita*, peonage, *encomienda* and tribal contract labor.[7] Some of these persist today in areas not fully transformed by the generalization of market relations.

Colonizing migrations belong to the early stage of capitalist penetration.[8] They are to be distinguished from forced-labor supply systems as well as from the international labor migrations that evolved at a later stage. Unlike both of these, colonizing migrations originated in core countries and colonists were viewed as a valuable resource.

The incorporation of most areas of the world into the capitalist system resulted in the disintegration or subordination of noncapitalist forms of subsistence (Amin 1974; Wallerstein 1974). This disintegration was more widespread in western Europe than in the periphery. But it was sufficient to move large masses of people in the periphery into the labor market, thereby creating a supply of potential migrant workers. Capitalism transforms land into a commodity. Land being the basis for noncapitalist modes of subsistence, its commodification left a mass of landless peasants with little alternative to becoming part of a rural or urban labor reserve. This was especially pronounced in periphery areas where the disintegration of noncapitalist modes of subsistence did not arise out of the expanded reproduction of capital in situ. As a result the transformation of labor into means of production that took place on such a large scale in western Europe and the United States occurred only minimally in the periphery.

The generalization of capitalist relations of production and the corresponding transformation of land into a commodity gave a "voluntary" quality to the resulting migrations.[9] This was in contrast with the forced population transfers of the earlier stage. The disintegration of autonomous modes of subsistence resulted in the creation of labor reserves willing to be mobilized into the labor market. There was no longer a need for the direct, physical subjugation of workers; in the new social structure, the same goal was accomplished by robbing workers of their means of subsistence. This process was not fully consolidated until the twentieth century (Zolberg 1979).[10]

The consolidation of a world system through the peripheralization of large areas of the world also brought about a shift in the flow of labor. The flows were no longer from one area in the periphery to another but went to satisfy the labor needs at the core. The labor supplying periphery expanded and came to encompass more and more parts of the world. The major western European countries first drew labor from their immediate peripheries: Irish went to England; Poles to German; Italians and Belgians to France. Eventually it included all of Eastern and Southern Europe—the main labor suppliers for western Europe and the United States. As these reserves were exhausted or their flows interrupted due to wars, China, Mexico and North Africa emerged as important labor suppliers. In the last two decades, the Caribbean Basin, the Mediterranean Basin, and Asia have become major labor suppliers.

An important new pattern of labor flows has been added in the last two decades to the continuing flow from periphery to core. The export of jobs from core to periphery, generated in the process of recomposition of world capital, has brought about new domestic and international labor flows *within* the periphery.[11] Similarly, oil-revenue financed industrialization in OPEC members has generated major international migrations from Asian and non-OPEC Arab countries.

The shift from forced labor mobilization and colonizing migrations to international labor migrations reflects the complex internal differentiation of the world system. The labor market in the North Atlantic zone was more generalized than in other areas of the world. While 'free' labor replaced slavery in areas under British control, slavery actually increased in Latin America. There, slave imports rose from 22,450 a year for the period 1701–1810 to 29,700 a year for 1811–1870 (Curtin 1969:268). A variety of labor supply systems were instituted throughout the world economy. Nevertheless, the forms of labor supply dominant in the core eventually became dominant, though not exclusive, in the periphery. Suggestive here is Amin's (1974) proposition that the rhythm of expanded reproduction of the social system at the center determines the tendencies of the world system as a whole.

State policy on international migration is in part reflective of a state's location in the world economy, or, more concretely, in the international division of labor. Liberal laws regarding emigration were less common in semiperipheral states than in the core. Thus, while Britain relaxed its antiemigration stance after the Napoleonic Wars (1812–1815) and introduced the most liberal policy, other European states such as France, some of the German states, and Russia maintained strong anti-emigration policies (Zolberg 1979). France, for example, had good reasons to be opposed to emigration (Zolberg 1979). Industrialization and the generalization of the labor market were not as fully accomplished there as elsewhere in western Europe.[12] Agrarian subsistence remained widespread but was only viable with small families given the small size of the holdings. Yet France's ongoing need for soldiers in the struggle to create a colonial empire in North Africa and Eastern Europe clashed with the slow demographic growth resulting from its internal economic structure.

These conditions created interests regarding migration different from those of Britain (Thomas 1973).

Furthermore, even within the rather integrated north Atlantic region controlled by Britain, restrictions on the movements of goods and people were more commonplace and effective (MacDonagh 1961) than the laissez-faire view suggests (e.g., Hansen 1961). Britain did not suddenly abandon its mercantilist position restricting the emigration of skilled machinists or mill operators (Zolberg 1979). At least three factors contributed to this change: (1) a 15 percent population growth shown in the 1811 census; (2) continued internal migration supplying labor to the new urban industrial centers; and (3) the growing influence of the political economists who viewed emigration and settlement as a way of creating foreign markets for British goods.[13] Nonetheless, attempts to control emigration continued through regulations, preferential fares, and restrictions (MacDonagh 1961; Plender 1972).

The enforcement of national borders contributes to the peripheralization of a part of the world and the designation of its workers as a labor reserve. Border enforcement emerges as a mechanism facilitating the extraction of surplus value by assigning a status of formal or informal powerlessness to foreign workers generally and criminality to illegal immigrants (Petras, 1980). Foreign workers undermine a nation's working class when the state renders foreigners socially and politically powerless. At the same time, border enforcement meets the demands of organized labor in the immigration country insofar as it presumes to protect native workers from unfair competition. Yet *selective* enforcement of policies can circumvent general border policies and protect the interests of capital sectors relying on immigrant labor. This points to the contradictory role of the state in the accumulation process.

Although the generalization of the labor market evolving out of the consolidation of the world economy created the conditions for international migrations as a global labor supply system, the development of the nation–state created the conditions for immigrant labor as a distinct category in a nation's labor supply. This distinctiveness rests on (1) the institutional differentiation of the processes of labor-force reproduction and maintenance and (2) a particular form of powerlessness that meets the social control requirements of a type of organization of the labor process that, though usually defined as backward, is a significant component in most core countries—notably in the service sector.

*184*

## A New Phase in International Capital and Labor Flows

Two significant trends in the United States since the middle of the 1960s point to what is possibly a new type of articulation between international capital and labor flows. First, there has been a significant increase in U.S. direct foreign investment, both in absolute terms and as a share of all U.S. investment. Northern manufacturing centers have been particularly affected by this capital emigration, including domestic capital migration to the Sunbelt (Nash; Safa, this volume). Second, there has been a large influx of Third World immigrants that reached massive levels towards the end of the sixties and continued throughout the seventies. Most of these immigrants come from the Caribbean Basin and Southeast Asia. These are also the areas of destination for a growing share of U.S. direct foreign investment. The large majority of Caribbean Basin immigrants and a very large share of Asian immigrants reside in New York City, also a location that has experienced very high levels of capital emigration.

The coexistence of large rates of labor immigration and capital emigration, as illustrated by the case of New York City, is both historically and analytically unusual. The main propositions in the migration literature hold that migration will tend to flow towards areas of economic growth, not towards those in decline. Though formulated differently, this view is present both in marxist and classical models of the relationship between capital and labor mobility.

And it is historically unusual both for the past, as discussed in the two preceding sections, and for today. The other major labor migrations of the last two decades rest on a direct relationship between capital and labor flows: the migrations to Western Europe after World War II; intraperiphery migrations to the Arab oil-exporting countries and to Venezuela; the migrations to the U.S. Sunbelt, mostly from Mexico and internal to the United States; the migrations, both internal and international, to areas with export processing zones and world market factories. These flows are, in a way, not unlike the earlier flows discussed in the preceding section. What is novel, is the particular location of economic growth in the world economy: a shift from core to periphery areas, including internal periphery areas as in the case of the United States Sunbelt.

In contrast, the large Caribbean Basin and South East Asian migrations have been directed mostly to areas with high levels of capital emigration: London in the 1950s and early 1960s, New York City since the middle of the 1960s, and Los Angeles—in the case of the major traditional manufacturing sectors—in the 1970s. This raises questions as to how these cities can absorb a large labor inflow under conditions of pronounced unemployment, the loss of jobs traditionally occupied by immigrants, and a severe deterioration of the economy generally, officially recognized in the case of New York City with the fiscal crisis of 1975–1976.

The image capital emigration is intended to emphasize one particular aspect of various processes affecting the old industrial centers of the capitalist world economy. This particular aspect is the production of goods for people and industries in the core through jobs located in the periphery. In many ways the international division between locations of consumption and locations of production has been a basic tendency in the capitalist world economy over the centuries. But the partial inversion of the role of manufacturing in this division over the last two decades, makes the present situation qualitatively different from earlier ones.Indicators of this shift are, among others, the large scale closings of factories in the old manufacturing centers in the Northeast and North of the United States (and in Western Europe), the development of export processing zones in the periphery, the pronounced increase in U.S. direct investment abroad with a significant shift towards certain periphery countries. These developments partly overlap and partly refer to processes that do not entail production for core markets through jobs located in the periphery. But they do provide data pointing to high levels of what I am here referring to, rather figuratively, as capital emigration.

Incorporating the variable capital emigration in an analysis of immigration requires a shift in focus away from immigration, and on to the urban economic structure as the focus where both capital emigration and human immigration take place and evolve into constitutive processes of that urban structure. Locations that have undergone intense capitalist transformation, such as the old manufacturing centers in the north, and subsequently experience decapitalization and severe economic decline, cannot revert to an earlier stage such as the farm communities they once may have been (Harvey 1978; Walker 1978). They remain in the capitalist circuit in a form not unlike that of the reserve of unemployed workers. Like these workers, they represent a concentration of use values that under certain conditions become exchange values—that is to say, they can become part of the value expansion process. In the case of the workers, the use values they represent may be quite basic: the internalization of the various attributes constitutive of the category wage labor and the possession of skills and experience. In the case

*186*

of places, the use values include a physical infrastructure, a social organization, and a labor supply that are all the result of capitalist development and hence at least somewhat supportive of capitalist modes of economic operation.

One way of describing economic decline would be to introduce a distinction between use value and exchange value as applied to places. New York City can be conceptualized as a place containing a large array of use values that during the last decade and a half have lost exchange value. As a consequence it is a location where a significant component of the economy has become part of the reserve of places for capital. This component is significant because it has submerged other components in the city's economy that have maintained their role in the process of value expansion and are perhaps even constitutive of novel processes of value expansion. The significance of the reserve status component can be gauged from the fact that aggregate data for a variety of economic measures for 1965–1975 show a generally declining economy in New York City. In this sense, it can be argued that by 1975 the whole city had acquired, at least ideologically, a reserve status.

Being part of the reserve of places for capital also entails a transformation in the relationship between capital and labor. Economic decline increases the power of capital over the resources contained in a place: a weakened working class, a weakened city government, an overall willingness to compromise in order to draw capital investment. Under these conditions capital investment may again become profitable. And the availability of immigrant labor assumes added significance: it is not simply labor being employed, but also a factor that may enhance New York City's potential for being "reemployed" by capital.[14] The fact that 60 percent of direct German, English, and Swiss investment in the U.S. in the last two years took place in declining Northeastern cities is suggestive in this regard (Bauer 1980).

A place like New York City, with a high level of capital emigration, is one location on a circuit that encompasses also new destinations of capital. This overcomes the tendency to see capital emigration as a one-way process that once accomplished, is over. It brings to the fore the dynamic element in the situation of economic decline. Though in the case of a boom town decline may well be a once-and-for-all process, decline in one of the centers of the capitalist world does raise important questions about modalities for readjustment and recomposition in the world economic system.

*187*

The reemployment by capital of a place in the reserve is not a simple mechanistic process where the same employers who left, and by leaving contributed to create anew conditions for profitable accumulation, are the ones who come back. The circuits through which a place like New York City becomes reemployed will probably tend to be complex ones, involving, for example, foreign investors.

As a way of organizing the data on capital emigration and human immigration, I will posit a capital migration circuit that contains New York City as one of its locations. The capital migration circuit, *as constituted in this location*, contains several moments: capital emigration and the resulting economic decline, the conditions for renewed profitable accumulation contained in that economic decline, and the possibility of the reemployment of this location by capital. The reasons for positing this in terms of a circuit are (1) to capture the dynamic elements in what is now a condition of economic decline in many of the old industrial centers and (2) to incorporate the world system as a background variable, that is, the capital migration circuit contains the locations of destination of capital, whether the Caribbean, South East Asia or any other major receiving area, in addition to those in decline, for example, the U.S. Northeast.

### Locating New York City in the New International Division of Labor

New York City has been disproportionately affected by the movement of jobs abroad and to the Sunbelt. Overall employment levels show virtually no growth since the mid-1950s and a considerable decline towards the end of the 1960s and early 1970s. Employment stood at 3.2 million in 1950, 3.3 million in 1960, and 3.1 million in 1970. By 1975 it had declined to 2.7 million and remains there today, 1981 (see Table 8–1). Unemployment was 4.8 percent in 1970; by 1976 it had reached 11.2 percent, and in 1981, 8.4 percent.

There were significant job losses in certain sectors of the economy. Netzer (1974) estimated that between 1968 and 1972, New York City lost 334,000 goods handling jobs and 99,000 retail and consumer service jobs. Between 1969 and 1977, Manhattan's central business district had a 15 percent decline in office employment, from 910,000 to 770,000, and a 30 percent decline in factory employment, from 570,000 to 400,000 (Tobier 1979: 15–16). In garment jobs alone, the New York region lost 158,000 jobs between 1950 and 1970 (Council on Wage and Price Stability 1978:26)

*188*

During this same period, the city experienced a large increase in immigration from the Caribbean Basin and Southeast Asia (Table 8–2). Since the 1965 Amendment to the Immigration Act went into full effect in 1968, annual legal immigration has risen, reaching 460,000 entries in 1979 up from 260,000 in 1960 (And these figures do not include legal entries under other classifications). Between 1966 and 1979, New York City received about one-fourth of all new arrivals, a level remarkably higher than that of the cities with the next largest concentrations–Los Angeles with 4.7 percent and Chicago with 4.4 percent. If we add the immigrant population of New Jersey, which in the last few years has been the third or fourth largest recipient, then the New York-New Jersey area has a disproportionate share of the total immigration (Table 8–3).

The composition of immigration also changed since the middle of the 1960s from a preponderance of high wage to one of low wage countries of origin (Table 8–4). Asia, which in 1950 supplied less than 2 percent of all legal immigrants, in 1979 accounted for more than a third. Asians had the highest rate of increase of all major immigrant groups from 1970 to 1980 (Table 8–5). Over that same period, the share of Latin America (excluding Mexico) went from 6.2 percent to 26 percent of all legal entries. While in 1960 Europe provided half of all legally admitted immigrants, by 1979 this share was down to one-seventh of the total and the numbers cut in half (see Table 8–4). New York City has received the largest share of immigrants from Latin America (excluding Mexico) and the Caribbean and to a small degree from Asia. Since undocumented im-

*Table 8-1.* New York City: Employment Level, 1950–1980. (In thousands)

| Year | Employed | Unemployed | As % of Civilian Labor Force |
|------|----------|------------|------------------------------|
| 1950 | 3,276 | 245 | 6.5 |
| 1960 | 3,307 | 180 | 5.2 |
| 1970 | 3,146 | 159 | 4.8 |
| 1975ᵃ | 2,761 | 327 | 10.6 |
| 1977ᵃ | 2,717 | 303 | 10.0 |
| 1978ᵃ | 2,741 | 268 | 8.9 |
| 1979ᵃ | 2,744 | 263 | 8.7 |
| 1980ᵃ | 2,726 | 257 | 8.6 |
| 1981ᵇ | 2,653 | 245 | 8.4 |

*Source:* U.S. Bureau of the Census, Census of the Population (1950, 1960, 1970) U.S. Department of Labor, Bureau of Labor Statistics (Middle Atlantic Region)
ᵃ Annual averages, unadjusted from the BLS (Middle Atlantic Region).
ᵇ Figures for September.

Table 8–2. Population by Race and Spanish Origin, 1980

| Regions | Total | White | Black | American Indian, Eskimo, and Aleut | Asian and Pacific Islander | Other | Spanish origin | As % of total |
|---|---|---|---|---|---|---|---|---|
| United States | 226,504,825 | 188,340,790 | 26,488,218 | 1,418,195 | 3,500,636 | 6,756,986 | 14,605,880 | 6.4 |
| Northeast | 49,136,667 | 42,328,154 | 4,848,786 | 78,182 | 559,759 | 1,321,786 | 2,604,260 | 5.3 |
| New England | 12,348,493 | 11,585,633 | 474,549 | 21,597 | 81,005 | 185,709 | 299,164 | 2.4 |
| Middle Atlantic | 36,788,174 | 30,742,521 | 4,374,237 | 56,585 | 478,054 | 1,136,077 | 2,305,110 | 6.2 |
| North Central | 58,853,804 | 52,183,794 | 5,336,542 | 248,505 | 389,747 | 695,216 | 1,276,400 | 2.1 |
| East North Central | 41,669,738 | 36,138,962 | 4,547,998 | 105,881 | 302,748 | 574,149 | 1,067,790 | 2.5 |
| West North Central | 17,184,066 | 16,044,832 | 788,544 | 142,624 | 86,999 | 121,067 | 208,610 | |
| South | 75,349,155 | 58,944,057 | 14,041,374 | 372,123 | 469,762 | 1,521,839 | 4,473,170 | 5.9 |
| South Atlantic | 36,943,139 | 28,647,762 | 7,647,743 | 118,656 | 260,038 | 268,340 | 1,193,820 | 0.3 |
| East South Central | 14,662,882 | 11,699,604 | 2,868,268 | 22,454 | 41,041 | 31,515 | 119,315 | 0.8 |
| West South Central | 23,743,134 | 18,596,691 | 3,525,363 | 231,013 | 168,083 | 1,221,984 | 3,160,094 | 13.3 |
| West | 43,165,199 | 34,884,785 | 2,261,516 | 719,385 | 2,081,368 | 3,218,145 | 6,252,040 | 14.4 |
| Mountain | 11,368,330 | 9,958,545 | 268,660 | 363,169 | 98,416 | 679,540 | 1,441,480 | 12.6 |
| Pacific | 31,796,869 | 24,926,240 | 1,992,856 | 356,216 | 1,982,952 | 2,538,605 | 4,810,565 | 15.1 |

Source: Bureau of the Census, 1980 Census of Population, Supplementary Report (1981: Table 3)

*Table 8-3.* Persons of Spanish/Hispanic Origin or Descent New York—New Jersey—Connecticut Region, 1970–1980

| | S/H Population | | | | | |
|---|---|---|---|---|---|---|
| | 1970 | Percent of Total Population | 1980 | Percent of Total Population | Change Number | 1970–1980 Percent |
| Total—N.Y.— N.J. Conn. Region | 1,694,020 | 9.4 | 2,043,976 | 11.9 | 349,956 | + 20.7 |
| N.Y. SMSA | 1,335,507 | 13.4 | 1,493,081 | 16.4 | 157,574 | + 11.8 |
| N.Y.C. | 1,278,630 | 16.2 | 1,405,957 | 19.9 | 127,327 | + 10.0 |
| Nassau—Suffolk SMSA | 77,352 | 3.0 | 101,975 | 3.9 | 24,623 | + 31.8 |
| Orange Co., N.Y. | 5,617 | 2.5 | 11,260 | 4.3 | 5,643 | +100.5 |
| Jersey City SMSA | 89,555 | 14.7 | 145,163 | 26.1 | 55,608 | + 62.1 |
| Newark SMSA | 90,559 | 4.4 | 132,356 | 6.7 | 41,797 | + 46.2 |
| Patterson— Clifton Passaic SMSA | 31,408 | 6.8 | 62,123 | 13.9 | 30,715 | + 98.7 |
| Long Branch— Asbury Park SMSA | 10,170 | 2.2 | 12,915 | 2.6 | 2,745 | + 27.0 |
| New Brunswick— Perth County— Sayerville SMSA | 21,529 | 3.7 | 34,138 | 5.7 | 12,609 | + 58.6 |
| Dutchess Co.— N.Y. | 3,977 | 1.8 | 5,853 | 2.4 | 1,876 | + 47.2 |
| Fairfield Co. Conn. | 28,346 | 3.6 | 45,112 | 5.6 | 16,766 | + 59.1 |

*Source:* 1970 Census Fourth Count—Spanish Language totals 1980 Census Public Law File
Prepared by: Population Research and Analysis Human Resources Division N.Y.C. Department of City Planning

migrants tend to settle in areas with high concentrations of legal immigrants, New York City's immigrant population is larger than official figures show.

If we disaggregate the data on New York City's overall economic decline, a more complex picture emerges. The data on capital emigration from the Northeast show several divergent trends. Firstly, not all components of labor intensive industries were affected equally by capital emigration. In the case of the garment industry, historically a key industrial sector in New York City, it was the larger shops with standardized production that moved while the less mechanized branches as well as the industry's marketing and design operations

Table 8-4. Immigrants Admitted by Origin, 1960, 1979

|  | 1960 | 1979 |
|---|---|---|
| Latin America and the Caribbean | 66,440 | 179,061 |
| Mexico | 32,684 | 52,096 |
| West Indies | 14,047 | 74,074 |
| Central America | 6,661 | 17,547 |
| South America | 13,048 | 35,344 |
| subtotal | 66,440 | 179,061 |
| Europe | 138,426 | 60,845 |
| Asia | 24,956 | 189,293 |
| Africa | 2,319 | 12,838 |
| Total | 265,398 | 460,348 |

Source: Same as Table 8-2.

Table 8-5. New York City Population (1980 census)[a]

|  | Total | White | Black | Asian | Other | American Indian | Hispanic |
|---|---|---|---|---|---|---|---|
| Brooklyn | 2,230,936 | 1,249,482 | 722,816 | 42,965 | 212,491 | 3,182 | 392,118 |
| Queens | 1,891,325 | 1,335,802 | 354,129 | 93,783 | 104,797 | 2,814 | 262,422 |
| Manhattan | 1,427,533 | 840,862 | 309,693 | 72,883 | 201,059 | 3,036 | 335,803 |
| Bronx | 1,169,115 | 554,015 | 371,870 | 15,165 | 225,656 | 2,409 | 396,730 |
| Staten Island | 352,121 | 313,534 | 25,616 | 6,709 | 5,879 | 383 | 18,884 |
| New York City | 7,071,030 | 4,293,695 | 1,784,124 | 231,505 | 749,882[b] | 11,824 | 1,405,957 |

Source: U.S. Bureau of the Census, 1980: Public Law File, 94–171.
[a]Census results are being challenged in court.
[b]This category includes a large number of Hispanics. Nationally, 40 percent of Spanish-origin persons reported their "race" as *other*.

remained in New York City. Secondly, types of production processes that make relocation easy and desirable also make it possible to continue operating in a place like New York City. Again a case in point is the garment industry, wherein the possibility of deskilling some jobs, low ratios of fixed assets per worker, and minimal economies of scale explain why it was easy to move certain shops to Hong Kong or Mexico and at the same time open new shops, especially sweatshops, in New York City. Thirdly, the severe shrinking of the production base of an industry resulting from the replacement of local production by imports, as in the footwear industry in the Northeast, may generate a whole range of new jobs associated with the import trade, a development of particular significance to New York City as a commercial center. These three trends do not by any means overcome the devastating impact of capital emigration from New York City. But they are elements in a larger explanation that seeks to identify an economic base for the absorption of immigrants in a situation of massive job loss in industries likely to employ immigrants.

Disaggregating the data on employment levels in New York City, we find sharp employment increases in certain sectors amidst the overall decline. Between 1977 and 1980, there was an overall 17 percent increase in nine white-collar industries in the service sector (includes the financial sector) (Table 8–6). Two-fifths of the jobs in these industries are in the higher-pay, higher-status professional, technical, managerial, and administrative occupations. Between 1977 and 1980, employment increased by 7.7 percent in finance, insurance, and real estate, by 9.4 percent in communications and media, and by 24.7 percent in business services. Employment also expanded by 8.9 percent in educational services and research institutions, by 7.4 percent in entertainment, culture, and tourism, and by 3.9 percent in social services.

Even in manufacturing, a sector with continuing employment losses, a more detailed analysis points to a number of growth trends. There has been an increase in foreign capital investment in manufacturing plants in New York City. Between 1976 and 1980, foreign capital added 196 plants in New York, compared to 161 in California, 87 in Texas, 94 in North Carolina, etc. (Table 8–7). Nationwide, New York and New Jersey had 18.6 percent of all foreign-owned manufacturing plants in 1980. This is not an insignificant share given

*Table 8–6.* New York City: Employment Trends in Selected Services, 1977 and 1980 (in thousands)

|  | 1977 | 1980 | Change in 000s | Change rate (%) |
|---|---|---|---|---|
| Finance, Insurance, Real Estate | 414 | 446 | 32 | 7.7 |
| Communications and Media | 212 | 232 | 20 | 9.4 |
| Business Services | 186 | 232 | 46 | 24.7 |
| Human Capital | 205.5 | 223.8 | 18.3 | 8.9 |
| Social Services | 617 | 642 | 25 | 3.9 |
| Entertainment, Culture, Tourism | 162 | 174 | 12 | 7.4 |

*Source:* U.S. Department of Labor Statistics, Middle Atlantic Region.

the severe economic decline of this region, and considering that booming states such as Texas and Georgia had 4.6 and 3.9 percent, respectively (Table 8–7).

Another example is the garment industry, one whose decline has been well documented. Yet amidst this pronounced overall loss of jobs, Chinatown's garment industry has been growing since the late 1970s. While in 1970 there were approximately 180 garment factories in Chinatown, by the late 1970s there were 400 (Wang 1979). And these figures exclude sweatshops and homework. There is a growing awareness in the industry that wages in New York City are increasingly competitive with those in the garment industry in Southeast Asia. And since a large share of production in Southeast Asia is for the United States market, the availability of immigrant labor in New York City makes location of factories here increasingly profitable.

The overall outcome of these decline and growth trends is an increasing polarization in the occupational structure and, hence, in the economic situation of the population. First, there has been a reduction in the upper segments of the manufacturing work force due to the shrinking, relocation or elimiation of those components of the production process that employed them. Second, there has been a reduction in the middle level white collar work force due to

Table 8–7. Foreign-Owned Manufacturing Firms, Selected States and U.S. Total, 1980

| | Cumulative Total Through 1975 | 1976 | 1977 | 1978 | 1979 | 1980 | Cumulative Total Through 1980 | | Net Increase 1978– 1980 |
|---|---|---|---|---|---|---|---|---|---|
| New York State | 222 | 42 | 45 | 36 | 50 | 23 | 418 | % US | 196 |
| New Jersey | 178 | 18 | 21 | 16 | 17 | 18 | 263 | 11.4 | 85 |
| NY-NJ Metropolitan Region | (234) | (9) | (17) | (18) | (28) | (16) | (322) | 7.2 | (88) |
| California | 103 | 16 | 22 | 43 | 50 | 30 | 264 | 7.2 | 161 |
| Texas | 82 | 6 | 14 | 16 | 31 | 20 | 169 | 5.8 | 87 |
| North Carolina | 90 | 6 | 11 | 16 | 25 | 36 | 184 | 5.0 | 94 |
| Pennsylvania | 125 | 10 | 16 | 14 | 19 | 30 | 214 | 4.6 | 89 |
| Georgia | 68 | 5 | 5 | 20 | 22 | 23 | 143 | 3.9 | 75 |
| Illinois | 92 | 10 | 5 | 6 | 10 | 13 | 136 | 3.7 | 44 |
| All Other | 1006 | 137 | 135 | 191 | 210 | 194 | 1873 | 51.2 | 867 |
| U.S. Total | 1966 | 245 | 274 | 358 | 434 | 387 | 3664 | 100.0 | 1698 |

Source: The Conference Board, Inc. The Port Authority of NY & NJ Planning and Development Department, Regional Research Section

*194*

the departure of corporation headquarters and other large office complexes. Third, there has been an expansion in the highly specialized professional work force employed in the advanced service sector. Fourth there has been an expansion in the low-wage work force employed in low-level service and manufacturing jobs that have been generated by the expansion of the advanced service sector and by the high-income lifestyles of those employed in it. Fifth, there has been an expansion in what I would call a downgraded manufacturing sector, notably sweatshops and industrial homework, developing from the conjunction of the victories of organized and unorganized workers in the 1960s which raised the cost of labor, the availability of immigrant labor and the fact that New York City is a key marketing center.[15]

The data on New York City's economy describe, in my view, not only the growth of certain sectors and the decline of others, but also a recomposition of the economic structure. It would seem that the configuration of resources represented by a city like New York generates a new, profitable use of such cities in the form of a service economy and a manufacturing sector largely oriented towards the servicing of the service sector. We need to re-examine the notion that New York City's economic decline is irreversible because its physical plant is inadequate for manufacturing. It is inadequate for the type of manufacturing that dominated the Northern cities up to World War II. As long as we use those categories and criteria that are rooted in an earlier phase of the development of urban economies, the outlook is gloomy. If we develop criteria to understand economies dominated by the production of advanced services mostly for export abroad and to other areas of the country, then New York may emerge as a rather different kind of place from what it appears when we emphasize the loss of the manufacturing base it once had.[16] The tourist boom, the hotel and restaurant boom, the gentrification process, the recent extension of international banking, the expansion of top-of-the-line services in advertising, economic and legal consulting, the art market, the selling of decision-making models to the rest of the world in terms of fashion, marketing, advertisement, investment: all of these point to growth and the desirability of the resources contained in a place like New York. In line with this, foreign investment in banking and financial institutions in New York City has grown by 42 percent from 1978 to 1980 (Table 8–8).

The importance of these developments is brought out by the growing share of services in United States exports over the last two decades. Between 1960 and 1980, the value of United States service

*Table 8–8.* Foreign-Owned Banks and Other Financial Institutions New York City (1978–1980)

| | CUMULATIVE INVENTORY | | | CHANGE FROM | |
| --- | --- | --- | --- | --- | --- |
| | 1978 | 1979 | 1980 | 1978 to 1980 | |
| Foreign Banks | 68 | 77 | 81 | +13 | 20% |
| Foreign Bank Agencies | 54 | 61 | 62 | + 8 | 14% |
| Subtotal: Combined Foreign Bank Branches and Agencies | 122 | 138 | 143 | +21 | 17% |
| Foreign-owned Trust Companies | 19 | 20 | 23 | + 4 | 19% |
| Total: Bank Branches, Agencies and Trust Companies | 141 | 158 | 166 | +25 | 18% |
| Foreign-owned Investment Companies | 6 | 6 | 6 | — | — |

*Source:* New York State Department of Banking, Foreign Banks Division
The Port Authority of NY & NJ Planning and Development Department
Regional Research Section

exports increased by an average of 12 percent a year. While in 1970 the value of service exports was $23.2 billion, by 1980 it had reached $120.7 billion.[17] The growing importance of the international trade in services led to the establishment in 1978 of the International Services Division within the Department of Commerce and to intensified pressure to lift barriers on service exports (U.S. Senate, Subcommittee on International Finance and Monetary Policy, 1982). Furthermore, the structure of direct foreign investment also changed towards a greater share of investments in services. While in 1960, 9.6 percent of the stock in U.S direct foreign investment was in Trade, Finance, and Insurance, by 1978 this share had increased to 25 percent (Table 8–9). The most significant relative increase in such investments was in periphery countries. This raises the possibility that the increased U.S. direct foreign investment in services and, more generally, the overall export of services during the last twenty years is partly associated with the location of manufacturing plants abroad during that same period of time. We see here an internationalization of the relationship between the manufacturing and service sector, historically a domestic one. The highly specialized services necessary for the management and operation of the new industrial zones in the periphery are largely produced in the core.[18] A similar situation can be seen within the U.S.: while the large headquarters left New York City, they continue to use the advanced services produced in the city (Cohen 1977; Drennan 1981).

*Table 8-9.* U.S. Direct Foreign Investment in Trade, Finance, Insurance: 1968–1978 (In million dollars)

|  | 1968 | 1978 |
|---|---|---|
| Foreign Investment | | |
| Position abroad | 61,907ᵃ | 168,081 |
| Manufacturing | 25,160 | 74,207 |
| Transport and | | |
| Communication | 2,586 | 3,693 |
| Trade | 4,872 | 17,585 |
| | 16% | 25% of total |
| Finance and | | |
| Insurance | 5,387 | 24,065 |
| Otherᵇ | 2,941 | 8,210 |

*Source:* U.S. Department of Commerce, Bureau of Economic Analysis, Selected Data on U.S. Direct Investment Abroad, 1966–1978. (1980)
ᵃItems do not add up to total because certain types of investment have been left out, e.g., Petroleum.
ᵇ*Other* includes a large area of services, e.g., business services.

The internal differentiation of the process of economic decline in the old manufacturing centers of the North and Northeast permits a parallel refinement of the role of immigration in this process. Saying that immigration provides cheap, reliable labor is correct. But it is a notion that needs refinement given the complexity of the socio-economic recomposition of these old centers.

Immigration plays distinctive roles in the three moments of the capital migration circuit postulated earlier in this paper. Recapitulating briefly, the capital migration circuit can conceivably incorporate the following moments: a) capital emigration and the resulting economic decline, b) the conditions for renewed profitable accumulation contained in that economic decline, and c) reemployment of the city by capital. The first is descriptive of many of these old industrial centers. The last two may or may not happen. They are partly empirical questions in that they need to be studied—especially in view of the usual conceptualization of economic decline as a rather unilinear process. These last two are also partly a historical question in that the decline of these old centers of the capitalist world economy is fairly recent, and what will happen with them is still history in the making. Nonetheless, I would venture that the argument I have developed here for the case of New York City may well hold for other large, complex cities, such as London or Los Angeles.

Correlating the functions of immigration with the different moments in the capital migration circuit gives us the elements for a

*197*

theoretical specification of the role of immigration in the old, declining centers of the capitalist world economy as illustrated by the case of New York City. These are as follows: (1) in the phase of economic decline, immigration provides cheap labor and therewith contributes to the survival of declining industries and of the backward sectors of capital generally; (2) having posited the distinction between decline and the conditions for renewed profitable accumulation, immigration can be seen as one of the factors promoting the reemployment of the city by capital; and (3) distinguishing between immigrant labor and immigrant community, immigration can be seen as an agent directly engaged in the reemployment of the city through the immigrant community. The first aspect has been widely discussed and studied in the migration literature—hence I will not dwell on it. The second and the third ones have not.

## Notes

1. The actual closing and moving of factories is only one component of the relocation of manufacturing, probably a relatively small one. More significant in terms of actual job losses are various kinds of disinvestment that amount to a gradual contraction of the manufacturing base: (a) the shift of profits and savings of a given plant to other plants in other locations, or their investment in other types of activities; (b) gradual moving of equipment and jobs, without necessarily closing the plant; (c) no new investments for plant maintenance or new equipment acquisitions.

2. Rapid industrialization has made possible a very high level of expenditure of oil revenues, much of it for imports from the core. Luxury consumption by the elites of these countries could not have generated such a large scale re-injection of oil revenues into the world accumulation process. On the other hand, the higher price of oil is being financed to a large extent by a higher cost of living and a decline in real wages in the core countries. Inflation, another name for this process, can then be seen as a mechanism for the transfer of these savings to the oil exporting countries and to transnational capital. This suggests that the interests of the states at the core and transnational capital no longer coincide to the extent they did at the turn of the century and up to the immediate post-World War Two period. (I have developed this argument in Sassen-Koob 1982). It is in this sense that the labor migrations into the oil-exporting countries are to be distinguished from the classical pattern of immigration into high growth areas.

3. Today's large-scale labor imports in Western Europe are typically seen as a reversal of the pre–World War Two period and the nineteenth century. But immigration started long before. Already in 1916 Lenin noted that one of the "special features of imperialism . . . is the decline in emigration from the imperialist countries and the increase in immigration into these countries from the more backward countries where lower wages are paid" (1975:127).

He went on to note that this decline had already started in the 1880s and that Germany, for example, had 1.3 million foreign workers by 1907. These facts have been overshadowed in our reading of history by the migrations into the New World, especially the U.S.

4. For example, of the 15 million Italians who emigrated between 1876 and 1920, almost half are estimated to have gone to other European countries, especially Germany, Switzerland and France (Cinanni 1968:29).

5. The use of immigrants to depress wages and weaken unions can already be found earlier in the United States. More generally, the emphasis on technological development as a variable explaining the organization of the labor process has obscured the importance of the struggle between workers and managers for control at the workplace in shaping that organization (Montgomery 1979; Edwards 1979).

6. Employment of a significant level of immigrant workers in these countries has an anti-cyclical effect because the possibility of exporting unemployment by repatriating immigrants in addition to their typically below average demand for goods and services exempts the economy from the need to build the kinds of infrastructure and service organizations that would be required by an equal number of national workers. This will tend to reduce the differences in levels of consumption, employment and utilization of the economy between cycles of expansion and contraction.

7. *Encomienda* was a system by which Indians under Spanish colonial rule in Latin America were forced to provide labor or tribute. *Mita* was a similar system but without the option to provide tribute.

8. I am here referring to a specific historical phenomenon. There were, for example, massive migrations in what is today China, involving many different ethnic nations and having a strong colonizing orientation dating from the early second millenium B.C. (Lee 1979:20). Furthermore, there are important differences among colonizing migrations (Omvedt 1973).

9. At the same time, a new, politically motivated type of involuntary migration emerged in the nineteenth century on a large scale. With fluctuations it has continued since then. The outcome was often the same: refugees became part of the labor supply in the receiving country. For an analysis of these migrations see Zolberg (1979).

10. This consolidation does not follow a fixed, lineal pattern. Rather, it is a historical process in which changing conditions generate new forms of incorporation. Thus, migrants in periphery countries today face new circumstances because the traditional modes of using the rural labor supply, such as factories in cities, have been exhausted or simply do not exist. McGee (1979) points out that the countryside, rather than the cities, has absorbed most of the population increase in highly populated countries in South East Asia. The historical nature of this process is further brought out by the technological transformation of the secondary sector and the shift towards service industries (Singelmann 1978).

11. The most extreme form of the large scale transfer of manufacturing jobs to the periphery is the development of export-processing zones and world market factories. In both of these, production is mostly for export to the core countries where the capital originated. This development began on a large scale in the late 1960s. By 1975, there were 79 export processing

zones, most of them concentrated in South East Asia and the Caribbean Basin.

12. After the Second World War, with industrialization fully under way (Savage 1979), France was one of the most liberal immigration countries in western Europe.

13. The growth of the "dangerous poor" expelled from the land and concentrated in urban centers was an important factor making emigration acceptable. Besides providing a means of creating new markets, emigration came to be seen as a way of applying redundant capital and redundant people to the colonies.

14. Of interest here is the argument that uneven development has been a strategy in capitalists' fight against labor, but one that has only really worked on the international level. That is to say, there has been an overall tendency towards evenness within the United States insofar as there are no regions that have undergone the "development of underdevelopment" (Frank 1972). This is a process that cannot be reproduced here (Fox 1978). In this context, the influx of immigrants from the periphery acquires an additional significance theoretically and politically insofar as it may be seen as a mechanism to introduce unevenness given the impossibility of generating it internally.

15. Two recent studies by the New York State Department of Labor (1982; 1982a) document the pronounced expansion in sweatshops and illegal industrial homework, not only in garments, but increasingly also in other industries, notably, toys, footwear, and electronics. Though inevitably incomplete, the findings are quite revealing.

16. Service industries in the United States that are important in international trade include: accounting, advertising, banking, communications, computer services, construction and engineering services, consulting and management services, educational services, franchising, health services, insurance, leasing, legal services, motion pictures, shipping and air transport, tourism (including the overseas development of hotels and motels) (U.S. Department of Commerce 1980:2–4). New York City is clearly a key producer of most of these services.

17. The data on the international service trade are inadequate. There have been growing surpluses in "invisibles" in the U.S. balance of payments. But these cannot be fully attributed to the sales of service industries abroad (U.S. Department of Commerce 1980). On the other hand, some of the receipts of service industries are reported under the merchandise account. Data on specific international service industries in the United States balance of payments accounts are limited to three disaggregated series, estimated from annual surveys. These are data on (a) foreign contract operations of construction, engineering, consulting and other technical services firms; (b) reinsurance by U.S. insurance companies; and (c) receipts from film rentals abroad. Furthermore, data on travel and passenger fares can be used for estimates of the tourist industry, as can be deduced from a recent study by the Department of Commerce (1980:5–6) that also gives data on ten major service industries selling abroad.

18. Banking, a key service industry, has expanded immensely. From 1971 to 1981 foreign branch assets of U.S. banks had a sixfold increase, from $55.1 billion to 320 billion. A study by the Centre on Transnational Cor-

porations (1981) of the United Nations, found that six countries accounted for 76 percent of the assets of all transnational banks in 1975 and in 1978. The Centre defines transnational banks as deposit taking banks with branches or majority-owned subsidiaries in five or more countries and/or territories. Using this definition, it identified 84 transnational banks in 1975 (Centre on Transnational Corporations, 1981:3).

19. For example, in interviews with landlords I found a common response to be that residents supposedly feel much "safer" with immigrants as building attendants than with inner-city blacks.

### References

Amin, Samir. 1974a. *Modern Migrations in West Africa.* New York: Oxford University Press.
——1974. *Accumulation on a World Scale. A Critique of the Theory of Underdevelopmment.* (vols. I and II) New York: Monthly Review Press.
Arrighi, G. and J. Saul (eds.). 1973. *Essays on the Political Economy of Africa.* New York: Monthly Review Press.
Bach, Robert L. 1978. "Mexican Immigration and the American State." *International Migration Review,* 12 (Winter): 536–558.
Bauer, David. 1980. "The Question of Foreign Investment." *New York Affairs* 6, 2:52–58.
Beckford, George. 1972. *Persistent Poverty.* London: Oxford University Press.
Burawoy, Michael. 1976. "The Functions and Reproduction of Migrant Labor: Comparative Material from Southern Africa and the United States." *American Journal of Sociology,* 81 (March): 1050–1087.
Centre on Transnational Corporations (United Nations). 1981. *Transnational Banks: Operations, Strategies and their Effects in Developing Countries.* New York: United Nations, Centre on Transnational Corporations.
Cinanni, Paolo. 1968. *Emigrazione e imperialismo.* Roma: Editori Riuniti.
Cohen, Robert. 1977. "Multinational Corporations, International Finance, and the Sunbelt." In Perry and Watkins (eds.). *The Rise of the Sunbelt Cities.* Urban Affairs Annual Reviews, 14:211–226.
Cohen, Steven M. and Saskia Sassen-Koob. 1982. *Survey of Six Immigrant Groups in Queens, New York City.* Department of Sociology, Queens College, CUNY.
Council on Wage and Price Stability. 1978. "A Study of Textile and Apparel Industries." Washington, D.C.: The Council on Wage and Price Stability (July), 27.
Curtin, Phillip D. 1969. *The Atlantic Slave Trade: A Census.* Madison: University of Wisconsin Press.
Drennan, Matthew. 1981. "Economy." In Horton and Brecher (eds.). *Setting Municipal Priorities 1982.* New York: Russell Sage Foundation, pp. 55–88.
Edwards, Richard. 1979. *Contested Terrain: The Transformation of the Workplace in the Twentieth Century.* Boston: Basic Books.
Emmanuel, Arghiri. 1972. *Unequal Exchange: A Study of the Imperialism of Trade.* New York: Monthly Review Press.
Fox, Kenneth. 1978. "Uneven Regional Development in the United States." *The Review of Radical Political Economics,* 10, 3:68–86.

Frank, Andre Gunder. 1972. *Lumpen-Burgeoisie, Lumpen-Development.* New York: Monthly Review Press.

Furtado, Celso. 1963. *The Economic Growth of Brazil: A Survey from Modern to Colonial Times.* Berkeley: University of California Press.

Glynn, Thomas and John Wang. 1978. "Chinatown." *The Neighborhood: Journal for City Preservation,* 1, 3:9–23.

Halliday, Fred. 1975. "The Ceylonese Insurrection." In R. Blackburn (ed.). *Explosion in a Subcontinent: India, Pakistan, Bangladesh and Ceylon.* Middlesex: Penguin, pp. 151–220.

Hansen, Marcus Lee. 1961. *The Atlantic Migration, 1607–1860.* New York: Harper Torchbooks.

Harvey, D. 1978. "Labor, Capital, and Class Struggle Around the Built-Environment in Advanced Capitalist Societies." pp. 9–37 in K. Cox (ed.), *Urbanization and Conflict in Market Societies.* Chicago: Maaroufa, pp. 9–37.

Jackson, J.A., 1963. *The Irish in Britain.* London: Routledge and Kegan Paul.

Kuo, Chia-ling. 1981. "A Study of the Coping Strategies of Immigrant Chinese Garment Workers in New York's Chinatown." Work in progress, Department of Anthropology, City College, City University of New York.

Lasserre Bigorry, J. 1975. *General Survey of Main Present-Day International Migration for Employment.* Geneva: International Labor Office, Department of Working Conditions and Environment.

Lee, James. 1979. "Migration and Expansion in Chinese History" in William H. McNeill and Ruth Adams, eds. *Human Migration: Patterns and Policies.* Bloomington, Indiana: Indiana University Press, pp. 20–47.

Lenin, V.I. 1975. Imperialism, the highest stage of capitalism. Peking: Foreign Language Press.

MacDonagh, Oliver. 1961. *A Pattern of Government Growth, 1800–1860: The Passenger Acts and Their Enforcement.* London: MacGibbon and Kee.

McGee, T.G. 1979. "Rural-urban mobility in South and Southwest Asia: Different formulations, different answers." In William H. McNeill and Ruth Adams (eds.), *Human Migration: Patterns and Policies.* Bloomington: Indiana University Press, pp. 199–224.

Marx, Karl. 1970. *Capital,* vol. 1. New York: International Publishers. (1867).

Montgomery, David. 1979. *Workers' Control.* Cambridge: Cambridge University Press.

Netzer, Dick. 1974. "The Cloudy Prospects for the City's Economy." *New York Affairs,* 1,4:22–35.

New York State Department of Labor. 1982. *Study of State-Federal Employment Standards for Industrial Homeworkers in New York City.* New York: Department of Labor, Division of Labor Standards.

———. 1982. *Report to the Governor and the Legislature on the Garment Manufacturing Industry and Industrial Homework.* New York: Department of Labor, Division of Labor Standards.

Omvedt, Gail. 1973. "Towards a theory of colonialism." *The Insurgent Sociologist,* 3 (Spring):1–24.

Petras, Elizabeth McLean. 1980. "The role of national boundaries in a cross-national labor market." *The International Journal of Urban and Regional Research*, 4(2):157–195.

Plender, Richard. 1972. *International Migration Law*. Leiden: A.W. Sythoff.

Portes, Alejandro (ed.). 1978. "Illegal Mexican immigrants to the U.S." *International Mitigation Review*, 12 (Winter): Special Issue.

Sassen-Koob, Saskia. 1978. "The International Circulation of Resources and Development: The Case of Migrant Labour." *Development and Change*, 9 (Fall):509–545.

————1979. "Formal and informal associations: Dominicans and Colombians in New York." *International Migration Review*, 13 (Summer): 314–332.

————1981. "Towards a conceptualization of immigrant labor." Social Problems, 29 (October): 65–85.

————1982. "Recomposition and peripheralization at the core." Contemporary Marxism, 5 (Summer): 88–100.

Savage, Dean. 1979. *Founders, Heirs and Managers: The French Industrial Elite in Transition*. Beverly Hills: Sage.

Schapera, Isaac. 1947. *Migrant Labour and Tribal Life*. London: Oxford University Press.

Singelmann, Joachim. 1978. *From Agriculture to Services: The Transformation of Industrial Employment*. Beverly Hills: Sage.

Thomas, Brinley. 1973. *"Migration and Economic Growth: A Study of Great Britain and the Atlantic Economy*. Cambridge: Cambridge University Press (2nd. edition).

Tobier, Emanuel. 1979. "Gentrification: The Manhattan Story." *New York Affairs*, 5,4:13–25.

U.S. Department of Commerce. 1980. *Current Developments in U.S. International Service Industries*. Washington, D.C.: U.S. Department of Commerce, International Trade Administration.

U.S. Senate, Subcommittee on International Finance and Monetary Policy. 1982. "Foreign Barriers to U.S. Trade: Service Export." Washington, D.C.: U.S. Senate, 97th Congress (Committee on Banking, Housing and Urban Affairs).

Walker, Richard, A. 1978. "Two Sources of Uneven Development Under Advanced Capitalism: Spatial Differentiation and Capital Mobility." *The Review of Radical Political Economics* 10,3:28–37.

Wallerstein, Immanuel. 1974. *The Modern World System. Capitalist Agriculture and the Origins of the European World-Economy in the Sixteenth Century*. New York: Academic Press.

Wang, John. 1979. "Behind the Boom: Power and Economics in Chinatown," *New York Affairs*, 5,3.

Williams, Eric. 1970. *From Columbus to Castro: The History of the Caribbean, 1492–1969*. London: Deutsch.

Wilson, Francis. 1976. "International Migration to Southern Africa." *International Migration Review*, 10 (Winter):451–488.

Wolpe, Harold. 1975. "The Theory of Internal Colonialism: The South African Case." In Oxaal, Barnett and Booth (eds.), Beyond the Sociology of Development. London: Routledge and Kegan Paul, pp. 208–228.

Zolberg, Aristide R. 1979. "International migration policies in a changing world system." In William H. McNeill and Ruth Adams (eds.), *Human Migration: Patterns and Policies.* Bloomington: Indiana University Press, pp. 241–286.

# CHAPTER 9

# Mexican Border Industrialization, Female Labor Force Participation and Migration

María Patricia Fernández-Kelly

Because of the significant theoretical and policy issues that it raises, migration has received considerable scholarly attention during the last decade. Two distinct and opposed modes of analysis have emerged. The first one is functionalist and views migrants as individuals who select the best among a series of alternatives by use of rational calculation. Explicitly or not, individualism and rationality have been stressed in this framework with an assumption that social organization is the sum of free-willed, goal-directed persons. Functionalism has oriented this perspective towards a study of the roles played by individuals in a social context. As a result, when studying migration, the tendency has been to emphasize the characteristics of migrants as well as their impact upon the areas of their destination.

Such analyses have evolved as part of a broader theory of industrialization and its corollary, modernization. Migration has been frequently interpreted as the effect of multiple rational choices leading large numbers of men and women to areas where industrialization opens new occupational opportunities, more attractive wages, better working conditions and other advantages. The best known metamorphosis of this view labels these phenomena as *pull factors*. In a complementary manner, groups are said to migrate also as a result of undesirable conditions in their areas of origin. Stagnation of the rural environment, progressive land erosion, diminishing agricultural productivity, and demographic growth are mentioned among these so-called *push factors*.

There are similarities between the perspective outlined above and a widespread understanding of social evolution in which various countries and/or geographical localities represent sequential stages of development. Migration occurs from "less developed" countries (or geographical areas) to those that have attained a higher level of development.

As with modernization theory, this framework sees the uneven growth of urban centers, the emergence of impoverished shantytowns, and the persistence of unemployment and underemployment (all linked to migration) as regrettable although inevitable consequences of progress, that is, the price of development. It is recognized that unemployment and underemployment result from the failure of industry to grow fast enough to absorb the labor that could be contributed by migrants, both within the domestic and international contexts (see for example Marshall 1978). At the same time, an unsympathetic portrayal of migrants is often attached to the same considerations. It is suggested, for example, that the inability to incorporate rural and/or ethnic groups into the industrial sector is due to educational, psychological, and cultural limitations of migrating individuals rather than to the shortcomings of the productive system as a whole. The policy implications derived from this view center around attempts to correct or reform the flaws of individuals and so to foster better assimilation of migrants and a more harmonious integration of society.

Because of its emphasis upon the individual and rational choice, as well as because of its functional purview, this perspective in large part fails to take account of the structural determinants imposed upon social classes by the accumulation of capital at an international scale. To consider migration as the result of aggregate individual decisions does not adequately explain why migration begins, increases, and diminishes at certain historical stages nor does it account for the direction of migratory flows, i.e., why migrants go where they go and why they tend to congregate predominantly in certain geographical areas.

A second perspective for the analysis of migration stems from Marxist theory. This approach does not necessarily deny the existence of individual rationality, personal limitations, and unique choices. But instead of focusing upon individual behavior, it emphasizes the interaction among social classes and the objective material constraints that ultimately determine personal actions (Safa 1975). It also facilitates the conceptualization of migration as a mechanism for the allocation of labor, particularly (but not exclusively) cheap, unskilled labor. In this process dynamism stems from the global requirements of capitalism and of the unequal relationships—economic, political, and ideological—among societies and among classes within societies (Petras 1979 and Safa 1975). Castells has argued (1975) that migration may be conceptualized as the effect of "the submission of the worker to . . . capital . . . and [of] the uneven development between sectors and regions, and between countries, in accordance with inter-capitalist competition."

More recently Portes (1979) has postulated the existence of several modes of structural incorporation of migrants into a segmented labor market in core countries. He notes that the channels accessible to foreigners who wish to acquire legal residence in the United States tend to draw professional and skilled workers whose services supplement those of U.S. citizens. These migrants enter the *primary* sector of the labor market which is characterized by relative stability of jobs, higher wages, possibility of promotion, due process, and a modicum of autonomy.

On the other hand, unskilled laborers—prevented by definition from legal entry into the U.S.—are channeled through informal networks in the *secondary* sector of the labor market. Once there, they tend to move in a circle of unstable or temporary jobs, low wages, undesirable working conditions, close supervision, and longer working hours. As Portes has demonstrated, the existence of a dual mode of structural incorporation of migrants has as much to do with the personal characteristics of individuals as with the nature of the labor market itself. The presence of labor market segments that operate according to distinct and frequently contradictory guidelines underscores the importance of an explanation of the structural constraints on migration.

A structural framework enhances the comprehension of certain crucial and much neglected issues. For example, it is only recently that the analysis of the differential participation of men and women in migratory processes has been attempted (Arizpe 1977, Jelin 1977). Contrary to widespread assumptions, it has now become apparent that in Latin America the majority of migrants are young women. In most cases, these women migrate and seek employment as members of kin networks for whose survival their earnings are vital (a phenomenon not unlike that of young nineteenth century European women extensively documented by Louise Tilly [1978] and others). As they enter the realm of paid labor, women bring forth particular kinds of behavior and attitudes linked to their socialization. Moreover, they move in a world pervaded by ideological notions about

*207*

women's work, femininity, and women's proper role in a social environment. Although they may share working and migratory backgrounds, women and men behave in and are expected to respond to their environment according to gender specific criteria. To overlook these distinctions may lead to limited and simplistic conclusions in the study of the participation of both men and women in social processes (for a differing view, see Leeds, 1976). Besides gender, class and family organization provide the indispensable scaffold for refining an understanding of migration.

These points, as well as the implicit connection between migration and the position of women and men within the domestic sphere and in the domain of wage labor are central to the purposes of this essay. Below, I have attempted to outline a schema for the conceptualization of migratory processes along the Mexican-American border in the context of its recent industrialization.

Until fairly recently, massive migration did not constitute a distinctive feature of the Mexican-American borderland. Only during the second decade of the twentieth century did migration, both legal and undocumented, become a quotidian aspect of Mexico–U.S. relations (Fernandez 1977). In the past this phenomenon was attributed to the pernicious effects of the Mexican Revolution, which presumably led exiles to abandon the country and at the same time forced dispossessed peasants to search for occupational alternatives by crossing the border.

More recently it has also been noted that the increase of Mexican migration to its northern neighbor coincided with the consolidation of the United States as an economic and political power on a world scale and with a need—particularly in the Southwest—for cheap labor to be employed in booming agricultural activities (Bustamante this volume; Fernandez 1977). It may be said that there has existed a measure of complementarity between the failure of the Mexican state to implement viable agrarian reform (a failure that in turn has generated increasing numbers of displaced agricultural workers) and the need of U.S. capital for abundant supplies of unskilled labor.

Put in a somewhat different way, there is little doubt that Mexican migrants attempt to cross the border—either legally or illegally—responding to expectations, motives, and calculations induced by personal experience and communications. But seen at a broader level and in an international context, their behavior can be said to be determined by the unequal relationship between Mexico and the United States.

In 1942 the Mexican Labor Program (commonly known as Bracero Program) was constituted by official bilateral agreement in order to regulate the transfer of Mexican agricultural workers to the United States. This program operated intermittently until December 31, 1964. During the same period undocumented Mexican migration to the United States grew at an alarming rate (Comercio Exterior 1978). According to government sources, it was precisely as a result of the termination of the Mexican Labor Program and of the high levels of unemployment that ensued in the border zone—40 to 50 percent— that a new effort under the rubric of the Border Industrialization Program was instituted in 1965. Its expressed objective was to generate the infrastructural and juridical conditions that would enable increased foreign investment in the area and, consequently, occupational opportunities for unemployed or underemployed Mexicans.

The Border Industrialization Program spurred an impressive proliferation of export manufacturing plants or *maquiladoras*[1] (mostly of the electric/electronic and textile/garment type). These plants operate as subsidiaries of multinational corporations under sections 806.30 and 807 of the U.S. customs code. *Maquiladoras* along the Mexican border may be seen as evidence of the growing contemporary tendency of international capital to invest in areas of the world where an abundant supply of cheap and docile, unskilled or semi-iskilled, labor is readily available. This movement represents an innovative trend that in Mexico, as well as in other parts of the world, has resulted in the incorporation of considerable numbers of women into the manufacturing industrial sector.

Thus, although international migration continues to provide labor for certain sectors of economic activity within the United States (for example agriculture in the U.S. Southwest), other economic interests rely upon the possibility of transporting the centers of production themselves to locations where costs can be reduced, productivity can be enhanced, and labor conflict can be brought to a minimum (as in the case of border *maquiladoras*). The most striking, although vastly neglected feature of this development, is its gender-specific nature. Although the majority of undocumented aliens working the fields of the U.S. Southwest continue to be male, 85 percent of those working in the export manufacturing plants along the Mexican border are female.

As may be seen, the Border Industrialization Program has effected a transfer of capital from the United States to the Mexican-American border by encouraging the operation of *maquiladoras*, which function as subsidiaries of multinational corporations. At a different level and

*209*

in a complementary fashion, the same process has accelerated the transfer of labor from the interior of Mexico to its northern frontier. Mexican border municipalities constitute the most rapidly growing region in the country after Mexico City. Luis Uniquel (1974) has indicated that population increases along the border have been fostered by intense migration rather than by internal growth. The proximity of the United States has weighed heavily in this process. In 1970, 15.3 percent of the total population in Mexico (48.2 million) had been born in areas other than those in which they resided. But the percentage of migrants in border cities was 29.3, almost twice the equivalent proportion for the country as a whole (Uniquel 1974).

Migration to the border zone is also related to the expansion of the service sector and to rising unemployment and marginality. Border cities where the service sector predominates have had the highest rate of population growth (5.3 percent in the decade of 1960 to 1970) in comparison to the average rate for the nation (which was 3.04 percent). Not surprisingly, the Mexican border shows considerable demographic concentration: 75 percent of those living in the borderland cluster in seven cities, and 50 percent live in Ciudad Juárez, Tijuana and Mexicali alone. These three cities have been the most important target of the Border Industrialization Program. The figures made available by the Mexican government (Secretaria del Patrimonio y Fomento Industrial, July 1982) show that of a total of 576 *maquiladoras* in Mexico, 290 (i.e., 56 percent) are located in Ciudad Juárez, Tijuana and Mexicali.[2] At the same time, indications are that migration, population growth, unemployment, and underemployment have intensified in these cities during the last decade, that is, during the same period that the *maquiladora* program has expanded.

What matters most for the purposes of the present discussion is to underscore the special dimension that the *maquiladora* industry has added to the complex picture of migration from the interior of Mexico to its northern border. Contrary to their alleged intent, *maquiladoras* have failed to generate employment opportunities for those left idle by the termination of the Bracero Program, that is, male agricultural workers. Nor have they provided employment opportunities for rural women. In Ciudad Juárez, for example, only 8 percent of migrant women working at *maquiladoras* come from a rural environment. While it is true that seventy percent of the total *maquiladora* work force in that city are migrants, the majority have urban or semiurban, not rural, backgrounds. Moreover, although *maquiladoras* generated more than eighty thousand jobs between

1960 and 1970 (Bustamante 1967a), in the same period, unemployment among the economically active in the area increased by 85 percent, that is, from 2.4 to 4.17 percent. It is known that the highest levels of unemployment are found among unskilled or semiskilled males and among migrants of both sexes coming from a rural to an urban setting (Barrera Bassols 1976).

The participation of women in border manufacturing acivities of the kind described earlier may be better understood by taking into consideration both gender and class deteminants. Class and gender define, to a large extent, the kinds of occupational opportunities available to different sectors of the working population, besides informing their distinct political and ideological practices. As stated in the introductory paragraphs of this essay, there is a logic underlying the division of labor by gender. This logic has been most evident when studying the interaction between unsalaried domestic activities and renumerated labor (Larguía and Dumoulin 1975), but it also has importance in the analysis of the particular positions of men and women in the waged work force (see, for example, Chaney *et al.* 1976). This is the same as saying that there are reasons rooted in historical and structural conditions why men or women predominate in certain branches of economic activity. It also means that capitalist development and penetration tend to affect men and women in substantially different ways (see Nash 1975).

What is, then, the specific relationship between the industrialization of the Mexican-American border and migratory patterns both within Mexico and from Mexico to the United States? Three interrelated but different cases must be distinguished. First, there are Mexicans who migrate to the border with the expectation (realistic or not) of, once there, being able to cross into U.S. territory. Second, there are those who migrate to seek border jobs and/or follow relatives and/or spouses. Finally, there are those who migrate to the border to acquire skills that may later enable them to migrate to the United States. Studies to clarify these phenomena are, unfortunately, still few and tentative. However, based on the existing information and field work conducted by this author in Ciudad Juárez, Chihuahua, it is possible to identify certain trends:

1. The migration of young unaccompanied males (or males who may later on be joined by their families) may be partly explained by the expectation (linked to objective socioeconomic conditions) that the border region might provide access into U.S. territory (Cornelius 1976). It has now been established that, contrary to modernization theory interpretations, people frequently do not mi-

grate believing that cities will provide them with a chance to progress and move up in the social ladder, but simply because survival in their hometowns has been severely impaired.

Thus, the position of certain sectors of the Mexican population within the international division of labor should be considered. When doing so, it becomes apparent that the convergence of the overall situation of underdevelopment in Mexico (particularly in the agricultural sector) and the requirements of U.S. capital for cheap, manipulable labor accounts for this aspect of migration. Mexican border municipalities are characterized by the highest minimum wages earned in the whole country.[2] Although this could be considered a powerful attraction for migrants, it should not be forgotten that the cost of living is also higher in the borderland. Moreover, higher minimum wages appear to be obtainable in the United States. As important as the relative appeal of minimum wages is, the labor requirements of U.S. agribusiness and the overall lack of employment alternatives for young, productive Mexican males along the border predominate as causal agents in male migration.

Gender intervenes in this complex panorama by defining overlapping areas of movement accessible to either men or women. Because of their relative autonomy from the household and particularly from domestic and reproductive functions, it is less difficult for men to risk the hazards involved in becoming *undocumented* or *illegal* aliens. As Cornelius has observed, male undocumented aliens very often migrate alone and tend to remain for extended periods of time in the United States (unless the Immigration and Naturalization Service (INS) prevents this). Female undocumented aliens, by contrast, cross the border daily in both directions more frequently. The majority of these women find employment as domestics in nearby U.S. border towns and return to Mexico every night or, at least, every weekend in order to care for their children and visit with their families.

Extensive interviews with women and men formerly or presently engaged in undocumented migration suggest that the appeal of higher minimum wages in the United States is sharply attenuated by the anxiety produced by possible harassment or detainment on the part of *migra* officials. As one woman, now working at one of the local *maquiladoras* in Ciudad Juárez, put it to me: "All I wanted was a job. But they made me feel like a criminal. Crossing the border was simply not worth the price; it is better to stay here and struggle."

Although the nervousness induced by INS policies is shared by both males and females, their experience with respect to migration is somewhat different. Men, socialized to act as *providers*, are expected to send money and/or presents to their families in Mexico and to visit occasionally. Women, on the other hand, are expected to take full responsibility for the daily care of their children and their homes. If they must migrate, they must also return to the homestead more frequently. Thus, the widespread ideological notion that "man was made to work, and woman to care for the house" (*el hombre para el trabajo y la mujer para la casa*) impinges upon the likelihood of female movement. It also reflects and reinforces a reality in which crossing the border illegally is a more feasible option for men than for women. Such is the nature of precarious alternatives.

Therefore, it is not surprising that the majority of female undocumented aliens who migrate alone and stay for longer periods of time in the United States are single and have either one or no children. These women can travel to more distant regions searching for better jobs and, once in the United States, they tend to live with relatives or friends. Their marital status and diminished responsibility with respect to offspring bring their experience and scope of alternatives closer to that of their male counterparts.

By contrast, the experience of those women with more than one child who migrate to the United States may be graphically illustrated by the story of Manuela. In late September of 1978, Manuela was desperately trying to find a job as a production operator at the largest electronic *maquiladora* in Ciudad Juárez, RCA Componentes de Television. She was twenty-four years old, single, with six years of schooling and two children (ages six and four) to support. A year before, when her common-law husband had deserted her, Manuela looked for a job in Juárez with little success. During most of the six months that preceded our encounter, she had been crossing the border every few days to work as a maid in El Paso, Texas.

Although many Mexicans cross the border without legal documentation, Manuela was at that time in possession of an international crossing card which had been issued in her name by immigration authorities. According to INS policy, such a card allows entry of Mexican citizens into the United States for a period of seventy-two hours and in a distance restricted to 12.5 miles. Holders of international crossing cards are explicitly forbidden from seeking or keeping jobs. The purpose of the cards is solely to stimulate tourism and purchases in U.S. border towns. Nevertheless, thousands of Mexicans, especially women, use them to gain access into the secondary sector of the U.S. labor market. Although she was able to earn up to twenty dollars a day, Manuela's problems grew over time.

Her mother, a widow of forty-four, also an undocumented maid, was not available to care for the children while Manuela was at work. This forced the latter's return to Juárez more frequently than safety advised. After a few months of what seemed like an untenable situation, Manuela's illegal activities were reported to the INS by an anonymous caller. She was promptly sent back to Mexico and her international crossing card was confiscated.

In the weeks prior to our conversation, Manuela had been supporting herself and her children by taking in laundry, up to three dozen garments a day for less than three dollars. She was understandably eager to start work at an assembly plant. I asked what she would have to do in order to surmount the problem of day care for her youngsters. Her answer was very revealing. An unmarried cousin from her hometown had already agreed to come to live in Ciudad Juárez and help out with the children in exchange for a weekly allowance. But this arrangement depended upon the uncertain possibility of Manuela getting a job at a *maquiladora*.

2. As the previous story suggests, the migratory background of women working at *maquiladoras* is a worthwhile, albeit complicated, field of study and one about which little information is presently available. The following paragraphs are, therefore, exploratory. They are based on data obtained by this author from a random sample of 510 women working at fourteen randomly selected assembly plants in Ciudad Juárez between September 1978 and March 1979. The questionnaire used includes more than one hundred items focusing on migratory background, income distribution, and family composition. Although the following propositions are tentative, they provide a useful context for future analysis and discussion.

The growth of the *maquiladora* program along with Mexican border has been impressive. To take but one example: in 1969 there were 13 *maquiladoras* in Ciudad Juárez, Chihuahua, which employed less than 2,000 workers. At the end of 1982, the number of plants in that city had risen to 257 and that of workers to approximately 50,000. Sixty percent of the *maquiladoras* in Ciudad Juárez are of the electric/electronic type, and 30 percent are involved in textile/garment manufacturing. The rest assemble miscellaneous products that include plastic sprays, toys, and asbestos yarn.

Nearly 85 percent of *maquiladora* workers are women whose ages vary between seventeen and twenty-five. Seventy percent are single and on the average they contribute more than half of their weekly earnings to the support of their families. Seen within the larger Latin American context, they represent an anomaly. One out of every

214

three Latin American women who work for a wage does so as a domestic. Of the 19.4 percent of women in industry, only 0.7 percent participate in manufacturing activities (Gonzalez Salazar 1976). In Ciudad Juárez, largely as a result of the *maquiladora* program, half of the labor force is female.

The general impression in Ciudad Juárez is that *maquiladoras* employ mostly migrants. This is a partially valid judgement: 70 percent of women engaged in assembly work were born outside of Ciudad Juárez. The main foci of outward migration were found in three northern Mexican states. Seventy six percent of migrant female factory workers were born in the interior of Chihuahua. The area surrounding Santa Barbara, Parral, and San Francisco del Oro was heavily represented in my sample as "place of birth". Next in importance were the states of Coahuila, Durango and Zacatecas with only a few migrants having been born in states further south. As indicated earlier, the majority of these women were born in cities smaller than Ciudad Juárez rather than in the countryside. Only 8 percent come from a rural background, although the majority of *maquila* workers in Ciudad Juárez are migrants, their median length of residence in that city is fourteen years. This reflects the interesting fact that the majority of migrants now working in Ciudad Juárez' *maquiladoras* arrived in that city at a very early age and in the company of members of their family, mainly parents and siblings. An average of five relatives (and, in a few cases, friends) came to Ciudad Juárez for every migrating female *maquila* worker. Only a small proportion of migrants left their hometowns as young women, unaccompanied and with the explicit purpose of finding a job in Ciudad Juárez. An even smaller number are presently living alone or with friends as opposed to families of orientation or procreation. In sum, the migration of women now employed at Ciudad Juárez 's *maquiladoras* cannot be fully understood without careful analysis of household needs and movement. Moreover, due both to their place of birth and because of their long period of residence in Ciudad Juárez, these women can be considered as urban rather than rural population.

The lengthy period of residence of these women in Ciudad Juárez also has an important bearing on issues such as educational background and labor experience. The vast majority of *maquila* workers, both migrants and nonmigrants, have attended school in Ciudad Juárez. Although the average educational level for Mexican workers in general is of 3.8 years,[3] most *maquiladora* operators have completed at least six years of schooling. Many have attended commercial

*215*

academies where they have acquired typing and accounting skills. Some have studied to be nurses, secretaries, computer technicians, beauticians, or seamstresses. This is not to say that all *maquiladora* workers have a relatively high educational background. Employment criteria vary from plant to plant. Important differences also emerge when comparing workers in textile/garment and electric/electronic plants. In the former there is a sizeable proportion of women who have less than six years of schooling whereas in the latter (where policies are generally stricter regarding educational qualifications of potential employees), it is nearly impossible to find anyone who has not completed primary school.

In part because of their youth, most assembly operators have limited work experience prior to their employment in the *maquiladora* sector. Particularly in the electric/electronic branch where the median age of workers is twenty-one years, the majority (about 60 percent) have not held jobs prior to their employment in the plant where they were interviewed. By contrast in the apparel manufacturing branch, where the median age of workers is twenty-six, only 30 percent of those interviewed had not had other types of jobs.

Among those who had worked for a wage before their employment at both kinds of *maquiladoras*, two distinct experiences were identified. The first group (about 40 percent) was formed by women who had worked in the service sector as clerks, cashiers, salespersons, beauticians, office auxiliaries, or secretaries. The second group was composed of those whose only prior experience was as domestics either in Ciudad Juárez or in El Paso. Among the members of the latter subgroup almost all had been undocumented aliens.

Although there is some overlap in the two kinds of labor experience outlined above, the predominance of one over the other is very likely related to variations in class background and household composition. It was found, for example, that although the average number of members per household for Ciudad Juárez in general is of 5.3, the equivalent figure for *maquiladora* workers' households is of 7. There is little doubt that the size of these households, large even by local standards, precipitates the entrance of young women into the wage labor force. Many find jobs as maids. In the meantime they try to acquire the qualifications necessary to become assembly workers (mainly more years of schooling) and wait for their chance to get a job at a *maquiladora*. For these women, work at a factory represents a step up in the occupational ladder: the possibility of obtaining higher, and regular incomes as well as the benefits granted by Mexican law to stable workers.

But for the large number of women who were clerical workers before becoming *maquila* operators, the situation is somewhat different. Seen from a broad perspective, their experience represents a curious transfer of labor from the so-called white-collar sector to blue-collar employment. This contradicts what has been regarded as the normal trend in occupational mobility according to modernization theory.

The explanation for this phenomenon may be found in the particular structure of the Ciudad Juárez labor market. As indicated in the initial section of this essay, the service (also known as *tertiary*) sector predominates along the Mexican border. However, the majority of jobs found in it lack stability, adequate earnings, and benefits, even in those slots endowed with more prestige than factory work. Most receptionists, salespersons, and secretaries in Ciudad Juárez earn less than *maquila* workers. The more prestigious and better paid occupations are only accessible to those who are highly trained and/or speak English. Thus, to a certain extent, service sector jobs available to most women are interchangeable with wage domestic work. The consensus is that *maquiladora* work offers the best employment alternative in Ciudad Juárez. This a striking revelation when noting that assembly operators earn an average of fifty-eight cents per hour in U.S. currency and work forty-eight hours a week.

If the majority of the women who work at Ciudad Juárez' *maquiladoras* were doing so primarily as *individuals*, that is, to fulfill personal needs or to supplement family income, it is probable that they would not opt for proletarian employment. The reality, however, is that these women enter the labor market as members of households for whose subsistence their wages are fundamental. In part this is so because of the size and age composition of the domestic unit. In part it is because of the scarcity of decorous employment alternatives for men in their families.

The importance of this last observation can be appreciated if one notes that the majority of men belonging to the same households to which female assembly operators in Juárez belong are either unemployed or underemployed. In order of importance, the occupations of these men were found to be unskilled construction worker, petty clerk, general unskilled worker, and street vendor. The convergence between labor market conditions and familial needs precipitates the flow of women as suppliers of labor for *maquiladoras*. As a result women have become the main providers of stable and regular income (however small this may be) for their families. Indeed, one out of three women working in the textile/garment manufacturing

217

branch provide the only means of support for their families. The abundance of women in search of jobs presupposes and is made possible by the fact that men are unable to gain access to stable employment. In a country where, for better or for worse, women aspire and are encouraged to become mothers and/or housewives, female factory employment does not necessarily indicate an expansion of alternatives for women.

3. A consideration of the limited alternatives of employment for males belonging to the same households of *maquila* workers brings us full circle to the subject of migration. The initial findings of my research suggest that it is precisely for those who cross the border illegally most frequently, that is, Mexican males of a productive age, that *maquiladoras* have had the least impact as sources of jobs. Thus, it is not surprising to find that more than half of the women interviewed in my sample reported having one or more male illegal aliens among their immediate relatives. The majority of these are brothers and fathers of *maquila* workers. Among married women and former common-law wives who work at *maquiladoras*, there are many who have been deserted (either temporarily or permanently) by husbands eager to begin a new life in the United States. In Ciudad Juárez there is a widespread tendency to condemn the irresponsible behavior of these men. However, when the objective realities of their lives are taken into account, it becomes apparent that many males who leave their families are prompted by their failure to meet the economic demands of wife and children. Luisa's plight is a case in point.

Luisa married Martín when she was nineteen and he twenty-two. At that time Martín was working as a mechanic in a car repair workshop. At age twenty-three, Luisa was expecting her second child. "Things went well for us at first, but then the workshop was shut down and Martín lost his job. He looked around for work but couldn't find anything. Then he started hanging out in bad company and drinking heavily. Finally he left us. He crossed the border as a wetback more than a year ago, and we haven't heard from him since. I believe he is in California. Maybe he's married to another woman. Men can't be trusted; that's the reason I'm working at the *maquiladora*." Luisa is now, at age twenty-four, working as a mainline operator in an apparel plant and her chances to achieve a more prosperous future are slim.

As Luisa's case suggests, single women who support their children through *maquila* work do so either because their male companions are unable to meet the economic needs of the family or because

*218*

they have been deserted. The absence of a male provider is a crucial factor that forces the entrance of women with children into the work force. Almost one-third of the women who work in the textile/garment manufacturing industry are heads of households and sole providers of income for their offspring.

These statements are central for an understanding of the effects of the Border Industrialization Program upon the living and working conditions of the laboring class. They clarify the relationship between women as a particular kind of labor reserve (see Safa 1978) and the occupational opportunities available to males. According to *maquiladora* managers and promoters, women are hired because of their putative higher levels of skill and performance; because of the quality of their handwork; because of their willingness to comply with monotonous, repetitive and highly exhausting work assignments; and because of their docility which discourages organizing efforts by union leaders. Men, on the other hand, are invariably described as being more restless and rebellious than woman; less patient; more willing to unionize; and, perhaps most importantly, less resigned to tolerate rigorous work paces and inadequate working conditions for a low wage.

Rather than being the result of inherent feminine or masculine psychological and physical determinants, these traits are explained by the economic and political position of men and women vis-à-vis international capitalism. The incorporation of women with acute economic needs into the *maquiladora* industry represents, in objective terms, the use of the most vulnerable sector of the population to achieve greater productivity and larger profits. The employment of men to perform similar operations would imply higher wages, better working conditions, and more flexible work schedules, all of which would increase labor costs and reduce capitalist gains. Furthermore, the use of female labor under the conditions described earlier diminishes the bargaining capacity of the working class as a whole. In the same vein, the employment of young women *who were not part of the work force* before the appearance of the Border Industrialization Program does not support the allegation that *maquiladoras* expand occupational alternatives along the Mexican border. It is in part because of this that unemployment rates continue to rise at the same time that the number of jobs opened by *maquiladoras* increases.

Another paradoxical feature of the *maquiladora* program should be mentioned. During the period that this type of industry has expanded, the age and composition of its work force has varied only slightly. This reflects the puzzling discovery that the majority of female workes tend to leave their jobs after a relatively short time. Permanence in a *maquila* job averages only three years. There exists a tendency within the *maquiladora* sector not to encourage the permanence of women in assembly operations over a long period of time. Women are often either laid off or persuaded to leave work voluntarily. In many cases, they are not hired permanently but on a temporary basis. The nature of the work performed at the plants is another contributing factor. Highly monotonous, repetitive operations; accelerated work rhythms; and lack of promotions and inadequate working conditions combine to prevent long term employment. In sum, it is not in the interest of the *maquiladora* industry to maintain a stable and permanently employed work force especially in an environment where assembly operators may be easily replaced. A recent study (University of Texas, El Paso 1977) calculates that there are at least three women with similar needs and skills for every *maquila* operator in Ciudad Juárez.

Other reasons given by women themselves for leaving their jobs are marriage, unwed womens' intention to have a child, and the desire of those who are married to give better attention to children and home. In both cases women, almost without exception, opt for this course of action to respond to the pressures of their male counterparts who urge them to leave their jobs in order to give full time to their homes, that is, to fulfill what is considered their "normal" or "proper" role. Such women rarely stay in a job long enough to acquire seniority benefits. It is in this sense that one of the functions of the domestic unit vis-à-vis industry may be better appreciated. At certain stages of its development, the domestic unit tends to produce and put into circulation young factory workers, that is, *daughters* who after a few years of work in one or several factories tend to be reabsorbed by newly formed homes as wives, while a new wave of younger women take their place along the assembly lines. But because of the inability of males to meet the economic needs of their newly formed households, many of these women have to reenter the labor force after becoming mothers. Their age and offspring at this point in their lives are handicaps in a highly discriminating labor market in which single childless women are preferred for *maquiladora* work. It is among these women who have previous factory work experience but who are unable to get new jobs in that sector that a large number of undocumented workers is found. Beatriz, a thirty-year-old-single mother who has worked in a *maquiladora* for seven years told me: If you are alone and have children to support, there is no future for you in Ciudad Juárez. That is why I am trying to go to the United States. It is not me I am thinking of; it is my children's future that worries me.

As may be seen from the information included in this essay, the impact of the *maquiladora* industry in deterring illegal migration to the United States is far from obvious. Not only because they do not provide jobs for the majority of males who need them, but also because of their somewhat temporary nature, *maquiladoras* are probably insufficient as a tool for retaining laborers in Mexico. Mexican government officials have recently stated that the *maquiladora* industry is an integral part of Mexico's development strategy. This is an ironic proposition in the context outlined above.

To conclude, it has been the objective of this essay to explore the crucial connections among gender, class, family sructure, and occupational alternatives for both men and women along the U.S.-Mexican border in the context of its recent industrialization. Only by taking into account these issues does the study of migration acquire its full significance. Migration is not a fortuitous phenomenon, nor is it the effect of multiple wills directed towards the same objective. Rather, migratory flows are the consequence of specified structural, economic, political, and ideologgical conditions that affect social classes in a differential manner.

## Notes

Revised version of a paper presented at the Annual Meeting of the American Sociological Association, San Francisco, September 1978.

1. Article 321 of the Mexican Customs Code defines a *maquiladora* (also known as *twin plant, in bond plant, offshore production plant* or *runaway plant*) as an industrial enterprise which: (1) with temporarily imported machinery, whatever the manufacturing costs, exports its total production or, (2) with a permanent industrial plant originally installed to supply the domestic market, now directs part or all of its production for exportation, and the direct manufacturing cost of its product at the time of exportation does not reach 40 percent (Bustamante 1976a:8)

2. Different wage levels prevail in different parts of the country. The highest minimum wages are to be found in the urban industrial areas (such as Mexico City, Monterey and Guadalajara) and along the U.S.-Mexico border.

3. This figure was offered by Lic. Jorge Bayer (Unidad Coordinadora para el Empleo, Capacitacion y Adiestramiento, Mexican Government) during an address at the Regional Convention of *Maquiladora* Associations (Ciudad Juárez, Chihuahua, February 9, 1979).

## References

Arizpe, Lourdes. 1977. "Women in the Informal Labor Sector: The Case of Mexico City." *Signs* 3, no. 1 (autumn): 25–37.

Barrera Bassols, Jacinto. 1976. "Maquiladoras y migración." In *Aspectos sociales de la migración municipal,* ed. Margarita Nolasco. Mexico: Instituto Nacional de Antropología e Historia.

Bustamante, Jorge A. 1975. "Espaldas mojadas: Materia prima para la expansión del capital Norteamericano." Centro de Estudios Sociológicos. Mexico, D.F.: El Colegio de México.

————. 1976. "*Maquiladoras*: A New Face of International Capitalism on Mexico's Northern Frontier." Revised version of a paper presented at the 6th National Meeting of the Latin American Studies Association, Atlanta, Georgia.

————. 1976b. "Structural and Ideological Conditions of Undocumented Mexican Immigration to the United States." In *Current Issues in Social Policy.* New York: Praeger.

Castells, Manuel. 1975. "Immigrant Workers and Class Struggle" *Politics and Society* Volume 5, no. 1, p. 353–66.

Chaney, E. 1973. Old and New Feminists: The Case of Peru and Chile *Journal of Marriage and the Family,* vol. 5, 1973, p. 81–95.

*Comercio Exterior.* 1978. "Las maquiladoras en el contexto económico de México" 28 (August).

Fernandez, Raul. 1977. *The United States—Mexico Border: A Politico-Economic Profile.* Notre Dame: University of Notre Dame Press.

Gonzalez Salazar, Gloria. 1976. "Participation of Women in the Mexican Labor Force." In *Sex and Class in Latin America,* eds. June Nash and Helen I. Safa. New York: Praeger.

Jelin, Elizabeth. 1977. "Migration and Labor Force Participation of Latin American Women: The Domestic Servants in the Cities." Signs 3, no. 1 (autumn): 129–141.

Jenkins, J. Craig. 1976. "The Demand for Alien Labor: Labor Scarcity or Social Control?" Paper presented at the Annual Meeting of the American Sociological Association, New York.

Larguia, Isabel and Dumoulin, John. 1975. "Aspects of the Condition of Women's Labor." *NACLA's Latin America and Empire Report IX* 6 (September): 4–13.

Leeds, Anthony. 1976. "Women and Migration: A Reductionist Approach." *Migration Quarterly.* Winter Issue.

Marshall, F. Ray. 1978. "Economic Factors Influencing the International Migration of Workers." In *Views Across the Border: The United States and Mexico.* ed. Stanley Ross. Albuquerque, New Mexico: University of New Mexico Press.

Nash, June. 1975. *Certain Aspects of the Integration of Women in the Development Process: A Point of View.* Conference Background Paper. World Conference of the International Women's Year. New York: United Nations.

Nash, June and Safa, Helen, eds. 1976. *Sex and Class in Latin America.* New York: Praeger.

Oliveira, Orlandina de. 1976. *Absorción de mano de obra a la estructura ocupacional de la Ciudad de México.* Mexico D.F.: El Colegio de México.

Palloix, Christian. 1975. "The Internationalization of Capital and the Circuit of Social Capital." In *International Firms and Modern Imperialism*, ed. H. Radice. New York: Penguin Books.

Petras, Elizabeth McLean. 1979. "Towards a Theory of International Migration: The New Division of Labor." In *The New Migration: Implications for the U.S. and the International Community*. New Brunswick, N.J.: Transaction Books

Portes, Alejandro. 1979. "Labor Market Segmentation and Migration." Paper presented for discussion at the Program on Comparative Studies of International Migration and Ethnicity. Duke University, Durham, North Carolina.

Ross, Stanley R. 1978. *Views Across the Border: The United States and Mexico*. Alburquerque: University of New Mexico Press.

Safa, Helen I. 1975. "Introduction" In *Migration and Development: Implications for Ethnic Identity and Political Conflict*, eds. Helen I. Safa and Brian M. Du Toit. The Hague: Mouton.

———. 1976. "A Comparison of Female Blue Collar Workers in Brazil and the United States." Unpublished paper. New Brunswick, N.J. Rutgers University.

———. 1977. "A Study of Women Garment Workers in New York and Mexico." Unpublished manuscript. New Brunswick, N.J. Rutgers University.

———. 1978. "Women, Production and Reproduction in Industrial Capitalism: A Comparison of Brazilian and U.S. Factory Workers." Unpublished Manuscript. New Brunswick, N.J., Rutgers University.

Sunkel, Oswaldo. 1973. "Transnational Capitalism and National Disintegration in Latin America." *Social and Economic Studies* 22, no. 1, pp. 132–171.

Tilly, Louise. 1978. *Women, Work and the Family*. New York: Monthly Review Press.

Uniquel, Luis et al. 1974. *El desarrollo urbano en México*. Mexico, D.F.: El Colegio de México.

University of Texas, El Paso. 1974. *The Ciudad Juárez Plan for Comprehensive Socioeconomic Development: A Model for Northern Mexico Border Cities*.

Villalpando, M. Victor et al. 1977. *A Study of the Socio-Economic Impact of Illegal Aliens on the County of San Diego*. San Diego California: Human Resources Agency.

Wallerstein, Immanuel. 1975. *The Modern World System*. New York: Academic Press.

CHAPTER 10

# Maquiladoras: *A New Face of International Capitalism on Mexico's Northern Frontier*

Jorge A. Bustamante

## The Binational Region of the United States-Mexico Border

A salient characteristic of the United States–Mexico border's history has been its permeability. People, goods, and values have gone through the border without much resistance.[1] This permeability has resulted in a contant process of social interaction between the people of the two countries. This social interaction has reflected the contrasts and conflicts between the two nations. Nevertheless, relations of interdependence have developed greatly with the growth of binational border communities.

The U.S.–Mexico binational border region is far from being homogeneous along the more than two thousand miles from the Pacific Ocean to the Gulf of Mexico. However, both sides share certain social and economic phenomena, the dynamics of which extend beyond the borderline as a result of processes of interaction between the two peoples. Not withstanding the differences between the two countries' economies and cultures, problems of unemployment, immigration, municipal services, overpopulation, and crime pervade both sides.[2]

## Population

The Mexican border region is not typical of the living conditions in Mexico, much the same as the U.S. border region is not typical of the whole country (each region tending to resemble the area right across the border). As is shown in Table 10–1, Mexican border municipalities constitute the most rapidly growing region in the country after Mexico City. Trends of population growth have been particularly impressive in the last five decades as can be seen in Table 10–2.

Some negative implications of this population growth in the Mexican border municipalities have been pointed out by Luis Uniquel, who suggests that these increases are disadvantageous in as much as they have responded to external rather than internal factors.[3] That is, rather than being a part of the overall national development, like in Mexico City, Guadalajara, or Monterrey, the growth in border municipalities is in response to their proximity to the United States. A comparative overview of the population of the U.S–Mexico border cities shows that in spite of important population increases in the U.S. border cities reported in the last three censuses, Mexican border municipalities show a far more rapid increase than their U.S. counterparts. One of the effects of this contrast is that all Mexican border municipalities except Reynosa are among the most *tertiarized* (where service activities are predominant) cities in Mexico.[4] The figures on the Economically Active Population (EAP) shown in Table 10–3 indicate the increasing predominance of the service sector in the Mexican border municipalities compared to the rest of the country. At the same time, the border cities where the service sector predominates had the highest rate of population growth (5.25 percent) in the decade 1960–1970 in comparison to the average rate for the nation, which was 3.04 percent.[5]

In industrialized countries, the phenomenon of tertiarization has corresponded to the economic development of the city. In the Mexican border municipalities however, this is hardly the case. Uniquel and his collaborators suggest, rather, that it indicates increasing unemployment and marginality.[6]

On the other side of the border, deviance from the typical tends to go in the opposite direction. The population in the U.S. border region is, with the exception of California, more economically deprived than the rest of the country. This, in particular is the case with the population of Mexican descent that lives in the border region. Along the U.S. border east of El Paso, the population of

*225*

*Table 10-1.* Mexico: Population of Border States and Largest Border Municipalities, 1950, 1960, and 1970

| | 1950 | | 1960 | | 1970 | | Rates of growth | |
|---|---|---|---|---|---|---|---|---|
| | Number | Percentages | Number | Percentages | Number | Percentages | 1950–1960 | 1960–1970 |
| 1. Mexican Republic | 25,792,017 | | 34,923,129 | | 48,313,438 | | 3.1 | 3.3 |
| 2. Border States | 3,762,963 | | 5,541,100 | | 7,912,930 | | 4.0 | 3.6 |
| 3. Border Municipalities | 849,135 | 100.0 | 1,508,187 | 100.0 | 2,274,085 | 100.0 | 5.9 | 4.2 |
| Tijuana | 65,364 | 7.7 | 165,690 | 11.0 | 340,583 | 15.0 | 9.8 | 7.4 |
| Mexicali | 124,362 | 14.6 | 281,333 | 18.7 | 396,314 | 17.4 | 8.4 | 3.4 |
| Ensenada | 31,077 | 3.7 | 64,934 | 4.3 | 115,423 | 5.1 | 7.6 | 5.9 |
| Ciudad Juárez | 131,308 | 15.5 | 276,995 | 18.4 | 424,135 | 18.7 | 11.1 | 4.4 |
| Nuevo Laredo | 59,496 | 7.0 | 96,043 | 6.4 | 151,253 | 6.7 | 4.9 | 4.6 |
| Reynosa | 69,428 | 8.2 | 134,869 | 8.9 | 150,786 | 6.6 | 6.9 | 1.1 |
| Matamoros | 128,347 | 15.1 | 143,043 | 9.5 | 186,146 | 8.2 | 1.1 | 2.7 |
| San Luis, R.C. | 13,593 | 1.6 | 42,134 | 2.8 | 63,604 | 2.8 | 12.0 | 4.2 |
| Nogales | 26,016 | 3.1 | 39,812 | 2.6 | 53,494 | 2.3 | 4.4 | 3.0 |
| Piedras Negras | 31,665 | 3.7 | 48,408 | 3.2 | 46,698 | 2.0 | 4.3 | −0.4 |
| Others | 168,479 | 19.8 | 214,926 | 14.2 | 345,639 | 15.2 | 2.4 | 4.9 |

*Source:* Secretaría de Industria y Comercio, Dirección General de Estadística, Government of Mexico.

*Table 10–2.* Mexico: Population of Border Municipalities' Urban Areas

| | 1930 | 1940 | 1950 | 1960 | 1970 |
|---|---|---|---|---|---|
| Mexicali | 14,842 | 18,775 | 65,749 | 179,539 | 263,498 |
| Tijuana | 8,384 | 16,486 | 59,952 | 152,473 | 277,306 |
| Ensenada | 3,042 | 4,616 | 18,150 | 42,561 | 77,687 |
| Piedras Negras | 15,878 | 15,663 | 27,581 | 44,992 | 41,033 |
| Ciudad Juárez | 39,659 | 48,881 | 122,566 | 262,119 | 407,370 |
| Nogales | 14,061 | 13,866 | 24,478 | 37,657 | 52,108 |
| San Luis Río Colorado | 910 | 558 | 4,079 | 28,545 | 49,990 |
| Nuevo Laredo | 21,636 | 28,872 | 57,668 | 92,627 | 148,867 |
| Matamoros | 9,733 | 15,699 | 45,846 | 92,327 | 137,749 |
| Reynosa | 4,840 | 9,412 | 34,087 | 74,140 | 137,383 |

*Source:* For the years 1930–1960, see *Dinámica de la población de México,* Centro de Estudios Económicos y Demográficos, El Colegio de México. For 1970 see *Censo general de población,* 1970 (Mexico: Dirección General de Estadística).

Table 10-3. Mexico: Economically Active Population (EAP) of Border Municipalities, 1950, 1960 and 1970

| | 1950 | | 1960 | | 1970 | |
|---|---|---|---|---|---|---|
| *Republic of Mexico* | 8,272,093 | 100.0 | 11,332,016 | 100.0 | 12,994,392 | 100.0 |
| Agriculture | 4,832,901 | 58.4 | 6,144,930 | 54.2 | 5,131,668 | 39.5 |
| Industry | 1,319,163 | 16.0 | 2,147,963 | 19.0 | 2,978,649 | 22.9 |
| Services | 1,774,093 | 21.4 | 2,957,332 | 26.1 | 4,134,405 | 31.8 |
| Not specified | 354,966 | 4.2 | 81,791 | 0.7 | 749,670 | 5.8 |
| *Border Municipalities* | 275,693 | 100.0 | 480,638 | 100.0 | 586,951 | 100.0 |
| Agriculture | 125,524 | 45.5 | 189,410 | 39.4 | 131,662 | 22.2 |
| Industry | 45,749 | 16.6 | 96,902 | 20.2 | 143,632 | 24.5 |
| Services | 86,883 | 31.5 | 180,839 | 37.6 | 270,461 | 46.1 |
| Not specified | 17,537 | 6.4 | 13,487 | 2.8 | 41,196 | 7.0 |
| *Ensenada* | 10,782 | 100.0 | 21,999 | 100.0 | 30,163 | 100.0 |
| Agriculture | 4,741 | 44.0 | 7,489 | 34.0 | 7,514 | 24.9 |
| Industry | 2,198 | 20.4 | 4,821 | 22.0 | 6,943 | 23.1 |
| Services | 3,256 | 30.2 | 8,320 | 37.8 | 14,056 | 46.6 |
| Not specified | 587 | 5.4 | 1,369 | 6.2 | 1,650 | 5.4 |
| *Tijuana* | 21,596 | 100.0 | 32,832 | 100.0 | 89,013 | 100.0 |
| Agriculture | 4,753 | 22.0 | 10,367 | 19.6 | 8,176 | 9.2 |
| Industry | 4,667 | 21.6 | 13,207 | 25.0 | 26,232 | 29.5 |
| Services | 10,175 | 47.1 | 24,937 | 47.2 | 46,688 | 52.4 |
| Not specified | 2,001 | 9.3 | 4,321 | 8.2 | 7,917 | 8.9 |
| *Mexicali* | 41,392 | 100.0 | 90,378 | 100.0 | 98,738 | 100.0 |
| Agriculture | 24,353 | 58.8 | 47,623 | 52.7 | 32,820 | 33.2 |
| Industry | 4,720 | 11.4 | 13,132 | 14.5 | 20,498 | 20.7 |
| Services | 10,456 | 25.3 | 25,411 | 29.2 | 38,701 | 39.3 |
| Not specified | 1,863 | 4.5 | 3,212 | 3.6 | 6,719 | 6.8 |

| | | | | | | |
|---|---|---|---|---|---|---|
| *San Luis Rio Colorado* | 4,869 | 100.0 | 13,030 | 100.0 | 16,422 | 100.0 |
| Agriculture | 3,548 | 72.9 | 7,745 | 59.5 | 6,775 | 41.3 |
| Industry | 304 | 6.2 | 1,502 | 11.5 | 2,212 | 13.3 |
| Services | 787 | 16.2 | 3,755 | 28.8 | 6,310 | 38.4 |
| Not specified | 230 | 4.7 | 28 | 0.2 | 1,125 | 6.8 |
| *Nogales* | 8,359 | 100.0 | 13,265 | 100.0 | 14,229 | 100.0 |
| Agriculture | 1,327 | 15.9 | 2,391 | 18.0 | 1,017 | 7.2 |
| Industry | 1,845 | 22.1 | 3,249 | 24.5 | 3,779 | 26.6 |
| Services | 4,718 | 56.4 | 7,610 | 57.4 | 8,315 | 58.5 |
| Not specified | 468 | 5.6 | 15 | 0.1 | 1,017 | 7.7 |
| *Juárez* | 41,977 | 100.0 | 85,989 | 100.0 | 108,078 | 100.0 |
| Agriculture | 7,231 | 17.2 | 16,518 | 19.2 | 9,342 | 8.6 |
| Industry | 11,547 | 27.5 | 24,621 | 28.6 | 29,085 | 26.9 |
| Services | 18,952 | 45.2 | 42,689 | 49.7 | 60,827 | 56.3 |
| Not specified | 4,247 | 10.1 | 2,161 | 2.3 | 8,823 | 8.2 |
| *Piedras Negras* | 9,751 | 100.0 | 13,381 | 100.0 | 12,130 | 100.0 |
| Agriculture | 3,717 | 38.1 | 4,293 | 32.1 | 1,957 | 16.1 |
| Industry | 1,948 | 20.0 | 3,290 | 24.6 | 3,711 | 30.6 |
| Services | 3,373 | 34.6 | 4,588 | 34.3 | 5,508 | 45.4 |
| Not specified | 713 | 7.3 | 1,210 | 9.0 | 954 | 7.9 |
| *Nuevo Laredo* | 19,178 | 100.0 | 30,576 | 100.0 | 39,463 | 100.0 |
| Agriculture | 3,537 | 18.4 | 7,090 | 23.2 | 4,397 | 11.1 |
| Industry | 3,953 | 20.6 | 6,862 | 22.4 | 10,789 | 27.3 |
| Services | 9,931 | 51.8 | 16,426 | 53.7 | 21,271 | 54.0 |
| Not specified | 1,757 | 9.2 | 198 | 0.7 | 3,006 | 7.6 |

Table 10-3. (Cont.)

| | 1950 | | 1960 | | 1970 | |
|---|---|---|---|---|---|---|
| *Reynosa* | 23,596 | 100.0 | 44,925 | 100.0 | 38,032 | 100.0 |
| Agriculture | 13,133 | 55.6 | 23,096 | 51.4 | 6,122 | 16.1 |
| Industry | 3,237 | 13.7 | 8,303 | 18.5 | 12,783 | 33.6 |
| Services | 5,769 | 24.5 | 13,455 | 30.0 | 16,511 | 43.4 |
| Not specified | 1,457 | 6.2 | 71 | 0.1 | 2,616 | 6.9 |
| *Matamoros* | 41,487 | 100.0 | 45,882 | 100.0 | 49,467 | 100.0 |
| Agriculture | 26,023 | 62.7 | 22,456 | 48.9 | 13,311 | 26.9 |
| Industry | 4,020 | 9.7 | 6,353 | 16.0 | 10,378 | 21.0 |
| Services | 9,166 | 22.1 | 15,969 | 34.9 | 22,851 | 46.2 |
| Not specified | 2,278 | 5.5 | 105 | 0.2 | 2,927 | 5.9 |
| *Others* | 52,706 | 100.0 | 68,381 | 100.0 | 91,227 | 100.0 |
| Agriculture | 33,161 | 62.9 | 40,342 | 59.0 | 40,231 | 44.1 |
| Industry | 7,309 | 13.9 | 10,562 | 15.4 | 17,221 | 18.9 |
| Services | 10,300 | 19.5 | 16,679 | 24.4 | 29,423 | 32.2 |
| Not specified | 1,936 | 3.7 | 798 | 1.2 | 4,352 | 4.8 |

*Source:* Mexican Censuses

Mexican descent has the highest unemployment rates (15 to 20 percent).[7] This region also has the highest percentage of people living below what has been established as the poverty level. The incidence of poverty in most of the Texas border counties is highest among the population of Mexican descent, (between 40 and 60 percent), whereas among the Anglo population in the same area the incidence is between 10 and 20 percent.[9]

Conditions of economic deprivation become particularly interesting when attention is focused on the strip of land that lies within two hundred miles to the north of the U.S.–Mexico border. According to the most recent data (April 1975) from the U.S. Census Bureau there are approximately 6,455,000 persons of Mexican origin in the United States; 86.3 percent of them live in the Southwest (California, Arizona, Colorado, New Mexico and Texas). In some of these states, particularly in Texas, the concentration of the population of Mexican descent is even greater. Seventy-five and a half percent of the total population of Mexican descent in the state of Texas live in an area within two hundred miles of the border[10] (the population of Mexican descent in Texas in 1973 was 2,190,000 or 19 percent of the Texas total.[11] The percentage of the U.S. population of Mexican descent that lives in that area within two hundred miles of the border is 55.2 percent of the total population.[12]

The Mexican border zone also demonstrates a great demographic concentration. Seventy-five percent of the population of the border region is concentrated in the cities of Tijuana, Mexicali, Ensenada, Ciudad Juárez, Matamoros, Nuevo Laredo, and Reynosa. Within these cities, the population in 1970 of Ciudad Juárez, Tijuana and Mexicali represented 50 percent of the total border population.

The migration rate to the border cities is very high. Of a total population for the country of 48.2 million in 1970, 15.3 percent came from different places than those in which they resided in January of the year in which the census was taken (1970). The total proportion of migrants for the border cities was 29.3 percent in that year. For the city of Tijuana, the proportion of migrants was 47 percent, Mexicali, 34 percent, Juárez, 23 percent, Ensenada, 35.7 percent, Matamoros, 21 percent, Nuevo Laredo, 33.2 percent and Reynosa, 30.9 percent.[13]

Regarding the economically active population, it is important to point out that in 1970 farm work occupied barely 29.2 percent in contrast with 39.4 percent for the whole nation. From 1950 to 1970, the economically active agricultural population in the Mexican border states was reduced from 50 percent to 29.2 percent. In contrast, the service activities of the economically active population grew from 15.2 percent in 1950 to 27.4 percent in 1970 (see Table 10–3).

In the context of this paradox, where the higher standards of living for one side represent the lowest for the other, we find a phenomenon of recent years: the *maquiladora*. This is the Spanish term for what in English has been called *off-shore assembly plant, in bond processing operation, twin plant,* and *runaway plant*. This phenomenon has been characterized as the most outstanding offspring of the Mexican Government Border Industrialization Program (BIP). The following section will focus on the issue of the *maquiladoras*.

## The Historical Context

In 1961 the Mexican Government initiated the first comprehensive attempt to improve the border region as a whole, with the Programa Nacional Fronterizo (PRONAF). At that time there was intensive bracero activity.[14] The U.S. established quota for 1960 was already declining (315,846) in comparison to previous years.[15] However, that figure signified approximately 6 percent of the economically active population engaged in agriculture in Mexico in 1960.[16] Mexican border municipalities, particularly Tijuana, Mexicali, and Ciudad Juárez, recorded an all-time high in immigration from the interior of Mexico. It was also a time of overcrowding and corruption in Mexican border towns and, concomitantly, manifestations of prejudice and discrimination against Mexicans and residents of Mexican descent on the U.S. side of the border.[17] Thus, the Mexican government decided to take action on the border situation.

The main objectives of PRONAF were
1. Gaining the market of the Mexican border by substituting Mexican products for U.S. ones to the limits of Mexican production.
2. Developing sales of Mexican handcrafts.
3. Transforming the physiognomy and the image of Mexican ports of entry.

From 1961 to 1970 PRONAF invested 40 million dollars in the construction of a new facade for the most important Mexican ports of entry. This part of the program was relatively successful in its correlation to an increase of U.S. tourism which went from almost 40 million dollars in 1960 to 56 million in 1970.[18] As for objectives one and two, PRONAF was nearly a complete failure if one considers the money invested by the government, the subsidies, the incentives given to Mexican entrepreneurs and the trends of the trade balance for the U.S.–Mexico border operations both in the free-trade zone (*perímetro libre*), which includes the borders of Baja California and part of Sonora and the rest of the U.S.–Mexico border.

Far from accomplishing its objectives, PRONAF failed in gaining the Mexican border market for Mexican products. According to a report of the Commission for the Two Californias, presided over by the governors of California and Baja California, the number of Mexicans buying on the U.S. side of the border in 1966–67 increased by 6 percent in contrast to an increase of 3 to 4 percent in previous years. It is difficult to establish whether or not this increase was due to the new jobs in *maquiladoras* in that period and consequently to an increasing purchasing power of the people from Mexican border towns. Should this be the case, it could be argued that the effects of the government's new policy seen in the Border Industrialization Program was working against the objective listed first in the old policy represented by PRONAF. It should be pointed out, however, that features for an employment policy were more prominent in the creation of BIP than in PRONAF. Certainly, the situation of unemployment facing Mexican border municipalities was considerably different at the time of the initiation of each program.

The year 1964 marks the end of the bracero program after twenty years of varied operation. Approximately two hundred thousand braceros were suddenly faced with unemployment; yet more landless peasants continued to migrate to the border. According to some sources, unemployment ran as high as 40 percent to 50 percent in Mexican border towns in 1965.[19] Since 1963 a new Mexican farm workers organization, Central Campesina Independiente (CCI), had begun organizing returning braceros in the border states. On the other hand, social unrest had been highlighted by some guerrilla operations that left several dead in the state of Chihuahua. President Díaz Ordaz failed in his attempts to revive the bracero program in 1965, candidly offering the U.S. cheap Mexican labor. It was fairly evident that something had to be done to neutralize the effect of increasing unemployment on the border. Then the Border Industrialization Program was announced by the Minister of Industry and Commerce, Octaviano Campos Salas, who later told the *Wall Street Journal* (May 25, 1976), "Our idea is to offer free enterprise an alternative to Hong Kong, Japan and Puerto Rico." The Border Industrialization Program was created in 1965 with the following objectives: (1) the creation of new jobs, larger incomes, and better standards of living for workers in the border area, (2) the improve-

Table 10-4. Mexico: Value of Imports via Free-Trade Zone at the Northern Border (in thousand of pesos)

| | 1950 | | 1960 | | 1970 | |
|---|---|---|---|---|---|---|
| | Value in pesos | Imports via free-trade zone as percentage of total imports | Value in pesos | Imports via free-trade zone as percentage of total imports | Value in pesos | Imports via free-trade zone as percentage of total imports |
| Total for Mexico | 405,278 | 8.4 | 1,368,769 | 9.2 | 4,176,115 | 13.5 |
| Total for border municipalities | 385,446 | 13.3 | 1,328,958 | 16.3 | 4,004,810 | 26.1 |
| Ensenada | 172 | 47.4 | 56,964 | 97.0 | 245,628 | 99.1 |
| Tijuana | 147,978 | 98.5 | 617,520 | 96.5 | 1,486,775 | 98.8 |
| Mexicali | 193,414 | 94.5 | 542,813 | 84.1 | 1,622,376 | 90.7 |
| San Luis Rio Colorado | 7,750 | 99.9 | 27,677 | 80.7 | 40,771 | 91.2 |
| Nogales | – | | 38,427 | 10.4 | 295,033 | 49.9 |
| Ciudad Juárez | – | | – | | – | |
| Piedras Negras | – | | – | | – | |
| Nuevo Laredo | – | | – | | – | |
| Reynosa | – | | – | | – | |
| Matamoros | – | | – | | – | |
| Other border municipalities | 36,132 | 39.3 | 45,557 | 22.1 | 314,227 | 29.5 |
| Other free-trade zones | 19,832 | | 39,811 | | 171,305 | |

Source: Government of Mexico. Dirección General de Estadística. Anuarios Estadísticos

Table 10-5. Mexico: Exports and Imports via Northern Border Customs Offices, 1950, 1960, 1970 (in thousands of pesos)

| | 1950 | | 1960 | | 1970 | |
|---|---|---|---|---|---|---|
| | Imports | Exports | Imports | Exports | Imports | Exports |
| Total | 4,808,647 | 4,337,405 | 14,830,598 | 7,895,848 | 30,760,140 | 14,702,765 |
| Frontera Norte | 2,900,091 | 2,740,001 | 8,129,329 | 3,112,280 | 15,318,875 | 7,524,803 |
| Ensenada | 363 | 29 | 58,756 | 324,245 | 247,681 | 308,026 |
| Tijuana | 150,278 | 166,912 | 639,793 | 79,441 | 1,505,109 | 539,013 |
| Mexicali | 204,566 | 347,059 | 645,575 | 211,903 | 1,798,637 | 653,653 |
| San Luis R.C. | 7,760 | 1,741 | 34,290 | 3,127 | 44,716 | 16,088 |
| Nogales | 132,156 | 110,703 | 370,919 | 443,492 | 590,894 | 1,339,300 |
| Ciudad Juárez | 260,107 | 261,193 | 454,673 | 315,482 | 614,231 | 842,912 |
| Piedras Negras | 133,206 | 103,388 | 261,261 | 105,542 | 733,380 | 447,054 |
| Nuevo Laredo | 1,666,835 | 628,976 | 4,802,306 | 569,526 | 7,604,183 | 1,950,677 |
| Reynosa | 77,274 | 28,064 | 290,367 | 153,714 | 182,376 | 300,770 |
| Matamoros | 175,696 | 566,106 | 365,104 | 755,353 | 1,362,643 | 813,413 |
| Mexican fisheries office in San Diego and San Pedro Cal. | – | 305,059 | – | – | – | – |
| Others | 91,850 | 220,771 | 206,265 | 150,455 | 634,930 | 313,897 |
| Acapulco | 57,544 | 22,720 | 264,056 | 60,165 | 485,263 | 22,652 |
| Coatzacoalcos | 13,524 | 102,935 | 218,326 | 647,087 | 484,147 | 822,682 |
| Mexico, D.F. (Customs office for importation) | 581,026 | 82,376 | 2,141,527 | 224,093 | 2,131,395 | 686,133 |
| Posta de Mexico | 53,149 | 10,201 | 69,226 | 39,089 | | |
| Tampico | 183,243 | 449,561 | 738,869 | 1,002,177 | 1,744,278 | 1,272,270 |
| Veracruz | 928,495 | 361,514 | 2,992,558 | 1,292,847 | 6,805,038 | 1,913,156 |
| Others | 91,575 | 568,097 | 276,707 | 1,518,110 | 3,791,144 | 2,461,069 |

Source: Dirección General de Estadística. Anuarios Estadísticos. Government of Mexico.

ment of labor skills levels through the acquisition of technology and training supplied by assembly plants, and, (3) the reduction of Mexico's trade deficit by increasing the consumption of Mexican components in *maquiladora* operations.[20]

Some U.S. economists expressed their views on the BIP as an idea, "simple in its approach":

> It intends to merge American capital and technical knowledge with relatively inexpensive Mexican labor. As such, attempts are made to lure American enterprise to the region by contending that labor costs are significantly lower. This program is analogous in many ways to other ongoing U.S. operations in Korea, Denmark, and Hong Kong.[21]

However, the U.S. Ambassador to Mexico during 1965, Fulton Freeman, found more complex implications in the BIP:

> Mexico's Border Industrialization Program offers a notable opportunity for providing Mexicans with jobs and reducing the incentive for them to enter the United States as wetbacks. . . . The braceros returned to Mexico with some concept of our type of democracy, with a knowledge of modern agricultural methods, and with positive friendly feelings about the United States. Just the reverse is true of the wetback; they inevitably develop enmities towards the system that outlaws them and deports them.[22]

*Maquiladora* operations entail basically the assembly of consumer products destined for exportation and exempt from export duties in Mexico. The attractiveness of *maquiladoras* for American industry derives basically from wage differentials. Minimum wages along most of the Mexican border region ranged from $3.52 to $5.52 per day in the late 1960s, whereas in the United States an average factory worker's wage plus fringe benefits, was then $25.12.[23] The proximity of the assembly plants in Mexico to the U.S. parent firm is also an important attraction.

The *maquiladora* system was helped by two important items in the U.S. Tariff Code, 806.30 and 807.00. Both items provide reduced tariff duties on imports which contain U.S. produced components and which have been assembled or processed abroad. The tariff duty, therefore, is applied merely to the value added in foreign operations. According to most reports[24] both 807.00 and 806.30 started with Canadian operation by U.S. firms. Actually, the story began with a Customs Court decision in 1954 that overruled a previous one in 1949 stipulating that work done abroad to assemble or combine an

American article with a foreign product added value or improved the condition of the American article.[25] The 1954 Court decision held basically that foreign labor in installing American marine engines in foreign built motorboats did not add value to the U.S. engines.[26] Therefore, the marine engines could be reimported duty free to the United States. The practice of importing duty-free products that had some finishing labor input abroad was started and finally became coded under item 807.00.

The use of these two items of the U.S. Tariff Code resulted in the relocation of some industrial plants on the Mexican Border. U.S. organized labor, however, expressed a growing disatisfaction in the following terms:

> Item 807 is one small loophole in the tax structure for the advantage of U.S. based multi-national companies. It operates as a lubricant for the growing export of U.S. capital, which is a major factor in America's balance of payments difficulties. It provides financial encouragement of foreign production, by U.S. firms, of goods that are sold in the U.S. market. It is a factor in the deterioration of both the volume and composition of the U.S. trade balance. . . . It encourages the mushrooming expansion of foreign subsidiary operations of the U.S. . . . with the displacement of U.S. production and employment.[27]

The point of view of U.S. industry on the same issue has been expressed as follows:

> It is economically sound that some countries concentrate on capital-intensive industries while others do the labor intensive tasks. . . . They (items 806.30 and 807) improve the competitive position of American industry by allowing a more efficient combination of factors of production through joint utilization of American capital and advanced skills with lesser skilled labor from less developed countries. . . . They preserve jobs in the United States in those very industries that otherwise would be even harder hit by foreign competition, thus allowing a more gradual adjustment to future trade patterns by industries that could not otherwise survive. . . . They do not add to the balance of payments difficulties of the United States because they generate two-way trade with friendly countries. . . . Mexico spends all the dollars it earns from us and even more for goods and services from the United States. We would gain nothing by preventing them from earning more and trading more with us.[28]

The differences between the views of organized labor and industry resulted in a request from the U.S. president (August 18, 1969), for an investigation of the economic factors affecting the use of items

806.30 and 807.00. These hearings were held in May 1970. By that time, imports from Mexico under these tariff items had increased 4,700 percent since 1966 (see tables 10–6 and 10–7).

As a result of these hearings the conclusion was reached that it was not in the best interest of the U.S. economy to discontinue items 806.30 and 807.00. The basic factor related to these decisions is best illustrated by a statement of a representative of the electronics industry who said, "In each case, the labor differentials are so great that the components would continue to be made abroad and imported into the U.S. even if item 807.00 were repealed."[29]

It should be pointed out that the same criteria apply for the actual conditions of operation of the *maquiladora* industry on the Mexican border, except for a change of economic conditions derived from the downswing trends of the U.S. economy in 1974 and 1975. The effects of these trends on the *maquiladora* industry have resulted in a revival of the *maquiladora* issue in Mexico. The socioeconomic context in which the issue is evolving will be seen in the following section.

*Table 10–6.* United States Imports from Mexico under Tariff Item 806.30, 1966–1974 (*Millions of dollars*)

| Year | Total value (1) | Duty-free value (2) | Dutiable value (3) | (3) as percentage of (1) (4) | Yearly increase (1) (5) | (3) (6) |
|---|---|---|---|---|---|---|
| 1966 | 0.1 | ª | ª | | | |
| 1967 | 0.2 | 0.1 | 0.1 | 50.0 | 100.0 | – |
| 1968 | 1.2 | 0.8 | 0.4 | 33.3 | 500.0 | 300.0 |
| 1969 | 4.8 | 2.1 | 2.7 | 56.3 | 300.0 | 575.0 |
| 1970 | 7.4 | 4.7 | 2.6 | 35.1 | 54.2 | –3.7 |
| 1971 | 9.8 | 6.2 | 3.6 | 36.7 | 32.4 | 38.5 |
| 1972 | 30.6 | 21.5 | 9.1 | 29.7 | 212.2 | 152.8 |
| 1973 | 59.2 | 39.1 | 20.1 | 34.0 | 93.5 | 120.9 |
| 1974 | 114.7 | 81.5 | 33.2 | 28.9 | 93.8 | 65.2 |
| Increase in percentage | | | | | | |
| 1969 over 1966 | 4,700.0 | – | – | | | |
| 1974 over 1970 | 1,450.0 | 1,634.0 | 1,176.9 | | | |
| 1974 over 1966 | 114,600.0 | – | – | | | |

*Source:* U.S. Tariff Commission, *Economic Factors Affecting the Use of Items 807.00 and 806.30 of the Tariff Schedules of the United States,* T.C. Publication 339 (Washington, D.C., September 1970), and unpublished data provided by U.S. Bureau of the Census.
ª Less than 50,000 dollars.

*Table 10-7.* United States Imports from Mexico and Central America under Tariff
Item 807.00, 1966-74 *(Millions of dollars)*

| Country and year | Total value (1) | Duty-free value (2) | Dutiable value (3) | (3) as per-cent of (1) (4) | Yearly increase | |
|---|---|---|---|---|---|---|
| | | | | | (1) (5) | (3) (6) |
| **Mexico** | | | | | | |
| 1966 | 7.0 | 3.6 | 3.4 | 48.6 | – | – |
| 1967 | 19.3 | 12.3 | 7.0 | 36.3 | 175.7 | 105.9 |
| 1968 | 73.4 | 49.7 | 23.7 | 32.3 | 280.3 | 238.6 |
| 1969 | 145.2 | 95.8 | 49.4 | 34.0 | 97.8 | 108.4 |
| 1970 | 211.4 | 133.6 | 77.9 | 36.8 | 45.6 | 57.7 |
| 1971 | 260.6 | 159.8 | 100.8 | 38.7 | 23.3 | 29.4 |
| 1972 | 395.8 | 234.8 | 161.0 | 40.7 | 51.9 | 59.7 |
| 1973 | 592.0 | 325.7 | 266.3 | 45.0 | 49.6 | 65.4 |
| 1974 | 918.2 | 487.4 | 430.8 | 46.9 | 55.1 | 61.8 |
| Increase in percent | | | | | | |
| 1969 over 1966 | 1,974.3 | 2,561.1 | 1,352.9 | | | |
| 1974 over 1970 | 334.3 | 264.8 | 453.0 | | | |
| 1974 over 1966 | 13,017.1 | 13,438.9 | 12,570.6 | | | |
| **Costa Rica** | | | | | | |
| 1966 | – | – | – | | | |
| 1967 | 0.1 | ʰ | ʰ | – | – | – |
| 1968 | 0.3 | 0.2 | 0.1 | 33.3 | 200.0 | |
| 1969 | 1.8 | 1.2 | 0.6 | 33.3 | 500.0 | 500.0 |
| 1970ᵃ | 2.1 | 1.5 | 0.7 | 33.3 | 16.7 | 16.7 |
| 1971 | 3.6 | 2.6 | 1.0 | 27.8 | 71.4 | 42.9 |
| 1972ᵃ | 5.7 | 3.9 | 1.7 | 29.8 | 58.3 | 70.0 |
| 1973 | 7.0 | 4.4 | 2.6 | 37.1 | 22.8 | 52.9 |
| 1974 | 11.3 | 8.0 | 3.3 | 29.2 | 61.4 | 26.9 |
| Increase in percent | | | | | | |
| 1974 over 1970 | 438.1 | 433.3 | 371.4 | | | |
| **El Salvador** | | | | | | |
| 1969 | 0.2 | 0.1 | 0.1 | 50.0 | – | – |
| 1970 | 0.4 | 0.3 | 0.1 | 25.0 | 100.0 | 0.0 |
| 1971 | 0.5 | 0.4 | 0.1 | 20.0 | 25.0 | 0.0 |
| 1972 | 1.6 | 1.2 | 0.4 | 25.0 | 220.0 | 300.0 |
| 1973ᵃ | 4.7 | 3.5 | 1.1 | 23.4 | 193.8 | 175.0 |
| 1974 | 20.4 | 12.5 | 7.9 | 38.7 | 334.0 | 618.2 |
| Increase in percent | | | | | | |
| 1974 over 1970 | 5,000.0 | 4,066.7 | 7,800.0 | | | |
| **Guatemala** | | | | | | |
| 1969 | ʰ | ʰ | ʰ | – | – | – |
| 1970 | ʰ | ʰ | ʰ | – | – | – |
| 1971 | ʰ | ʰ | ʰ | – | – | – |
| 1972 | ʰ | ʰ | ʰ | – | – | – |
| 1973 | 0.2 | 0.1 | 0.1 | 50.0 | – | – |
| 1974 | 0.8 | 0.4 | 0.4 | 50.0 | 300.0 | 300.0 |
| Increase in percent | | | | | | |
| 1974 over 1970 | – | – | – | | | |

*Table 10-7* (Cont.)

| Country and year | Total Value (1) | Duty-free value (2) | Dutiable value (3) | (3) as per-cent of (1) (4) | Yearly increase (1) (5) | Yearly increase (3) (6) |
|---|---|---|---|---|---|---|
| **Honduras** | | | | | | |
| 1966 | ᵇ | ᵇ | ᵇ | – | – | – |
| 1967 | 0.1 | 0.1 | ᵇ | | | |
| 1968 | 0.4 | 0.3 | 0.1 | 25.0 | 300.0 | |
| 1969 | 0.8 | 0.6 | 0.2 | 25.0 | 100.0 | 100.0 |
| 1970 | 0.8 | 0.6 | 0.2 | 25.0 | 0.0 | 0.0 |
| 1971 | 1.0 | 0.7 | 0.3 | 30.0 | 25.0 | 50.0 |
| 1972 | 1.3 | 1.0 | 0.3 | 23.1 | 38.0 | 0.0 |
| 1973ᵃ | 1.6 | 1.0 | 0.5 | 31.3 | 23.1 | 66.7 |
| 1974 | 1.9 | 1.4 | 0.5 | 26.3 | 18.8 | 0.0 |
| **Increase in percent** | | | | | | |
| 1969 over 1966 | – | – | – | | | |
| 1974 over 1970 | 137.5 | 133.3 | 150.0 | | | |
| 1974 over 1966 | – | – | – | | | |
| **Nicaragua** | | | | | | |
| 1969 | – | – | – | | | |
| 1970 | 0.1 | 0.1 | ᵇ | – | – | – |
| 1971 | 0.1 | ᵇ | ᵇ | – | 0.0 | – |
| 1972 | 0.4 | 0.3 | 0.1 | 25.0 | 300.0 | – |
| 1973 | 0.6 | 0.4 | 0.2 | 33.3 | 50.0 | 100.0 |
| 1974 | 1.2 | 0.9 | 0.3 | 25.0 | 100.0 | 50.0 |
| **Increase in percent** | | | | | | |
| 1974 over 1970 | 1,100.0 | 800.0 | – | | | |
| **Belize** | | | | | | |
| 1966 | 0.3 | 0.1 | 0.2 | 66.7 | – | – |
| 1967ᵃ | 0.4 | 0.2 | 0.1 | 25.0 | 33.3 | –50.0 |
| 1968 | 0.6 | 0.4 | 0.2 | 33.3 | 50.0 | 100.0 |
| 1969 | 0.8 | 0.5 | 0.3 | 37.5 | 33.3 | 50.0 |
| 1970 | 0.5 | 0.4 | 0.1 | 20.0 | –37.5 | –66.7 |
| 1971 | 1.4 | 1.0 | 0.4 | 28.6 | 180.0 | 300.0 |
| 1972 | 1.9 | 1.4 | 0.6 | 31.6 | 35.7 | 50.0 |
| 1973 | 2.1 | 1.5 | 0.7 | 33.3 | 10.5 | 16.7 |
| 1974 | 2.7 | 2.0 | 0.7 | 25.9 | 28.6 | 0.0 |
| **Increase in percent** | | | | | | |
| 1969 over 1966 | 166.7 | 400.0 | 50.0 | | | |
| 1974 over 1970 | 440.0 | 400.0 | 600.0 | | | |
| 1974 over 1966 | 800.0 | 1,900.0 | 250.0 | | | |

*Source:* United States Tariff Commission, *Economic Factors in Affecting the Use of Items 807.00 and 806.30 of the Tariff Schedules of the United States.* T. C. Publication 339 (Washington, D.C., September 1970), and unpublished data provided by United States Bureau of this Census.

ᵃ (2) and (3) do not add to total (1) because of rounding.

ᵇ Less than $50,000.

## The Maquiladora Issue in Mexico

Article 321 of the Mexican Customs Code defines a *maquiladora* as an industrial enterprise which: (1) with temporarily imported machinery, whatever the manufacturing costs, exports its total production or, (2) with a permanent industrial plant originally meant to supply the domestic market, later on directs part or all of its production for exportation; and the direct manufacturing cost of its product at the time of exportation does not reach 40 percent (Regulation of October 31, 1972).

According to the original idea, the *maquiladoras* were to be established in the industrial parks administered by the Mexican Border Industrialization Program in 1965. From the beginning, the foreign investors who established the *maquiladoras* rented the land where they were installed and were prohibited by law from owning more than 49 percent of the capital stock of the enterprise. In March 1971 an executive decree was issued which in effect changed these conditions. It permitted: (1) that the capital stock of the enterprise could be 100 percent foreign owned and (2) that the foreign investors could obtain the right of possession over land destined for the establishment of *maquiladoras* for a period of thirty years, within the border fringe restricted by Article 27 of the Mexican Constitution by means of a trust relationship with a Mexican bank.

In December 1965 there were twelve *maquiladora* enterprises in the Mexican border area, which employed 3,087 workers. In 1971 the number of *maquiladoras* climbed to 209 and the number of employed workers increased to 29,000. By December 31, 1974, the number of *maquiladoras* in operation was 516; and the number of employees was 56,253 (data from the Chamber of Commerce of Mexico, *Newsletter* 2, no. 2 [February 1975]). The relevancy of these figures that demonstrate the growth of the *maquiladora* industry in the last nine years is deduced from two circumstances. First, approximately 90 percent of the total work force employed by the border *maquiladoras* is female, with an average age between sixteen and twenty-four. Second, At least 30 *maquiladora* enterprises have closed since October 1974, leaving some 20,000 workers unemployed.

The administrators of the *maquiladora* industries have maintained in recent conferences (Binational Conference of *Maquiladoras*, Chihuahua, Chihuahua, Mexico, March 7, 1975; seminar organized by the American Chamber of Commerce of Mexico, entitled: Labor Panorama for 1975, Mexico, D.F., April 22, 1975) that the closing of *maquiladoras* is due principally to two factors: (1) the economic

*241*

recession in the United States and (2) the Mexico's "loss of competitiveness" vis-à-vis other countries, due to salary increases and the creation of additional incentives in other countries that are not offered by ours. The reality is that there is a lack of objective information to determine whether the closing of the *maquiladoras* in recent months is caused solely by the economic recession in the United States or whether it is a strategy to pressure the Mexican government to negotiate better operating conditions.[30]

Whatever the case, the growth of the number of *maquiladoras* has drastically diminished and the threat exists that this will become an irreversible tendency. This situation suggests clearly the need to review the effects that to date the *maquiladoras* have produced upon the socioeconomic conditions of the Mexican northern border.

## Frame of Reference for an Evaluation

To evaluate the *maquiladora* industries program, it is first necessary to define the criteria needed for such appraisal. It is logical to search for these criteria in the Mexican government's motives and legislation regarding *maquiladoras*.

In the hearing that President Echeverría held with the industrialists of the northern border on March 21, 1974 in Los Pinos, Attorney Eliseo Mendoza Berrueto, the under secretary of commerce, indicated that the main objectives of the Mexican government in the promotion of the *maquiladora* industries were (1) gaining a transfer of technology through the training received by the workers of the *maquiladoras*, (2) increasing the number of jobs in the border area, and (3) improving the income of the border population. In drawing up these objectives, it was added that the *maquiladoras* should not be considered a sign of dependency (see Presidencia de la República, *El Gobierno Mexicano*, vol. 40, p. 94).

In April 1975, the secretaría de industria y commercio (SIC) published a monograph, *La Frontera Norte: Diagnóstico y Perspectivas* [The northern border: diagnosis and perspectives]. In this monograph the SIC reached the conclusion that *maquiladoras* are advantageous for Mexico because of the following reasons:

1. Employment is being promoted in areas with strong demographic pressure.
2. Income from foreign exchange is being increased, strengthening the balance of payments.

3. Industrial jobs are being generated that train personnel extracted in large measure from primary activities [e.g., farming].
4. The market for national products is being enlarged, as more income enters the area.
5. Commerce, banking, and services are being augmented, as well as tourism.
6. Prejudice regarding the quality of the Mexican labor force is vanishing.
7. More taxes are being collected at all levels as a result of the economic expansion.
8. Maquiladoras promote investment in spin-off activities in Mexico.

Notwithstanding the conclusive character of the eight points that summarize how the SIC considers *maquiladoras* advantageous for Mexico, these points can serve as a frame of reference in evaluating the industrial program and as a guide in the search of data with which to measure its success. With these criteria in mind we now review the affirmation contained in the first point of the summary of advantages that the SIC attributes to the *maquiladora* program.

The American Chamber of Commerce of Mexico affirms that on December 31, 1974 there were 516 *maquiladoras*, which employed 56,253 workers. It is important to point out the concentration of *maquiladoras* in five border cities: Tijuana, Mexicali, Ciudad Juárez, Nuevo Laredo, and Matamoros. It was calculated that on April 30, 1973, 82.9 percent of all jobs provided by the *maquiladoras* were concentrated in the five cities according to information from the Administration of Industries of the SIC. It is known that the population census does not permit a precise count of overt unemployment and that data supplied by the census underestimate unemployment. It is possible, however, to establish that unemployment is growing in the border municipalities. In 1960 it was observed that the proportion of unemployed among the economically active population (EAP) in the border municipalities was 2.4 percent, whereas in 1970 it was 4.17 percent (see table 10–3). Among the EAP of the border municipalities, the highest proportion of unemployed is found precisely in Tijuana, Mexicali and Ciudad Juárez, which contain 53.6 percent of the total unemployed.[31] Regarding the underemployed (that is, all those that only work part of the year and/or that receive an income lower than the minimum wage), we are confronted with border areas where 34.3 percent of the EAP in the industrial sector are underemployed (ibid.). These facts tell us that notwithstanding the jobs opened up by the *maquiladora* industries up to 1970, the unemployment and underemployment in the border cities is growing more rapidly than the national average.

This is, however, a question that requires deeper investigation. Is the attraction posed by the *maquiladoras* for migration to the border proportional to their real demand for labor? The census data leads us to believe not. In a different vein we could ask if this disproportion between migration and real demand for labor is an inevitable consequence of all industrial development processes? The history of migration to the large urban industrial centers indicates that this is the case during the initial periods of industrial expansion. However, in the case of the *maquiladora* industry the question should be whether the *maquiladoras* have the degree of permanency and stability that would generate economic development and absorb the labor force that the industry has attracted to the large industrial centers. In the March 1975 issue of the *Mexican American Review* published by the American Chamber of Commerce of Mexico, it was acknowledged that one of the characteristics of the *maquiladoras* is their great geographical mobility. In the same issue, Joseph B. Mackinnon, author of the article "Investment at the Border—the Maquiladoras," reported that in September 1975 a whole *maquiladora* plant disappeared in Ciudad Juárez during the national independence holidays. By their very nature and given their function in the industrial process, maquiladoras are extremely sensitive to fluctuations in the international labor market. This was demonstrated by the recent disappearance of the Magnavox and Packard-Bell plants. They simply moved their piecework operations from Mexico to other countries where wages were lower. These two companies alone left behind approximately five thousand unemployed.

Let us move now to the second point in the summary of "advantages" by the SIC: "Income from foreign exchange is being increased, strengthening the balance of payments."

The annual preliminary report of the Bank of Mexico for 1974, published in *Excelsior*, February 27, 1975, indicates that the balance of exchange from the exports of the maquiladoras was $278 million in 1973 or 5.8 percent of the total income in the current account of the balance of payments, and 443 million in 1974 or 7.1 percent of said income. Figures from American sources for 1974 indicate that the *maquiladoras* exported an added value of one billion dollars, which made up 28 percent of all the sales of manufactured products for export and 17 percent of all exports from Mexico. Although the figures from Mexican sources are approximately half of what the American sources indicate,[32] findings in Mexico suggest a considerable contribution of the *maquiladoras* to Mexico's balance of payments. These contributions don't take into account losses caused by the sale of tax-free imports (machinery and equipment) for *maquiladora* operations, in the interior of Mexico. The same appraisal would have to be made with respect to the occasional sales of products manufactured in the *maquiladora* plants for national consumption. It is not easy to determine the extent to which these practices take place.

In either case, the importation of duty-free machinery, supposedly, would not substantially modify the situation with respect to the contributions that the *maquiladora* industry makes to the Mexican balance of payments. The question comes to mind, then, of how the *maquiladora* contributions can be considered a factor in the strengthening of the Mexican balance of payments. It can be maintained that as long as the *maquiladoras* are characterized by the high mobility of their installations, their contributions to the balance of payments will be very unstable and certainly not enough to be counted among programs for independent development.

Regarding the third point of the summary of advantages as seen by the SIC, "Industrial jobs will be generated that train personnel extracted in large measure from the primary activities," it will be necessary to return to the census data on the dynamics of the economically active population in the border cities.

By natural growth and immigration, the population of the border cities has increased in the last three decades over the average population growth for the rest of the country. Between 1950 and 1960 the actual average rate of demographic growth of the border cities was of 6.3 percent (against 3.1 percent for the country as a whole). Between 1960 and 1970 it declined to 4.1 percent, probably because of the termination in 1964 of the Bracero Program, which was the main stimulation for border migration. Although all the border cities were affected by this decline, Tijuana maintained a growth rate of 7.5 percent and Ensenada 5.9 percent, whereas the national rate was 3.4 percent.

It can be argued that the migration to the border and the increase in the EAP originates in the primary sector. However, to state that the *maquiladoras* employ peasants and transform them into industrial workers is a great exaggeration. In any case, it is a question that has not been measured empirically. Given the dynamics of the EAP in the services area, it is probable that this area absorbs the major part of the population proceeding from primary activities that migrates to the border and a somewhat smaller proportion of the same population is absorbed by industrial activities. The promotional campaigns that originate in the Chambers of Commerce of border cities make it clear that the main attraction offered to the investors is an inexhaustible source of unskilled and semiskilled labor.

When evaluating the advantages of the training received in the *maquiladora* industry, the degree of specialization has to be taken into account; no matter how high the level of training obtained in the *maquiladora* industry, the degree of specialization required in most piecework operations raises serious doubts about the extent to which maquiladoras effectively train workers for other sectors of national industry.

The argument (contained in the fourth point of SIC's summary) that *maquiladoras* enlarge the market for Mexican products is very difficult to prove in light of the recent tendency of the coefficients of retention of foreign exchange, resulting from border transactions. These coefficients of retention measure the proportion of each dollar that enters the border region that is retained in the country. The coefficients are calculated by dividing the positive balance (difference between the entry and exit of foreign exchange) by the total income originating from border transactions.[33] According to SIC data, the retention in Mexico, of foreign exchange income from border transactions has been deteriorating steadily since 1968. From 1955 to 1970 the coefficient of retention has been reduced from 42.2 cents a dollar to 33.4 cents. This means that the persons that earn money in the United States are spending an increasingly large proportion of it in the United States. This does not indicate an enlargement of the market for Mexican products. On the contrary, it indicates that the increase in dollar income in the border region that the SIC attributes partially to the *maquiladoras* is favoring economic development on the U.S. side of the border. The *maquiladoras* have contributed to the increase in buying power of the Mexican on the border, but that power is being increasingly exercised in the purchase of American products in the United States. The growing orientation toward American products in the consumer patterns of the Mexican border population is easily understood, if one considers the isolation of the border economy from the rest of the country. The lack of integration between the Mexican border economy and the national economy is in turn related to internal shortages of products and limited production on the one hand, and the disproportionate competition of American products on the other.

"Commerce, banking, and services are being augmented as well as tourism" (point five of the summary earlier cited). The importance of each item warrants separate evaluation. It could be argued that the only route by which commerce is related to the *maquiladoras* is through the wages paid to labor. Expenditures for nationally produced imput are generally insignificant. Given the highly fragmented nature of piecework *maquiladoras* depend on imput from the United States. Benefits for Mexico such as the purchase of nationally produced imput are almost inexistent. *Maquiladoras* are only one component in a process of production that originates and ends in the United States. The basic relation between *maquiladoras* and the Mexican national interest comes as a result of the availability of cheap labor in Mexico.

Therefore, the relation between commercial activity and *maquiladoras* occurs through the wages paid to workers. The relevance of this point is underscored by our earlier consideration of the coefficients of retention of foreign exchange for border transactions as derived precisely from commercial activity. The Department of Industry and Commerce itself has recognized that since 1968 there has been a deterioration of the coefficients of retention in Mexico.[34] Contrary to SIC's allegations, maquiladora's role in promoting commercial activity is not clear or unambiguous.

It is probably true that there has been an increase of banking on the Mexican border due to the *maquiladoras*. The size of investment in *maquiladora* industries ($3,675,400,000) suggests that part of the management of that investment includes participation by Mexican border banks. Nevertheless, it is important to point out that the extent to which banking activity has increased as a result of *maquiladoras* has not been measured by Mexican agencies. Mention was made early in 1976 of an increase in the savings account deposits in border banks on the Mexican side. This has been attributed to the favorable interest rates offered by Mexican banks. That is to say, increase in banking activity certainly has occurred. How much of this increase is due to the *maquiladoras*? Facts that would permit verification of this point are not available.

When we ask ourselves what has been the effect of the *maquiladoras* on the dynamics of the service sector, we have to consider the relation between the increase of migration to the Mexican border and the changes in the occupational structure of border cities' economically active population (EAP). We know through SIC data that the proportion of the increase of the work force that finds employment in the border cities has diminished in the manufacturing sector, whereas, it has increased in those sectors that generate services. The same source makes it clear that *maquiladoras* have only employed

2.4 percent of the recent arrivals to border cities.[35] These facts support the hypothesis that *maquiladoras* operate as a magnet in the migration to the border cities, but that the population attracted to the border is not absorbed by the *maquiladoras*. Instead it is employed by the service sector or not employed at all. In determining whether the proportion of the increase of the EAP in the service sector is due to the *maquiladoras* or to the real or imaginary demand of labor by the American side, we are confronted again with a measurement problem and a lack of data. In any case the important question here is whether the increase of the absorption of employees by the service sector, in the context of the border economies of Mexico and the United States, is an indication of Mexican economic development or an indication of dependency.

The last part of the fifth point of the summary of advantages that according to the SIC the *maquiladora* program offers Mexico, is the increase in tourism. According to SIC figures, the annual average number of border visitors is growing, especially border Mexicans visiting the American border zone. The SIC reports that as of 1965 (the year that the *maquiladora* program was initiated), for each 100 American residents that visited our border cities, 145 Mexicans visited the U.S. border cities; in 1971 the proportion of visitors was 148 Mexicans for every 100 Americans. In that period the annual average growth rate of border visitors was 3.8 percent for the American visitors and 4.3 percent for the Mexican visitors.[36] This means that if the *maquiladoras* are exercising some effect on border tourism, this effect is favoring the American side. Again, we point out that the advantages referred to by the SIC as attributes of the *maquiladora* lack empirical substantiation.

The influx of tourists and their expenditures are manifested in different proportions at different points of the border. Nevertheless, the points of greatest traffic of border visitors are Tijuana and Ciudad Juárez with 53.6 percent of the total of American visitors. Although the average expenditure of the tourists in Tijuana increased between 1967 and 1970 by a rate of 16 percent, the amount of Mexican expenditures on the American side surpassed the American expenditures due to the disproportionate augmentation of the number of Mexicans spending their money on the U.S. side. Data compiled by the Mexican Department of Industry and Commerce, shows that this occurred because the number of Mexican tourists from Tijuana increased at a rate of 8.3 percent while the number of American visitors to Tijuana only grew 2.2 percent annually.[37] The same source suggests that the situation in Ciudad Juárez is even more critical. Here the Americans diminished their annual average expenditure after 1967 by 2.1 percent while the annual average expenditure in the United States by residents of Ciudad Juárez increased in the same period by 12.8 percent.[38] These figures call into question the SIC's appraisal of the indisputible advantages of the *maquiladoras*.

The sixth point says: "The prejudice regarding the quality of the Mexican labor force is vanishing." This statement assumes that there is a general negative prejudice regarding the quality of Mexican labor. Again, the SIC cites a phenomenon without saying who measured it or how it was measured, or on what basis the affirmation was made. Nevertheless, the mentioning of prejudices is useful because it directs our attention to the relationship between the *maquiladora* program and the Mexican labor force on both sides of the border.

Investors in *maquiladora* plants have fully recognized that, as much in Mexico as in other Latin American countries, Taiwan, and southeast Asia, the main reason for setting up a productive process outside the United States is to reduce production costs by paying very low wages. If there has been some prejudice regarding the quality of Mexican labor, this has not been strong enough to neutralize the advantage of the low wages in Mexico. In fact, the 1968 fall issue of the official publication of the Development Authority for Tucson's Expansion, entitled *Date Line* offered this headline: "INEXHAUSTIBLE LABOR SUPPLY 30 CENTS AN HOUR." As an explanation to a picture of the Mexican border customs station in Nogales, Sonora, the publication stated, "The Mexican Border Station at Nogales, Sonora, just seventy miles south of Tucson, Arizona marks the gateway to an inexhaustible 30 cents an hour labor supply." On page 3 appeared an article entitled: "U.S. Manufacturer says Mexican Labor is Outstanding." Dr. C. Lester Hogan, president of Fairchild Camera, is quoted in this article in reference to his experiences with the Motorola *maquiladora* plant in Nogales, Sonora. Among other things, Dr. Hogan says: "All our workers are of an extremely high caliber under any criteria". Then the writers say:

> Considering the history of Mexican excellence in manual craftsmanship, this is not surprising. The same hands which can carve an intricate design from wood, silver or leather can successfully assemble a shirt. . . . or any other product. More than one manufacturer has cut training schedules in half and halved them again because of the speed and skill of his Mexican employees. There's more to it than just innate ability. A condition of extremely high unemployment (9,000 currently available)

exists in the Sonoran border area. The resulting competition for jobs, combined with pride in workmanship and the desire to work hard to please management, add up to capable productive employees whose loyalties lie with the companies which hire them.

To judge from recent promotional publications such as the one circulated by the State National Bank of El Paso, Texas (winter 1974 issue), entitled "The Mexican Border Industrialization Program: Twin Plant Concept," the point of view quoted above in the letter by Mr. Hogan (at the time he wrote, he was secretary of the Mexican American Border Cities Association) has not varied substantially. Moreover, there is an important connection between the lure of skill and low wages. According to the State National Bank, the best incentive offered investors by the Mexican Border Industrialization Program is "an abundance of inexpensive labor." From this we may conclude that advantages listed under point six of the SIC summary (regarding prejudices against Mexican labor) are irrelevant.

The seventh point of the summary of the SIC attributes an increase of tax revenues at all levels to the *maquiladoras*, which alledgedly have caused the broadening of economic activities. It is very probable that to a certain extent the *maquiladoras* are increasing the amount of taxes collected. To partially prove the declaration of the SIC it would suffice to take into account the collection of income taxes that are deducted from the workers' pay checks. We do not have the necessary data that would allow us to establish the volume of the tax collections derived from *maquiladora* operations. The data on which the SIC based the seventh point are not provided. Nonetheless, it is questionable that the increase in tax collection that the SIC attributes to the *maquiladoras* has taken place on all levels, given the fiscal incentives and tax exemptions decreed by the federal government in favor of these types of industries. This does not mean that tax collections have not increased as a result of the expansion of *maquiladoras*. It means that an evaluation of the effects of these industries requires quantitative data regarding such collections. As of now, we know that in 1974 the *maquiladora* industries exported approximately 12,500 million pesos in value added to piecework products and that this amount represents approximately 17 percent of the total value of the exports. We know that the *maquiladoras* should have paid taxes to Mexico on the added value of their operations. We also know that, like all other industries in Mexico, they should have used a sum equivalent to 5 percent of the wages paid to their workers in order to affiliate them to the Instituto

Nacional para el Fomento de Viviendas para los Trabajadores— INFONAVIT (National Institute for the Promotion of Housing for Workers). An additional one percent should have been paid for education, and other sums for social security. On the other hand we know from the publication of the American Chamber of Commerce of Mexico, (Mexican American Review, vol. 2, No. 2 [February 1975] that representatives of the *maquiladoras* are negotiating with the federal government for the reduction or abolition of sales taxes. It is also known that the government of the state of Tamaulipas has interceded with the Mexican Institute of Social Security to have the debt of some *maquiladoras* located in that state pardoned. We do not have precise information on the success or failure of such negotiations: nevertheless, the fact that these negotiations have taken place raises questions that the federal government should answer in its evaluation of the *maquiladoras.*

The eighth and last point of the summary of advantages of the SIC states that the *maquiladoras* promote investment in spin-off activities in Mexico. If the SIC is referring to the bulk of government expenditures used to facilitate the growth of *maquiladoras* then it probably is correct in its assertion. It is unquestionable that the investment of the Mexican federal government in industrial parks in border cities, for example, has been very costly and has probably been promoted by the growth of the *maquiladora* industries. We cannot tell if the SIC is referring to private or public investment on the Mexican border as a consequence of the *maquiladora* operations, since unfortunately also in this eighth point no reference was made to facts or to the criteria that were used to reach the conclusion. Nevertheless, it is very likely that the investments made in Border Commercial Centers were caused by the need to stop the money drain flowing from *maquiladora* workers' expenditures on the U.S. side of the border. As of May 1970, Commercial Centers have been constructed in Tijuana, Mexicali, and San Luis Rio Colorado at a cost of 5.3 million dollars and two more are being constructed, one in Rio Grande and another in Ciudad Juárez, the latter at a cost of 9.4 million dollars.

### Female Labor in the Maquiladoras

At the beginning of this essay, we indicated an important reason for assessing the impact of the *maquiladoras* on the socioeconomic conditions of our country, that is the *maquiladoras* hire predomi-

*251*

nantly female labor. We know that the concept of the *maquiladoras*, as it was presented by the government of Mexico on May 2, 1971, in launching the Border Industrialization Program did not include the proposal that such predominance be given to female labor. This preponderance could have been predicted if the hiring practices of similar plants in other underdeveloped parts of the world had been examined. In the case of our border, it is a de facto situation, the unperceived effects of which have made indispensable a reconsideration of the governmental conception of *maquiladoras*.

The number of *maquiladoras* had increased by 288 percent from 1970 to 1974. By 1975 the number of employees reached 56,253, and the proportion of female labor approximately 90 percent. But with the recent closure of many *maquiladoras* caused by the U.S. recession, many workers (20,000) lost jobs. Under these circumstances we need a study of the effects of *maquiladoras* on the socioeconomic conditions of the women who have worked in them.

Without any claims towards broader generalization and only as a means to illustrate what may well be the effect of maquiladoras on female workers, we transcribe the following narrative of a woman interviewed by the author in Tijuana in March 1975.

I am from Zamora, Michoacán. I am twenty years old and I got to Tijuana in January of 1972. Even though I finished high school in Zamora, the best job that I could get there was as a maid. I think that if I had known how to dress up as I do now, I could probably have found a better job there. My cousin, who had come to Tijuana before me and had begun to work in a brassiere factory, got me excited about coming. I started to work in the factory where my cousin was without any problem. They hired me on a trial basis for a week, along with fifteen other girls; and the ten of us that worked the best and produced the most while we learned were given the job. Even the ones that weren't hired found work later in another factory. It was a good time for almost all the girls that arrived; if they were just a little smart, they could get a job easily. It started going real well for me. I had never earned as much as I was making here. I started buying myself new clothes and I learned how to dress well. You know, to "discover my charms," like the advertisement says. For the first time in my life I felt like a real woman. I dressed just like the richest woman in Zamora would have dressed. I had a hard time at first because I roomed with six other girls in a single room, but later I moved into a better place with two other girls. I started saving up money to appease my parents. I had come against their wishes. They didn't want me to come because my father had been here as a bracero and said that Tijuana was like Sodom, a city of sin. I was frightened when I came, and to a certain point kind of sad, thinking that maybe something would happen to me that would keep me from seeing my parents again. But, as the saying goes, sorrows go down easier with a piece of bread.

I started to get acquainted with the surrounding area and to visit San Diego and even Los Angeles. Nothing made me happier than to go into a shopping center and start looking at things and buying. I was very content in the factory because there was a lot of work. They'd give us a bonus for the pieces we produced above the quota and they'd let us work up to twelve and thirteen hours a day. One day they told us they were giving us a two week vacation, during which I decided to go to Zamora. It had been almost a year since I had left home. I was scared to death because I didn't know how my father would react. I had already reconciled with my mother through our correspondence and I had been sending her a monthly amount. As soon as my father saw me, he accused me of being a prostitute. He couldn't see how I could dress the way I did working at a decent job. When I was telling my father what I did with the four hundred dollars I averaged a month, my mother ruined everything by reproaching him for not earning as much money as I, even though he is a man. To make a long story short, since then things haven't been the same between my father and me. He lost faith in me and no longer considered me with affection. After I had come home, my whole manner of being seemed to him to be a lack of respect on my part. Even the fact that I dated the son of one of the rich families in Zamora seemed a shameful act to my father, just because he had worked as a servant for the same family when he was a boy. Anyway, when I got back to Tijuana, it seemed as if a curse had fallen over me. At work they gave me the story that I had signed my resignation with my last pay check. So I was fired along with everyone else that had gone on vacation at the same time as I. It took me about a month to find another job in a shirt factory. In the factory I had worked in before, all the foremen were gringos, but in this one there were one or two Mexicans. Unfortunately, I got a Mexican. It turned out that this guy was the manager of a section of the factory and he managed it as if it was his private territory. He insulted us; and if anyone protested, he'd fire them without giving explanations. This guy would charge the gringos our salaries by the hour, but paid us by the piece. He would cheat us with the figures and in general was a calamity. Anyway, I couldn't take it any longer so I quit that job. I took a third job and I was doing alright until I took on the payments for a color television and started taking English lessons, which were very expensive. Here, they also gave me the story about giving me a vacation. This time I did take notice and I told them I wouldn't sign where it said I would voluntarily resign from my job. They fired me anyway for raising such a stink. They even threatened to blacklist me so I wouldn't be able to work in Tijuana and they accused me of associating with some guys from a union who had the reputation of being Communists. I was doing alright on the fourth job too, until they started giving us less work; and since they paid us by the piece, I wasn't even making enough to pay my debts. It turned out, they fired more than half of us, that was around October, also with the same story about the vacations. This time I didn't say anything and signed my so-called voluntary resignation. Since then I haven't had a steady job; I work a few days here and there. To top it off, I got involved with a guy who said he was going to help us because he was from the CTM (Confederación de trabajadores Mexicanos, the largest workers union in the country) and that they were going to fight the factory. I had already been warned that the guy was a swindler; but I, the fool, thought that he would change with me. I got pregnant, and had to borrow money to get an abortion. I wouldn't have been able to do anything with a baby to care for. May God forgive me. I still don't have a job; I just wait to be called by the factory to work for a few days. I can't think of going back to Zamora. I just don't want to work as a maid anymore. Things are getting serious here for us. Some of the girls have gotten into prostitution in order to make some money. But they say that things will get better, and I hope its true.

More questions than certainties can indeed be drawn from this narrative. Some of these questions are: (1) what is the real impact of *maquiladoras* on unemployment in the Mexico border municipalities? (2) are the *maquiladoras* operating like a magnet for further immigration to the U.S.–Mexico border region?, (3) are they absorbing migrant workers?, (4) is there an impact of *maquiladoras* on the cultural values, sex roles, family structure, and ethnic identity of the labor force in the Mexican border municipalities?, (5) is there an impact on the unionization process of the workers on the Mexican border as a result of the *maquiladoras*, (6) are the *maquiladora* operations going to affect the legal status of Mexican workers in federal legislation?, (7) what is the real impact of *maquiladoras* on the economy of the U.S.–Mexico border?. Without implying an order of importance, these are some of the questions that remain to be answered by researchers, social planners, and policy makers on the increasingly growing issue of the Mexican border *maquiladoras*.

### Notes

1. The disruptive affects of *operation interception* in 1969 demonstrate the extent to which the life of the binational border community depends upon permeability.
2. This situation has been recognized in a recent conference of mayors of U.S. border cities held in El Paso, February 6 and 7, 1976.
3. Luis Uniquel et al., *El desarrollo urbano en México*, preliminary version (Mexico: El Colegio de México, 1974), p. 2.42.
4. Ibid.
5. Uniquel et al., op. cit., p. 5.30.
6. Ibid.
7. U.S. Office of Economic Opportunity, *Poverty in Texas* (Austin: Texas Department of Community Affairs, 1974).

8. Texas Institute For Educational Development, *Chicano Almanac* (San Antonio: 1973).

9. Ibid.

10. U.S. Department of Commerce, Bureau of the Census, "Spanish Origin Persons as a Percent of Total Population by Counties of the U.S.," map (Washington D.C.: U.S. Government Printing Office, 1970).

11. U.S. Department of Commerce, Bureau of the Census *Current Population Reports*, Series P-20, no. 264 (Washington D.C.: U.S. Government Printing Office, 1974), p. 2, Table B.

12. Texas Institute For Educational Development, op. cit., (compilation).

13. Secretaría de Industria y Comercio, *Zonas Fronterizas de México: Perfil Socioeconómico* (Mexico, D.F.: Government of Mexico, 1974), pp. 18–19.

14. The best historical account of the bracero program is Ernesto Galarza, *Merchants of Labor* (Santa Barbara: McNally and Loftin, 1964).

15. Julian Samora, *Los Mojados: The Wetback Story* (Notre Dame: University of Notre Dame Press, 1971).

16. VIII Censo General de Población, Mexico: 1960.

17. Galarza, op. cit. p. 87.

18. For more recent trends of U.S. tourism to Mexico, see Table 10-7.

19. B. Taylor and M.E. Bond, "Mexican Border Industrialization," *Michigan State University Business Topics*, spring, 1968, p. 36.

20. Jorge Farias Negrete, *Industrialization Program for the Mexican Northern Border*, Mexico: Banco Comercial Mexicano, S.A., 1969.

21. Taylor and Bond, Op. cit. p. 34.

22. NACLA, *Latin America and Empire Report*, 9 no. 5 (July and August 1975).

23. Ibid.

24. Ibid.

25. Nathaniel Goldfinger, director of the AFL-CIO Department of Research, statement before the U.S. Tariff Commission Hearings, May 5, 1970.

26. Ibid.

27. Ibid.

28. Ibid.

29. Statement by Trude C. Taylor, director of a trade association—WEMA—that includes six hundred companies engaged in electronics, Proceedings of the U.S. Tariff Commission, May 13, 1970.

30. This possibility has been recognized by authors sympathetic to the *maquiladora* program such as Benjamin J. Taylor and M.E. Bond in their article, "Mexican Border Industrialization," *Michigan State University Business Topics*, Spring, 1969. They say: "As a result of the rate of U.S. firm proliferation in the border region, legal changes permitting U.S. sales may be brought about with little effort. Given an influx of Mexican workers into the border area, greater dependency will be placed on relocated U.S. firms to provide employment opportunities. Accordingly the drive to secure more favorable market conditions in Mexico for U.S. products might be obtained by use of subtle pressures" (p. 42).

31. Victor L. Urquidi and Sofia Mendez Villareal, "Importancia Económica de la Zona Fronteriza del Norte de México," *Foro Internacional* 5 no. 2. (October–December 1975), p. 165.

32. American Chamber of Commerce of Mexico, *Mexican American Review*, March, 1975, p. 75.

33. Secretaria de Industria y Comercio, La Frontera Norte (Mexico, D.F.: Government of Mexico, 1974), pp. 111–114.

34. Op. cit., pp. 112–113.

35. Op. cit., pp. 48–49 and 96.

36. Op. cit., pp. 122.

37. Secretaría de Industria y Comercio, op. cit., pp. 94–95.

38. Ibid.

CHAPTER 11

# The Formation of an Ethnic Group: Colombian Female Workers in Venezuela

MARGALIT BERLIN

Recent social studies inquiry has shifted the focus for analysis of migrant labor systems from the individual migrant's adaptation in the urban environment to structural considerations related to an unevenly developing world market (Mangalam and Schwarzweller 1968). This analysis reveals the interdependence of all regions of the world and the corresponding sensitivity of each to changes in investment and production in any single one (Amin 1977, Wallerstein 1976). The resulting flow of capital causes people to move across frontiers in search of better job opportunities and in order to take advantage of currency exchanges. In the context of a fragmented household economy, chronic unemployment, and an alien government that assigns them a semilegal status, immigrants tend to accept subordinate positions in an alien economic system in which they have few alternatives. In this way they contribute to a general lowering of the wage level. That they are often not unionized hinders indigenous collective efforts (Castells 1974, Keeley and Tomassi 1978, Newland 1979).

These basic theoretical premises guided my research on Colombian female labor in the Venezuelan garment industry. I questioned whether the premises held for these immigrants and if so, to what degree did migrants accept working conditions in the factories? What individual strategies were developed by these workmen to cope with life in an alien environment and how did these affect their relations

257

with Venezuelan factory workers? But more importantly, I tried to tie these relations in production to the changes in capital accumulation on a world scale.

## Participant-Observation Research

My research in Caracas, Venezuela, can be divided into three phases: first, I carried out a study of the political economic context in which Colombian immigration takes place. Of special interest was the growth of the manufacture and construction sectors. Both are important in absorbing Colombian labor, and the category of *Colombian* or *illegal immigrant* is always associated with housing policies in Venezuela. Extensive interviews with financial and construction entrepreneurs, private and government policy makers, as well as Venezuelan social scientists were carried out in the field from May to November 1979. Later I spent three months working in a large garment factory in Caracas. With the consent of the owners, I became a seamstress's helper without revealing my identity as an investigator, from June to August 1980. During this period I participated in the closing and reopening of two sections of this firm. After leaving my employment, I spent two months from September to October 1980 visiting some of the women with whom I had developed close contacts at work. During this period I was a participant-observer of an overall mobilization of resources promoted by the state and private institutions to locate the undocumented population and change them from nonproduction and self-employed activities such as street trades and so forth to the secondary labor market (Piore 1979) with its low-paying wage-earning occupations. This paper will be an account of these events and the people involved in them. In the process of my investigation I became both a participant-observer as a factory worker and as a stranger in my own country. I was always an outsider, a researcher, trying to capture any detail that could help me understand the situation in which I found myself.

## The World Outside the Factory

When the factory was founded in 1966, Venezuela was going through a period of direct state intervention to enhance the nation's capital growth. This was a period of "import substitution" when the government utilized some of the oil revenues to strengthen the image of peace and stability so as to attract foreign investment to a democratic regime that gained public acceptance through a populist ideology. In fact, political participation through unions and parties enabled the government to hold in check the demands of a growing proletariat in the expanding industrial sector.

One populist strategy of political parties was to lead invasions of squatter settlements in order to gain new political constituencies. Today some of these *barrios* are the only housing available for factory workers. Immigrants who rent these houses pay up to 300 bolivars (Bs.) (U.S.$69) for a tiny corner in a four-person bedroom. The owner makes Bs.3000 (U.S.$690) out of the ten immigrants that live in his house.

During the seventies the housing situation of thousands of Colombians in other parts of the city changed. The increase in all revenues attracted large inputs of capital both to manufacturing and the construction industries, increasing the purchasing power of the middle and upper classes. Urban renwal projects in the center of Caracas were designed and executed through state expropriation of land. Middle income housing projects and large highways intensified land use and increased land values, thus strengthening the political and economic position of the promoters—powerful construction groups closely allied with financial and governmental elites (Bolivar and Lovera 1979 and Lander 1976).

Some squatter settlements got in the way of these projects. They were moved to temporary *barracas* that have already been occupied six years. In these large concrete row houses with no windows at the end of the rows, squatters in San Jose parish raised their families (Facultad de Arquitectura, 1979). Squatter settlements have also been demolished by the national guard, with the illegal status of some of their residents used as the rationale. In these cases there was no compensation, and immigrants had to return to Colombia or stay with relatives. As in the case of South Africa, these housing policies induced immigrants to return to their homeland when their labor was no longer needed (Wilson 1978).

The tall glass buildings of Parque Central—resort hotels, shopping malls, and luxury apartments—reflect the social contradictions of Venezuelan housing policy. One can see mirrored in those walls the living conditions of the majority of the population that does not benefit from the accumulation of petrodollars. Even when the new government reduced loans and credits for middle-class housing construction, the unintended consequences were to exacerbate the already difficult situation in working-class housing since the older housing that might have been made available to low-income residential units was no longer released. Instead of leveling single family houses to construct large projects, landlords evicted tenants and subdivided these smaller dwellings into "cases de vecindad," or multiple occupancy units, where immigrant workers pay up to Bs.600 (U.S.$139) a month. The chief complaint of residents was the lack of proper ventilation and cooking facilities.

Economic expansion in the mid-seventies included a government policy to subsidize the textile industry's growth with loans for the purchase of modern machinery. This in turn decreased the number of workers required by industry. Both of these factors—a capital-intensive industry and mass layoffs—brought about the labor laws of 1979–1980: the "Law of Unemployment Compensation" (*Ley del Despido Injustificado*) and the "Law of Wage Increase" (*Ley de Aumento de Sueldos y Salarios*).

The financial assistance for textile plant expansion was cut in 1980 by the present government. The resulting crisis aroused both entrepreneurs and workers. The former declared the crisis was due to high labor costs caused by the recent labor laws that did not consider productivity rates to be the main wage determinant. Moreover, they claimed sales were low due to the smuggling of fabrics, which were sold at prices much lower than what the Venezuelan wage structure and cost of living allowed them to charge. The workers organized a strike under the leadership of the leftist textile industry union, *Union de Trabajadores de la Industria Textil* (UTIT) to protest the precarious position of workers. They also tried to force the government to again permit imports.

Prominent economists such as Merhav (1969) question import substitution policies as increasing monopolistic and oligopolistic structures. As a result of such criticism, the new administration has lifted the tariff barriers on foreign textiles, with resulting pressure on local industry.

Like the textile industry, garment manufacturers employ foreign female labor, mostly from Colombia but also from Ecuador, Peru, and the Dominican Republic. In order to compete with products from areas where labor is cheap—such as Hong Kong, Indonesia, the Philippines, and so forth, small and medium-size factories employ illegal immigrants who continue to enter despite selective migration policies.[1] In order to avoid union, legal and wage requirements, entrepreneurs pay these illegal workers for stitching done in their own homes. The finishing is done at the factory so that the seamstresses will not sell the product on their own. Large factories, through their linkages with government, receive permission to bring workers from Medellín and Bucaramanga, both large textile centers of Colombia, in special one-year contracts that include the cost of the trip plus one-month's rent in a pensión or *casa de vecindad* whose owners are connected with the management of the factory.

### The Factory Site

The bonanza resulting from the increased flow of petrodollars in the mid-seventies was also felt in the factory. Those who reaped new benefits in those years were now required to play an increased role in Venezuelan society and had to dress for the part. Elegant suits were in great demand.

Elegant suits are made in a section of a factory which employed immigrant women from Colombia brought in under contract. The section began with thirty women supervised by Enriqueta, a Colombian woman who worked under an Italian shop manager. She had been a legal secretary in Colombia; her first job in Venezuela was as a school teacher in a Catholic school. Although she would rather deal with students than with workers, she changed jobs in search of better wages. An ambitious woman, Enriqueta works her country-women hard in order to ingratiate herself with the manager. Some of the Venezuelan female workers are favored, however, because Enriqueta, as a foreigner, needs certain favors. For example, one helped her to get a license for her friend's taxi. Another Venezuelan took her to a follower of the popular Venezuelan cult figure Maria Lionza to get some idea of what her future might bring. The women in the section do not take Enriqueta seriously. She is there only to maintain discipline, she does not even know how to sew. Enriqueta makes twice as much as the average seamstress (Bs.2000, U.S.$460).

Nieves, the seamstress's helper in the section, came from Colombia with her mother and her younger sister. The job alternatives for Nieves as an unskilled worker were very few; domestic service was her most likely prospect. Her mother's contacts as a pattern maker in a Venezuelan textile factory helped her to get her present job. Nieves contributes most of her weekly salary (Bs.231, U.S.$53) to her family's budget. Every morning she receives cut fabrics from the floor below; she classifies and distributes it with matching thread to the seamstresses whom she assists. The day goes from 7:30 to 5:30 and by the end of it two hundred elegant suits are finished and

*261*

cleaned on the shop floor. Each is sold for about Bs.1000 ($232) in local boutiques. The factory worker can buy one for Bs.600 (U.S.$139). This is obviously a rarely used fringe benefit because the reduced price is almost half the seamstress's monthly wage. But workers do purchase jeans, men's shirts, and sport jackets at the factory. The price of a sport jacket is Bs.600, and the factory worker may purchase one for Bs.300 (U.S.$69).

Towards the end of 1978, as we have seen, the state cut back its aid to the construction and textile sectors of the economy. It reoriented its financial policies towards encouraging the production of mass-consumption goods. These changes were felt in the factory. The elegant suit section was temporarily closed and most workers were laid off. Some were rehired to sew sport pants to match jackets in stock at the factory.

The new product required different skills and different machine operations. Engineers took their time to price these new operations. Piecework rate wages were delayed. The distribution of tasks was disorganized. Supervisors would complain that the work should be done in another section. Chaos and misconceptions were prevalent.

Strong competition from foreign markets demanded the presence of a quality-control supervisor, but his presence provoked a crisis of authority. Neither supervisors nor workers were willing to take orders from a stranger. Also, the informal exchanges of favors between supervisors and workers, which were often more beneficial to the worker than to the factory, were no longer possible. Venezuelan workers complained. Immigrants accepted the changes; but nonetheless they resented the delay in wages, and were angry at the native workers. The faults in the assembly line were blamed on the Venezuelan seamstresses' laziness and carelessness. The lowering of wages was interpreted as a consequence of Enriqueta's preference for the Venezuelan workers with whom she had developed close relations.

Florinda, a Venezuelan seamstress, was a hard worker. She operated one machine and made Bs.360 (U.S.$83) a week, (the base wage of Bs.280 (U.S.$65 plus the piecework wages of Bs.80 U.S.$19)). She only stayed one year at the factory because she could not stand the pressure of learning the new operations entailed in making sport pants. She had been under a lot of emotional stress. She separated from her husband during the period when he was building houses (ranchos) for Colombians all over the huge barrio where they live. She hates Colombians. Her husband is building a house right next-door to hers for his new Colombian woman.

Cilia and Gladiola were brought by the factory from Medellín to make elegant suits. By the end of the one-year contract they were operating an extra machine, for which they were not paid. The end of the one-year contract coincided with the closure of the elegant suit section. They were laid off and got paid their social security benefits. Because they had demonstrated both skill and a good disposition, they were offered the opportunity to stay on a different basis, receiving basic wages with no extra piecework rates. This meant a decrease in Bs.140 from their weekly pay ($32 U.S. or 1400 Colombian pesos). In order to rehire them, a new company was opened within the same factory and with the same management. This procedure allowed them to evade the Venezuelan law that requires that laid-off workers be unemployed at least three months before being rehired by the same firm.

The new section reorganized as a separate company, opened about the time I entered the factory. My job was to assist Cilia, Gladiola and Omeira, a newly arrived seamstress. I supplied them with matching colored threads and clasps. As time went by, the new and the old section became one. The sewing machines had been moved from the old to the new section space. Enriqueta and Nieves from the old section became respectively the supervisor and the helper of the new sport pant section. Towards the end of my stay at the factory, I became the cutter in the old section space for leftover pieces of the sport pants.

Thus changes in State policies in response to changes in the international market brought about factory reorganization in Venezuela. This affected the lives of many workers who were caught up in closing and reopening of the section. Their position in a skill hierarchy that assigned them to semiskilled jobs in which they knew only one machine limited their ability to respond to change. Their careers at the factory reveal the constant need for retraining to satisfy changing production requirements.

Cilia and Gladiola remained in the factory after the closing, accepting apprenticeship wages until the sport pants section became stabilized. They learned to operate new machines during an eight months' apprenticeship. The garment industry union (led by the leading democratic party, *Acción Democratica* ) limited apprenticeship wages to two months. However, the women did not contact the union. They saw unions as corrupt, never operating for the worker's benefit, and even less concerned with the immigrant's welfare. This evaluation was not far from the truth. Union officials argue that Colombian women are better workers than Venezuelan women. Rather than promoting a different wage system or instituting broader training programs for the native women, the union promotes labor migration. On one hand, the union struggles for wage increases before collective contracts are signed and in this way they capture native workers under the union umbrella. On the other hand, the union sponsors selective migration policies; and the industry gains workers who, even if formally employed under union contract, will not ask for union intervention.

Venezuelan women do not believe in unions either. Many left the shop when there were increasing pressures at work, such as strict control and wage regulations in the sport pants section. They preferred to stay home with their extended families upon whom they could rely for support for their children. They felt that the union disregarded their household tasks. Wages do not reflect the "invisible labor" (i.e., child rearing, cooking, laundry, etc.) that they must perform at home in addition to sewing at the factory. Being paid at piecework rates reveals this fact. It is the finished product that gets paid, not the person. Employment at such low wages is only worthwhile for the immigrant women who send the pay home and gain from the currency exchange.

The resulting inability to attract an indigenous labor force serves as a rationale for the reinforcement of existing labor importation policies. Immigrant women produce at a high rate as if they were getting extra piecework wage rates because they want to stay in the country and are waiting for the management to make good its promise of a wage increase. They compete against one another in search of high piecework rates, playing, as Burawoy (1979) calls it, "make out" games resulting in "manufacturing consent"—a tacit compliance with management objectives.

Not all Colombian seamstresses were brought into the country by the factory. Many came after hearing about the opportunities oil has opened in Venezuela. Omeira, the new worker in the sport pant section, came on her own from a rural town on the Colombian coast. She had worked as a maid in Caracas for five years, earning Bs.1200 (U.S.$200) a month. She saved almost all her monthly wage because board and room were free. Because she took good care of her employer's children, they helped her to get a visa when she decided to be on her own, migrate to Venezuela, and work in a factory. She did not know sewing when she entered the factory, but in three months she learned to operate two machines and earned Bs.33 a day, or Bs.924 a month. This was Bs.276 less than what she used to earn as a maid, and she also had to pay room and board, which cost as much as Bs.600 (U.S.$139) a month. Nevertheless. she decided to bear with the factory's wage and training regulations, because she was determined to do anything to avoid working as a maid.

## The Immigrant

From any perspective Cilia and Gladiola, who stayed at apprenticeship wages for almost a year, are not typical cases. However, they illustrate how the linkage to the domestic unit in Colombia determines the behavior of immigrants in the host country. Like most other women whom I met at the factory, they come from large families headed by the mother. Father had left their homes soon after the loss of their jobs. The wages of women in the Colombian textile or garment factories were too low (one-fourth of what they make in Venezuela) to make ends meet in their homes. Food for seven siblings costs about 6,000 Colombian pesos a month. Rent costs about 4,000 Colombian pesos. Cilia and Gladiola, as well as most of the women at the factory, managed to save and send home more than half of their monthly wage.

The women who are brought in by the factory were part of the active urban labor force in Colombia, where they were recruited in their work places through representatives of the Venezuelan factory. In contrast, those like Omeira, the former maid, who have come through the *caminos verdes*, or illegal paths, tend to come from rural areas. Their histories reveal land expropriation by the new financial large holders. Small farmers who acquired credits and loans for the purchase of fertilizers and modern machinery were often forced to sell their crop to the banks at very low prices even before the harvest period, a process that one could see happening at an earlier period in Mexico (Warman 1972). Immigrant women from rural areas tend to stay in Venezuela longer than those from urban areas. They first became maids and then found jobs in the factory. They do not have to send part of the wages they earn to their homes because their households have been dispersed—the members having gone either to Colombian cities, to Venezuela, or to the United States (Cardona 1980).

Acceptance of miserable working conditions and austerity characterizes the lives of these women in Venezuela. They prepare their food at home and take it to the factory. Lunch at the factory cafeteria is very expensive, costing about Bs.10, or U.S.$2.50. They often sit on the stairs of the factory, eating in a hurry in order to utilize some of the thirty minutes allowed for lunch to iron some of their own clothing at the plant.

The immigrant women form sexual alliances with foreigners, either Italians, Spaniards, or other Colombians. Venezuelan men, they say, are careless about their families. Ethnographies reveal that male desertion is common in Colombia as well, but stereotypical notions inhibit their forming permanent relations with Venezuelan men. They believe that such relationships with Venezuelan men could result in the loss of ties with their household in Colombia.

Most of these women range in age from twenty to thirty years. They see themselves as future housewives, not as factory workers. In marriage they envision an end to their hardships, although past histories reveal abandonment and abuse from alliances with men. But there is always hope, as Fernández–Kelly (1980) points out when writing about Mexican workers in *maquiladoras*, of "someone out there who is worth living for." Ideology reinforces these women's view of themselves as future housewives. Historically, Latin American women have had low rates of participation in the wage labor market except as domestics. Although this has been changing in recent years, hope is built around the belief that they can attain the life of the middle-class women often projected in the media. Ignoring the different economic realities, these women with scarce resources envision a life as the lady who is queen of her home.[2] Some of the soap operas and other television programs are attempting to change these views of women. The trend toward employment in the wage labor force in the U.S. to which inflation and the women's movement have both contributed and the encouragement of women's participation are beginning to be felt in Latin America. However, immigrants who lives in two worlds tend to be cut off from the new trends in each area.

In the course of time, these immigrants learn to operate the machines and adjust to working conditions. They acquiesce in what employers want, and see native coworkers as being against them, almost like an enemy, because they are not willing to endure as much as they, the immigrant labor force. Hope is based on a future return to Colombia; but every return trip has shown the immigrant, once more, the oversaturation in the Colombian labor market. This cultivates the illusion that they will find a man who will save them from hardships of the labor market. Given the limited opportunities for them in Colombia, this is also a fruitless hope since men too often migrate to Venezuela where they develop relations with Venezuelan women so that they might have access to housing. Hope for a redeeming man delays participation in collective action with native coworkers.

### Colombian, Immigrant or Factory Worker?

Housing is scarce, expensive, hard to maintain, and usually contingent on the labor contract. (This situation results from the dependency of the construction industry on government bureaucracies [Perez Perdomo 1979]). The women perceive legal immigrant status as ineffectual in solving their personal problems because access to housing terminates when their job contract ends. Cultivating paternalistic relations with management offer the possibility of extending their contract as well as maintaining access to basic necessities such as housing and health facilities.

Gladiola left the house that management provided. She wanted to try a cheaper place. She moved to a ranch in Baruta, and for eight months she travelled three hours a day to work in order to pay Bs.50 less a month. Towards the end of my employment, Gladiola moved to a cleaner place, where Cilia rents a bed in a boarding house close to the factory. The latter got this place through the aid of the factory social worker.

The maintenance of both patron-client relations with management and contacts through people and letters from Colombia to Venezuela constitute the accepted "structuring," in Vincent's (1974) terms, of Colombian ethnicity. Social contacts are limited primarily to Colombian women and men. Sundays are spent writing letters or seeing other Colombians seeking ways to increase savings.

Native women, as Florinda's case shows, have the advantage of being owners of their own housing or of living with relatives. This enables them to change jobs or stay home, making about the same money as Colombian women working full-time in the factory, by working a few hours at home doing laundry, taking care of other people's children, or sending their children to work in the streets. Colombians are seen as "social climbers" (*jala mecate*) who want to get ahead through their factory contacts, and as thieves for not wanting to remain in Venezuela.

Ethnic boundaries serve to obscure the crude realities of economic oppression. Beyond the control of these workers, both immigrants and natives, lie work patterns following the uneven distribution of resources. These infrastructural conditions determine an international division of labor that, with the help of the law, assigns Colombians to the lower echelons in the Venezuelan occupational structure. The ethnic boundary determines the immigrant's fate before she decides to leave home.

Ethnic identification feeds on the immigrant's perception of her life as one of progress and improvement. The native woman sees the immigrant coworker as an enemy, not realizing her incapacity to fight inequality, because confrontation with factory management is avoided, there is almost unimpeded exploitation of the labor force.

The role of the press is crucial in crystalizing this ethnic pattern. Language is not an obstacle to ethnic assimilation, with Spanish the native language of both countries; the sense of separation is cultivated rather by stereotyped images. Journalists create an image of a delinquent Colombian, emphasizing the importance of purifying Venezuelan identity from foreign elements, which, they maintain, confuse and destroy the cultural heritage (*Resumen*, articles in the June, July, August, and September 1980 issues, among other journals carrying this message). The dispute over jurisdiction of the waters flowing from the Venezuelan Gulf adds to ethnic conflict even though the dispute originates in claims by foreign companies. This site of so many historic events involving both countries must now be redefined by foreign companies competing for rights of oil extraction.

In the strange world reproduced in the daily interaction at work and outside the factory and embroidered by the press, the Colombian immigrants constitute a subordinate minority, that is, a sector of national and ethnic differences that fulfills specific tasks that are different from those of the workers of the national majority (Guerrero and Lopez Rivas 1980). They constitute the cheap labor force that sharpens competition in the context of a growing international division of labor.

Paradoxically, the growing trends of unemployment that follow a capital-intensive industry in one country create the conditions that motivate Colombian women to migrate to higher wage areas in Venezuela. Because of the favorable monetary exchange for Venezuelan money in Colombia, the low wages from labor intensive industries such as garment making can draw women from middle class professions in Colombia. As I have attempted to show in this paper, Colombian women can not get housing without the factory's assistance. Hence they make the factory their homes.

## Notes

In developing my understanding of Venezuelan political economy and urban anthropology, I have drawn on conversations with several friends and teachers, among them, Bela Feldman-Bianco, Maria Lagos, Leith Mullings, Peter Marcuse, June Nash, Domingo Alberto Rangel, Salvador Rosillo, Jagna Scharff, Joan Vincent, Arturo Warman, and particularly Marvin Harris. I thank them all. I am grateful to June Nash and Julius Silverman for their critical reading of an earlier draft of this paper.

1. Sassen-Koob (1978), working with official figures, has shown how the number of illegal entries increases with the institution of selective policies of immigration.

2. Compare with media research published in *El Nacional*, June 13, 1980.

## References

Amin, Samir. 1977. *La acumulación a escala mundial, critica la teoría del subdesarrollo*. México, D.F.: Siglo Veintiuno Editores.

Azcargorta, Jesus. 1980. "La concentración industrial en la industría de la confección," Mimeographed paper of the Institute de Administracion Caracus.

Bolivar, Teolinda and Lovera, Alberto. 1979. "De Pérez a Pérez: contribución al estudio de las politicas urbanas en el período 1948–1978. Working Paper of the Faculty of Architecture, Universidad Central de Venezuela, Caracas.

Burawoy, Michael. 1977. *Manufacturing Consent: Changes in the Labor Process under Monopoly Capitalism*. Chicago and London: University of Chicago Press.

Cardona, Ramiro. 1980. "Aportes sobre la migración de Colombia a Venezuela," Documents prepared for the Centro Latinoamericano de Ciencias Sociales. Buenos Aires.

Castells, Manuel. 1975. "Immigrant Workers and Class Struggles in Advanced Capitalism: The Western European Experience," *Politics and Society*, fall.

Facultad de Arquitectura. 1979. "Barracas Area Metropolitana de Caracas. Caso, Los Mangos de la Vega." Information paper for the Consejo de Facultad de Arquitectura y Urbanismo. Mimeographed. Caracas: Universidad Central de Venezuela.

Fernandez-Kelly, Maria Patricia. 1980. "*Chavales de Maquiladora*; A Study of the Female Labor Force of Ciudad Juarez Offshore Production Plants." Ph.D thesis, Department of Anthropology, Rutgers University, New Brunswick, N.J.

Guerrero, Javier and Lopez y Rivas, Gilberto. 1980. "Las minorias étnicas como categoría politica en la cuestión regional," Monograph prepared for the Seminario sobre la Questión Étnica y la Cuestión Regional en América Latina.

Harris, Marvin. 1979. *Cultural Materialism: The Struggle for a Science of Culture*. New York: Random House.

Keeley, Charles and Tomassi, S. 1978. *The Disposable Worker: The Cyclical Nature of the Mexican American Immigration*. Mimeographed monograph.

Lander, Luis. 1976. "La vivienda popular en Venequela." Mimeographed paper of the Centro Nacional de Estudios Scientificos (CENDES). Caracas: Universidad Central de Venezuela.

Mangalem, J. and Schwarzweller, H. 1968. "General Theory in the Study of Migration: Current Needs and Difficulties." *International Migration Review* 3, 1, pp. 3–18.

Merhav, Meir. 1969. *Technological Dependency, Monopoly and Growth.* New York: Oxford.

Newland, Kathleen. 1979. "International Migration: the Search for Work," World Watch Institute Paper.

Pérez-Perdomo, Rogelio 1979 *Derecho y Propiedad de Vivienda en los Ranchos de Caracas*: Editorial Ateneo 1979 Caracas. Monto Avila, Editores.

Piore, Michael. 1979. *Birds of Passage: Migrant Labor and Industrial Societies.* New York: Cambridge University Press.

*Resumen* Articles in issues from June to September, 1980.

Sassen-Koob, Saskia. 1978. "Economic Growth and Immigration in Venezuela." *International Migration Review* 13, 3: pp. 455–74.

Vincent, Joan. 1974. "Structuring of Ethnicity," *Human Organization* 33(Winter): 375—79.

Wallerstein, Immanuel. 1976. "Semiperipheral Countries and the Contemporary World Crisis," *Theory and Society* 3, pp. 461–83.

Warman, Arturo. 1972. *Los campesinos, hijos predilectos del régimen.* Mexico: Editorial Nuestro Tiempo.

Wilson, R. 1978. *Migrant Labour in South Africa*: Cambridge University Press.

*Part IV*

# Case Studies in
# Electronics and Textiles

Comparison of the cases of electronics and garment workers throughout the United States, Asia, and Latin America reveals striking similarities in the emergent global integration of production. Susan Green, Naomi Katz and David S. Kemnitzer, and John Keller analyze the home and work environment of women in the Silicon Valley electronic factories. The incipient trend toward contracting out elements of production can be found from San Jose in California to Taiwan. The superexploitation of young, unorganized female workers is found in different degrees from the Caribbean to Malaysia, Taiwan, and the Philippines. These articles provide a basis for further global comparisons.

# CHAPTER 12

# Silicon Valley's Women Workers: A Theoretical Analysis of Sex-Segregation in the Electronics Industry Labor Market

SUSAN S. GREEN

The internationalization of manufacturing industries over the last several decades has transformed labor market structures in both the United States and the Third World. The electronics industry, one of the more labor-intensive and geographically dispersed of the global manufacturing industries, provides a useful focus for examining the impact of labor market transformations. In both Third World export-oriented industrial sectors and in the United States, industries such as electronics now employ a predominantly female work force. The following discussion focuses on two bodies of theory that shed light on the situation of women workers, specifically at the U.S. end of the global electronics assembly line. The issues explored here are relevant not only to the role of American workers in the electronics industry, but also to the situation of women workers in similar industries in many different parts of the world.

In the Third World, the electronics industry hires a highly homogeneous wage labor force characterized by a large proportion of young, unmarried, poorly skilled, and minimally paid female production workers. A much greater degree of diversity characterizes the U.S. electronics work force including a wider age range among workers; a higher proportion of males, especially minority males; and a significant number of married women. What are the circumstances that have led to both similarities and differences between the domestic labor market and the Third World labor market? Is there a single theoretical model that explains the roles of women workers in the "world market factories,"[1] as well as in domestic manufacturing centers? On the one hand, segmented labor market models (see below, p. 277ff.) that seek to explain divisions in the U.S. labor market are too narrowly confined to the domestic economy to explain the trend toward internationalization of production and the development of a female work force on a global scale. On the other hand, theoretical discussions of the new international division of labor have yet to link domestic labor market theory with analyses of labor market structures in the Third World export-oriented industrial sectors. To date, discussions of the new international division of labor have focused primarily on the development of an international hierarchy of production processes where less-skilled manufacturing operations are being relegated to the Third World, and research, development, and other more-skilled operations are becoming the principle tasks of the U.S. work force. This tends to ignore the role of the predominantly female, low-skilled U.S. production work force in internationalizing industries. Two important questions have not been adequately answered:

1. Why are predominantly women employed as the production work force in both the U.S. and the Third World, in industries which are rapidly being internationalized?

2. Why and how does the character of this international work force vary between the U.S. and the world market factories?

Answering these two questions requires a deeper exploration into the sexual division of labor in both the public (i.e., the market) and the private (i.e., the family or domestic) spheres. Only by linking the organization of production processes and labor markets to the sexual division of labor can the predominantly female character of the global manufacturing work force be better understood.

This paper has a dual focus. First, it will examine the status of female electronics workers in the United States within the theoretical context of the segmented labor market model. And second, it will argue the need for a reformulation of this body of thought along socialist feminist theoretical lines in order to provide clearer answers to the above two questions. Building on the base of the segmented labor market model, the socialist feminist perspective provides a theoretically unified foundation for analyzing women's roles within both domestic labor market structures and the international division of labor.

The conclusions and conjectures that follow are based on a limited pilot study carried out in the San Jose area[2] of California among a small, yet diverse group of female electronics[3] assemblers. Their employers varied in size and organizational structure. Not all of these firms had plants in other countries or even in other parts of the United States, although all offered employment opportunities that were quite uniform as to the level of skills involved, the pay scales, and other job characteristics. In depth interviews were conducted with seventeen women, all but three of whom lived and worked in this area commonly known as Silicon Valley, where many American owned electronics corporations are headquartered. (For a summary of demographic and other information concerning the women interviewed, see Appendix A.)

The first section of this article briefly traces the development of the segmented labor market model, which provides some of the most accurate and relevant explanations for the channelling of groups of less advantaged workers into largely low status occupational categories. The character of women's employment in the domestic electronics industry, specifically in the San Jose area, supports many of the contentions of this model.

The second section describes the Santa Clara County electronics production work force; case studies illustrate the variety of personal characteristics, experiences, and attitudes of the women employed there. An evaluation of the case study material tests the tenets of the segmented labor market model. It is difficult on the basis of this model alone, to answer fully even the first of the two questions posed above, as it relates to the U.S. work force: Why are predominantly *women* employed as production workers in electronics? Further, segmented labor market concepts, having a principally domestic focus, stop short of being able to link domestic and international labor market structures. Lacking this theoretical connection, it is difficult, if not impossible, to understand why the international expansion of capitalist production has taken the particular form of export-oriented industrialization with a predominantly female work force.

The third section of this article attempts to address some of the shortcomings of the segmented labor market model. A small yet growing body of socialist feminist literature has begun to criticize domestic labor market theories for their lack of attention to the causes of occupational sex-segregation and for their seeming inability to bridge the gap between the existence of sex segregated jobs in the United States and the rise of a predominantly female manufacturing

275

work force in the world market factories. The views of socialist feminist writers provide a transforming new depth to the segmented labor market model.

Radical theorists of the segmented labor market school added an historical class analysis component to the more static dual labor market model developed in the 1960s to explain poverty and unemployment. The dynamic of class conflict, upon which the segmented model rests, is the crucial determinant of the evolution of capitalist production. Analyzing class conflict does not adequately explain, however, the differential employment of women versus men in either the domestic or the international labor market. Examining the historical interplay of capitalists and workers cannot tell us why women in particular have been singled out—as opposed to minorities, teenagers, or any other group—as the new and growing sector of the manufacturing work force in international industry. Socialist feminist analysis attempts to answer this question by identifying the mechanisms used to channel women into the production work force of these industries. Fundamental to this perspective is the notion that a full understanding of capitalist social relations, of the roles of power and class in the organization of production, must also include an analysis of social relations within the family, of the role of men and women in a distinct division of labor within the family unit. The evolution of the family structure has shaped the social valuation of women's labor power, consigning women to positions of subordination both within the family and in the marketplace. This ideological assignment of women to a secondary status within the family has provided the basis for the differential exploitation of men and women in the work force. It has allowed women to be singled out for recruitment into the least advantageous job sectors and exclusion from the better paying, more highly valued job sectors as the segmented labor market has developed. In order to analyze the role of women within the new international division of labor, therefore, the concepts of *both* the segmented labor market theorists and their socialist feminist critics are important.

It is commonly assumed that by providing women with access to employment in modern industrial sectors, their social and economic position will be advanced. In evaluating the case study material presented, this assumption is implicitly tested. I believe it to have only limited validity. In any event, it is important to look at the precise nature of jobs available to women before making broad generalizations about the benefits of expanding female employment. Certainly, the expansion of employment opportunities for women lessens their economic dependence on men and in turn effects the structure of the family. Yet, there are serious limits to this process. The interplay of power relationships between the sexes and between classes has placed women at the bottom of the social and economic hierarchy, a position not likely to be changed by the expansion of job opportunities primarily in the lowest status, lowest paying occupational categories. The importance of socialist feminist theory here is that it provides a basis for identifying the structures that continue to keep women in a subordinate social and economic position and thus identifies those that must be altered or dismantled in order to effectively enhance women's status.

The case study material presented is a small sample of women's experiences in the U.S. electronics work force. However, it provides valuable insights into the nature of blue-collar female occupations in domestic manufacturing industries and supports many of the contentions of the radical and socialist feminist theorists. Hopefully, the following arguments will help to pose appropriate questions for the further examining of the internationalization of industry and its impact on women.

## 1. The Segmented Labor Market Model: A Review of the Literature

A host of theoretical models have been proposed, spanning the ideological spectrum, to explain differentials in income and occupational status in the U.S. labor force. Basing their models on a view of industrial society where these differentials are reduced to the level of individual variables, neo-classical theorists assume a basically homogeneous labor market. Empirical evidence and, I believe, commonsense observations, weigh against them. (See Beck 1978, Bibb 1977, Gordon 1972, Reagan 1979, and Piore 1975, among others, for empirical and observational challenges to the concept of a homogeneous labor market.) The analysis of case studies to follow assumes the existence of fundamental, structural divisions within the domestic labor market based on class and sex.

David Gordon, in his 1972 survey of labor market theories, reviews the dual labor market models put forth by Pierre Doeringer, Michael Piore and others writing in the late 1960s, which suggested a dichotomization in the American labor market. Piore defined the two distinct labor markets accordingly:

> . . . the primary market offers jobs which possess several of the following traits: high wages, good working conditions, employment sta-

bility and job security, equity and due process in the administration of work rules, and chances for advancement. The . . . secondary market has jobs which, relative to those in the primary sector, are decidedly less attractive. They tend to involve low wages, poor working conditions, considerable variability in employment, harsh and often arbitrary discipline, and little opportunity to advance. [Gordon, 1972:46]

The level of skills, the degree of employment stability and discrimination on the basis of "superficial characteristics" such as race or sex mark key differences between the two sectors. Mobility between the sectors is quite limited.

Changes in industry structure have been both the cause and the result of continuing work force dichotomization. The more highly concentrated industries in the monopoly sector can afford to pay higher wages and invest more in employee training because they can pass such costs on to consumers. The more competitive or marginal industries, on the other hand, can little afford the expense of offering primary sector concessions, and thus, through their lower level of remuneration encourage a greater amount of worker turnover. In this manner, structural divisions in the labor market are maintained and deepened.

The dual labor market theory is essentially historical in approach in that it traces the development of certain occupational and personal characteristics in labor market operations. However, the early dual labor market model defined little in the way of explanatory historical mechanisms leading to the kind of structural divisions in the labor market that it described. In other words this theory does not incorporate class conflict as part of the process that leads to the formation of labor markets. Gordon notes critically that "dual market theory . . . does not provide an explicit analysis of conflict in society . . . as if a harmony of interest was driving the evolution of a dual structure." [Gordon 1972:87]

Dual theorists, however, did lay the foundations for the more dynamic and less rigid segmented labor market model of the radical school. Many of the earlier "dualists," Piore, Wachtel, Gordon among others, have gone on to incorporate their original concepts within a more general radical framework. Depending heavily on dual market concepts, radical analysts differ primarily in their emphasis on the historical impact of class relations in shaping the structure of the U.S. labor market and on the consequences of the process of capital accumulation in creating divisions in the American workforce."

According to the radical perspective, the goal of capital is the extraction of the greatest possible surplus value from the work force.

This is accomplished, simplistically speaking, by increasing the rate of productivity more rapidly than increases in the real wage rate. This creates the *potential* for rising wages, realizable only through the collective pressure of wageworkers to gain access to a greater share of the surplus. Thus, it is in the interests of capital to create as many divisions among workers as possible to forestall the strengthening of worker organizations:

> As a result, employers were likely to try to develop a stratified labor market in order to accomplish two complementary objectives. . . . If they could, they would try to segregate white-collar workers from blue-collar workers, create or permit the development of a class identity among more advantaged white-collar workers to distinguish them from blue-collar workers, and to impose some sharp barriers between the different kinds of jobs, . . . And employers were likely to seek, on the other hand, to sharply segregate those blue-collar or secondary workers who were not likely to develop class consciousness, in order, obviously, to limit the potential costs of concessions to workers who made determined demands. [Gordon 1972:73]

Many methods have been employed to create such divisions; the increasing hierarchization and proliferation of job classifications has increased the degree of separation between and control over individuals in the workplace (Gordon 1972, Edwards 1979, Wachtel 1975, and Piore 1975) The development and employment of select technologies has furthered divisions in the working class, increasing capital's ability to control, while "proletarianizing" many primary occupations and further deskilling secondary jobs. (Braverman 1974, Zimbalist 1979). Discriminatory hiring and wage policies, based on sex, racial or ethnic origin, and language ability have further diminished the ability of workers as a class to develop a common identity. Braverman and others emphasize that during the development of labor market divisions as they exist today, the primary goal of capital has been to increase social control. The central position of class conflict in determining relative access to surplus capital has meant that capital traditionally places the goal of social control above that of efficiency when it comes to making decisions regarding specific technologies or forms of workplace organization (Braverman 1974:112–121; Edwards 1979:139–140; and Gordon 1972:130–131).

The important contribution of radical analysts has been the formulation of a methodology for analyzing the processes and trends which have shaped the formation of the U.S. labor market. Current labor market divisions, are a product of earlier attempts by capital to create and reinforce subjective distinctions among groups of work-ers, "[channelling] into secondary jobs those workers who were least likely to identify with more advantaged workers" (Gordon 1972:74–75). Consequently, employers are both subject to the char-acter of the workforce which has developed, and act consciously or otherwise, to reinforce divisions in the market structure through hiring and promotion policies, personnel management techniques, discriminatory job classifications and certain forms of internal organi-zation. The institutionalized encouragement, through various social and economic disincentives, of job instability among secondary work-ers has been an important part of these overall trends, supporting the isolation and limited mobility of the secondary workforce. Or-ganized worker opposition to these policies, practices and trends acts to modify the nature and degree of control which employers have over their workers.

Specifically, where and how do women fit into this radical analysis? Most radical theorists have lumped women, minorities, teenagers and non-English speaking people into one loose category (often together with the (urban poor or simply the poor), that of the traditionally disadvantaged worker:

> [Employers] would seek to stratify jobs in order to objectively separate job clusters from each other and consequently to establish "fire trails," as it were, to limit the potential spread of costly concessions. . . . They were likely to try to fill the worst jobs with those who were least likely to identify with advantaged workers. Gradually, as the composition of the American labor force changed, it became relatively easy for employers to reserve the most "secondary" jobs for teens, women and minority group workers with quite confident expectations that they would not identify with more advantaged workers and develop a common con-sciousness about the disadvantages of their jobs. [Gordon 1972:73–74]

Edwards, whose somewhat more complex analysis segregates the labor market into three fractions (having further subdivisions within each fraction), adds refinements to the description of categories within the secondary sector where the predominantly female occupations prevail. The secondary position of female and minority workers has been reinforced by discrimination at the time of hiring, preventing them from obtaining employment in the primary sector. Entering the wage labor force in the era of monopoly capitalism, he argues, these groups were channeled into the beginnings of what would later become, in part through their own presence in increasing numbers, a rigidly separate and distinct labor force. In other words, employers have taken advantage of preexisting discrimination, leading to the development of segregated occupational categories that preserve and foster sexually and racially discriminatory social patterns.

> [The] lack of any effective bargaining strength among blacks and women made discrimination possible. . . . racism and sexism prevented them from being able to enter the wage labor force on equal terms with white males. Their increasing numbers relative to the jobs open to them necessarily implied low wages . . . and high unemployment. [Edwards 1979:195]

This notion of "crowding" into sex- or racially segregated occupations, advanced initially by F. Y. Edgeworth in "Equal Pay to Men and Women for Equal Work," in the *Economic Journal*, in 1922 has been the concern of many labor market analysts (Stevenson 1975b:199; Blau 1975:257; Lloyd 1975:16; Edwards 1979:194). Stevenson, among others, recognizes that even the historical approach of most radical researchers fails to explain the origins of the crowding phenomenon, though societal prejudice and job completion do partially explain the maintenance of job segregation over time.

As Gordon pointed out earlier in the 70s, until recently, labor market analysts of every ideological leaning have lacked the empirical evidence with which to support their claims about the structure of labor markets. Data examining and explaining the particular position of women workers within a stratified labor market were equally scarce. More recently, a number of researchers have presented historical and demographic data which supports the existence of occupational satification by sex (see Kessler-Harris 1975, Oppenheimer 1973, Stevenson 1975b, Ferber and Lowry 1976, Blau 1975, Zellner 1972, and Reagan 1979). Others have provided empirical evidence linking job segregation by sex to wage differentials between men and women workers [Stevenson 1975a, Beck et al. 1978, and Bibb and Form 1977].

Bibb and Form treat the issue of women's predominance in the secondary job sector in some detail. They characterize the dual sector economy in terms of an enterprise's "material and organizational resources and [its] ability to pay high wages"; the primary sector is composed largely of "capital intensive, oligopolistic firms which practice economies of scale and earn relatively high and stable profits," whereas the secondary sector includes typically small, highly competitive, labor-intensive, and geographically dispersed firms with unstable profits. As a consequence of these characteristics, the secondary sector work force lacks the organizational power of the more homogeneous, advantaged primary sector work force. With reference to the position of female workers, consigned predominantly to the secondary sector, Bibb and Form present evidence in support of the claim that:

> The low income of blue-collar women cannot be explained by individual variables in a human capital model but by merging of three low strata: economically weak enterprises in the peripheral sector, occupational groups with weak organizational power and the subordinated estate of women in society. [Bibb and Form 1977:979]

Thus, the radical model provides a set of theoretical propositions, a framework for analysis, backed up by a growing body of historical and empirical research, which can be applied to the situation of women in the American work force. Such applications focus primarily on sex segregation among occupations and industries, women's lack of occupational mobility and male-female wage differentials. In the sections to follow, this framework is tested with respect to the structure of the electronics industry and the reality of blue-collar women's work within the industry.

## 2. The U.S. Electronics Industry

*Industry Structure.* How does the structure of the electronics industry correspond with the salient characteristics analysts have outlined as the determinants of a secondary labor market: a high degree of industry competition, geographic dispersion, labor intensiveness, instability of profits and small firm size?

A U.S. Federal Trade Commission report stated in 1977 that the semiconductor industry, the heart of the electronics industry, was as perfectly competitive as any industry could get (Hancock 1979:10). As of 1977, nearly six thousand electronics firms existed nationwide. However, because of increasing capitalization costs, the scarcity of venture capital, and the growing difficulty of "catching up" with the technological leads of major companies, the number of firms in the industry as a whole is no longer growing quite so rapidly. In the semiconductor industry in particular, firms maintain or increase their relative market shares through constant innovation. The development of new technologies depends more on a firm's previous research and development record now than at any time in the past (New York

*Times* 1979, *Business Week* 1979. pp. 89) The need to control market stability and to obtain greater access to a wider range of technologies and skills is transforming the industry. Currently, the industry stands at a threshold; the trend is now towards vertical integration and concentration within the different sectors of electronics production (Pacific Studies Center 1977, Hancock 1979, and *Business Week* 1979). But to date, competition is still quite marked.

An interesting phenomenon has accompanied industry development that places electronics in two camps, in both the primary and secondary sectors in terms of labor market participation. On the one hand, these firms exhibit many of the features of oligopoly that are associated with the primary sector; relatively few companies dominate the market in several major electronics sectors. Six companies accounted for more than 92 percent of sales of all mainframe computers in 1975 and one firm alone, IBM, controlled over 65 percent of this market; in consumer electronics only seven U.S. television producers were operating in 1977 (NACLA 1977:6); in 1972, four out of 289 semiconductor firms accounted for just over 53 percent of the industry's value of shipments and many of the larger companies exhibited considerable economies of scale in production processes (Webbink 1977:20). In recent years the semiconductor industry has moved to consolidate its oligopolistic structure through the increase in mergers and corporate acquisitions by semiconductor firms and by electronic equipment producers in general (*Business Week* 1979, pp. 89). Control of market shares depends to a large extent not only on a company's ability to innovate but on the ability to predict the market for new technologies. Thus, research and development and marketing are of primary importance. Because of this, the industry employs a large proportion of "primary" employees: highly educated, well trained professionals and technicians. Labor shortages in the San Jose area among this kind of worker have resulted in considerable "head-hunting," with substantial benefits and high salaries offered as bait. The scientific and technical work force (engineers and scientists, technicians, draftsmen, etc.), grew from 16 to 27 percent of the total semiconductor workforce between 1964 and 1971 (U.S. Department of Commerce 1979b:31). Few sectors of electronics depend quite so heavily on research and development to maintain their competitive edge. However, rapid technological innovation and a large and growing professional job sector characterize the entire industry.

On the other hand, such aspects as stable market shares and oligopolistic price setting are not characteristic of the electronics industry. Although technological prowess provides the potential for acquiring larger market shares in particular product lines, the ease of entry into the market (which is only beginning to decline); the large number of firms; and, as in most areas of electronics production, aggressive price cutting strategies mean the continuation of an extremely competitive sales market for some time to come. Pressure to reduce production costs translates into low wages and secondary working conditions for the bulk of the blue-collar work force.

Between 1967 and 1974, in semiconductors the cost of materials rose from 29 percent of total production costs to 36 percent. The share of salaried workers remained about the same, yet the share of the wage work force dropped from 26 percent to 11.7 percent. Production workers average hourly earnings in the U.S. rose by 6.2 percent a year between 1967 and 1976, from $2.60 to $4.46 an hour, more slowly than average wage increases for all U.S. manufacturing industries (U.S. Department of Commerce 1979:13–32). The real decline in labor costs, according to a U.S. Department of Commerce report, is in fact due to the widespread trend towards offshore assembly. Primarily competition in the area of pricing policies together with rapid technological change and the precise demands of production processes have therefore resulted in the development of an extremely labor intensive, low-skilled production process. Corresponding with radical segmented labor market notions, the jobs offered fall primarily to the less advantaged workers. In the United States in 1978, 76.4 percent of electronics operatives were women and 27.1 percent of the total number of operatives were minorities. (U.S. Equal Employment Opportunity Commission [EEOC] 1967–1978.) In Asia, Grossman and others have estimaed that close to 90 percent of production workers are female (Grossman 1979:3). Table 12-1 illustrates the degree of labor intensiveness in U.S. semiconductor manufacturing compared with all U.S. manufacturing industries:

Not only does the electronics industry straddle the two major labor market sectors outlined here with a fairly clear delineation between primary and secondary workers, it has gone a step further in the process of segmenting the work force by creating international divisions within the secondary work force itself. Certainly, portions of the industry are highly concentrated geographically (see Snow 1980 for details), primarily the research and development and more complex production processes, which are centered around the twin industry capitals in Boston and San Jose. Yet the industry exhibits a high degree of geographic decentralization overall, both within the

*Table 12-1.* Comparative Labor Intensive: U.S. Domestic Semiconductor Manufacturing versus All U.S. Manufacturing[a] 1967, 1972–1976 (Percentage)

| | Payroll/Value of Output[b] | | | | | |
|---|---|---|---|---|---|---|
| | 1967 | 1972 | 1973 | 1974 | 1975 | 1976 |
| Semiconductors (3674) | 46.7 | 33.5 | 31.6 | 32.1 | 38.3 | 30.4 |
| All Manufacturing[a] | 21.9 | 21.0 | 20.0 | 18.1 | 18.3 | 17.8 |

*Source:* U.S. Department of Commerce, 1976b:33.

[a] The data are for "operating manufacturing establishments" and exclude central administrative offices and auxiliaries.

[b] The value of output is equal to value of U.S. domestic industry shipments adjusted for the inventory change over the year.

United States and more dramatically on an international scale. Offshore sourcing has clearly resulted in a vertically integrated international division of production and labor with relatively sophisticated, more capital intensive and more highly skilled production in the industry's domestic centers, whereas the labor-intensive, semiskilled production is carried out increasingly in Third World industrial centers. This notion, however, tends to minimize the existence of a similar division of labor within the domestic industry itself and even within the highly concentrated research and development centers like Silicon Valley and Boston's Route 128. The decentralization of the industry on both a domestic and an international scale helps to maintain the secondary character of blue-collar workers in the centers as well by further adding to the divisions among all production workers.

Because so much of a company's competitive standing, particularly in semiconductors and consumer electronics, is based on innovation and the market demand for new technologies, sales and profits are extremely susceptible to fluctuations in the business cycle. Cost cutting to maintain acceptable profit rates and to balance output with demand requires cutbacks in production. Thus, the secondary sector production jobs offer no guarantees in the way of job security and stability. (See pp. 301ff. below, for a more detailed discussion of fluctuations in employment of production workers in the San Jose area electronics industry.)

Firm size is probably the most indeterminant characteristic among electronics companies in terms of defining the structure or character of labor markets. In California during 1977, 408 out of 1,175 firms employed more than twenty people. These 408 firms probably employed the majority of all electronics workers in the state. Data on the San Jose area provide an indication of the dominance of the large firm as employer. There, only 8 percent of the total number of firms (or 38 companies) employed over five hundred workers each; together they employed three-fourths of the local electronics work force in 1979 (Axelrad 1979:4). Little that can be substantiated, however, can be said about the connection between firm size and the character of the labor force or of the jobs offered. Only in a few cases does the greater size of a firm correspond with better working conditions, higher pay scales, and increased job security in the production occupations. Most noticeably, Hewlett Packard operations in the San Jose area have gained a Valley-wide reputation for more nearly providing the kind of primary sector production opportunities described by the segmented labor market theorists. As one worker commented, "Everyone in the valley wants to work for Hewlett Packard."

Many theorists link larger firm size with a greater degree of unionization, as it is assumed that workers in larger firms can more easily develop a sense of solidarity. The larger unionized firms are expected to bring primary sector benefits to blue-collar workers. Unfortunately, data are not available that compares firm size with the degree of unionization in electronics. However, the industry, especially the younger manufacturers, have remained remarkably union free. Nationally, about one-fifth of semiconductor workers are represented by union contracts. The younger establishments, primarily in the South and West have a much lower degree of union representation. In the San Jose area, it has been estimated that, at most, 6 percent of production workers are union members (Axelrad 1979:12). Many large firms, such as Hewlett Packard and Texas Instruments, remain, for very different reasons, nonunion, while smaller, less competitive firms are under union contracts. In sum, the kinds of employment opportunities open to production workers seem to depend little on actual firm size. In this regard the radical model does not appear to hold true. The actual size of firms seems to matter less than other factors in shaping the work force. For example, a firm's personnel management philosophy and policies concerning internal plant organization appear to have a greater impact on the type of work force employed and the compensation workers receive. Additionally, as in the case of Hewlett Packard and other firms that offer characteristically primary employment opportunities, a virtually stable market share in certain product lines assures the firm of more stable profits. In this sense, they are more closely able to approximate the theoretical primary employer. Thus, it is risky to assume that firm size rather than oligopolistic market standing, for example, is the underlying determinant of particular employment practices.

*The Female Labor Force.* Since 1940 the entrance of women into the paid labor force has risen dramatically. In 1940 approximately 30 percent of all women aged eighteen to sixty-four were employed (Oppenheimer 1973:185); according to the Bureau of Labor Statistics in 1970, 42.8 percent of all women over the age of sixteen were in the paid labor force (U.S. Department of Commerce 1971:211); and in 1979 this figure rose to 50.7 percent (U.S. Department of Labor 1979b:2). Two recent features mark this rise in female employment rates: the entrance of large numbers of women aged thirty-five to fifty-nine and the rise in work force participation of younger married women with pre–school-aged children. These trends can be attributed to several factors. Increased economic development has resulted in a more rapid demand for female labor, as the major, traditionally female occupations have expanded considerably. And a declining relative supply of younger unmarried women, traditionally the most commonly employed among women, has necessitated the hiring of older women and married women with children (Oppenheimer 1973:192–194).

This does not necessarily imply a shortage of female workers, merely an increase in relative demand that has brought older and married women into the workforce, where they would not easily have found employment before. As Braverman points out:

> . . . in a process which cuts across racial and national lines, the female proportion of the population has become the prime supplementary reservoir of labor. In all the most rapidly growing sectors of the working class, women make up the majority of the workers. Women form the ideal reservoir of labor for the new mass occupations. The barrier which confines women to much lower pay scales is reinforced by the vast numbers in which they are available. [Braverman 1974:385]

However, for the electronics industry, nationwide employment figures show that occupations employing predominantly females have grown more slowly than employment in the industry as a whole. Between 1966 and 1978, total employment in electronics grew from 326,993 to 453,576, an increase of 38.7 percent. The blue-collar work force grew from 203,950 to 230,911, or about 13.2 percent and the category of operatives, where most blue-collar women workers are found, appeared to grow even more slowly, increasing from 141,835 to 153,678 or 8.3 percent (U.S. Equal Employment Opportunity Commission 1966–1978). When overseas expansion is taken into account, however, the picture changes. Since 1962 when the first semiconductor firms began moving to Asia, the growth of production overseas has expanded rapidly. In 1979, it was estimated that somewhere between 200,000 and 300,000 women production workers were employed by electronics firms in southeast Asia alone (Grossman 1979:3).

Growth in blue-collar occupations in the San Jose area between 1966 and 1978 has been much more rapid than the national rate, with an increase of approximately 92 percent, in that period from 7,495 to 14,391 (U.S. EEOC 1966–1978). Although data is not available which provides information on the age and marital status of electronics workers in the San Jose area, this survey and corporate hiring policies indicate that women of all ages, married and unmarried are to be found in significant proportions among the production workforce.

*Silicon Valley's Women Workers: Case Studies.* The case studies begin with a look at Alice, a young, married woman who has recently entered electronics and who is optimistic about her future in the field. Nina's story follows. A spanish-speaking immigrant to this country, she has, after a series of low-paying, highly insecure jobs, landed a position as an assembler. Her experiences illustrate the obstacles faced by minority and non-English speaking women. Finally, we look at Ruth, who has worked in one electronics firm in the Valley for over twenty years. Her insights about the opportunities open to women who stay in electronics provide a revealing contrast to the views of the two previous, young newcomers. These case studies describe just three perspectives but they relate many of the common experiences of assembly line workers in Silicon Valley and other U.S. electronics manufacturing sites. The names of the women interviewed and the company names have been changed to protect the confidentiality of the women interviewed.

*Alice.* Alice's experiences typify those of many hardworking, optimistic young women in Silicon Valley. Now in her second electronics job at a small firm, Microtech, she has been working for the last eight months as a wafer tester. Twenty eight years old, caucasian, with a high school education, Alice lives with her husband and her two children, aged six and four, in Sunnyvale the site of a large number of Silicon Valley's electronics firms. She and her husband, a technician at another local high technology firm, moved to the

Bay area just over two years ago from the east coast. They have been renting a small, comfortable, two bedroom house in a residential area of Sunnyvale near their workplaces. Recently, they have begun to worry about keeping their house as rents in the area have been increasing rapidly. Many of Alice's coworkers live up to twenty miles farther south in San Jose where housing is somewhat less expensive. Not having to commute long distances daily, however, is an advantage that outweighs the higher cost of rents, in Alice's eyes.

Before having children, Alice held a variety of jobs—as a nurse's aid, a clerk, and a telegraph operator. But with the birth of her first child, she dropped out of the work force for several years. Once the children were old enough to attend day school, Alice began to look for a new job. In the San Jose area, electronics seemed to offer the best opportunities for women. Her first job as an assembler, easily obtained with no prior experience required, was in the wafer fabrication division of a small Silicon Valley firm. Unfortunately, after little more than a year, she found it necessary to leave because of the prolonged illness of her son. Some months later, she reapplied at the same company but was offered only a training position at a cut in pay. The job offered then was a more boring and repetitive one than her previous position and was therefore not appealing. Hearing about openings at Microtech through a local employment agency, she applied and was hired immediately by the woman who was to be her supervisor. A female supervisor, she felt, would be more understanding and provide a better working environment. Microtech manufactures a variety of electronic components and instruments for biomedical, environmental, and other uses, including the electronic wands used by cashiers in retail establishments.

The training period for wafer testers at Microtech lasts six months. Trainees learn to operate delicate machinery that automatically tests wafers received from an Intel facility in the Philippines. The starting wage was $3.50 an hour when Alice was hired, but with her previous experience, she was able to start at a slightly higher wage.

The tasks of a tester are fairly varied, involving the use of both automatic and manual equipment for testing, plating, and sawing the wafers. In hindsight Alice feels the training process was fair, though during the six month period she had felt frustrated about not having been given more responsibility. What makes her job interesting is that she has continued to learn about the equipment and various fabrication processes from the engineers she works with daily.

At Microtech employee evaluations are carried out every six months. Workers are judged largely on the basis of their attendance records and on whether they meet quotas, where the latter exist. After her initial training, Alice was awarded a raise bringing her hourly earnings up to $4.80. Together with her husband's wage of $9.00 an hour and with the extensive overtime that he works, they are fairly comfortable financially.

For Alice the pay is not the most attractive aspect of working for Microtech. Being in a position to learn more about the industry, and the particular benefits package that the company offers are the most appealing factors. Extensive medical coverage for herself and her children, one part of Microtech's benefits, is extremely important because of her son's poor health. The company also offers a credit union with a savings plan for all employees. They do not, however, offer any standardized or built in merit increases nor any cost of living increase. These, she feels, are considerable deficiences.

About twenty people work in production at Microtech, out of a total of perhaps two hundred employees. The company is owned by a large conglomerate, but does not itself have any branches in other areas of the United States or abroad. All of Alice's coworkers are female except one eighteen-year-old high school student.

Alice had never given much thought to the different ethnic backgrounds of the women in her area. And although they are varied, English is the language spoken by nearly everyone. Most of the women in the area get along well and morale is usually quite good. As a group they are extremely well disciplined; talkativeness and lack of concentration reflect negatively on a worker's performance. "You have to work hard or you get fired." Testers are not subject to quotas because of the variability of their work, but most others have charts on the floor and are required to log their daily performance to compare with established quotas. Most of the workers seem to feel that the quotas are fair. The group has been fairly stable, with neither layoffs nor much new hiring since Alice's arrival.

Work hours are slightly flexible, allowing those with commitments at home to come in half an hour late as long as they work a full eight hours each day. This gives Alice the time to drop her children off at the sitter before leaving for work. The sitter, who lives several blocks from their home, takes the children to school and picks them up in the afternoon. Alice collects them on her way home from work. She and her husband have heard rumors of a possible child-care center at her husband's workplace; this would be a new and innovative ideas for the area. Alice is all in favor of it, but skeptical that it will ever happen.

For Alice the advantage of this kind of work is the financial security that on-the-job experience brings. She sees quite a variety of opportunities for women in electronics, and feels there is room for advancement to more interesting and better paying jobs. A sense of family among the workers in her own plant as well as among women working in similar jobs for different companies marks both the work place and the community. The "female orientation" of the work place is a valued aspect for Alice and many of her friends.

However, Alice is not one to look at her daily life through rose-colored glasses. Significant problems exist as well. The tedium of assembly work is one major disadvantage. A positive attitude and coworkers with whom she can laugh and joke are Alice's way of coping with the rules and regulations and the boredom of her job.

Alice talked openly of other problems. "Safety is the biggest issue for electronics. It has to be. Especially in the wafer fab areas." Working closely with a wide range of hazardous chemicals, hot furnaces, and frequently poor safety equipment, health, and safety issues have become paramount for women working in plants all across the Valley. At Microtech the biggest problem has been lack of access to information. For example, many of the women had been working with chemicals for years, only recently discovering (if they are fortunate) that the chemicals may be highly dangerous and that extreme caution and proper safety procedures should be exercised. Since her arrival the company's management has shown signs of becoming more aware of work site health problems. This, she suspects is due to recent public outcries and worker organizing in response to glaring safety problems at a nearby plant. Yet still, she notes, "small companies can do what they want. If you get on them, then sometimes things change." And there are problems for which she doesn't see answers. For the women in her area who work constantly with microscopes, vision problems are inevitable. Such things are accepted as the price of wanting and keeping a job. At least in a small firm like Microtech, she reasons, the workers have a greater chance of influencing management to resolve problems.

Unionization is not an option Alice would like too see her co-workers pursue. From past experience she holds unions ultimately responsible for layoffs and feels the structure they bring stifles individual initiative and effort. Instead, Alice would prefer to see employer-sponsored programs take the place of the benefits a union might provide. Right now, she attributes the lack of a stronger benefits package to the youth of the company and feels the situation will change. If not, she thinks, there are other firms and better job offers. "That's the thing about electronics. It's constant moving around and changing to get better money somewhere else. In a few years time you can really make good money if you work hard."

Ideally, she says, she would like to return to school in the field of electronics. Having only a high school diploma, further education would be a faster route to job promotions. But for now Alice intends to spend another full year at Microtech before moving on. Her reluctance to return to school is understandable. With a worried look, she acknowledged that it will be extremely difficult to adjust her time to meet her family's needs, school requirements, and the responsibilities of full-time work.

Like many other women in the area, Alice is not particularly aware of the "offshore sourcing" trend that the industry has pursued during the last two decades. Microtech does receive wafers and components from overseas, but workers at their plant hear little about foreign industrial sites or about the lives of women in other countries who are doing quite similar work.

Alice's view of women's employment in electronics is a complex and ambivalent one, based on a mix of perceptive observation, personal expectation, and the industry's own ideology:

> Women make the best workers at this kind of thing because you have to be patient, you have to be good with your hands, and the work is so tedious. Isn't raising children and doing housework tedious? I mean, women are good at this. And, I guess [women are hired] mainly because the labor is cheap, and you don't have to have a good education behind you to get a good start. But it isn't bad, it's something that can work out well for a woman who hasn't worked—you know, women who have raised their families, who are working now and are out of the house. It's good for them, they'd go crazy if they didn't get out.

Indeed, these are the only kinds of jobs many women in the area can get, especially when reentering the work force after a number of years in the home. In comparison with many of the alternatives— such as cannery work, domestic service, or fast food employment— electronics work appears quite attractive. The industry offers a measure of financial security in a seemingly clean and pleasant environment, and for many women it provides companionship with other women which they do not find as housewives.

Alice, like many of the other women interviewed, views herself apart from the majority of assemblers. Although she implied that most women in the Valley who begin assembly work remain in these positions, for herself she sees a more interesting and promising future.

*Nina.* Nina, thirty-six years old and Spanish speaking, came to the United States with her husband and three children, aged sixteen, seven and three, nearly two years ago as a political exile. Her background is solidly middle class. In Chile where she was born and raised, Nina had several years of vocational training in nursing. Her husband, Jorge, was a lawyer. Since their arrival she and Jorge and their sixteen year old son have worked as house painters and car washers; Nina herself has held down jobs in local canneries and in a furniture refinishing establishment. Four months before our interview, she began working as a janitor for $5.00 an hour at a medium-sized electronics firm, Davis Instruments, which manufactures lasers and electronic instrumentation for laser equipment. Through friends there, she was able to get her husband hired on as well, inspecting products in the optic division at $5.65 an hour. The friends who introduced him to the firm received $100 bonuses for recruiting him. Because of the labor shortage in technical occupations, even untrained people, if they are highly educated and are willing to work their way up from a very low level, are highly valued.

One month before the interview, Nina was able to transfer to an assembly position in her husband's area. In her present job, English is not a requirement. Several of the line leaders speak Spanish and many of Nina's coworkers speak little English. However, to acquire this job, Nina agreed to a substantial cut in pay; now she earns the starting wage of $3.50 an hour.

Although Nina's political experiences and outlook set her apart from many of her coworkers, in most aspects, her situation is not particularly unique. State licensing problems preclude the possibility of nursing until she can master English and study for the state exams. Without the necessary language skills, her professional experience and education mean nothing. Many immigrants have similar problems, sometimes even when their ability to speak English is quite good. For example, surveys among the Filipino community in Mountain View, the heart of Silicon Valley, have shown that 37 percent of employed Filipinos now work as assemblers in the electronics industry. Of those, only one percent held assembly-line jobs in the Philippines before emmigrating, and 47 percent held professional or managerial positions (Filipino Association of Mountain View 1978:99–100). Without significantly improving her English and with little other skilled experience, it will be very difficult for Nina to move far beyond her current position as an assembler. Her highest priority now is, of course, to learn English; but with three children and a full time job, finding the time for classes or the money for private lessons is difficult.

In some ways however, Nina is fortunate, her son takes care of the two younger girls when they are not in school or the day-care center. Nina works the day shift and Jorge works the swing shift so that they can balance their time to take care of their children. The biggest advantage has been finding an affordable day-care center. At her daughter's elementary school there is a state funded center that charges a total of only $11 a week to care for both children during after-school hours until Nina or Jorge can come for them. As far as she knows, this is the only child-care center of its kind in the Valley. Other women who don't have family or friends to care for their children, commonly pay up to $70 per week for full-time services for each child. For many women who work as assemblers, this can mean close to half of their net weekly earnings.

Nina is now working forty to forty-five hours each week. Her production area has about twenty-five workers, all but three of whom are women. As a group, they assemble entire vacuum tubes for lasers and some of the electronic components that go into the laser equipment. Each person rotates between tasks so that everyone eventually learns the entire assembly process. Each worker keeps track of his or her own performance; there are no established quotas. The workers in her area get along quite well, but Nina feels a form of subtle control in the group process. Because they are working as a team, assemblers check on each other's work and through this, word gets to the supervisors of each individual's performance.

Davis Instruments is a rapidly growing company. Twenty people were hired with Nina and she has seen no layoffs. The benefits provided by this firm, when compared with many other local firms, are quite good. Besides having flexible hours, full medical coverage and one week's vacation after six months, workers are granted one day sick leave per month. This was more than most of the women interviewed for this study received; some received no paid sick leave at all.

Stepping into Nina's work area is like walking into an international organization. The workers are of varied racial and national backgrounds; Mexicans, Chicanos, Vietnamese and Filipinas make up the majority with a few blacks, white North Americans and Europeans as well. The management, she notes, is comprised heavily of Caucasian North Americans.

Discipline on the shop floor is fairly relaxed. Talking is permitted as long as it doesn't negatively influence work performance. Work is varied enough to keep them interested and the company seems to prefer careful, precise work and does not encourage greater output at the expense of poorer quality goods. Nina noted that in her area the quality of work has been improving with time.

Although she is optimistic about the potential for advancement within the company, two problems overshadow the benefits at times. Foremost, in Nina's opinion is the low pay and the arbitrary structure for assigning pay raises. After six months workers typically may be earning $4.25 an hour. If they remain with the firm, after eight years or so, they may be able to earn as much as $8.00 an hour, she has heard. But wage increases are at the discretion of individual supervisors and are based on personal evaluations. No standard wage increases of any kind exist. Further, workers are instructed not to discuss their wages, so Nina has no way of knowing what the longer term workers there are actually being paid. As to the arbitrary nature of this system, Nina cites her husband's experience as a case in point. He has been working there just over six months and already earns as much as many women who have worked there for three or more years in comparable posiitions.

The second problem is the workers' lack of access to information and services within the plant, and even more importantly, the inability of the women there to articulate their needs. For example, child care is of great concern to many of the women, yet few would be willing to pressure the company to become involved with this issue. In contrast, in Chile under the Allende administration, she recalls that such services as child care and housing were supported in part by employers. It is upsetting to Nina that problems such as these are accepted (and are often not even recognized as such) by most of the women at Davis Instruments.

Nina's political views do set her apart: "People don't know how to put into words the injustices they feel. For example, what is a just salary? In a socialist society, this is defined." But she knows that to keep her job and to get ahead, it is best to simply keep quiet and attend to her own future. As a janitor for three months, she was able to observe and work in all the production divisions in the several buildings Davis Instruments occupies. From this experience and from talking with friends in other firms, Nina has learned that her employer and her job are considered among the best that Silicon Valley has to offer women.

Why are women the ones hired to do this kind of work? "Women work in production—work that is most difficult, lowest paid, and most detailed—because men don't have the patience, and it's precisely patience that is why women do the work better. Women are accustomed to doing what they're told. . . . No, we're never told that's why we're hired. I can see and feel it, that's all." If men don't like these kinds of jobs, they leave for more interesting or better paid work. Nina saw this in the canneries in San Jose where she worked previously. All of the men left after the first day, but not one of the women left at first. When asked if she feels the opportunities for work are discriminatory, Nina responded, "I can't say that there's sex discrimination. I can only say what I've observed." And she went on to note that all of the owners of the company are men, the heads of the various divisions and most of the engineers and supervisors, including her own, are all men. Most of the women who work there, she observed, are no more than "little specks" giving their labor and their overtime hours to reach positions usually no higher than line leader in production areas after years of employment.

For Nina, like Alice, electronics work conjures up ambivalent feelings. Personally, she is fairly confident of working her way up into a more advanced and better paying job. But for most of the women in electronics, she knows the future holds little in the way of advancement or the opportunity to be creative at work. For those like Nina who speak little English, the structure of the industry locks them tightly into low paying, deadend positions. They must overcome both language and educational obstacles before they can realistically expect to find more rewarding jobs. With family and/or work demands, theirs is a difficult future.

*Ruth.* Ruth, a 55 year old, Caucasian, native of Georgia, has worked for ACI Corporation in Mountain View, California for twenty-one years now. Although the firm is headquartered on the east coast, it is one of Silicon Valley's oldest electronic establishments. The firm employs over 57,000 people in the United States and overseas, producing electronic components and major appliances. By now, Ruth thinks she has worked in nearly every production area in the plant. When she began, starrting wages were $1.89 an hour, now she receives $6.19 an hour. A lot has changed at ACI over the years and Ruth is in a position to know what the firm has to offer the woman who makes electronics her life's work.

Ruth grew up in the south, quitting school after the tenth grade to find a job. Except for the five years when her two children were young, she has worked ever since. With her husband, a $9.50 a hour teamster with a local dairy firm, she has lived in the San Jose area for over 25 years.

Ruth is now working in the classification and storage division, logging and storing finished components and handling the distribution of materials for the next stages of production. All categorizing and ordering information is computerized so Ruth's time is spent largely in front of a computer terminal. In her previous position, she had been an operative in the mask making area of ACI's wafer fabrication division where she worked for five years.

About five hundred workers are employed at ACI's Mountain View facility, not including the workers in Quality Control whose jobs are actually quite similar to those of assemblers in terms of skill, pay scales, and the repetitive nature of the work. From what Ruth has seen and heard, the company appears to have been downgrading some job classificatons over the last several years. The jobs haven't changed, but the lower classification puts them on a flatter pay curve. The number of job categories has expanded tremendously over the years and have in Ruth's words been, "chopped up so bad it's impossible to tell what's what." Starting wages over the years have been slowly raised to remain competitive with wages offered by other local firms. Now, inexperienced workers start at $3.01 an hour. But with down grading, the flatter pay curves mean that the longer term female employee can expect to earn little more than Ruth does after a comparable working career.

Working at ACI, as with so many other plants in the area, seems like "working in a foreign country" to Ruth. There are quite a few minorities represented, many non-English speaking people and many recent immigrants. In all of her previous work areas, Ruth's coworkers were always solely women. Now, she works with two others, one Caucasian woman who has been at ACI for twelve to thirteen years and a Filipino man who has been with the company six to seven months. In most areas one or two men are beginning to be employed now. Ruth thinks the company likes hiring minorities, especially recent immigrants because "they work hard, don't complain, and follow orders well."

The company has expanded tremendously since Ruth's arrival. One of the most notable changes in this process has been that the production floor, which used to be entirely open, is now sectioned off by work areas. Ruth speculates that this is a reaction to the various union drives that have occurred over the years. With the

*297*

partitions people can no longer meet and get to know one another quite so easily.

Another change Ruth has noticed with some disquiet, has been a slow shift in management's emphasis from high quality output to greater quantity. She surmised that management must be able to utilize some form of tax write-off to enable them to handle the costs of rejected material.

What are the advantages to working with a firm like ACI? Ruth's rueful response was similar to many of the other women interviewed; "Saturdays and Sundays." Wage work has been a way of life for Ruth; and in general, she enjoys the companionship of coworkers and the workplace atmosphere. "Any place is a good place to work if you're making a decent living out of it and you're being treated right." But in her own case, she does not feel that she is being treated fairly. Ruth sees herself as a "cog in a wheel, just a number." She has stayed so long with the same firm because she does not believe conditions would be much different in other electronics companies. From the experiences of other women interviewed, this perception is fairly accurate.

Ruth's dissatisfaction and relative lack of loyalty to the company has been a long time in developing. In the past the International Brotherhood of Electrical Workers (IBEW) has conducted a series of organizing drives at ACI's Mountain View plant. (The IBEW represents workers in several of ACI's plants on the east coast.) Only in the most recent campaign did Ruth become an active supporter. The primary reason for her involvement is that with time, Ruth came to realize that nearly every aspect of personnel management and corporate policy is arbitrary in relation to the worker. Everything that affects her own life: company discipline, the seniority system, pay scales and benefits, evaluations, promotions, and transfers are all beyond her control. She has come to understand that conformity, "brownnosing," and quiescence mark the character of the "good" worker. A concern for profit maximization mixed with personal favoritism appears to guide the decisions of managers and supervisors.

Ruth has not always gotten along well with her supervisors because she has been apt to speak up when she sees problems. In her eyes though, individual managers escape much of the direct blame for their poor and arbitrary treatment of workers. An ideology that presents the firm as an entity in its own right, as somehow above the control of any set of individuals within it, pervades the workers' views. "They [the supervisors] do what they're told to do; they have no choice either."

Ruth campaigned for the union during the last drive because she hoped to see institutionalized some legitimate body that could argue grievances on behalf of the workers in a forceful and systematic manner. To the worker, company policy seems to be founded on a set of arbitrary distinctions. No uniform grievance procedures exist and this works to management's advantage in controlling their employees. One example Ruth gave in explaining the need for a union concerned the overall wage structure. As in both Nina's and Alice's case, workers are presently discouraged from sharing information about the wages they receive. When inequities are revealed, the workers tend to express their frustrations in the form of resentment against one another, rather than against the company for its arbitrary wage policy. This is common among the workers of many plants and serves to keep them from developing a stronger sense of solidarity.

Ruth cited example after example. Evaluations are conducted every six months; but transfers, promotions, and raises that depend on these evaluations are left up to the discretion of individual supervisors. No cost-of-living increases or standardized wage-incentive programs exist. None of the workers seem to know the maximum level of wages in their own work areas or classifications. Although Ruth applied for a routine transfer out of the mask-making area after her six months there, it took over five years before her transfer was granted. In areas with strict production quotas, she has seen some people harrassed by their supervisors, and even fired, when others doing comparable work were treated well or simply ignored. Rather than promoting people from within certain work areas, the company often brings in outsiders, frequently men, to fill supervisorial positions. Highly qualified women in those areas may be passed over and then be required to train the new supervisor. Ruth feels that many women who were working for the union were passed over in this manner. The seniority system, which supposedly guides many supervisorial decisions concerning promotions, transfers, and so forth, is a joke in Ruth's opinion.

Although she feels secure in her job, Ruth expressed much concern about the scattered, seemingly arbitrary, layoffs she has seen. "After you're there for ten years or more, they don't really want you there anymore because you're going to start accumulating retirement benefits, and they don't want to have to pay that. And after fifteen years, you're going to get four weeks vacation, and they don't want that either. . . .If you complain about things, it's, 'Why don't you quit?'" She has seen and heard of people at Raytheon being laid off close to retirement age, or in response to their involvement with the union. More frequently, management succeeds in pressuring people to quit through subtle harrassment and discrimination. One older woman who worked in Ruth's area was put in this situation when her work performance was impaired by a work related injury. Ruth felt they had made her so miserable that she resigned, forfeiting the retirement benefits she would have received within several years.

Some years before, the company produced a booklet describing personnel policies. Ruth thought it so irrelevant as to be totally useless. "One person is told one thing, and another something else. You never know what to expect and after awhile you cease to care about it."

Ruth's biggest complaint concerning this whole issue of arbitrary work rules and procedures is that the women workers are treated as "school children." Supervisors at times seem to avoid the responsibility of dealing with individual's work problems by confronting their entire production group. In this manner a worker's colleagues are pressured to take the responsibility for making that worker "shape up." Ruth would like to see a more responsible and systematic method for addressing problems and complaints, for both workers and managers. The union, she had hoped, would provide the structure to accomplish this. However, in this last election, the union was defeated by an even larger margin than in some of the previous elections. In Ruth's eyes, fear—of a bad work record, of being fired, or of simply losing the little they do have—and communication problems between the people of different nationalities stymied the union's efforts. Extremely high turnover hindered the campaign as well, making it very difficult for the union to determine what percent of the workers' votes they could count on.

Cynicism clouds the hindsight of union supporters like Ruth. "People don't seem to want to be bothered. A lot of people have no interest in staying in the first place." And this is the crux of the matter: with rapid turnover, with the persistant myth that there is actually opportunity for advancement on an individual basis, many women in Silicon Valley will only halfheartedly support efforts to unionize. For many of these women, putting up with the problems and negative aspects of their jobs are simply part of the reason they are being paid. Lack of knowledge and access to information about the many problems and dangers associated with their work and a

300

perceived lack of better alternatives shapes their self-perception and their attitudes towards their working roles.

Ruth, like many others, acknowledges and simultaneously downplays many work related problems. For example, she knows that she has been in numerous dangerous and unhealthy situations at work. Evacuations due to fume problems occur periodically. After a period of constant microscope use, she needed eyeglasses for the first time. Safety training in areas where workers use highly hazardous chemicals has been minimal and enforcement of safety regulations intermittent. Ruth has not heard any particular expressions of concern from management about health and safety issues at the plant. Yet, overall, her evaluation of the company's record in this regard is that there have not been any significant safety problems or threats to the health of workers.

Most of the women who work in Silicon Valley seem resigned to the general situation of women's employment, though many are personally optimistic. About other women in electronics, Ruth comments,

> I feel sorry for the ones who are just starting. . . . They [the companies] use people. They really take advantage of women. And I don't know why more women don't see it. I suppose maybe I didn't when I was younger. But some of the women there are supporting kids by themselves. And they're not even making as much as I do. I don't know how they do it on what we're paid. I really don't.

Besides the day-to-day routine, electronics work has meant a long process of observation and realization for Ruth. After twenty one years, she feels she understands the basic motivations of and the powerful control exerted by Silicon Valley employers over their women workers.

*Job Mobility Among Female Assemblers.* Corporate recruiting propaganda, a scattered number of individual success stories, and the overall expansion of jobs may have helped to perpetuate a myth of upward mobility among women in Silicon Valley. Of the women interviewed, certainly one of their more common aspirations is to advance within the field of electronics. Most realize that this necessitates further schooling, although few indicated how they would manage to return to earn college degrees. State Employment Development Department publications reveal that,

. . . local employers hiring electrical and electronics technicians usually require two years of college with emphasis on math, physics and electronics or related military training and experience. The demand for electronics technicians is closely tied to trends in the electrical and electronic equipment industries, which are influenced by government contracts and the level of consumer and industrial demand for goods. Because of this, future demand for the technicians can fluctuate noticeably. [California Employment Development Department 1979:39]

For women with families, attempting to fulfill the prerequisites of technical jobs often means the triple burden of work, family, and school responsibilities. In the professional and scientific occupations, corporations are more likely to invest in the upgrading of employee skills. But for the "secondary" worker, the corporation's willingness to invest in "human capital" is largely limited to covering the costs of local vocational training school programs for their employees. However, nearly all community college programs in the San Jose area which offer electronics AA degrees are tuition-free and are supported by local, state, and federal funds.

In many cases, it appears that the college degree requirement is used more as a screening device than as a necessary requirement for on-the-job tasks. In effect, it provides one of the structural barriers to mobility between what may be considered, in terms of social status, secondary and primary occupations, that is, assembly work versus technical work.

Female electronics technicians in the United States do in fact receive approximately 38 percent more in average hourly earnings than female assemblers, the difference between $5.56 and $4.04. And, their positions are somewhat more secure than those of assemblers (U.S. Department of Labor (DOL) 1979c:7—8). However, their opportunities for further advancement within the firm and the nature of their daily work are often quite similar to those of assemblers. Several of the women interviewed felt they could easily and competently perform the duties of the technicians in their areas with only a minimal amount of additional training. Increasingly, the tasks of the technician have been routinized and automated.

Nevertheless, a technician's job is a step up in the electronics work force hierarchy; and it is a job less occupied by women. How realistic is the common expectation of advancement in electronics for the female assembler? Statistically, the growth in technical openings in electronics has been much more rapid than the expansion of assembly jobs in the San Jose area. The number of female technicians between

1966 and 1978 increased by nearly ten times. Table 12-2 illustrates this growth for selected years.

However, the number of new technicians hired in recent years has been falling; in fact, between 1975 and 1978, only 224 new female technicians were hired, while the number of male technicians employed by the industry in the San Jose area dropped by 292. The percent of technicians who were female rose from 8 percent in 1966 to 24 percent in 1978, although, overall, between 1974 and 1978, this percentage has remained fairly stable. Thus, women have been gaining ground relative to men among the technical occupations in the field. However, when viewed in terms of the blue-collar production force, upward mobility within electronics for female assemblers remains quite limited. Assuming from the aggregated data between 1975 and 1978 that an average of nearly 100 new female technicians were hired each year, this would be equal to approximately 1.4 percent of the female operative work force in 1975 and about 1.6 percent in 1978. Certainly, not all of the new technicians hired come straight from assembly line jobs. Although data on the previous work experience of female technicians is unavailable, the comments of women interviewed indicated that technical positions are frequently filled by young men and women just out of college and by women entering the work force after some years in the home. The latter have had the advantage of being able to acquire appropriate degrees while being housewives, before seeking employment. These technicians are likely to be of higher class backgrounds than most assembly workers. By starting out in primary jobs, they may find it easier to advance further in the field than assemblers are generally able to do so.

*Table 12-2.* Electronics Workers in the San Jose Area

| Year | Technicians | | | | Operatives | | | |
|------|-------|-------|--------|----------|-------|-------|--------|----------|
|      | Total | Male  | Female | % female | Total | Male  | Female | % Female |
| 1966 | 1,956 | 1,809 | 147    | 8%       | 5,755 | 736   | 5,019  | 88%      |
| 1969 | 3,172 | 2,838 | 334    | 11%      | 3,438 | 957   | 2,481  | 73%      |
| 1970 | 3,832 | 3,198 | 634    | 17%      | 6,209 | 1,087 | 5,122  | 83%      |
| 1971 | 3,642 | 3,075 | 567    | 16%      | 5,325 | 866   | 4,459  | 84%      |
| 1972 | 3,724 | 3,031 | 693    | 19%      | 5,422 | 812   | 4,610  | 85%      |
| 1973 | 4,668 | 3,788 | 880    | 18.9%    | 9,227 | 1,544 | 7,683  | 83.3%    |
| 1974 | 5,494 | 4,195 | 1,299  | 23.6%    | 11,510| 1,940 | 9,570  | 83.1%    |
| 1975 | 6,147 | 4,941 | 1,206  | 19.6%    | 9,185 | 1,808 | 7,377  | 80.3%    |
| 1978 | 6,079 | 4,649 | 1,430  | 23.5%    | 8,226 | 1,896 | 6,330  | 77.0%    |

*Source:* U.S. Equal Employment Opportunity Commission Reports, 1966–1978. The E.E.O.C. has not compiled comparable data for 1966, 1967, 1968, 1976, 1977.

It appears that relatively very few women rise each year from the ranks of assembly line workers to technical positions. Furthermore, although increasing proportions of women have been hired as technicians, many of the women interviewed felt that automated processes and the reorganization and reclassification of technical jobs have begun to deskill the work of technicians, rendering their tasks little different from those of assemblers.

Few female assemblers, especially married women with family responsibilities, appear able to overcome the many obstacles to job advancement that they face. Although many of the women interviewed realize that assembly jobs are dead-end positions for the majority of women, most seem unwilling to give up hope that things will be different for themselves. The attitude that advancement is purely a matter of personal motivation prevails:

> In electronics, without a certain amount of education you are really not going to go very far. If you started off as an assembler, the only way you can get out of it or go on to something is to go back to school. So, it's kind of a locked-in position. If you're doing this today, you're going to be doing it for years. But I do think the opportunities are there for women if they want them. [Electronics Assembler]

Unfortunately, job opportunities for Silicon Valley women with only high school diplomas or little work experience in other fields are to be found largely within the secondary occupations of the manufacturing and service sectors. This kind of limited occupational mobility clearly supports the tenets of the segmented labor market model.

As outlined above, other salient characteristics of secondary sector jobs include low pay, frequently poor working conditions, a low level of work force organization or unionization, a high degree of job instability and insecurity, little in the way of skills acquisition, and a predominance of women and minority workers. These characteristics match quite closely the situation of the San Jose area electronics work force. Snow has provided detailed documentation on the trend toward increasing minority hiring and the constantly high proportion of females in blue-collar occupations within the electronics industry (Snow 1980). Briefly, as of 1978 approximately 77 percent of Silicon Valley's operatives were female, 6,330 out of 8,226; and 44 percent of the total number of operatives were minority members, or 3,648 out of 8,226 (U.S. Equal Employment Opportunity Commission 1966–1978). Other characteristics of the secondary sector workforce are treated below.

304

*Wage Rates.* Nationally, gross hourly earnings for production workers in electrical and electronic equipment industries averaged $5.51 in 1977 (U.S. Department of Labor 1979c:2). Table 12-3 indicates the range of earnings among different segments of the industry. According to the Bureau of Labor Statistics,

> . . . the middle 50% of workers earned between $3.34 and $5.83 and hour. . . . three levels of assemblers, accounting for 55% of all production workers, averaged $4.08 an hour. Inspectors and testers, numerically the second largest job, averaged, $4.84 an hour. [U.S. DoL 1979c:2]

National average hourly wages for men in assembly, inspection and testing positions in the semiconductor industry were approximately 12 percent higher than women's wages in those same occupations (Table 12-4).

In 1978, the San Francisco Bay Area average hourly wages for assembler ranged from $4.06 to $5.58, depending on the grade of assembly position. For inspectors and testers, the average hourly wage was slightly higher, up to $6.38 for senior level employees (Axelrod 1979:25). The medium wage rate of the women interviewed in 1980 for this study was approximately $5.00 an hour, varying from $3.00 to $6.50 (The Federal minimum wage is $3.10 an hour.).

Table 12-5 gives an indication of the maximum amouint of earnings women in the San Jose area can expect to receive. The table lists the employer, the duration of employment, and the hourly wage rates of the top four earners among those interviewed. Several of

*Table 12–3.* Earnings: Electrical and Electronic Production Workers

|  | Average gross hourly earnings of production workers |
|---|---|
| Electric and electronic equipment | $5.51 |
| Miscellaneous electrical equipment and supplies | 6.62 |
| Communications equipment | 6.35 |
| Electrical industrial apparatus | 5.61 |
| Electrical distributing equipment | 5.57 |
| Household appliances | 5.44 |
| Electrical lighting and wiring equipment | 5.13 |
| Radio and TV receiving equipment | 4.97 |
| Electronic components and accessories | 4.58 |
| Semiconductors and related devices | 5.09 |

*Source:* U.S. Department of Labor 1979c:2.

*Table 12-4.* Wages in the Semiconductor Industry

| | Average Hourly Earnings | | |
|---|---|---|---|
| Occupation | All | Men | Women |
| All Assemblers | $4.08 | $4.52 | $4.04 |
| Class A (Skilled) | 4.53 | 6.02 | 4.39 |
| Class B (Semiskilled) | 4.16 | 4.78 | 4.12 |
| Class C (Unskilled) | 3.90 | 3.97 | 3.90 |
| All Inspectors and Testers | $4.84 | 5.32 | 4.77 |
| Class A (Quality control) | 5.11 | 6.36 | 4.63 |
| Class B (General testing) | 4.58 | 4.72 | 4.55 |
| Class C (Specialized testing) | 5.02 | 5.21 | 5.01 |

*Source:* U.S. Department of Labor, 1979c:7–8.

*Table 12-5.* Maximum Earnings, San Jose Area

| Employer | Duration of Employment | Previous Education and Experience of Worker | Gross Hourly Wage Received |
|---|---|---|---|
| Rolm Corporation | 4 years | 7 years assembly experience, some junior college (no degree) | $6.00 |
| ACI Corporation | 21 years | completed 10th grade | $6.19 |
| GTE Lenkurt (Union shop, IBEW) | 7 years | 1½ years assembly experience, competed 12th grade | $6.36 |
| Hewlett Packard | 5 years | 4 years assembly experience, 2 years junior college (no degree) | $6.40 |

*Source:* Interviews.

the women interviewed expected eventually to receive wages up to $7.00 or $8.00 an hour as senior assemblers. None of them, however, indicated that they knew of others receiving this level of pay. In comparison with the lower paying employers, the above figures would indicate that firms most interested in employee stability, such as Rolm and Hewlett Packard, and those that are unionized present the best paying options for female assembly workers in the Valley.

The low level of earnings in the electronics production work is compounded by the high cost of living in the San Jose area. Housing costs are one of the most rapidly increasing burdens on family income. Average home prices in the city of San Jose had risen from

$33,000 in 1973 to $92,000 in 1979 (*Electronics* 1980:99). The cost of rental units in Santa Clara County in recent years has increased slightly faster than incomes (Pacific Studies Center 1977:43). Housing is scarce in the immediate vicinity of electronics plants, resulting in additional transportation costs for those who live farther away and commute longer distances. Full-time child care for one child can run between 25 percent and 50 percent of a worker's net weekly income. For many women, unless they are merely supplementing the family income electronics production work offers a meager living indeed. Yet few better paying options are open to many of these women. Of these seventeen women interviewed, ten were members of households with more than one income earner; two were heads of households with at least one dependent; four were single women; and, one, aged eighteen was, herself a dependent in a household to which she did not regularly contribute a portion of her income.

*Working Conditions.* At first glance working conditions in the electronics industry appear relatively pleasant. The clean and spacious physical surroundings in most U.S. electronics plants have given the industry a reputation as a good place to work. The workers interviewed in this study by and large described their work areas as roomy and well lit. Most did not feel under continual pressure to increase their productivity, although a few noted that periodically their jobs have been quite stressful when deadlines approach and the pace of production is stepped up.

However, aspects of working conditions that have little immediate effect on productivity are those most easily overlooked by management. As both Alice and Ruth described above, the fastest growing concern to women working in the Valley is workplace safety and health. Of the women interviewed, ten complained of problems with chemical fumes and poor or faulty ventilation systems. Feelings of dizziness, nausea, burning eyes, and other problems are not uncommon among those who work with chemicals. Several of the women had been evacuated at various times because of dangerous fume problems. Two of the women interviewed experienced eye problems after constant microscope use, and both must now wear eyeglasses. Five of the women work in places where they were given little to no safety instruction and six felt that safety regulations at their work site were only periodically or haphazardly enforced.

Although considerable educational efforts have been carried out by independent occupational health organizations in the area as well as by a few of the firms' many of the Valley's female workers still lack information regarding the health hazards they face on a daily basis. In the experience of the women interviewed, the typical management response to health hazards has been largely ineffective and piecemeal. Workers' responses, like Ruth's, have often been to psychologically minimize the personal dangers because they seem unresolvable and because keeping one's job often seems of greater immediate importance. An extreme example of this among those interviewed is the case of Sally, who has worked now at three different electronics firms. At her first job, what she identifies as ammonia fumes were nearly always present and large containers of acids, metals, and solvents were routinely left uncovered. Many mornings when she arrived, she could see a thin mist of chemical vapors in her work area. Her second day of employment, she remained at home, sick from the fumes of the day before. Once in a while, she described, the company would bring in large fans to ventilate the area. The drainage system at the plant was also in need of repair; chemicals were dumped down corroded, leaking pipes. At her second job, safety conditions seemed much better, although safety regulations, such as wearing improtective glasses and clothing, were rarely enforced. Now, in her present job, Sally is under strict safety supervision. The use of safety equipment and proper procedures is regularly enforced. She works with potentially carcinogenic solvents but feels that the safety precautions she takes remove any danger from her working situation.

Clearly, Sally is in a safer position now than in her first job. The remarkable feature of her story is that despite the range of her experiences, she feels that in *all three cases* her employers were quite concerned with health and safety issues and the welfare of their employees. Sally is eighteen and at her first job she was earning less than $4.50 an hour. In the words of another women interviewed

If you're going to have your health involved, they should pay you for it or at least tell people and give them a choice. But these kids, . . . they don't tell [them] that it's dangerous, and they don't pay them anything. I think this thing of paying these wages to women—[with] the health hazards, it's a total disgrace. . . . If they're that way here, I can imagine what they're like in other countries. In relation to the profits involved, the wages are ridiculous. They're making one hell of a lot of money, and they're not giving one pinch to the production workers.

Most of the workers interviewed felt that if employees complained long enough, management would respond eventually. Though, of course, complaining too often or too loudly may mean running the risk of a bad work record or eventually even of being laid off. In the meantime, the workers must put up with many dangerous and annoying situations. Cutbacks in the budgets of state and federal occupational health and safety agencies and legislative battles that threaten the powers of these agencies will mean a slower rate of improvement in working conditions.

*Unionization.* As noted above. less than 6 percent of Silicon Valley's production work force is represented by unions. Wage scales in one of the few unionized plants in the Bay Area are above the local average. Among the women interviewed, however, reactions to union representation were quite mixed. Although a few worked actively in support of unions, the majority were either disinterested, unaware of or actively opposed to union organizing at their plants. The IBEW member interviewed had mixed feelings about her own union's ability to deal effectively with workers' grievances. Workers at her company, GTE Lenkurt, have been represented by the IBEW for over seven years and the workers have gone out on strike several times. The amount of pay lost during strike periods, she felt, was not compensated for by the minimal gains the union had made. Wage scales at GTE Lenkurt, however, were above the local average. At GTE Lenkurt and at many other facilities managements have recently turned toward active minority recruitment campaigns, including nonEnglish speaking peoples. Many of these new workers are much less likely to take action against employers for fear of losing their jobs. And language problems between worker's help to isolate them from each other even within the same work areas. Constantly high turnover rates, encouraged by low wages and poor working conditions, facilitate the companies' endeavors to remain nonunion (*Electronic Business* 1979).

*Job Instability.* For the national industry in 1978, an average of 2.2 per 100 employees quit per month, signifying a national average quit rate of over 25 percent a year. The average number of monthly layoffs per 100 employees was 0.4 employees, representing a 4.8 percent annual layoff rate. Because this accounts for workers in all occupational categories, it can be assumed that production workers experience substantially higher rates than these. Both quit and layoff rates tend to fluctuate widely, trends in the business cycle apparently having a significant impact on both. Contrary to what might be expected, electronics workers experienced initially higher quit rates (as well as layoffs) in the recession year of 1974. During that year, the average monthly number of quits per 100 employees rose to 2.7 for a 32.4 percent annual average rate, and the same figure for layoffs increased to 1.8, an annual average rate of 21.6 percent. In the following year, with the continuing recession, the quit rate dropped to its lowest point in nearly twenty years, with a monthly average of 1.2 quits per 100 employees or 14.4 percent per year. Layoffs, on the other hand, rose to a monthly average of 1.8 per 100 employees or 21.6 percent. From November 1974 to January 1975, the national industry experienced its highest layoff rates since 1958, levels that on an annual basis would have meant 46 percent to 54 percent of the work force being laid off annually—the average monthly layoffs per 100 employees ranged from 4.5 to 3.8 in that period (U.S. Department of Labor 1979a:335–336). The unexpectedly high quit rate at the onset of the recession may reflect two factors. First, the women interviewed in this study indicated that workers can frequently predict coming layoffs through slowdowns or other changes in work patterns. Thus, many choose to seek other employment, quitting voluntarily in an effort to avoid periods of unemployment that might result should they wait to be laid off. Second, many women for whom overtime is a financial necessity may be forced to seek other employment as slowdowns cut back on overtime hours available. A third factor may also enter in: women for whom electronics employment is not a financial necessity (the truely "secondary" income earners), may choose to drop out of the workforce voluntarily during such periods when faced with inevitable layoffs.

Table 12-6 indicates the depth of fluctuations in the employment of operatives in the San Jose electronics industry for selected years. As can be seen, the changes in employment levels among operatives, as compared with the total workforce, have varied more widely. Overall growth in employment for operatives in the San Jose area has not kept pace with the total growth in employment. However, looking simply at the San Jose area understates national trends in electronics production employment shifts, as Snow has described in great detail (Snow 1980).

Currently, most of the women in this survey do not feel threatened by imminent layoffs. Although several had been laid off in the past for various reasons, it was generally felt that layoffs present no serious problem. Presently, jobs can be found quite easily, usually involving from one day to one or two weeks worth of job hunting,

Table 12-6. Fluctuations, San Jose Electronics Industry

| Year | Total Employees | Percent Change in Number of Employees From Previous Year | Total Operatives | Percent Change in Number of Operatives From Previous Year |
|---|---|---|---|---|
| 1966 | 15,317 | – | 5,755 | – |
| 1969 | 19,758 | – | 3,438 | – |
| 1970 | 25,610 | 29.6 | 6,209 | 80.6 |
| 1971 | 24,504 | -4.3 | 5,325 | -14.2 |
| 1972 | 24,601 | 0.3 | 5,442 | 1.8 |
| 1973 | 33,420 | 35.8 | 9,227 | 70.2 |
| 1974 | 38,122 | 14.1 | 11,510 | 24.7 |
| 1975 | 39,852 | 4.5 | 9,185 | -20.2 |
| 1978 | 41,088 | 3.1 | 8,226 | -10.4 |

Source: U.S. Equal Employment Opportunity Commission. The E.E.O.C. has not compiled comparable date for 1967, 1968, 1976, and 1977.

depending on the particular preferences of the worker. A few of the larger, more established firms have "no layoff" policies. During short term periods of higher output, they hire "temporaries," thus avoiding having to layoff permanent personnel when production slacks off. In times of more severe cutbacks, work hours are reduced (and therefore earnings), but layoffs are avoided.

In general, however, the production worker has no guarantee of job security. The San Jose area is one of the more secure areas in which an electronics worker can be employed. (See Appendix B for information about benefits for workers). But as shown above, the level of employment in the area has been known in the past to drop as much as 20 percent from year to year. In any case, it is the production worker who first feels the impact of industry or firm cutbacks.

*Skill Levels.* In government and industry publications, the work of assemblers is described as semiskilled. The tasks of the women interviewed ranged from, for example, moving thousands of similar parts with tweezers from one place to another, eight hours a day, to working with fairly delicate and varied fabrication and testing equipment. For most, especially in larger firms with greater division of job specificity, training takes place on the job. Within the first several weeks, the worker usually acquires nearly all the skills necessary to perform her assigned tasks. Many skills are acquired within a matters of days. Only with some of the more complicated procedures, such as working from blueprints or operating precision instruments, does training take several months.

*311*

By and large, specific, full-time skills training programs for production workers are not a part of company procedures. Five of the women interviewed obtained training through local community colleges and job training centers. They learned the rudiments of assembly work before seeking electronics employment. All but one of the remainder, received training from their line leaders or immediate supervisors, learning their duties largely through trial and error. This seems to be fairly standard training procedure especially among firms that emphasize the quantity of products over quality. In some firms, new employees are easily trained by coworkers with little more than two weeks experience themselves, indicating that these jobs require minimal skill. Where jobs are repetitious, require little actual skill and where the firm offers the least chance for advancement to more skilled positions, a company gains little through investing in employee training and, in turn, encourages greater worker turnover.

Standard policy, regardless of the requirements of on-the-job training, usually defines the first three to six months as a probationary period. Pay is maintained at the starting or "training" level, regardless of the actual length of training involved. The justification for this is that a worker is only expected to reach maximum efficiency after a period of some months. Edwards emphasizes that the importance of such probationary periods appear to be less the acquisition and improvement of manual skills and more the smooth integration of the probationary worker into a secondary occupational slot within the hierarchy of the workplace (Edwards 1979:137, 179).

Although jobs in Silicon Valley are often less tedious, more varied, and involve a slightly higher level of skill than "offshore" production jobs, the emphasis during training periods is much the same. Like offshore workers, domestic production workers are taught that a positive attitude and regular attendance are the keys to good work performance. They learn little in the way of actual skills, especially in terms of skills that are transferrable to other occupations. Thus, what skills training does exists, helps to maintain occupational segregation, as workers become trapped in dead-end jobs that offer little in the way of skills upgrading beyond the particular requirements of their job.

*The Silicon Valley Work Force as a Microcosm of the International Electronics Workforce.* Compared with the industry nationally, the San Jose area work force is much more heavily white-collar. Thus, women's changes for advancement into low level management may be somewhat better than the national average. (Although, as described

*312*

above, opportunities for upward mobility are quite limited even in the Sane Jose area.) Fluctuations in total employment appear to be more dramatic in the peripheral areas of the country, meaning San Jose's women workers may also have a somewhat greater degree of job security (Snow 1980). Pay scales, benefits, and working conditions differ regionally according to the degree of unionization and to some extent, differences in the cost of living (U.S. DoL 1979c:2; based also on the comments of Santa Rosa, Californian workers regarding comparative pay scales between Santa Rosa and San Jose).

The distinctions between American workers, on the average, and offshore production workers are quite clear. The U.S. work force shows a much greater diversity in composition, with variations in age and marital status being considerably more pronounced. The U.S. electronics production work force also includes a substantially higher proportion of males. Pay, benefits, working conditions, and so forth are better in the United States, as are chances for advancement. The offshore production sites have a very low relative proportion of managerial, professional, and technical positions.

*Evaluating the Segmented Labor Market Model.* Production employment in the electronics industry corresponds quite directly with the segmented labor market model's schema of employment characteristics in the secondary sector. Low wages, poor working conditions, relative job instability and insecurity, arbitrary work rules, and little opportunity for advancement characterize the situation of Silicon Valley's production workers quite well. However, certain formulations of this model, especially with respect to analyzing the position of women, seem in some ways to lack both comprehensiveness and precision. In particular, returning to Bibb and Form's presentation, described in some detail in Section 1 above, several fairly substantial criticisms can be made. The first of their "three low strata" (which merge to explain women's low position in the work force hierarchy), that of economically weak enterprises in the peripheral economy, seems less relevant to electronics than perhaps to other female dominated manufacturing industries in the United States, for instance, the garment or textiles industries. Indeed, the electronics industry promises to be among the more vital and central industries in U.S. manufacturing. A Department of Commerce report on the semiconductor industry comments that in "only 32 years of product and process development, semiconductors have emerged from the laboratory to touch the lives of nearly everyone in the industrial world," not to mention significant portions of the Third

World. By 1976 it was estimated that the semiconductor industry's output was critical to the production of more than $200 billion worth of goods and services in manufacturing (including ordinance) and communications industries (U.S. DoC 1979b:1 and 103).

> According to industry analysts, the biggest growth era in its history is yet to come: the strongest predicted future growth markets are the telecommunications and automative industries, which when combined with a resurging military/aerospace demand should provide a tripling of semiconductor usage over the next five years. The traditional markets—computer, industrial, consumer and international are also growing strongly. [Saxenian 1979:2]

Other theorists have emphasized the monopoly versus nonmonopoly status of industries over their "peripheral" or "weak" economic stature. This seems more accurate in the case of electronics and perhaps for all industry.

The second element in Bibb and Form's explanation of women's secondary sector predominance corresponds accurately with the reality of electronics industry: the female work force is characterized by occupational groups with relatively weak organizational power. This does, however, raise the question of why. If developed further, the authors' third explanation might offer insights into this question. The third feature, "the subordinated estate of women" in industrial society touches on more fundamental causes of this phenomenon. Yet, Bibb and Form, like many other segmented labor market theorists, tend to pay lip service to this concept rather than explore the cause for and the impact of this reality. Pearson and Elson critically summarize such arguments in a somewhat simplified, but not inaccurate, manner: "Women are used as cheap labor because women's labor is cheap," which in various writings has been presented alternatively: women are discriminated against in the labor force because they have been discriminated against in the past (Pearson and Elson 1978:25). The segmented labor market model, although accurate and useful on many levels, suffers from a lack of analytical depth, especially in explaining the role of women in the domestic labor market. Because of this, many radical theorists obfuscate distinctions between the causes and the characteristics of sex-segregated occupations and divisions in the labor market structure. The following section addresses these problems in somewhat more detail, applying the theoretical criticisms and suggestions of socialist feminist theorists.

### III. Socialist Feminist Labor Market Theory

> We hire mostly women because they are more reliable than men; they have finer fingers, smaller muscles and unsurpassed manual dexterity. Also, women don't get tired of repeating the same operations nine-hundred times a day [Fernández Kelly 1979a:8]

So says an electronics firm manager in the Mexican Border Industrial Zone. This is a common international impression, from the fast-fingered Malay girl to the dexterous, diligent women of Silicon Valley. Many of the women interviewed from the San Jose area agreed that manual dexterity was a key factor in hiring women. But as Fernández-Kelly responds, "By distorting and oversimplifying complex phenomena, ideology obviates the need to center attention upon economic and political realities." Such can also be said of the greater portion of radical labor market theory when it comes to answering the important question of why predominantly women occupy secondary jobs within the hierarchy of the labor market today, in both the United States and the Third World.

In the last few years, socialist feminist commentators have provided two important contributions towards answering this question. First, they present an historical framework that goes farther in exploring and explaining women's subordinate status within the division of labor in both the family and the economic market place. Second, they bring a new interpretation of the theoretical concept of the reserve army of labor, providing the link between women's labor force roles in the United States and the Third World. Socialist feminists argue that there is a dialectical relationship between two mutually dependent systems, capitalism and patriachy, which together have shaped and reinforced the existence of economic classes and male dominance in capitalist economies (Ferguson 1979:279). There are, of course, a wide range of views within the socialist feminist camp and a number of definitions of patriarchy itself and how it interacts with capitalism to shape social relations. The following discussion leans heavily on Hartmann's definition of patriarchy and treats the interactions between capitalism and patriarchy only as they relate to the structure of labor markets. Hartmann defines patriarchy as "a set of social relations between men, and solidarity among them, which enable them to control women. Patriarchy is thus the system of male oppression" (Hartmann 1976:138).

The writings of many of the segmented labor market theorists either ignore or only briefly allude to social relations within the family, and few authors would include such an analysis as part of the core of economic relations shaping our society (Ferguson 1979:289–290). In contrast, others (see Ferguson 1979, Mitchell 1972, Eisenstein 1979, and Hartmann 1976) assume that the historical development of the family unit (satisfying such basic human needs as sexualilty, biological reproduction, the socialization of children, and domestic maintenance) has been equally as important in determining the particular form of productive relations as has been the historical development of the marketplace (which satisfies basic material needs). In effect, the interlocking relationship between the socially defined division of labor within the family and within the economic sphere has shaped the particular structures and characteristics of both the family and the labor market.[5]

Where the radical segmented labor market model falls short is in its primary reliance on the concept of economic class conflict as the *only* dynamic factor which shapes the character of social relations. Thus, the distinctions between men's and women's roles are blurred.

> The radical view, in particular, emphasizes the role of men as capitalists in creating hierarchies in the production process in order to maintain their power. Capitalists do this by segmenting the labor market (along race, sex and ethnic lines among others) and playing workers off against each other [Hartmann 1976:139].

> This ignores the role of men, men in general, as both capitalists and workers in maintaining the subordination of women in the labor market. Hartmann adds:

> Recent work on labor-market segmentation theory provides a framework for looking at the role of employers. According to this model, one mechanism which creates segmentation is the conscious, though not necessary conspiratorial, action of capitalists; they act to exacerbate existing divisions among workers in order to further divide them, thus weakening their class unity and reducing their bargaining power [Hartmann 1976:166].

On the basis of the segmented labor market model, as we can see from regional and national electronics industry employment statistics, the impact of this "mechanism" has been to channel women and minorities (with no necessary distinction between them) into the least desirable, lowest-paying job categories. This model, in its somewhat limited scope, focuses solely on the role of capitalists, the processes of capital accumulation, and class conflict in creating occupational segregation by sex. In fact, these processes should be seen not as causative but as perpetuating mechanisms in the continuing subordination of women in the marketplace. They reinforce a cycle of limited opportunities and lower wages for female workers. They encourage women to float in and out of the paid labor force in response to the varying needs of the marketplace and family requirements. To capital the sex of the worker matters only when the differences between sexes can be exploited to render greater profits. It is patriarchal relations, not class relations, that provide the bases for such differences.

The origins of sex-segregated occupations are to be found in the unequal division of labor within the family. Two mechanisms have been described by socialist feminists to explain the origins of sex-segregated occupations: (1) the narrow circumscription of women's access to paid employment resulting from male domination in the economic sphere and, originally , within the family; and (2) the inferior valuation of women's labor power (when compared with men's) resulting from women's economic dependence within the family.

Hartmann speaks generally about both of these mechanism, although her comments focus more specifically on the former. Tracing the development of patriarchal capitalist relations from the creation of waged labor to the present in England and the United States, she emphasizes the role of male workers in restricting women's access to certain segments of the labor market. The interplay between capitalist and patriarchal relations has meant that men, working men, responded to the capitalist's segmentation of labor markets by excluding women from those jobs that lend support to overall male dominance, that is, the primary sector jobs. Hartmann describes the ways in which male workers have been instrumental in restricting women's labor force participation. She argues that capitalists inherited rather than created a system of job segregation by sex that was already clearly defined by the powers of early craft guilds and was later reinforced by the policies and practices of trade unions. Capitalists have then been able to use such divisions to their own advantage, employing cheap labor in female-stereotyped positions, thereby weakening the working class as a whole. At times, capitalists have been able to buy the allegiance of male workers with patriarchal benefits; that is, employers have been willing to grant primary sector concessions to a relatively small sector of organized male workers, whereas rapid economic expansion in other sectors has depended heavily on the employment of cheaper female labor. Although Hartmann downplays the role of capitalists in her analysis, she would no doubt agree that it is men of all classes who have been instrumental in channelling women into certain limited sectors of the work force, either through conscious design or through their acceptance and thus their de facto support of patriarchal social relations.

Given that women in the electronics industry and other secondary sector manufacturing industries are not hired because their cheaper labor reflects an inferior level of productivity, it must therefore be argued that "women enter the capitalist (and other) labour market already determined as inferior *bearers of labour*" (Pearson and Elson 1978:29). Male control over familial relations and their long-standing dominance in the market sphere determine women's economic dependence and, thus, the lower value of their labor power (Beechey 1978, West 1978, Pearson and Elson 1979). Beechey's conclusion are worth quoting at length:

> [B]y virtue of the existence of the family, women are not expected themselves to bear the costs of reproduction. Since male wages are paid on the assumption that men are responsible for the costs of reproduction, and since it is generally assumed that women have husbands to provide for them and their children, the value of labour power can be lowered. . . . As far as women are concerned, it is only possible to pay wages below the value of labour power [i.e. below the market cost of reproducing labor power]. . . because of the assumption that a woman is partly dependent upon her husband's wages within the family. . . . The point is that even where women do not have husbands—or fathers—to support them, in patriarchal ideology their social position is defined in terms of the family as a patriarchal system. [Beechey 1978:186]

That this ideology persists quite strongly can be seen from the comments of many of the women interviewed. One, a single head of household with a fifteen year old son to support and no outside income, finds it extremely difficult to make ends meet on her wage of $6.42 an hour. She is often just able to pay her necessary expenses and rarely has money for leisure activities. Yet she commented, "It's okay pay for a woman."

West describes how the role of capitalist development has been influenced by the patriarchal family structure:

> Those attributes that women bring to the labour market by virtue of family obligations and socialisation are used by employers to select them for the secondary sector [That is, dispensibility and socially differentiable characteristics such as docility, patience, and obedience.]. . . . Conditions in the labour market, deskilling and other such factors do not explain why women are drawn in rather than migrants, or school leavers or indeed men displaced from other sectors of the economy. . . . Women's cheap, flexible and disposable labour power,

their situation both when employed and unemployed, stems funda-
mentally from their actual and assumed role in the family. [West
1978:247]

Women's opportunity costs are lower as well, based on the socially
available alternative uses of their time. Therefore, they are more
willing to accept the low wages, poorer working conditions, and
tedious tasks of secondary work. Alice's comments above support
this argument. Women are, after all, raised to handle the repetitive,
demanding, and occasionally thankless tasks of raising children and
doing housework. Why should they not then be willing to accept
similar jobs in the paid labor force?

In sum, women's segregated role in the segmented labor market
is better understood when one recognizes the fundamental reasons
why women form a cheap, relatively docile, and dispensable work
force. The patriarchally defined division of labor within the family
(and, therefore, the socially defined role of women in general) together
with male dominance in the economic sphere act to undervalue
women's labor power and to limit the options open to women in
the labor force.

The relatively recent influx of substantial numbers of women into
the wage economy and the unstable and insecure nature of the
majority of female occupations have resulted in the formation of a
new and rapidly growing reserve army of labor (Beechey 1978, Braverman 1974, Pearson and Elson 1978). For Marx, a surplus working
population was both a product and a reinforcement of the continuation of capital accumulation. Braverman points out that the relative
level of male labor force participation in the United States has been
declining since the 1940s, noting a drop of 87 percent to 80 percent
in the proportion of males who are employed. This phenomenon
"indicates that a portion of the male working population (and the
figures point to white workers almost as much as to black) has been
and is being moved into the reserve army of labor without this
showing up in the unemployment statistics" (Braverman 1974:391).
As discussed above, in this same period, women's labor force participation rates have risen dramatically. This is attributed to the
recruitment of women into the female-stereotyped jobs of the rapidly
expanding service, trade, and labor-intensive manufacturing sectors,
whereas blue-collar males continue predominantly to fill the higher
paying, more craft-oriented occupations in the relatively stagnant
sectors of mining, construction, capital-intensive manufacturing, and
other heavy industry. The outcome is twofold: on the one hand, a

319

growing "stagnant" army of male unemployed and, on the other, an increase in the ranks of female labor drawn from a population that previously did not work and that can be dispensed with or drawn from according to the dictates of the process of capital accumulation. Women, it is assumed, can "disappear virtually without trace back into the family" (Beechey 1978:190).

That women, who are paid on a substantially lower scale than men, occupy the fastest growing occupational sectors illustrates the blending of the capitalist and patriarchal systems. Capital takes fullest advantage of the patriarchal system by hiring women whose labor costs tend to be lower even than the costs of reproducing labor power (that is the cost of feeding, clothing and otherwise supporting an able worker). At the same time, male domination in the marketplace and also within the family is reinforced by restricting women to the weakest economic position possible. Unfortunately for the blue-collar male worker, it would appear that this direction in capitalist development is turning the advantages of the patriarchal system over primarily to the capitalist class, as working class males suffer job losses in the more stagnant sectors of the economy and their overall work force participation rates decline. (This sort of impact on the development of labor market structures, it may be assumed, will result in a renewal of working-class male opposition to large-scale female labor force participation.) In the future, however, as Oppenheimer has suggested, the quantitative and qualitative changes in women's labor force participation have been of such significance and have been such an integral part of capitalist expansion in recent years that a return to the days when the actual position of most women was indeed in the household will probably not be possible (Oppenheimer 1973:198).

In conclusion, what the socialist feminist perspective contributes to the discussion of the development of labor market structures under capitalism is the conceptual wedding of class and patriarchal analyses. Now, we can come closer to answering (leaving tautologies behind) the question of why women are predominantly employed in secondary sector jobs. And we can better understand the particular form which the internationalization of capitalist production is currently taking. Women form what Marx referred to as a "floating" reserve, a flexible and disposable work force that can be repelled or attracted by particular branches of industry depending on the dictates of production (Beechey 1978:188). In the case of the electroncis industry, as with other export-oriented internationalized industries, the emergence of capitalist production in relatively new branches of industry or in noncapitalist economic sectors has resulted in the creation and expansion of new and greater reserve armies of labor. In the United States, the employment of women, especially married women, has created this reserve; whereas in the Third World, the expansion of Western capital has meant the creation of an entirely new work force sector of young, largely unmarried women. "The fact that women's wages can be paid below the value of labour power means that women, as part of the industrial reserve army, constitute a particularly intense pressure on wages. It appears, therefore, that women form a specific element of the industrial reserve army by virtue of the sexual division that consigns them to the family and inscribes a set of assumptions abouit women's roles" (Beechey 1978:191). Describing the role of expanding female labor in this manner, as a unique aspect of surplus labor, highlights the theoretical link between the employment of women in the domestic secondary job sector and the employment of women in secondary jobs in the world market factories. As capitalist production expands globally, the interplay of established patriarchal relations and capitalist relations has resulted in the recruitment of women into the waged labor force, where traditionally women may have worked little or not at all outside the home. In the Third World, the "social relations of imperialism" add to the complex of capitalism and patriarchy, allowing capital to offer women workers real wages well below that of their Western counterparts (Pearson and Elson 1978:25). Third World workers of both sexes are paid below the level of sustenance because, assumably, they are able to gain the remaining margin of necessary income in the traditional sector outside the scope of capitalist relations. Women's ideologically defined roles as socially and economically dependent beings is a further justification for lowering the wage rate, thus compounding the process of primitive accumulation and exploitation in these areas.

> The labour requirements of capital in international subcontracting plants do not specify that women should be employed because the jobs offered are women's jobs; rather they specify that labour required should be the cheapest—that is the most productive, exploitable and dispensable in order to maximize the opportunity for cutting costs without confronting the resistance of organized labour. . . . women are invariably proved to be the source of the cheapest labour, regardless of the type of society we consider. [Pearson and Elson 1978:29]

The importance of the family structure in determining sex-segregated employment, the concept of a growing "floating" reserve army of labor, and an understanding of the symbiotic relationship between patriarchal and capitalist relations provide an important theoretical foundation for analyzing the development of the 'new international division of labor." Whereas radical segmented labor market theories were developed to explain the workings of the domestic labor market and alone are inadequate even there, adding the socialist feminist perspective provides the necessary depth for analyzing both domestic and international capitalist labor market structures and their impact on women. The dictates of capital accumulation, the search for cheaper labor, have led to the development of export-oriented industrial centers all over the "free" and not so "free" world. The particular forms of patriarchal relations within Third World cultures, interacting with the demands of Western capital, have resulted in an extremely homogeneous work force of young, unmarried women. But in both the United States and the Third World, the same general pattern can be seen: women are becoming a new sector of the work force at wages that undervalue the costs necessary to maintain their own labor power. They are becoming a new, flexible reserve army of labor acting to lower the average wage rate and probably ultimately (and inadvertantly), acting to bring about a resurgence of hostility on the part of working-class males towards wage-earning females.

In many Third World countries, as in the United States, there is a common assumption that the employment of women in capitalist production will have the effect of breaking down preexisting traditional structures that subordinate women: the notion that wage labor will give women greater power within their own families. In some ways, this is true in many countries at the level of the individual. Personal access to the means of subsistence can give a woman greater control over her own life in a social sense. But as Pearson and Elson point out, and as the above case study material and theoreticasl analysis supports,

> . . . there are structural limits to the extent to which the development of capitalism decomposes the forms of women's subordination so that the overall effect is a transformation of women's subordination rather than its dissolution. The extent to which women becoming wage earners decomposes the forms of women's subordionation depends principally on how large the wage is; how regular and secure the employment is; the extent to which the wage earner has control over the spending of the wage; and the extent to which the capitalist form of social production is compatible with the responsibilities of bringing up children. The lower the wage, the more unstable the employment, and the less control which the wage earner has over the spending of the wage, the less likely is

waged work to free women from pre-capitalist forms of dependence on men. The type of employment offered in the industries we are considering is not, and does not seem likely to become, high wage, high security employment. [Pearson and Elson 1978:35]

The costs of bearing and raising children, for instance, are still the responsibility of the family with its patriarchally defined division of labor. To illustrate, few electronics firms in the United States provide child care for women workers; fewer of these firms operating in the Third World are willing to hire married women or women with children. The advantage of hiring women, single or married, however, for secondary sector jobs is precisely that they bring with them the characteristics of subordination within two spheres, the family and the marketplace. They are willing therefore, to accept the kinds of secondary jobs offered and they possess the training and socialization that enables them to productively undertake such work.

This sort of analysis suggests that the net effect of wage work within the international capitalist system may mean a double burden for women rather than a lessening of restrictions and control mechanisms that keep women in socially and economically inferior positions. For married women in the United States, this is particularly clear; it is less so for Third World women. For the latter, employment in the world market factories may be used to delay marriage in order to take advantage of the kind of limited freedoms that factory work offers relative to the duties of domestic maintainance, childbearing, and raising (Snow 1977). But in either case, changes in labor market structures that have drawn women into the secondary sector work force in increasing numbers, cannot even begin to actually bring about the emancipation of women from their traditionally defined status as dependent social beings. Because capitalist and patriarchal institutions have developed historically in a mutually supportive manner, substantial redefinitions of women's position within the family must necessarily accompany changes in the hierarchical structure of the labor market before women's overall status will improve.

### APPENDIX A: Data on Women Interviewed

I.   Total number of women interviewed:                    17

II. Source of introductions to interviewees:
   A. Church organization or affiliated individual      5
   B. Labor organization or affiliated individual      3
   C. Social service/job placement organization      3
   D. Community activist organization      2
   E. Other women interviewed      2
   F. Personal acquainance of author      2

III. Demographic data:
   A. Median age:      34 years
   B. Age distribution: (18, 22, 23, 25, 28, 30, 33, 34, 36, 37, 39, 40, 41, 45, 55, 58)      18–58 years
   C. Racial/ethnic/national background:
      1. American      15
         a. Caucasian      12
         b. Black      1
         c. Chicana      2
      2. Foreign born      2
         a. Chilean      1
         b. Chinese      1
   D. Language spoken as first language:
      1. English      15
      2. Spanish      1
      3. Cantonese      1
   E. Language spoken as second language:
      1. English      1
      2. Spanish      2
      3. Mandarin      1
   F. Recent immigrant to U.S.:      2
   G. Religious affiliation:
      1. None      7
      2. Protestant      8
      3. Catholic      1
      4. Mormon      1
   H. Formal educational background:
      1. Less than high school graduation      2
      2. High school graduation      9
      3. Some college      5
      4. College degree (AA)      1
   I. Vocational training:
      1. In electronics      5

       2. In other field                              3

  J.  Marital Status:

       1. Single                                  3

       2. Married                             10

       3. Divorced/widowed                4

  K.  Place of origin:

       1. San Jose/area in which currently employed          2

       2. Northeast U.S.                     4

       3. Southern U.S.                      2

       4. Midwest U.S.                       2

       5. Other parts of California        5

       6. Outside the U.S.                   2

IV.  Household Data

  A.  Range of household sizes             1–6

  B.  Average household size              3.1

  C.  Single person households            4

  D.  Single heads of household with one or more dependent          2

  E.  Male head of household present     10

  F.  Dependent in household            1

  G.  Women with children               9

  H.  Women with preschool-aged children    4

  I.  Have family members in electronics jobs   8

V.  Employment Data

  A.  Median length of employment with current or most recent employer     1 year

  B.  Range of employment tenures with current employer   3 months to 21 years

  C.  Held previous positions in electronics     10

  D.  Reasons for having left previous positions:

       1. Seeking/offered better job (not necessarily in electronics)         6

       2. Laid off from permanent position     5

       3. Laid off as temporary worker       5

       4. Pregnant                          3

       5. Family illness                     2

       6. Return to school                 2

       7. Geographic move               2

|  |  |  |
|---|---|---|
| 8. | Married | 1 |
| 9. | To stay at home with children | 1 |
| E. | Status in most current job: | |
| | 1. Part time | 2 |
| | 2. Temporary | 1 |
| | 3. Second of two jobs | 1 |
| | 4. Working at home | 1 |
| | 5. Full time, permanent factory workers | 7 |
| F. | Not working | 5 |
| | 1. Laid off, as temporary worker | 1 |
| | 2. Disability (work related) | 1 |
| | 3. Quit | 3 |
| G. | Working in union shops | 1 |
| H. | Older women who entered work force after having raised children | 3 |
| I. | Other kinds of employment held by interviewees prior to electronics: | |
| | 1. Restaurant/bar | 5 |
| | 2. Cashier/sales | 7 |
| | 3. Clerical | 3 |
| | 4. Factory production | 3 |
| | 5. Laundry | 2 |
| | 6. Agriculture/cannery | 2 |
| | 7. Nurse's aid | 2 |
| | 8. Domestic worker | 2 |
| | 9. Telephone/telegraph operator | 2 |
| | 10. Bookkeeping, house painting, car washing, furniture refinishing, teaching (Taiwan), nursing (Chile), dog grooming, taxi driving, ranch hand, saddle making, shipyard welding | 1 each |

VI. Income Data

|  |  |  |
|---|---|---|
| A. | Median personal income per hour | $5.00 |
| B. | Distribution of incomes | $3.00–6.50 |
| C. | Range of current starting wage offered by employers of women interviewed where known (no prior experience) | $3.00–4.01 |
| D. | Households with more than one income | 10 |
| E. | Single-income earners with no dependents | 4 |

F.  Single-income earners with one or more
    dependents                                              2
G.  Dependent income earner; doesn't con-
    tribute to family income                               1
H.  Women who chose to work out of per-
    ceived financial necessity                            13
I.  Women for whom electronics work is sec-
    ondary job; income is not perceived as
    necessary                                              4
J.  Median combined family income, where
    are two or more income earners            $13.50/hour
K.  Range of combined family incomes where  $7.25–20.00+/
    are two or more income earners                 hour

## Appendix B: Benefits for Workers

The standard benefits package typically includes one week of vacation after six months or two weeks after the first year, rising to three weeks after five to ten years and four weeks after fifteen years of employment with the same firm. Paid sick leave varies usually between five and twelve days per year, although several of the women interviewed received no paid sick leave and such absences were deducted from vacation time.

Medical coverage, with the employer paying full or nearly full cost, was the rule. Medical plans varied in the extent that they included pregnancy, dental, or optical coverage. The latter two are usually not included.

Many San Jose area firms now offer some form of profit sharing or subsidized stock option programs and a few operate credit unions for their employees. Cost-of-living adjustments are not a standard part of most San Jose electronics employer's pay scales. Raises, although commonly based on 10 percent per year averages, were largely discretionary, depending on the individual's work performance and relationship with her supervisor. At GTE Lenkurt, the only union shop among the employers of the women interviewed, contract specifications called for a yearly cost-of-living adjustment. This was the only case among those of the women interviewed, where this was offered. (It was felt, however, that this never actually kept up with inflation rates.) Several of the women interviewed were aware of pension plans at their company. Usually these involve benefits that accrue only after ten or more years of employment.

## Notes

This paper was part of the Impact of Transnational Interactions Project of the Cultural Learning Institute at the East-West Center in Honolulu. My appreciation and thanks to Dr. Robert Snow, Mary Alison Hancock, and Joyce Chinen for their helpful comments and criticisms of an earlier draft, and to Jenny Ichinotsubo and Judith Seo of the Institute for their help in typing and preparing this final version (July 1980).

1. Fröbel, Heinrichs, and Kreye (1978:139) have defined the term *world market factory* to mean factories that are installed in industrial enclaves, such as export processing zones, and elsewhere in order to utilize abundant cheap labor in manufacturing for markets of the traditional industrialized countries.

2. The use of the term *San Jose area* is synonymous with the San Jose Standard Metropolitan Statistical Area and Santa Clara County.

3. By *electronics*, in all but this particular example, I refer to the Department of Labor's Standard Industrial Classification code number 367, electronics components and accessories. In this case, some of the employers of the women interviewed fell outside of this classification, into the more general code number 36, electrical equipment and supplies. In terms of the kinds of jobs open to production workers and the experiences of women workers in the San Jose area, this distinction is of minimal importance. Most of the women interviewed did not themselves distinguish between jobs in these two categories. Several had held quite similar positions in firms of the more general classification as well as in the specific electronics components category.

4. Much has been written about the confusion surrounding class delineations in American society. (See Walker 1979, *Between Labor and Capital*, for a collection of quite recent articles on the subject.) This kind of discussion is beyond the scope of this paper. Rather, the point here is to outline the general processes shaping the work force and to identify the role of women within the work force.

5. * See Ferguson 1979:291–294 for a more complete justification of the claim that "social relatins of sex/affective production [i.e. the social relations within the family] are *as formative* in shaping the other social relations of society as are the social relations of material production." This discussion is concerned only with demonstrating how an analysis that shares this basic assumption adds depth to theoretical models of contemporary labor market structures.

## References

Axelrad, Marcie and the PHASE Staff. 1979. "Profile of the Electronics Industry Workforce in the Santa Clara Valley." Mountain View, Calif.: Project on Health and Safety in Electronics (PHASE).

Beck, E.M.; Horan, Patrick M.; and Tolbert II, Charles M. 1978. "Stratification in a Dual Economy." *American Sociological Review* 43:704–720.

Beechey, Veronica. 1978. "Women and Production: A Critical Analysis of Some Sociological Theories of Women's Work." In *Feminism and materialism*, eds. Kuhn and Wolpe, pp. 155–197. Boston: Routledge and Kegan Paul.

Bibb, Robert and Form, William H. 1977. "The Effects of Industrial, Occupational, and Sex Stratification on Wages in Blue-Collar Markets." *Social Forces* 55:974–996.

Blau, Francine. 1975. "Sex Segregation of Workers by Enterprise in clerical Occupations." In Edwards, et al. 1975:275–278.

Blaxall, Martha and Reagan, Barbara. 1976. *Women and the Workplace, the Implications of Occupational Segregation.* Chicago: University of Chicago Press.

Braverman, Harry. 1974. *Labor and Monopoly Capital.* New York: Monthly Review Press.

Brecher, Jeremy. 1979. "Roots of Power: Employers and Workers in the Electrical Products Industry." In Zimbalist 1979:206–227.

*Business Week.* 1980. "More Elbowroom for the Electronics Industry." (March 10):94–100.

———. 1979. "Can Semiconductors Survive Big Business?" (December 3):66–81.

Cahn, Ann Foote. 1979. *Women in the U.S. Labor Force.* New York: Praeger.

California Employment Development Department. 1976. *Manpower 1975–1980, Santa Clara County.* Santa Clara County: State of California Employment Development Department, Northern California Employment Data and Research.

Edwards, Richard C. 1979. *Contested Terrain,* New York: Basic Books.

Edwards, Richard C.; Reich, Michael; and Gordon, David M. 1975. *Labor Market Segmentation.* Lexington: D.C. Heath.

Eisenstein, Zillah. 1979. *Capitalist Patriarchy and the Case for Socialist Feminism.* New York: Monthly Review Press.

Electronics. 1980. "Silicon Valley is Filling Up." *Electronics* (February 28):99–100.

*Electronic Business.* 1979. "How Elecronics Companies Repudiate Unions." (July):30–34.

Ferber, Marianne A. and Lowry, Helen M. 1976. "Women: The New Reserve Army of the Unemployed." In Blaxall and Reagan 1976:213–232.

Ferguson, Ann. 1979. "Women as a New Revolutionary Class." In Walker 1979:279–309.

Fernández Kelly, María Patricia. 1979a. "Francisca Lucero: A Profile of Female Factory Work in Cuidad Juárez." Dept. of Anthropology, Rutgers University.

Fernández Kelly, María Patricia. 1982. "Mexican Border Industrialization, Female Labor Force Participation and Migration." Working Paper Series, Center for the Education Study and advancement of Women. University of California, Berkeley.

Filipino Association of Mountain View. 1978. *"The Filipinos in Mountain View, California: a Census Type, Socio-economic Survey.* Mountain View: Filipino Association of Mountain view.

Fröbel, Folker; Heinrichs, Jurgen; and Kreye, Otto. 1978. "The New International Division of Labour." *Social Science Information* 17, no. 1 (1978):143–144.

Gordon, David M. 1972. *Theories of Poverty and Underemployment.* Lexington: D.C. Heath.

Grossman, Rachael. 1979. "Women's Place in the Integrated Circuit." *Southeast Asia Chronicle* 66:(January–February):2–17.

Hancock, Mary. 1979. *"Electronics: The International Industry: An Examination of U.S. Electronics Offshore Production Involving a Female Workforce in Southeast Asia."* Honolulu: East-West Center.

Hartman, Heidi. 1976. "Capitalism, Patriarchy and Job Segregation by Sex." In Blaxalll and Reagan 1976:137–170.

———. "Women in Mexican Border Industries: The Search for Cheap Labor." Dept. of Anthropology, Rutgers University.

Kessler-Harris, Alice. 1975. "Stratifying by Sex: Understanding the History of Working Women." In Edwards et al. 1975:217–242.

Keyserling, Mary Dublin. 1979. "Women's Stake in Full Employment: Their Disadvantaged Role in the Economy—Challenges to Action." In *Women in the U.S. Labor Force*, pp. 25–39. New York: Prager.

Kuhn, Annete and Wolpe, AnnMarie. 1978. *Feminism and Materialism*. Boston: Routledge and Kegan Paul.

Lloyd, Cynthia B. 1975. *Sex, Discrimination, and the Division of Labor*. New York: Columbia University Press.

Mitchell, Juliet. 1972. *Woman's Estate*. New York: Random House.

*New York Times.* 1979. "Winning and Losing at Texas Instruments." (May 13) Peter J. Schuyten.

North American Congress on Latin America (NACLA). 1977. "Electronics: The Global Industry." *Latin American and Empire Report* 9, no. 4 pp. 1–25.

Oppenheimer, Valerie Kincade. 1973. "Demographic Influence on Female Employment and the Status of Women." In *Changing Women in a Changing Society*, ed. Joan Huber. Chicago: University of Chicago Press.

———. 1969. *The Female Labor Force in the United States.* Berkeley: Institute of International Studies, University of California.

Pacific Studies Center. 1977. *Silicon Valley: Paradise or Paradox? The Impact of High Technology Industry on Santa Clara County.* Mountain View: Pacific Studies Center.

Pearson, Ruth and Elson, Diane. 1978. "Internationalisation of Capital and its Implications for Women in the Third World." Sussex, England: Institute of Development Studies, Conference on the Subordination of Women (Mimeo).

Piore, Michael J. 1973. "Notes for a Theory of Labor Market Stratification." In Edwards, 1975:95–122.

Reagan, Barbara. 1979. "De Facto Job Segregation." In Cahn, 1979:90–102.

Safa, Helen I. 1978. "Women, Production and Reproduction in Industrial Capitalism; A Comparison of Brazilian and U.S. Factory Workers." Unpublished manuscript. Dept. of Anthropology, Rutgers University.

Saxenian, AnnaLee. 1979. "Overview of Trends in the American Semiconductor Industry." Dept. of Urban and Regional Planning, University of California, Berkeley (Mimeo).

Seigel, Lenny. 1979. "Microelectrics Does Little for the Third World." *Pacific Research* 10, no. 2, (second quarter, 1979):15–21.

Snow, Robert T. 1980. *The New International Division of Labor and the U.S. Workforce: The Case of the Electronics Industry.* Honolulu: The East-West Center.

————. 1977. ::Dependent Development and the New Industrial Worker: The Case of the Export Processing Zone in the Philippines." Dissertation. Department of Sociology, Harvard University.

Stevenson, Mary. 1975a. "Women's Wages and Job Segregation." In Edwards et al. 1975:243–256.

————.1975b. "Relative Wages and Sex Segregation by Occupation." In Lloyd 1975:175–200.

U.S. Department of Commerce. 1979a. *1977 Census of Manufactures.* Washington D.C.: Department of Commerce, Bureau of Labor Statistics.

————.1979b. *U.S. Semiconductor Industry.* Washington D.C.: Dept. of Commerce, Industry and Trade Administration.

————. 1971. *Statistical Abstract of the U.S., 1971.* Washington D.C.: Bureau of the Census.

U.S. Department of Labor. 1978a. *Marital and Family Characteristics of Workers, March 1977.* Washington D.C.: Department of Labor, Bureau of Labor Statistics.

————. 1978b. *Women Who Head Families: A Socioeconomic Analysis.* Special Labor Force Report, 213. Washington, D.C.: Depart. of Labor, Bureau of Labor Statistics.

————. 1979a. *Employment and Earnings, U.S., 1909–1978.* Washington D.C.: Dept. of Labor, Bureau of Labor Statistics.

————. 1979b. *Employment in Perspective: Working Women.* Report 572. Washington D.C.: Dept. of Labor, Bureau of Labor Statistics.

————. 1979c. *Industry Wage Survey: Semiconductors, September 1977.* Washington D.C.: Department of Labor, Bureau of Labor Statistics.

U.S. Equal Employment Opportunity Commission. 1966–1978. Reports for San Jose Standard Metropolitan Statistical Area and for the United States, "Employment Analysis Report Program."

Wachtel, Howard M. 1975. "Class Consciousness and Stratification in the Labor Process." in Edwards et al. 1975:95–122.

Walker, Pat. 1979. *Between Labor and Capital.* Boston: South End Press.

Webbink, Douglas W. 1977. *The Semiconductor Industry: A Survey of Structure, Conduct and Performance.* Washington D.C.: Federal Trade Commission Bureau of Economics, January.

West, Jackie. 1978. "Women, Sex and Class." In Kuhn and Wolpe 1978:220–253.

Zellner, Harriet. 1972. "Discrimination against Women, Occupational Segregation, and the Relative Wage." *American Economic Review* (May).

Zimbalist, Andrew. 1979. *Case Studies on the Labor Process.* New York: Monthly Review Press.

# CHAPTER 13

# Fast Forward:
# The Internationalization
# of Silicon Valley

NAOMI KATZ AND DAVID S. KEMNITZER

> O'dāy, chôn'g Têcħ vó Lỳ
> Cun'g laṁ mót xiṗ coñ g'i xú'ong hoñ
> (Here, the husband is a technician, the wife an assembler.
> Together, working the same shift, nothing is happier)
(in C.R. Finnan, 1980)

The electronics industry, based in the Santa Clara Valley of California and depending to an overwhelming extent on the labor of women, has played a major role in fostering the highly integrated international division of labor. The flexibility afforded by its overseas expansion has enabled the electronics industry to develop in the United States alternatives to traditional patterns of factory labor—alternatives that operate to the advantage of employers. These new relations of production are the consequence of wide-ranging employer strategies that have kept wages lower than those in U. S. manufacturing as a whole, have encroached upon institutionalized workers' guarantees and benefits, and have lengthened the working day.

Radical critics of multinational corporations have developed an important and powerful analysis of the internationalization of Capital, an analysis which points to the ways in which off-shore production has both enhanced corporate profits and at the same time contributed to domestic unemployment (cf. Fröbel, et al, 1980). But this is only part of the story. The other part concerns the negative impact of this internationalization on the ongoing production labor force at home. To better understand this process, we report here on an ongoing field study in the Santa Clara Valley.

In more traditional, high wage industries, like automobiles, the pressure to cut wages is portrayed as capital's asking labor to "share the costs of hard times." By contrast, changed working conditions in electronics are portrayed by a curious ideological mix incorporating positive images of the intangible benefits of alternatives to traditional work patterns, along with fairly blatant gender and ethnic stereotyping. The latter are successful just because of the preponderance of women, particularly Third World and immigrant women, in the bottom rungs of the industry (production work on the assembly line). Indeed, playing on the fragmentation of the labor force, with an emphasis on gender and ethnic, rather than class, markers is one of the employers' strategies about which we will have more to say below.

A key element, unlikely in this highly technological industry, has been the spread of the "pre-industrial" practice of cottage industry: industrial work, performed at workers' homes, often in contravention of safety and health standards, paid for by piece-work wages, often in cash. Although it is easier to move capital than people, the current internationalization process has not only relocated managerial and technical personnel abroad, but has encouraged widespread immigration *to* the US, including large numbers of "unskilled" Asian women — a dramatic reversal of recent U. S. immigration policies and something of an anomaly in these times of accelerating domestic unemployment. The meshing of all these factors allows the trend-setting electronics industry the advantages over labor that it currently enjoys.

In Silicon Valley some seventy thousand women make up the bulk of the production work force, and are variously estimated to hold from 80 to 90 percent of operative and laborer jobs on the factory floor (Snow, 1980:14–16). Of these women production workers, 45 to 50 percent are estimated to be Third World, particularly newly arrived Asian immigrants. These are the legal immigrants; undocumented immigrants are employed as well, cash-payment fashion and in cottage industry. Of the male employees, many are also Third World and immigrant; white men, from all accounts, rise rapidly to positions of technician and supervisor. Wages in general have not kept up with wages for U. S. industrial workers as a whole (*ibid*), and union organizing has been slow and only minimally successful. Only one major plant in the area is organized, by the International Brotherhood of Electrical Workers (IBEW). Despite higher wages and somewhat closer adherence to safety standards there, IBEW recently lost a closely contested election at a nearby Raytheon plant. The difficulties encountered in organizing, despite the apparently noncompetitive efforts of the three major unions involved in the area and of the many devoted organizers, is a complex matter which calls for further study; some of the dynamic discussed below is doubtless involved.

As Patricia Fernández–Kelly has pointed out, race, ethnic, and gender differences are all used by this industry to identify and seek out particular groups of people to perform tedious, unrewarding, and poorly paid work. Bolstered by ethnic and gender stereotypes (for example: "Women—and especially Asian women—are unusually dextrous," not to be recruited as brain surgeons, to be sure, but "suited for tedious work since they're so patient and docile.") and by the deskilling of production work, the electronics industry seeks for itself a source of cheap labor. For the answer as to why women are the mainstay of this labor force in Silicon Valley, one must look to a combination of social and economic factors, to gender and ethnic stereotypes, to the struggle for class mobility bolstered by the very messages that devalue production labor, and in all of this to the women's own perception of their overall situation.

When any assembly worker is asked, "Why are you working at this job?" the answer is, "I need the money." The answers immediately become more complex, to be sure, but the well-known facts of the inadequacy of a single income to support a family, the large number of single mothers and other self-supporting women, and recent layoffs in other nearby industries such as auto, have led in Silicon Valley to a large population of potentially employable women, many of whom, in the last decade and even now, are seeking work for the first time. Ironically, the very presence of the electronics firms with their demand for labor has drastically raised the cost of living in the Santa Clara Valley area, adding to everyone's need for income.

The industry, in its efforts to recruit these women to their low-paid jobs, both utilizes and circumvents sexist stereotypes in a number of interesting ways. One ingenious example is a recruiting commercial shown on television in the area. A young boy is complaining to his father, a personable white man in his mid-thirties, that he wants to talk to his mother. The father tells him just to call her at work; she has this good job now; and if you need her, she's easy to reach at this job we're all so glad she has. The cultural, and indeed male, legitimation—indeed, downright manipulation—of a mother's working needs no further comment.

In training programs and in managerial comments to us as interviewers, the unskilled and therefore "easy" nature of the job, and even its tediousness, were explained as virtues, again in terms of gender stereotyping. Bypassing the definitional problem that all assembly jobs are called "unskilled"—even rather complex soldering under microscopes that requires substantial training—whereas "experience" is neccessary and important and is supposed to lead to better pay and job stability, [1] trainers tell new recruits, and managers told us, that the work was "really easy," "just like following a recipe." The only skills needed were those of manual dexterity—doubtless acquired knitting and crocheting—and which women had anyway, particularly Asians, along with their tolerance for tedious work. The tedious, "easy," work, again, was a virtue because women wouldn't be so tired when they got home and had all those household chores (naturally) to do. In fact, the so-called nontiring work, requiring little training, along with the "pleasant" surroundings, choice of shifts, and "mothers' shifts"[2] all combined, in the jargon of managers, to make these jobs ideal "supplementary" activities for women.

As part of being supplementary, women's needs for jobs is also portrayed by management as temporary—"until the orthodontist's bill is paid," or the TV, or "until she gets married or marries again." Because their working is temporary, women, it is said, prefer an undemanding, go-nowhere job. Thus, women seldom get on-the-job training, and some of the deepest resentments that we heard expressed concerned just this issue of being an experienced assembly worker, "and then a white man comes in," is soon up for advancement, "and you end up training your boss."

The women's perception of the work situation as a whole is in many ways more complex than the expressed, paternalist managerial view. Their interviews chronicle a subtle awareness of the interplay of the advantages of their jobs and the limited options for other employment, as well as a thoughtful, cool appraisal of the benefits and advantages of their possible choices. Ease of getting or changing a job is acknowledged, and two women did voluntarily point out that after so boring a day, one welcomes rather than resents the activities of one's children. Choice of shifts was, in fact, a big plus, making possible shared child care for mothers and overtime and moonlighting for everyone.

But the low pay, neccessitating regular overtime and/or moonlighting, meaning for almost everyone a six or seven day work week,

335

made the management construct of women's work as supplementary activity both laughable and bitterly resented. For the women workers interviewed, far from being a supplementary or temporary activity, the job represents or is part of a *lifelong* strategy for coping with or overcoming low class, race, and/or gender status.

"Compensations" most frequently mentioned were the friends and companionship on the job, with "lunchtime" parties, potlucks, and gifts to mark all possibly celebratable events. On the other hand, the workplace itself was more likely seen as dreary than pleasant. One worker suggested that a "women-at-work" film project should be of women painters—"something pretty," "artistic." Another woman mused that she would really like a job selling flowers, and yet another, that she planned to volunteer at a hospital, "cuddling babies." Finally, health hazards were frequently alluded to, and always acknowledged although there was a reluctance among our informants to dwell on this issue at length, the matter soon being summed up by rather fatalistic statements like ". . . but every job has its hazards," or ". . . when your number is called . . .".

If job benefits and advantages are somewhat coolly viewed by the women interviewed, much more highly charged are those issues having to do with status and class, specifically issues of condescension to them and devaluation of them *as* production workers, both on the job and in the outside world. Statements like, "When you get on the production floor, you feel like less," or "It's easy to dump on someone who makes $3.85 an hour," were never far from the surface of people's conversations about their work. Several times we heard comments about clerical personnel like, "The secretaries think they're someone with their skirts and high heels and going out to lunch with the managers; but with overtime, we make more." And in one plant an issue was raised over production workers' pictures being displayed on a bulletin board *below* those of managers.

This apparent disjuncture between managerial use of ethnic and gender stereotyping and the women's repeated emphasis on status and class was dramatized last summer when one of us, Naomi Katz, applied for a production job in the Valley. In the course of seeking work, she had to admit that she had had some college background, and had been married to a teacher. On three separate, independent occassions, she was told by personnel people interviewing her—all women, as it happens, trying to help and be friendly to her—"You won't like the work," and then, in a single breath, "They're a lower class of people—they don't even all speak English." Needless to say, it was the helpfulness of her coworkers that allowed her to survive her brief stint when she did get hired as a "temporary"—working the graveyard shift at Raytheon—and who reminded her not to work even fifteen seconds into her break and to go to the bathroom as allowed, on their time rather than during her lunch half hour. More to the point, however, is the fact that the off-the-cuff comments of the personnel managers, not for public consumption but to an apparently misguided "class"-mate, revealed the core of the class condescension that underlies the more strategic management stereotyping—condescention lost, by the way, on no worker.

Moreover, that very stereotyping—"It's easy, just like following a recipe"—defines the work not only as women's work but as trivial, insignificant, not even, properly speaking, work at all—and surely not a trade or skill. The gender stereotyping does not mask the status devaluation of the worker as at first seemed to be the case, but rather reinforces and communicates it.

The workers combat their devaluation as workers *by increasing their income* in the most immediately available ways: job-hopping, overtime, and moonlighting. Assertion of positive status and of pride in themselves as persons are clearly tied to making more than survival pay, thus underscoring once again the symbolic as well as practical attributes of money in our culture. The most overwhelming example of this sort of effort is that of a Tongan woman who works three jobs, and uses her income to participate simultaneously, if a bit tiredly, in three cultures. When one of us commented on how little sleep she must get, she answered that she gets top pay at Lenkirk— "I'm trained and experienced and it's a unionized plant"; top pay for cleaning houses "And I only clean clean houses"; and that, moreover, in addition to sending money home to Tonga and participating generously in Tongon community affairs in the Bay Area; also, "I'm putting money away for my son's college." Similar sentiments were expressed by three women, all married with employed husbands, who regularly worked fifty-eight hours a week, also for top pay, at Lenkirk. "Despite what we look like when we get off, with that big check, you feel like somebody." "It's for the house payments. . . . But we're buying a good house in a good neighborhood—for the children." "I dropped out in high school. My son goes to private school and won't have to do like me."

The commitment to the strategies and symbols of mobility for themselves, perhaps, and at least for their children is once again seen as a way out of, or at least a way to cope with, the practical difficulties of their lives and simultaneously a counter assertion of self and status in the context of the devaluation and condescension from above. At the same time, working overtime or moonlighting in the attempt to escape from or modify their social/class position, on a more basic level, serves to intensify the collective and structural distinctions against which they are struggling as individuals.[3]

Although the workers approach their work and work situations as *workers*, there is an entrepreneurial aspect to the relations many have to their jobs. (This differs markedly from the assumptions and strategies of workers in those industries where status mobility for the individual is more tied to collective efforts and practices, emphasizing seniority, security, promotion, collective bargaining, and pride in skill.[4]) Here, much more in accord with the devaluation of work and of the work place, mobility is sought via efforts more akin to "hustling"—that is, job-hopping, moonlighting, and branching out as independent contractors on a putting-out, cottage-industry basis. In recent years in Silicon Valley, this approach has both encouraged and been reinforced by the resurgence, as the underside of this highly technological industry, of older manufacturing practice and an associated "underground" economy.

At first glance, the mushrooming of homework (as it is called) is a management strategy analogous to offshore production, providing flexibility and a means of getting work done more cheaply, with no benefits, no sick leave, no paid breaks, with piecework rates, and with no threat of unions. And it is all this and more, a point to which we shall return shortly. From one perspective, however, it must be acknowledged that homework is in fact a preferable option to factory labor for some women, revealing again many of the felt inadequacies of work on the production-room floor. It appeals to some as a way to tailor their need to work more closely to their life situation; for example, to mothers who do not want to leave small children: to women who want, for whatever reason, greater flexibility than any of the shifts allow; and to those who prefer continued isolation at home to spending all day in a closed-in, supervised plant. It also appeals to those women who *do* wish to define their paid work as supplementary: "I do it only after my husband has left in the morning and after I've picked up the house."

From a contrasting perspective, the subcontracting side of homework is seen by some experienced workers as a way out of their low position in the plants as women. Two young mothers emphasized that for them subcontracting was a means to independence and status, as well as to a less alienated relationship to their work. They discussed becoming "independent" after having trained a series of bosses while they worked in the plants, stressing repeatedly that subcontracting was the way that they, as women, could achieve *outside* the factory the levels of income, initiative, excitement, job satisfaction, and "something to show for it" that capable men could achieve, via promotion, *inside* the plants. And, of course, from a management viewpoint the energies of two experienced, restless, dynamic women who might have been just the ones to challenge authority effectively *within* the plant—as union organizers, for example—are effectively diverted elsewhere.

Nonetheless, the conditions and "costs" of homework reflect an erosion of the protections and benefits we have come to associate with industrial work and merit some further attention. Plants may send work home with full-time workers on a cash-payment basis, as, for example, rush orders or, more usually, contract work out via subcontractors. Pay is by piecework or job lot, with no legally mandated protections such as minimum wage, unemployment insurance, workers' compensation, guaranteed overtime, paid breaks, sick leave, or paid holidays, and certainly no fringe benefits like health insurance. The independent employee frequently has to provide her own tools and equipment, often has to pick up and return work at her own transportation cost and time, is held responsible for the safety of parts and materials, and always pays her own overhead—heat, electricity, cleaning, and so forth. Plants can thus be proportionately smaller and save on both construction and maintenance, in effect transfering these costs to workers. Finally, because the entire practice is at best semilegal and thus not even under the minimal surveillance otherwise provided by government agencies, health and safety protection is nonexistent, and instances have been documented of women in ignorance heating toxic chemicals on their kitchen stoves.[5] The advantages for management are clear; in the words of one frustrated investigator for the California State Labor Practices Commission, "They do it because they're getting away with something."[6]

The conventional wisdom in Silicon Valley—from managers, muckraking liberals, and Marxists alike—is that these entrepreneurial excesses and underground features of the Valley economy can be explained by the relative youth and competitiveness of this particular industry. It is thus interesting that in a recent article in *Radical America*, Phillip Mattera notes similar developments in Italy in a variety of industries including textiles, apparel, footwear, and also metalworking, electronics, and automobile parts construction (1980). Mattera links, as we do, overtime, moonlighting, and homework. He points to the recent proliferation of practices almost identical to those just noted in Silicon Valley. Although not acquainted with our data, he discusses as well other features found by us that become exceedingly interesting for analysis in a comparative context—that is, the increasing use of immigrant labor, both legal and illegal; the importance of the underground economy in the more highly industrialized and technologically advanced areas and industries; and the fact that, despite surface appearances, the independent or decentralized firms are not genuinely independent at all but on a more basic level ". . . are external departments of the big plants or, to use the Italian term, a diffused factory" (p. 72–3). He also strongly emphasizes, as do we, the critical importance of the lengthening of the working day and the erosion of workers' historically won benefits.

The similarity of the developments in the two areas seems to confirm both Mattera's and our suggestion that we are witnessing not a recapitulation of earlier forms of capitalist development in a new industry but the further development of contemporary capitalism as part of capital's efforts to deal with current economic conditions. Moreover, industry's strategies are simultaneously political, related to the successful struggles of workers in the past; they affect both "above ground" and "underground" workers by their individualizing and antiunion impact and are, properly speaking, part of the class struggle as traditionally understood.

The similarities between the situation Mattera described and that in Silicon Valley suggest that at this juncture the initiative is in the hands of employers and that the options open to workers are not of their own making. Although in one way this formulation is true, and available options allow workers to find a livable strategy only within narrow limits, this does not give "the system" total dominance, with no role for the perceptions, actions, and choices of real human beings. Indeed, quite the reverse; as we have seen, individual workers quite knowingly take advantage of the contradictions and interstices of the situations they confront. Thus, they make choices for themselves that allow not only survival, but assertion of self and flexibility in the arrangement of their work, compatible with their life situation and with their definition and understanding of it. In this sense they may, and frequently do, shape the form of their labor and expand the range of options open to them.

At the same time, the individualized choices workers *can* make have only the most limited potential for transforming the system. On a more fundamental level, however, the gains of the metropolitan working classes over the last century—economic, social, and political—have affected real structural changes in capitalism. It is to these changes, in significant part, that the current undermining and erosion of institutionalized workers' benefits is a response. Moreover, one element of this response is the displacement of class conflict, away from confrontation at the work place and toward issues of social status that the workers confront as individuals, or as members of a cultural "type"—women, Vietnamese, and so forth—in a broader, more diffuse arena. The increasing speedup and the transforming of labor relations, bolstered by the diffussion of class into social issues with other markers, such as gender or ethnicity, underscore the fact that the "institutionalized indirect wages" (Wolpe 1975:247) won by metropolitan workers over the last century are not so secure as had been previously assumed.

In a more theoretical vein, these de facto wage cuts suggest that the metropolitan/peripheral model of the 1960s and 70s is no longer applicable to the international scene. Many observers since World War II have pointed out that imperialism has operated to the economic advantage, not only of metropolitan capital, but of the stable American and European working classes as well. Thus, for example, Samir Amin (1975), basing his argument firmly on a class rather than an ethnic or "cultural" analysis, located what he called the "dominant cleavage" between the metropolitan world and its neocolonial periphery. Low wages and political suppression in the Third World were seen by Amin, and by such different other commentators as George Meany, as making possible the higher wages and apparent political clout of organized labor in Europe and the United States. Runaway shops and offshore production—the so-called international division of labor—although in part seen as a threat to jobs, were also seen as financing the relatively high standard of living of the metropolitan working classes and their "aristocratization" as well as the growth and dynamism of metropolitan capital. In the last few years, however, as the consequences of this strategy have come home to roost, these same practices are pointed to as contributing to problems of domestic unemployment, stagnation, and inflation. Further, the costs of supporting both the welfare state at home and the international presence, particularly in the context of Third World economic nationalism, have added to the strains on the domestic economies of the metropoles. In this context, it is hardly surprising that the "benefits" of offshore production are now being sought by capital at home.

Just as offshore production bypasses the high costs of metropolitan labor and provides increased flexibility for management, so too the new combination at home of underground labor and selective recruiting of women and Third World immigrants. As Wolpe points out,

> ... the means of subsistence acquired by the laborer can be divided into two parts—the direct wages paid to the worker in and during employment, and indirect wages he receives in the form of social security benefits ... unemployment payments, family allowances ... and so on. In its most advanced form indirect wages are institutionalized in the social welfare arrangements of the welfare state, but obviously, these arrangements are the outcome of a lengthy historical process.
>
> Under certain conditions, the capitalist mode of production is able to avoid, to a greater or lesser extent, the payment of indirect wages; that is, it is obliged to pay only the immediate sustenance of the laborer ... it can avoid paying for his subsistence during periods of unemployment, or for the subsistence of children or costs of education, etc.
>
> The most important conditions enabling capitalism to pay for labor-power below its cost of reproduction in this way is the availability of a supply of labor-power which is produced and reproduced outside the capitalist mode of production. [1975:247]

As with the overseas runaway shops, the underground economy at home evades or circumvents legal, institutionalized, or contractual agreements that add to indirect wages. It is essential to remember, however, that there is a clear and significant difference between an imperialist situation in which capitalism has been imposed upon a noncapitalist, typically subsistence-based mode of production that bears much of the burden of reproducing the working class and the situation in the metropoles, where we witness differentially powerful sectors of a single working class within a single mode of production. Nonetheless, in the latter situation, an analogous *ideological* redefinition occurs, allowing the job and its income to be defined as other than the basis of support of the "comfortable" working-class family. There is thus a clear relationship between the substandard wages paid and the fact that the work is done by women whose work is supplementary; or by nonwhites, whose life-styles are ideologically defined as different and cheaper. These two groups can continue to be "defined out" of the old industrial system and thus be targets and/or instruments of the ideological shift of conflict away from class and toward national/ethnic/gender lines.

At the same time, given the differences in modes of production, relations of production, culture, and ideology in the metropolitan areas, the *forms* that efforts to intensify production and increase extraction of surplus take differ from those in the Third World (Rey 1971). To take one example, in Malaysia the electronics industry recruits young women directly from agricultural villages to work in large plants, with intense labor discipline and dormitory residence— the factory writ large (Grossman, 1979). In the metropolitan areas, savings on indirect wages are more appropriately achieved through underground methods. In Silicon Valley, the accompanying ideology emphasizes the close fit with those strands of American culture that stress individual maximization of options for personal success. These more individualistic strands of American culture seem to be on the rise generally and are clearly making inroads on the working-class world view that for many decades linked personal betterment with union activity, political struggle, and collective relations.

When this study was begun two years ago, the electronics industry portrayed itself as a trend setter, whereas others believed that, with regard to work relations and wages at any rate, it had not yet "caught up" with U. S. industry as a whole. The industry's official perception has proven more accurate, at least in the short run. Often with the use of different ideological supports, the trend throughout the country has been a lowering of wage rates and a worsening of working conditions, constituting a dual assault on labor, both political and economic. However, although these tendencies increase surplus extraction and undermine the benefits and standard of living of American workers and threaten their ability to fight back, they also narrow the gap of interest between them and their counterparts overseas.

On one level, we seem to be witnessing an increasing physical and ideological *fragmentation* of the working class. The powerless sectors—women, the very poor, nonwhites generally, and recent and/ or undocumented immigrants in particular—seem once again played off against the more entrenched, traditional industrial working class to the detriment of both. Moreover, the internationalization of capital appears as a further constraint on labor, as offshore production along with the "reserve army of the unemployed," marginal or outsider groups of workers, and even different unions can all be played off against one another. But what appears as a forceful initiative of capital is at the same time a response to the twin challenges it has received from metropolitan organized labor on the one hand and Third World nationalism and antiimperialism on the other. So far, the strategy of capital has been effectively to keep these two struggles separate. In the process of its own necessary internationalization, however, capital may be undermining this very strategy. We suggest that we may be witnessing a real shift in the "dominant cleavage" toward a starker class lineup as the international division of labor of the 60s and 70s becomes the international speedup of the 80s.

In the words of Korean garment worker Min Chong Suk, "We all have the same hard life. We are bound together with one thread" (in Ehrenreich and Fuentes 1981).

## Notes

1. Although this confusion between skill and experience seems to be a managerial strategy to divide workers, the women themselves are divided on the question of the skilled or unskilled nature of their jobs, an ambiguity which has wide-ranging ideological consequences deserving of separate treatment. The interested reader is referred to Harry Braverman's excellent *Labor and Monopoly Capital* (New York: Monthly Review Press, 1974) for a groundwork for such an analysis.

2. The term "mothers' shifts" applies to a number of different arrangements, ranging from shortened day shifts to Friday–Saturday–Sunday, 6:00 A.M. to 6:00 P.M. shifts. With regard to the latter, there has been some dispute as to the companies' pay policies, in at least one case leading to successful litigation against an employer for failing to pay overtime rates then required by law.

3. This argument is developed at greater length by Marx in *Capital*, volume 1: "The Length of the Working Day."

4. This has, in effect, been the case at least since the 30s in steel, auto, mining, and garment industries among others (see, for example, Safa 1980). At a meeting with six shop stewards at Lenkirk, the only unionized factory in Silicon Valley, this traditional view was presented.

5. Personal interview. Staff Reporter, Pacific Studies Center, March 25, 1980.

6. Personal interview with California Bureau of Labor Standards employee, who wishes to remain anonymous (January 1981).

## References

Amin, S. 1975. *Unequal Development: An Essay on the Social Formations of Peripheral Capitalism.* Translated by B. Pearce. New York: Monthly Review Press.

Ehrenreich, B. and Fuentes, A. 1981. "Women and Multinationals: Life on the Global Assembly Line." *Ms.* 9, no. 7 (January).

Fernández-Kelly, M.P. n.d. "'*Maquiladoras*' and Women in Ciudad Juárez: The Paradoxes of Industrialization under Global Capitalism." MS, Program in Comparative Studies of Immigration and Ethnicity, Duke University.

Finnan, C.R. 1980. "Community Influence on Occupational Identity Development: Vietnamese Refugees and Job Training." Paper presented at the Annual Meeting of the American Anthropological Association. MS.

Grossman, R. 1979. "Women's Place in the Integrated Circuit." In *Changing Role of S.E. Asian Women. Southeast Asia Chronicle/Pacific Research* (joint double issue, January)

Marx, Karl. 1867/1967. *Capital, vol I: A Critical Analysis of Capitalist Production.* New York: International Publishers.

Mattera, P. 1980. "Small Is Not Beautiful: Decentralized Production and the Underground Economy in Italy." *Radical America.* 14:5 (Sept./Oct.)

Safa, H. 1980. "Work and Women's Liberation: A Case Study of Garment Workers in New Jersey." Presented at the Annual Meeting of the American Anthropological Association. MS.

Snow, R. 1980. *The New International Division of Labor and the U.S. Workforce: The Case of the Electronics Industry.* Honolulu: East-West Center.

Wolpe, H. 1975. Urban Politics in Nigeria. Berkeley: University of California Press.

CHAPTER 14

# The Division of Labor
# in Electronics

JOHN F. KELLER

The rise of the semiconductor electronics industry in the United States, its place in the international division of labor, and the specific occupational, gender, and ethnic divisions of labor in electronics production have all been conditioned by post-World War II political and economic strictures.

Perhaps the most significant development in international economic relations resulting from the war was the dismantling—under United States urging—of the European colonial systems. As a result, former market restrictions for the United States were significantly reduced. Under these conditions the undamaged United States economy entered into a long and relatively stable period of expansion and domination in the world market, a period that now appears to be coming to an end.

This period posed two major political-economic problems for the United States, and solutions to both were sought in the development and application of new semiconductor electronics technology: the main political problem was how to effectively project military power into all areas of the globe in order to manage the political stability of the capitalist world market and restrain further expansion of the socialist market; the main economic problem was how to efficiently

This is excerpted from the author's Ph.D. dissertation, *The Production Worker in Electronics: Industrialization and Labor Development in California's Santa Clara Valley* (University of Michigan, 1981) and appears here with his permission.

346

manage and service the circulation of capital and commodities in a period of unprecedented expansion of production.

The answer to the political problem was to place increased emphasis on aircraft and missile warfare systems, the most versatile means for exerting military power on a world scale.[1] The most important new technology for aerospace use was semiconductor electronics. Following the Korean War (which confirmed to the military the centrality of aerial warfare in modern military planning), the Department of Defense began funding high technology development and production with an orientation toward the military aerospace market. By the mid-1960s electronic components and systems accounted for as much as 30 percent of the value of military aircraft and missiles; the aggregate electronics content of annual United States military procurement reached over 40 percent; and electronics sales to the Department of Defense and the National Aeornautics and Space Administration accounted for approximately 60 percent of sales by the United States electronics industry (Freeman 1967:94–6).

The spin-off from military electronics research and development also provided an answer to the second problem, that is, the application of semiconductor and computer technology to management, service, and information needs. These two fundamental applications of electronics technology underlie the two most prominent trends in the postwar development of American society, the militarization of the economy (Schiller and Phillips 1972) and the proliferation of white-collar service employment (Budish 1962). A major feature of these developments has been the large-scale entry of women—especially minority women—into both the electronics production and the service industry work forces.[2]

Since the 1960s, financial and industrial planners have been trying to restructure the place of the United States in the international division of labor on the basis of these domestic trends and in conformity with other world trends. Foremost among the latter was the fact that the reconstructed capitalist countries with newer, more efficient plants and facilities in the basic industries were beginning to penetrate the North American market for steel, textiles, automobiles, and so forth. Furthermore the postwar decolonization process had essentially done away with the limitations on capital investment inherent in the old system of single nation financial control of direct colonies, and as a result the unrestricted flow of capital from the financial centers of North America, Europe, and Japan into all parts of the undeveloped world made stepped-up industrialization

347

in low wage countries a possibility and reality (Mellman 1976). Thus, competitive goods began entering the United States not only from the revitalized European economies but also from the world's developing countries.

The immense problems involved in generating new capital, investing in new plants, and regaining competitive positions vis-à-vis European and other commodities were circumvented to a large extent by the development and pursuit of a world economic strategy involving a new division of labor among nations. Wall Street's conception of this new economic order—based on the differential production of either high-technology or basic industrial goods—is clearly reflected in policy statements such as *The Rockefeller Report on the Americas* (Rockefeller 1969:102):

> At present, the United States is producing, at high cost behind tariff walls and quotas, goods which could be produced more economically by other hemisphere nations. The U.S. is short of skilled labor and, if anything, this shortage promises to get worse. The shortage of skilled labor is intensified when the U.S. continues to keep workers in lines which are, by definition, inefficient, since production can only be carried on here behind tariff or quota barriers. National productivity would be enhanced by shifting workers and capital out of protected industries into industries where advanced technology and intensive capital investment permits the U.S. to pay high wages and still remain competitive in world markets. The goods the United States is now producing inefficiently would be imported, mainly from less developed countries.

The actual implementation of this policy has required the constant precipitation of structural changes in the economies of the developing countries—and much has been written on this subject—but what is focused on here are some of the complementary processes and developments in the United States, especially the establishment of various divisions of labor in the electronics industry in the Silicon Valley (Santa Clara County, California).

## The International Division of Labor

The historical connection between the military aerospace market and the rise of the semiconductor electronics industry is reflected today in a clear international division of labor in electronics production. In particular, research and development operations (R & D) and security-sensitive production remain concentrated in the

348

United States whereas production and assembly of consumer electronics commodities are generally carried out in low wage areas abroad.

One of the common conceptions regarding the international aspects of electronics production is that any and all labor-intensive production and assembly operations are eligible to become concentrated in low wage countries in especially Asia and Latin America, whereas R & D operations are mainly left in the United States (Bernstein et al. 1977:35–6; NACLA 1977:4–5). If this were the case, it would be expected that most U.S. based electronics firms would maintain few production facilities here; but a compilation of actual production plant locations does not bear this out (Table 14-1). Indeed, the five largest semiconductor firms in the United States maintain nearly as many production facilities in the three states of California, Arizona, and Texas as in the whole of Asia. The picture is further complicated by the presence of nearly as many plants in Europe—another high labor cost area—as in Asia. In sum, the number of plants in North America and Europe total 50 percent more than in the rest of the world combined.

*Table 14-1.* Principal Worldwide Production Facilities of the Five Largest U.S. Semiconductor Manufacturers, 1976

| Plant Locations (Area Totals) | Santa Clara County Firms | | | Other Firms | |
|---|---|---|---|---|---|
| | Fairchild | National | Intel | Texas Instruments | Motorola |
| Europe (18) | 1 | 2 | — | 6 | 9 |
| N. America (43) | | | | | |
|   Canada | — | — | — | 1 | 2 |
|   U.S.: | | | | | |
|     Northeast | 4 | 1 | — | 1 | 1 |
|     Midwest | 1 | — | — | — | 8[a] |
|     Southwest[b] | 8 | 2 | 1 | 4 | 7 |
|     South | — | — | — | — | 1 |
|     Puerto Rico | — | — | — | — | 1 |
| S. America (12) | 2 | 1 | — | 4 | 5 |
| Asia (25) | 6 | 6 | 2 | 6 | 5 |
| Africa (2) | — | — | — | — | 2 |
| Mideast (1) | — | — | — | — | 1 |
| Totals (101) | 22 | 12 | 3 | 22 | 42 |

*Source:* Moody's 1976; 1977.
[a]Includes older vacuum tube plants.
[b]Includes Texas.

The real basis for an international division of labor in electronics is not between labor-intensive operations (abroad) and R & D (at home); rather it is between government-oriented military and space production (including both R & D and production) conducted mainly in the United States and consumer commodity production and assembly carried out largely abroad (there are of course exceptions). Historically it has been the case that all the chief developments in electronics technology have been funded and fostered by the Pentagon. The breakthroughs have always first been put to use in the manufacture of military-quality components and systems in the United States. Only when the cost of manufacturing such components has been brought down (i.e., by the development of reliable mass-production techniques) do they begin to find application in consumer-oriented commodities (OECD 1968:63–7). Furthermore, because there is no guaranteed federal market for consumer items as there is for military electronics, the success of consumer electronics sales depends to a large extent on underselling competitors and capturing the market through the lowest possible prices. Thus a tendency within consumer electronics production is for assembly operations to become concentrated in low wage labor markets abroad. Some of the consumer spin-off from military production has remained in the United States, but from 1950 to 1968 the portion of U.S. electronics output sold to consumer markets declined from nearly 56 percent to only 21 percent (Malito 1970:14–5).

Security restrictions and procurement regulations applicable to government related electronics production explains the heavy concentration of military and space production in the United States (Freeman 1967:103). However, other factors underlie the concentration of plants in Europe where a great deal of electronics goes into automated industrial systems (one of the factors which has since WW II made European hard goods competitive with the products of older, less efficient plant facilities in the United States). One of the chief concerns in the United States is the problem of high tariff barriers aimed at keeping U.S. electronics out of the European market. One of the main ways for circumventing this problem has been the construction of manufacturing facilities in various European countries to service national markets there (NACLA 1977:15). More recently, U.S. and European electronics firms have begun signing joint licensing, production, and marketing agreements, thus enabling the cooperating firms to have their own patented products sold by each other in the other's home market while circumventing tariffs and duties. For example, between 1976 and 1978 Fairchild entered into at least six such joint ventures with English, French, Italian, Japanese, and Hungarian firms (*Horizons* 1976, 1977, 1978a, 1978c, 1978d).

Except for Common Market tariff barriers, consumer electronics production remains relatively unhindered and free to be carried out wherever the lowest production costs (usually based on the lowest wage scales) can be achieved. This explains the large numbers of consumer electronics commodities manufactured in Asian and Latin American countries. Government statistics underscore the huge difference between imports of consumer and military electronics: in 1972, 44 percent of all electronic imports to the United States were consumer items while only 11 percent were military/industrial commodities (U.S. Bureau of Domestic Commerce 1974:10).

Still, even in electronics production in the United States and Europe, the determination of plant locations is heavily influenced by regional differences in wage rates. For example, most U.S. semiconductor operations are concentrated in the Southwest and form a kind of belt stretching between the West Coast (i.e., southern California) and the newer Texas aerospace center (around Dallas–Ft. Worth). This also places them in a geographic position such that they are able to take advantage of the large reserves of low-paid Mexican and Mexican-American labor in the Southwest. In Texas and Arizona, companies can also be relatively sure that the labor forces there will remain nonunionized because of the impact of so-called right-to-work laws in those states. Similarly in the southern United States, there are a number of potentially important electronics centers just developing around Huntsville, Alabama; Orlando, Florida; and Greensboro, North Carolina—all cities in states with right-to-work laws (Keller 1980:43–4). Even in Europe electronics companies tend to locate in the countries with the lowest wage scales (e.g., Spain, Portugal, and Ireland) or in low wage regions of countries, for example, in Scotland within the United Kingdom (NACLA 1977:13).

Such is the general organization of world electronics production today. However, there are forces at work which over the next decade could conceivably force much of the consumer electronics production back to the U.S. alongside the already heavy concentration of government-oriented production. First of all, the inflation rate for labor costs in Asia and Latin America runs much higher than in the United States; thus in the 1970s, starting wages at new electronics facilities in Asia were as low as 10 cents per hour in some countries, but were increasing by half each year. Because of transport costs and duty fees, some firms claim it is not economical to maintain offshore facilities when wages rise above 60 cents per hour. At the afore-mentioned inflation rate for wages, that gives foreign plants a useful life span of only five or so years before a new cheaper location must be found or the production lines brought back to the U.S. (*Electronic News* 1976). The consequences of rising wage rates overseas are already being seen in other industries, for example, the German and Japanese auto industries, which are currently relocating some of their production in the United States.

To delay the costly shifting of production lines back to the United States, the biggest electronics companies have made numerous legal (and also illegal) attempts to reduce foreign production costs. Illegal activities became commonplace by the early 1970s, with Fairchild, Texas Instruments, and Motorola all engaging in transport agreements involving unlawful rebates or customs bribes for understating the value of imports for tariff purposes (*Electronics News* 1977). After having been called up before the U.S. Securities and Exchange Commission for investigation of these violations, companies sought other legal means for extending the useful life of foreign plants. Such means, combined with political repression of the labor movement for better wages and conditions, for example, in Korea and the Philippines (Bernstein et al. 1977:37–8), have continued to produce profit margins that justify continued foreign production operations.

These legal means, like the illegal methods before them, tend to center around the reduction of transport and duty costs. In this regard, a foreign trade zone was opened in San Jose to service the area's electronics industry beginning around 1976. These zones, which are authorized by the federal Foreign Trade Zone Act of 1934, are enclosed areas located physically within the United States but considered outside U.S. Customs territory. Foreign Trade Zone #18 in San Jose consists of 30 acres of the 375 acre International Business Park on the northern border of the city near Santa Clara. The advantages a foreign trade zone offers to a manufacturer are numerous; but, most importantly, goods may be processed or manipulated there in various ways in order to qualify for the lowest duties. Furthermore, companies may actually set up manufacturing facilities in the zone, and the rate of duty on the finished product may be applied to either the entire finished product or to just the foreign component materials, whichever best benefits the manufacturer (International Business Parks n.d.:5). Additionally, an April 1980 amendment to U.S. Customs regulations has cut the normal tariff on foreign trade zone imports by half to 3 percent (Zausner 1980), a decision which will favor continued overseas consumer electronics production by U.S. companies.

Because of the impact of foreign trade zone operations on the electronics business, the chance of any immediate return of offshore production work to the United States has been significantly reduced. Consequently, the character of electronics production carried out in Santa Clara County can be expected to remain relatively unchanged over the near term, that is, it should continue to be heavily oriented toward production for the military/space market in the United States. It is this particular orientation which has determined—and likely will continue to determine—the internal occupational division of labor within the county electronics industry.

### The Occupational Division of Labor

One of the major consequences of the retention of R & D and military production in the United States has been an intensified structural division of labor between *mental* and *manual* workers in the U.S. section of the industry. Thus, although foreign assembly plants employ almost exclusively production workers, in Santa Clara County, California—the "Silicon Valley"—the percentage of non-production jobs in electronics and related industries is exceptionally high, even compared to other U.S. industries. As a result, the labor force in U.S. electronics is polarized between nearly equal-sized blocs of college-educated professionals or technicians and unskilled blue-collar workers. This is a distinguishing feature of the occupational structure of all military-oriented electronics production, whether carried out in the United States or Europe (Freeman 1967:97–8).

Census data for the period 1950–1970 in Santa Clara County shows the development of the occupational structure in local electronics production (Table 14-2). There was a dramatic shift in this structure following the Korean War, a shift which corresponded to the new military and space orientation of the industry from that point forward.[3] Whereas in 1950 nonproduction workers accounted for 38 percent of all employees in county electronics (half of those being professional and technical workers), by 1970 the figure reached nearly 60 percent. This was due almost entirely to relative increases in professional and technical employment.

In contrast to the highly technical requirements of military electronics research, development, and production control, major aspects of the production process itself have actually remained relatively

*353*

Table 14-2. Occupational Structure of the Electronic Component and Equipment Industry in Santa Clara County, 1950-1970

| Occupational Group and Gender of Employees | Percentage of Total Employment | | |
|---|---|---|---|
| | 1950 | 1960 | 1970 |
| Nonproduction Workers: | 38.5 | 55.8 | 59.2 |
| Professional/Technical | (19.4) | (34.5) | (34.7) |
| women | 0.9 | 2.8 | 4.0 |
| men | 18.5 | 31.7 | 30.7 |
| Managerial/Sales | (4.5) | (7.0) | (8.7) |
| women | – | 0.5 | 0.5 |
| men | 4.5 | 6.5 | 8.2 |
| Clerical | (14.6) | (14.3) | (15.8) |
| women | 8.7 | 9.8 | 11.9 |
| men | 5.9 | 4.5 | 3.9 |
| Production Workers: | 61.5 | 44.2 | 40.8 |
| Skilled/Supervisors | (27.1) | (17.8) | (11.5) |
| women | 0.7 | 1.0 | 1.1 |
| men | 26.4 | 16.8 | 10.4 |
| Semiskilled/Unskilled | (34.3) | (26.4) | (29.3) |
| women | 8.3 | 14.9 | 19.2 |
| men | 26.0 | 11.5 | 10.1 |

Source: U.S. Bureau of the Census 1952: Table 84; 1963: Table 125; 1973: Table 180.

labor-intensive due to problems in imparting human hand-eye co-ordination capabilities to automated production machinery. Thus, some of the fundamental production tasks are still virtually done by hand, require little or no previous experience or formal training, and can be easily learned on the job. The persistence of labor-intensive work in electronics in this age of automation is another of the industry's distinguishing features (Freeman 1967:97).

One of my main objectives in working in electronics was to become familiar with and analyze trends in the production process itself and on that basis to be able to explain and predict changes in the composition of the production line work force.

There are different stages in semiconductor production and they exhibit distinct differences in the degree of capital-intensity or labor-intensity of production. These different stages include the manufacture of silicon wafers, the fabrication of integrated circuits on these wafers, the assembly of the individual integrated circuit chips into usable components, and the testing of the final product (Bernstein et al. 1977:25–6; Robinson 1980c). If a firm also manufactures systems, it will further assemble these components into communications equipment, computers, instruments, or weapons systems.

In the decade following the development of the integrated circuit (IC) and the beginnings of large-scale production (i.e., after about 1962), the proportion of semiskilled and unskilled workers in all stages of electronics production increased more than for even non-production workers in county electronics, from 26.4 to 29.3 workers per hundred employees (Table 14-2). However in the fabrication stage of production, automation has in fact forced a decline in the proportional employment of workers, that is, machine operators. Data show that their proportion in the county electronics industry declined from 13 to 9 individuals per 100 employees between 1960 and 1970. The growing machine-intensive nature of IC fabrication underlies this employment trend.

In the initial production steps, round silicon wafers up to four inches in diameter and a fraction of an inch thick are sliced from a long, artificially grown crystal ingot. After polishing, wafers are sent in racks to fabrication areas where each wafer is thinly coated with a photosensitive, fast-drying liquid. Then using what is called a masking machine, an operator works from a glass template to photoengrave hundreds or even thousands of identical IC patterns side by side on a single wafer surface, a process which usually takes no more than thirty seconds. After etching out the pattern in an acid bath, special chemicals are diffused under intense heat into the crystalline structure of the IC patterns remaining on the wafer surface. These chemicals alter the electrical conductivity properties of the circuits at given points, and each of these points becomes part of a transistor. By varying the masking and diffusion process, each transistor type in the circuit can be given different amplifying and switching characteristics, which are activated by the input of minute electrical signals. After the diffusion oven operators have done their job, the photo-resist, masking, etching, and diffusion processes are repeated between six and nine more times as other circuit patterns are layered on top of and connected to previous ones.

Increased productivity in fabrication areas has historically been achieved in several ways. First, either miniaturization of components or enlargement of the wafer surface make it possible to fit more ICs on each wafer; thus the industry converted from two-inch to three-inch diameter wafers in the early 1970s and now is converting to four-inch wafers (*Horizons* 1978b:7). Secondly, better precision masking machines may be introduced to improve production speed and reduce the rejection rate by increasing masking accuracy (because each plane or layer of circuitry must be perfectly aligned with those below it in order for the proper circuit connections to be made). Thus, for example, one bi-polar memory fabrication area at Fairchild Semiconductor in Mountain View converted from Kaspar to Cobilt masking machines in the summer of 1977 and, before the last Cobilt was in place, began installing even newer, more efficient (and more costly) direct-projection Perkin-Elmar machines.

Likewise, slow and messy acid etching baths are being replaced with plasma etching equipment (Penn 1980), and in the diffusion areas, automatic ion implant machines (produced by a satellite company controlled by Fairchild) are supplanting manually loaded ovens. In every instance, the result has been increased output per worker-hour, thus permitting production goals to be achieved by fewer and fewer personnel. As a result of fabrication improvements ongoing since the 1960s, the proportion of machine operators in electronics has been steadily declining, and the forces effecting this drop continue to operate.

In contrast to the fabrication process trends, the assembly process has remained relatively labor intensive. Here each of the finished wafers is cut into separate chips or dies (each bearing a complete IC), every chip is individually mounted in the center of a one-inch square gold or silver-plated metal frame, and minute wires are bonded from input and output points on each IC to metal leads extending from the frame. Finally, the chip is encapsulated in plastic or ceramic, leaving only the leads of the metal frame exposed; these leads are then used to plug the whole component into circuit board sockets in electronics systems.

These assembly steps require a great deal of labor performed on each separate IC by workers using microscopes and hand-manipulated wire-bonding devices. A number of semiconductor equipment suppliers have developed prototype machines for the automation of bonding tasks, but, because of the variety of electronics circuits being manufactured today and because of the very different operations required to be carried out on each, no sufficiently versatile line of machines has as yet been devised that could accommodate the switch from one item to another in normal production scheduling and still maintain a high degree of bonding accuracy. Consequently, of the estimated twenty-four thousand bonding machines in use worldwide in 1976, fewer than one hundred were fully automatic (*Electronic News* 1976). Thus, semiconductor assembly has remained relatively labor-intensive (ABAG 1981:42). Similarly, in the manufacture of electronics equipment, assemblers typically plug in IC units and hand solder these and various discrete semiconductors (i.e., the old-style pronged transistors and diodes) along with other electrical components (e.g., resistors and capacitors) into printed circuit (PC) boards. This area of electronics equipment assembly has also remained relatively labor-intensive over the years.

Although automation has tended to reduce the percentage of fabrication personnel in electronics, the greater output achieved conversely necessitated more employment in the labor-intensive assembly process where each component must be worked over separately and then individually worked into systems. Consequently, during the 1960s the proportion of assemblers in the county electronics work force increased from 10.6 to 12.5 per 100 employees.

This was not, however, the only area of production employment showing gains within the industry. Due to increased fabrication productivity, more personnel were also added between the fabrication and assembly stages to inspect for and identify faulty IC patterns on wafers, and other workers were added to conduct tests on the rising volume of finished components. Thus, during the first decade of semiconductor production, the proportion of inspectors and testers in the county industry increased more than for any other occupation, from 1.3 to 5.4 workers per 100 employees. Presently however, there is a trend toward introducing automatic testing equipment in the industry (*Horizons* 1976b, 1976c), and so the proportion of testers and inspectors should level off and possibly decline in the near future.

Projections regarding the future employment trends of semiskilled and unskilled workers in electronics are mixed. On one hand, the perfection of automatic bonding equipment will eventually result in a proportional reduction of assemblers in the electronics work force; but offsetting this, new complications in wafer fabrication techniques could very well result in a proportional increase in machine operator employment. This is especially due to problems arising from the continuous miniaturization of ICs and the increasing densification of chips on wafers. The newest masking machines in use in the industry (the aforementioned Perkin-Elmar Micralign machines) are called projection printers because they use an optical system to focus the array of identical patterns from a glass mask or template onto the wafer surface. However, as IC feature sizes have been steadily reduced through engineering developments, these conventional optical systems have proven less and less able to project and maintain high-resolution patterns across a widening wafer surface (now four

*357*

inches in diameter), the result being distorted images at the wafer edge and a consequent growing rate of rejections.

Because the needed improvements in optical technology are not yet forthcoming, the industry has developed a couple of other options for solving the problem of image resolution. One is to use a computer-controlled electron beam to inscribe circuit patterns directly on the wafer surface, but machines of this type are currently far too costly (about $1.5 million apiece) for widespread installation. By comparison, the Perkin-Elmar machines sell for $250,000 whereas the older Cobilt and Kaspar equipment sold for about $120,000 and $60,000 respectively. Another more widely adoptable production solution is the "direct step-on" fabrication method. In this process, circuit patterns are imparted to just a few or even one chip at a time rather than simultaneouosly to hundreds or even thousands on a single wafer (Robinson 1980a:482).

Naturally, this latter production process is less productive than other masking techniques, so if it were to be widely adopted it would necessitate a tremendous expansion in the number of projection machines and operators just to meet production demand. On the other hand, the present methods, if continued, allow for little more *intensification* of production, so output can only be increased *extensively*, that is, by putting more and more machines and operators into service. In either case, the result is a likely proportional rise in labor employment in the fabrication stage of semiconductor production, which would probably easily offset any other decline in assembly and testing employment due to automation in those areas of work.

The only other immediate alternative is to hold back on the mass production of a new generation of smaller ICs until the needed optical technology is developed or the cost of electron beam technology is reduced to an economical level. Of course, either choice would entail foregoing growth opportunities in an industry whose products seem to be confronted by an ever more demanding market— especially the huge military aerospace market—so this is really no alternative at all. It is an interesting contradiction in an industry producing such a sophisticated technological product that key aspects of production should be so heavily labor intensive and, despite the probable introduction of automated assembly machinery, likely to remain so.

## The Gender Division of Labor

Because much electronics production work requires little or no previous experience and because the electronics work force has remained largely unorganized, production workers in this industry have become one of the lowest paid sections of the industrial labor force in Santa Clara County. With the growth of well-paid scientific and technical positions in the industry and the development of some unionized manufacturing and construction industries in the area, the predominance of Anglo-American males in electronics production jobs during the industry's early years steadily gave way to the concentration of historically less skilled and lower paid sections of labor in electronics. Especially since about 1960, women workers have entered the work force in huge numbers whereas men have come to occupy most of the technical and engineering positions in the industry. Consequently, a sexual division of labor has developed in the industry corresponding to the division of labor between mental and manual work.

United States census data show that between 1950 and 1970 the ratio of men to women in production area tasks became reversed from roughly 3:1 in 1950 to 2:3 in 1960 to 1:2 in 1970 (Table 14-2). In all other occupations in electronics the preponderance of men—and in the case of clericals, women—persisted over the same period. The continuation of this trend through 1977 was confirmed in an occupational survey of five Santa Clara County semiconductor plants by the Pacific Studies Center in Mountain View (Bernstein et al. 1977:29). These results indicate the almost total absence of men from all but skilled crafts jobs in production.

This sexual reconstitution of the production work force cannot be understood apart from the long-term impact of labor-intensive production on levels of productivity, industrial monopolization, labor unionism, and wages. In other industries with production processes more amenable to automation, heavy capital investment after World War II typically resulted in rapidly rising productivity and the capture of greater shares of a commodity market by the most technically advanced firms. In the continuous search for maximum profit, investment capital has always gravitated toward such firms, and monopolization of production has usually followed (Eaton 1949:73–5). It is precisely in these technically advanced, most productive, and highly monopolized sectors of industry where labor unions have flourished and where wages are generally greatest (Green 1976:59–61).

*359*

There are some basic reasons for this relationship. Increased automation in industry would seem to lead to a lower demand for skilled labor and a concomitant decrease in the value of labor power utilized in industry. However, automation also makes possible greater productivity per worker-hour and an increase in the rate of surplus value extracted in production (Eaton 1949:153). Coupled with established control of markets and pricing, this yields enormous possibilities for capital accumulation in monopolized sectors of industry, and it is here (most notably in auto, steel, rubber, chemicals, and other so-called basic industries) that workers have most concertedly formed combinations to bargain for higher wages, that is, for a return of a portion of the increased surplus value extracted on the basis of capital-intensive production.

In turn, having achieved monopoly or cartel domination of an industry, giant firms are able to accede to certain of these wage demands to mollify the workers confronting them as an organized force; they can safely absorb the added expense of union-scale wages by raising prices without fear of placing themselves in a competitive bind (Perlo 1974:26–33). This is exactly the process taking place today in the southern textile industry (Green 1976:89) and underlies the development of union drives there. Given the eventuality of automation in all areas of electronics production, it is undoubtedly a process that the electronics industry and labor force will also one day experience.

However, the current mixed nature of the electronics industry suggests it is in a developmental stage transitional to monopolization, as evidenced by the domination of some product markets by a few firms while intense competition by a large number of companies continues for other commodity markets (Bernstein et al. 1977:12–4). My own conversations with workers at Fairchild Semiconductor Corporation revealed that much of the anti-union sentiment there was based precisely on the belief—reinforced by company promoted anti-union campaigns (Leeke 1980)—that any demands for union-scale wages might undercut the competitiveness and viability of the company, thus directly threatening the continuation of their own jobs. This of course neglects the likelihood that an absorbed company would continue operations but under a different name. Nevertheless, workers had a strong sense of the still competitive aspects of the industry, and this gained ideological expression in various pro-company attitudes and negative opinions about trade unionism.

In contrast, there was also a certain sense of the growing monopolization of the industry's business by a few big firms, especially in the realm of IC manufacture. Two important events in 1979 underscore this trend: first, the original and once largest semiconductor company in Santa Clara County, Fairchild, was acquired by the French conglomerate Schlumberger; second, Mostek, a leading producer of random access memory (RAM) chips, was absorbed by United Technologies (Robinson 1980a, 1980b). In short, the competitive position of even some of the biggest firms in electronics is being eroded by others today, and from this point forward the trend will likely be toward greater consolidation and monopolization in the industry.

Some workers, therefore, think that there might be some real advantages and fewer risks in labor organizing today, but this is a newly emerging outlook. So at this point, despite years of organizing efforts in county electronics by the United Electrical Workers (UE), the International Brotherhood of Electrical Workers (IBEW), and the International Association of Machinists (IAM), it is estimated that only about 5 percent of electronics production workers in the county are organized in unions (Axelrad 1979:12–4). However, recently stepped up organizing efforts by the aforementioned unions (Shiras 1977), and now by the United Auto Workers (UAW) union (Sachar 1980), suggests that changes in the industry structure and the attitudes of the work force are being recognized and reacted to in the circles of organized labor.

As indicated, trends toward greater automation and productivity underlie monopolization and lay the basis for union organizing. However, in the period before the introduction of the integrated circuit, the labor-intensive character of all aspects of transistor production exerted a definite drag on productivity in electronics compared to other industries amenable to automation. This was reflected in a widening gap between the rate of surplus value extracted in electronics compared to other industries in the San Jose metropolitan area between 1954 and 1967. During that period, the ratio of the rate of surplus value in electronics to the rate of surplus value in other local industries declined from 0.98 to 0.71, indicating a relative decrease in the profitability of electronics production compared to other industries.[4]

However, in the late 1960s, this trend was reversed due to the beginning of IC production, whose preliminary photoetching stages were subject to increased capital investment and automation. Still, given the labor intensive character of IC assembly, the rate of surplus value in electronics remained below that for all other manufacturing sectors until the mid-1970s. Since then the gradual introduction of automatic testing and assembly equipment has begun to achieve greater productivity in even the formerly technically backward phases of the production process. Thus, in the late 1970s, the rate of surplus value in electronics pulled even with and surpassed for the first time the rate of surplus value in all other local industries. It is this increased profitability of electronics production which the labor force itself will eventually demand to share in, as manifested in the development of an organized labor movement.

However, lacking such organization, electronics workers have seen their wages steadily outstripped over the years by gains in production pay won by workers in other organized industries (auto, construction, printing, etc.). Indeed, since the 1950s, wages in electronics—although rising—have gone from the highest in Santa Clara County manufacturing to almost the lowest today. By 1972 only production workers in local canneries and at the Levi's garment factory in San Jose earned less per annum. As an example of the kind of wages one could expect to earn in electronics, starting pay for assembler and inspector trainees at Fairchild in 1973 was just $2.10 per hour and $2.45 per hour after achieving a certain daily production standard.

Even four years later, despite the slashing effect of the nation's inflation woes, trainees were being started out at just $2.65 per hour, to be raised to $2.95 per hour upon reaching and maintaining standard. Thus after 1976, average annual electronics wages had even fallen below those for seasonal cannery work, which is also heavily labor intensive. Without organization, the production work force in electronics has been unable to gain any significant share in the fruits of the industry's increased productivity.

Like the unorganized apparel industry, electronics is not only extremely low paying but, as a consequence of the low wage scales, has also tended to become one of the largest employers of women workers, the most universally accessible and one of the least skilled sections of the labor force (Green 1976:235). As wages in electronics fell behind pay in other industries in Santa Clara County, and as better-paying technical positions opened up in electronics itself (accounting for over one-third of all electronics jobs) male breadwinners who dominated electronics production lines during the 1950s and who might have remained so employed instead sought other more remunerative opportunities.

To achieve these goals, many men used financial resources they had saved up or GI Bill educational benefits due them to pursue the necessary technical training to advance themselves in the expanding electronics complex. Thus, the formation of a large bloc of technical personnel in the county labor force occurred not just through migration from the East but also through the implementation of training programs at a half-dozen junior colleges built in the valley since the mid-1950s. Indeed, a study of the local junior college system in its formative years confirmed how this institutional setup systematically facilitated the transformation of a section of the blue-collar work force in the area into a corps of electronics technicians: 62 percent of enrollees at San Jose Junior College (later renamed San Jose City College) came from blue-collar families, and 55 percent of all job placements were as electronics technicians in the industrial and service sectors of the county economy (Clark 1960:53–6, 78–9).

Men nevertheless continued to be hired into semiskilled and unskilled production jobs in electronics and occupied almost half of such jobs in the industry as late as 1960. Still, the long-term trend was for them to be steadily replaced by women workers.[5] It might be expected that residual evidence of the earlier heavy employment of men in production could still be observed; but in two years of work at Fairchild, virtually the only workers who were encountered with more than five years production line experience were women (Table 14-3). As can be seen from the data, it is rare to find male production line workers over the age of thirty, especially ones with more than three or so years of experience. This suggests that not only has the number of men seeking production employment in electronics declined over the years, but virtually all men originally employed in production areas in the 1960s (other than better-paid maintenance personnel) have either left the industry or at least changed jobs within it.

In fact, the only departments where one finds a high percentage of men today (aside from engineering and maintenance) are those doing the most physical work, for example, electroplating. Some electronics-related electroplating operations are run as separate businesses, like the specialty houses which manufacture production equipment, but the largest semiconductor firms maintain their own plating departments in-house. These provide needed materials not only for a firm's own operations but may also sell plated lead frames (on which IC chips are mounted) or pins and cannisters (which become the familiar metal cap and prongs of discrete transistors) to smaller companies. Plating involves much lifting (by hand and by small crane) of heavy boxes and reels of unfinished parts, hoisting barrels of these parts in and out of large acid-clean, cyanide-plating and rinse-water tanks, and making high voltage (440 Volts AC) electrical connections throughout the plating process.

*Table 14–3.* Work Experience of Production and Inspection Personnel in the Automotive and Plating Departments at Fairchild Semiconductor, 1976

| Department, Gender of Workers, and Years of Work in Electronics | | Number of Workers, by Age | | | | |
|---|---|---|---|---|---|---|
| | | 16–19 | 20–29 | 30–39 | 40–49 | 50+ |
| Automotive | | | | | | |
| Women: | 0–2 | 2 | 11 | 2 | 1 | 1 |
| | 3–5 | – | 11 | 9 | 5 | – |
| | 6–10 | – | – | 1 | – | – |
| | 11–15 | – | – | – | 1 | – |
| Men: | 0–2 | 1 | 1 | 1 | – | – |
| | 3–5 | – | – | – | – | – |
| | 6–10 | – | 1 | – | – | – |
| Plating | | | | | | |
| Men: | 0–2 | 4 | 5 | – | – | – |
| | 3–5 | – | 6 | 1 | 1 | – |
| Women: | 0–2 | – | 3 | – | – | – |
| | 3–5 | – | 1 | 2 | 1 | – |
| | 6–10 | – | – | – | 2 | – |
| | 11–15 | – | – | – | – | 1 |

*Source:* Author's survey.

It is physical and noxious work, and height, reach and strength requirements are listed on plating job descriptions by the company in order to discourage women from applying for these jobs. In the same line, the wages for the lowest grade plater (Electroplater A) are more than for many operator, assembler and inspector positions. These higher rates play an important part in encouraging at least some men to apply for work—especially young men just getting started in their working lives—in a side of the industry where strength is assumed to influence productivity.

However it was also found that the recruitment of men in plating and in other assembly areas served another purpose: those individuals who proved most adept at solving minor equipment problems in order to keep up their own production performance were often advanced to low level maintenance positions. This was precisely the route I followed during two years of employment in a big semiconductor firm in order to carry out participant observation work in both production and maintenance departments.

Still, although men continue to occupy some production line positions in electronics, the long-term trend has been for them to leave production area work. The major consequence of this trend was the development of a shortage of unskilled labor for Santa Clara

County electronics manufacturers. The main new source of labor to be drawn on was the local female population, but after 1960 even the character of this labor supply began to change.

## The Ethnic Division of Labor

In 1950 Santa Clara County agricultural employment stood at about eleven thousand compared to eight thousand in durable manufacturing, but by 1960 the boom in electronics had increased durable goods employment to nearly fifty thousand compared to a decline in agricultural jobs to fewer than eight thousand. Soon, however, the demand for unskilled industrial labor surpassed the available supply of women workers, and there began a tremendous influx of new labor from outside the valley. Between 1955 and 1960 alone, the population of Santa Clara County increased by sixty percent with two-thirds of the rise due to net migration. In 1965 fewer than one percent of all metropolitan residents in the United States lived in the San Jose area, but this south Bay Area metropole alone received over 5 percent of all migrants to metropolitan areas in the United States (Morrison 1974:18).

The content of migration to the San Jose area in recent decades exhibits one of the chief characteristics of international and national migration since World War II and especially since the passage of the 1965 Immigration Act., that is, the "brain drain" of scientifically and technically skilled individuals from other countries to the United States and from east to west within the United States.

By 1973 about 32 percent of all immigrants to the United States came from Asia, up from 7 percent in 1965, and of all the nations outside the Western Hemisphere, four of the five largest contributors were Asian countries—the Phillippines, Korea, China/Taiwan and India. Italy (completing the top five) and Portugal showed the most significant increases among European nations in the number of emigrees to the United States. Within the Western Hemisphere, Mexico has remained the single largest source of immigrants (Dinnerstein and Reimers 1975:90, 166–70).

These new immigration trends are also reflected in the electronics industry in Santa Clara County as illustrated by data on the ethnic composition of the work force culled from official anniversary and service award lists published by Fairchild Semiconductor. Every month the company newsletter would print the names of persons celebrating five, ten or fifteen years of employment with the company.

*365*

During the twelve month period from July 1976 through June 1977 these lists were compiled to show exactly how many persons still with the company were hired five years earlier (between July 1971 and June 1972), ten years earlier (between July 1966 and June 1967) and fifteen years earlier—that is, before the passage of the 1965 Immigration Act (Between July 1961 and June 1962). The number of five, ten, and fifteen year annivesaries during the period under investigation totaled 202, 158 and 74 respectively.

Through a combined method of relying on informant identification of listed individuals known to bear a self-ascribed ethnic identity and by tabulating other names according to their national language characteristics and gender, an analysis of general trends in the employment of ethnic workers in electronics was made possible. Some ethnic identifications were too few in number to permit any conclusions about employment trends (e.g., there were no more than two each of Swedish, Arab, Greek, and German immigrants in the sample). It is the trends for those groups that form distinct ethnic communities within the San Jose metropolitan area (usually reflected in settlement concentrations or the organization of social clubs) which are most revealing (Table 14-4).

When the population groups with similar employment trends are clustered, the hiring percentages show the following: first, those groups with the longest immigration histories (going back to the early 1900s, i.e., the Japanese and Italians), manifest a declining presence in the work force, possibly due to the long-term tendency to move upward socially and be replaced by others in the plants; second, there is the countervailing tendency exhibited by recent international migrants (Filipinos, Koreans, Chinese, Indians, and Portuguese) who have gained a real presence in the plants only since 1965; third, there are rising numbers of Latinos (mainly Mexican-Americans) plus some blacks in the electronics work force. The latter two trends—based mostly on a rising percentage of women operatives—point to the declining Anglo-American composition of the production work force and the relatively greater importance of domestic vis-à-vis international migration of unskilled labor.

Thus the differential operation of two general migration processes corresponding to the fundamental division of labor along occupational and gender lines is indicated: not only is there a brain drain of skilled men (especially Anglo-Americans) from the eastern United States to Santa Clara County electronics, but also a concurrent in-migration of unskilled women (especially minority women, arriving

*Table 14-4.* Trends in the Ethnic Composition of the Electronics Workforce, Fairchild Semiconductor Corporation, 1961–1972

| Ethnic Groups Clustered by Trend | Date of Hire (Total Still With the Company) Minority Totals by Gender Minority Cluster Percent of Total | | |
|---|---|---|---|
| | 1961–2 (74) | 1966–7 (158) | 1971–2 (202) |
| 1. Declining proportion, significant before 1965 | | | |
| Italians—males | 2 | 2 | 3 |
| females | 2 | 2 | 3 |
| Japanese—males | 2 | 0 | 0 |
| females | 4 | 4 | 3 |
| Cluster percent of total | 13.5 | 5.1 | 4.5 |
| 2. Rising proportion, insignificant before 1965 | | | |
| Filipinos—males | 0 | 1 | 3 |
| females | 2 | 6 | 4 |
| Koreans/Chinese/ E. Indians | | | |
| —males | 0 | 3 | 3 |
| females | 0 | 1 | 3 |
| Portuguese—males | 0 | 0 | 1 |
| females | 0 | 1 | 5 |
| Cluster percent of total | 2.7 | 7.6 | 9.4 |
| 3. Rising proportion, significant before 1965 | | | |
| Latinos—males | 1 | 1 | 4 |
| females | 8 | 16 | 25 |
| Blacks—males | 0 | 1 | 2 |
| females | 1 | 2 | 4 |
| Cluster percent of total | 13.5 | 12.7 | 17.3 |
| Clusters 2 and 3 percent total | 16.2 | 20.3 | 26.7 |

*Source: Microwire,* Service Awards column July–Oct 1976
*Pacific Circuit,* Anniversaries, column Jan.–June 1977.

singly or as part of a family unit) who take production jobs in electronics.

Some surveys indicate that as many as 83 percent of all professionals and technicians employed in Santa Clara County semiconductor firms are Anglo-American males, whereas half of all unskilled workers in the same firms are minority women (Bernstein et al. 1977:29). My own survey of several production departments in one of the largest semiconductor firms confirms that 50 percent of the unskilled workers today are minority women. Moreover, 60 percent of the unskilled workers in these departments proved to be in-migrants from out of state or from another country.[6]

The heavy domestic migration of unskilled workers is a particularly important process often overlooked in connection with brain drain. Yet it is an historical fact that restrictions on the international migration of unskilled workers have almost always been accompanied by the countervailing tendency for domestic migration (migration internal to the United States) to increase. In this country the best historical examples of this process were the movements of rural southern blacks into northern industry during the world wars (Thomas 1972:141–2). Today with immigration law written to favor entry by professionals and skilled workers, internal migration of unskilled workers has once again become a key element in U.S. economic development, especially as it relates to the building up of new, high technology–producing industries as part of the international division of labor.

As noted earlier, the shortage of unskilled electronics workers created by the exit of men from production line jobs led first to the large-scale entry of women into production work. This trend began in the 1950s and was clearly evident by 1960. But the industry continued to grow and so did the need for production workers, a need which after a point simply could not be met by further drawing on the resident female population. Thus, in the late 1950s, a wave of migration to the county began to develop and resulted in a net population gain of 155,000 persons between just 1955 and 1960 and of another 176,000 persons between 1960 and 1965. Massive population transfers continued to accompany (and facilitate) the growth of the county electronics industry into the 1970s. Census data show an additional population growth of 149,000 persons between 1965 and 1970 plus another 53,000 in the following five years (bringing the county total to just over one million).

At first, during the 1950s, the main minority and ethnic population groups detailed in the census were augmented by in-migration and natural increase in such a way as to result in 1960 population proportions almost identical to those in 1950. For example, Latinos (mainly Mexican-Americans) represented a constant 12 percent of all residents in 1950 and 1960, and all minority population groups (Latinos, Blacks, Japanese, Chinese, Filipinos, American Indians, and others) accounted for a constant 15 percent of the population.

By 1970 these Santa Clara County population proportions had changed dramatically due especially to the sharply rising number of Latino and black migrants from the U.S. South and Southwest. In 1960 these two groups accounted for 13 percent of the county population; between 1960 and 1970 they accounted for almost 30 percent of the population increase; and in 1970 they accounted for nearly 20 percent of the total population. Other minority groups made up almost 3 percent of the population in 1960, accounted for 6 percent of the 1960–1970 population increase, and totaled 4 percent of the population in 1970. Today all minority population groups account for about one-fourth of county residents.

Thus, the continually pressing shortage of labor in electronics, which was first met by the entry of women into production, began to be met by the domestic migration of minority workers, especially Latinos, to the south Bay Area. From among these in-migrants, the electronics industry continued to draw upon mostly women as workers (as dictated by wage scales), whereas the men in in-migrating families moved into the main unionized industries locally (canning, motor vehicle production, and construction). Latino men are heavily overrepresented in these industries (and also in more traditional farm labor) relative to their proportion in the male labor force; conversely, Latino women are overrepresented in the electronics and computer industries (as well as in canning) relative to their proportion in the female labor force.

Black men and women show somewhat similar patterns of industrial employment vis-à-vis Latinos, but Anglo-Americans and Asians exhibit distinctly different patterns. Anglo-American men are overrepresented in the high-technology industries (i.e., as engineers, etc.) and very underrepresented in the unskilled but unionized industries which minority working men rely on for high wages; Anglo-American women tend to be underemployed in the unskilled electronics work force because fewer—especially the wives of well-paid professionals and technicans—need to go to work in the low wage industries to earn a complementary income than is more typically the case among women from blue-collar backgrounds. Census data for Asians (undifferentiated by national background) indicates a different pattern obtaining for male/female employment, in which both sexes are overconcentrated in the elecronics and computer industries and (with the exception of the old agricultural sector) underconcentrated in the others. Personal observations suggest this is in part due to a heavy concentration of women from the Philippines in production work, offset by a large number of Chinese and other Asian engineers in nonproduction work.

*369*

## Conclusion

What I have tried to outline here are the systematic interconnections among the main divisions of labor in U.S. electronics production today. These divisions have devolved in the post–World War II period from a particular political-economic foundation and in a particular sequence. Indeed, the special position of the United States in the postwar world market gave initial impetus to the pronounced military and space orientation of U.S. electronics production.

The U.S. electronics industry as a whole developed a different occupational structure compared to consumer production–oriented operations of electronics multinationals in other countries. For the main electronics complex in California's Silicon Valley, this meant the organization of a work force around two occupational poles: scientific R & D and unskilled fabrication and assembly. However, production techniques in electronics remained relatively labor intensive and low paying and resulted in the exit of men from production lines and their replacement by less privileged women workers.

Finally, the post-1965 legal restrictions on unskilled migration to the United States have stimulated the domestic migration of a rising proportion of unskilled, minority workers from the least developed regions of the United States to supply the electronics industry's labor needs. The result has been a developing ethnic division of labor in congruence with the occupational and gender division of labor in electronics.

The social division of labor in Santa Clara County today provides a glimpse of structural features that could become basic in U.S. society as the country pursues a special position in the international division of labor as a militarized, high technology–producing power.

## Notes

1. Every major development in army and navy organization also shows the impact of this policy, from the development of field operated tactical nuclear rockets and the formation of an airborne rapid deployment force to the centering of naval fleets around powerful aircraft carriers and the transformation of the submarine fleet into a leg of the missile-launching triad.

2. Marvin Harris's (1981) populistic contention that postwar growth in the "service" sector is due alone to the declining quality of U.S. manufactured

goods and that the rise in women's employment undercuts minority employment are both contradicted by this analysis.

3. It should be noted that dating back to Lee DeForest's invention of the vacuum tube (the precursor of the transistor and the integrated circuit) in Palo Alto in 1912, the Santa Clara County economy has had an electronics manufacturing sector. For a brief history, see Keller 1981:63–7.

4. Rates of surplus value in manufacturing were computed from U.S. Census of Manufactures data by subtracting total hourly wages from the value added in an industry and then dividing the result by total hourly wages. For a discussion of this method and its meaning, see Keller 1981:304–11.

5. For a discussion of social patterns in the recruitment, hiring, and laying off of women workers in electronics, see Keller 1981:123–53.

6. For a discussion of the geographical and social origins of production workers in several representative semiconductor departments, see Keller 1981:210–61.

## References

Association of Bay Area Governments (ABAG). 1981. *Silicon Valley and Beyond.* Working Papers on the Region's Economy, no. 2. Berkeley.

Axelrad, Marcie. 1979. *Profile of the Electronics Industry Workforce in the Santa Clara Valley.* Mountain View, California: Project on Health and Safety in Electronics (PHASE).

Bernstein, Alan; DeGrasse, B.; Grossman, R.; Paine, C.; and Siegel, L. 1977. *Silicon Valley: Paradise or Paradox?* Mountain View, California: Pacific Studies Center.

Budish, J.M. 1962. *The Changing Structure of the Working Class.* New York: International.

Clark, Burton R. 1960. *The Open Door College: A Case Study.* New York: McGraw-Hill.

Dinnerstein, Leonard, and Reimers, David M. 1975. *Ethnic Americans: A History of Immigration and Assimilation.* New York: Harper and Row.

Eaton, John. 1949. *Political Economy.* New York: International.

*Electronic News.* 1976. "See No Quick Return of Offshore Work." 16 February, p. 70.

———. 1977. "Texas Instruments, Motorola Cite 'Payments'." 28 March, p. 75.

Freeman, C.A. 1967. "Situation of Manpower in the Electronics Industry Working for the Aircraft Industry." In *Geographical and Occupational Mobility of Workers in the Aircraft and Electronics Industries,* pp. 89–109. OECD Social Affairs Division. Paris: OECD.

Green, Gil. 1976. *What's Happening to Labor.* New York: International.

Harris, Marvin. 1981. *Why America Changed: Our Cultural Crisis.* New York: Simon and Schuster.

*Horizons.* 1976. "Newsclips." July/August, p. 3. Fairchild Semiconductor Corporation magazine.

———. 1977. "Newsclips." Summer, p. 3.

———. 1978a. "Newsclips." Spring, p. 3.

———. 1978b. "On The Way to South San Jose." Spring, pp. 4–7.

————. 1978c. "Newsclips." Summer, p. 3.

————. 1978d. "Newsclips." Fall, p. 3.

International Business Parks. N.d. *Passport to Foreign-Trade Profits.* San Jose, California: International Business Parks, Inc.

Keller, John F. 1980. "The Militarization of the Southern Economy." *Appeal To Reason* 6 (Summer):31–47.

————. 1981. *The Production Worker in Electronics: Industrialization and Labor Development in California's Santa Clara Valley.* Ph.D. dissertation, University of Michigan. Ann Arbor: University Microfilms.

Leeke, Jim. 1980. "Silicon Valley's Anti-Union Sentiment Remains Strong." *Peninsula Times Tribune,* 25 March, sect. D., p. 1.

Malito, Anthony E., Jr. 1970. Characteristics of the Electronics Industry. In *Potential Civilian Markets for the Military-Electronics Industry: Strategies for Conversion,* ed. John E. Ullmann, pp. 11–43. New York: Praeger.

Mellman, Larry. 1976. "Contradictions within Finance Capital." *Appeal To Reason* 2 (summer):11–20.

*Microwire.* Monthly Newsletter published for the employees of Fairchild Corporate Headquarters. Mountain View, California (through 1976; succeeded by *Pacific Circuit*).

Moody's. 1976. *Moody's Industrial Manual.* New York: Moody's Investors Service.

————. 1977. *Moody's Handbook of Common Stocks.* New York: Moody's Investors Service.

Morrison, Peter A. 1974. *Urban Growth and Decline in the United States: A Study of Migration's Effects in Two Cities.* Rand Paper Series, P-5234. Santa Monica, California: Rand Corporation.

NACLA (North American Congress on Latin America). 1977. *Electronics: The Global Industry.* NACLA Report on the Americas, 11 (April). Special Issue.

OECD (Organization for Economic Co-operation and Development). 1968. *Electronic Components: Gaps in Technology.* Paris: OECD.

*Pacific Circuit* (formerly *Microwire*). Monthly Newsletter published for the employees of California facilities of Fairchild Camera and Instrument Corporation. Mountain View, Calif. (since 1977).

Penn, T.C. 1980. "New Methods of Processing Silicon Slices." *Science,* 23 May, pp. 923–6.

Perlo, Victor. 1974. *The Unstable Economy.* New York: International.

Robinson, Aurthur L. 1980a. "Giant Corporations from Tiny Chips Grow." *Science,* 2 May, pp. 480–4.

————. 1980b. "Perilous Times for U.S. Microcircuit Makers." *Science* 208: 582–6.

————. 1980c. "New Ways to Make Microcircuits Smaller." *Science,* 30 May, pp. 1019–22.

Rockefeller, Nelson A. 1969. *The Rockefeller Report on the Americas.* Chicago: Quadrangle.

Sachar, Emily. 1980. "The Woman Who Wants to Unionize Silicon Valley." *Peninsula Times Tribune,* 5 March, sect. B, p. 11.

Schiller, Herbert I. and Phillips, Joseph D., eds. 1972. *Super-State: Readings in the Military-Industrial Complex.* Urbana: University of Illinois.

Shiras, Natalie. 1977. "Labor in the Valley: Closing the Open Shop." *Plowshare Press* 2 (Summer):1–7.

Thomas, Brinley. 1972. *Migration and Urban Development*. London: Methuen.

U.S. Bureau of Domestic Commerce. 1974. *Industrial Growth and International Trade Balanced for Selected Electronics Industries, 1967 to 1972*. Washington, D.C.: Government Printing Office.

U.S. Bureau of the Census. 1952. *Census of Population: 1950*. Vol. 2, *Characteristics of the Population*, pt. 5, "California."

———. 1963. *Census of Population: 1960*. Vol. 1, *Characteristics of the Population*, pt.6, "California."

———. 1973. *Census of Population: 1970*. Vol. 1, *Characteristics of the Population*, pt. 6, "California," sect.2.

Zausner, Robert. 1980. "Firms Rediscover Duty-free Ports as Savings Havens." *Ann Arbor News*, 28 December, sect. D, p. 1

# CHAPTER 15

# The Impact of Industrialization on Women: A Caribbean Case

## Eva E. Abraham–Van der Mark

In the beginning of the century Curaçao had a castelike society (Hoetink 1958:149–157). With industrialization and modernization, however, an *open* class structure with increased social mobility both for individuals and groups has developed. Nevertheless, stratification by race and ethnicity has persisted; and the black population that previously had been characterized by a considerable amount of sexual equality (see Sanday 1973; Schlegel 1977; Sutton 1977) developed an increasing inequality in this respect.

### Colonial Commercial Economy.

Because of poor soil and irregular rainfall, plantations never flourished and were often rather a status symbol than a source of income. Until the 1920s the island's economy was based on large-scale international trade and shipping, operated by a small group of white elite families. Within these elite groups there was a highly patriarchal family system. Women were completely subordinated to their husbands and fathers, and their primary biological and social role was that of wife and mother of legitimate heirs. Such women led lives of enforced leisure. In the black population, however, many house-

Ronny Martina provided much helpful information; and June Nash, Constance Sutton, Bob Scholte, and Derek Phillips read an earlier version of this paper and made valuable remarks for which I am most grateful.

holds had a female head, who often was the chief provider for herself and her children. Men, in various roles (father, husband, son, brother, lover) might make material contributions to one or more households (Abraham—Van der Mark 1973:155). In the beginning of the century, however, because of the constraints of poverty, many men were forced to emigrate, often leaving women behind to fend for themselves.

Before industrialization came to the island, women performed many of the agricultural tasks, engaged in crafts such as weaving straw hats for export, and sold the agricultural products, fish, homemake foodstuffs, and handicrafts. Apart from their important economic roles, they played a leading role in rites of passage, in various voluntary organizations, and as healers and as specialists in *brua*, which includes black and white magic.

The prestige and authority of women as mothers and as focal role bearers in the kinship network is celebrated in a great variety of old songs, proverbs, sayings, and expressions in Papiamentu, the local language of the Dutch Leeward Islands. Similar indications of men's position are lacking. Women held the family together during slavery and afterwards. The emotional bond between mother and child was strong, intense, and permanent. There is a saying that a child without a mother is food for the warawara (a bird of prey); adult men lament their miserable existence after their mother's death in such songs as: "*Ai, Dios*, my mother has died; *ai, Dios*, I have no longer a mother in this world; a stray dog is better off than I am," or "If my mother were still alive, I would not roam about drinking rum and having nowhere to go", and "Who will wash my clothes? Who will do the ironing? I'm a desperate and destitute man: I have lost my mother."

The sexual alliances between the men and women, on the other hand, were often not enduring and marriage was the exception rather than the rule. In 1864, one year after the emancipation of slaves, illegitimate births were estimated to be 81 percent. In order to promote legal marriage the Roman Catholic Church introduced and maintained a number of cruel, punitive measures against the offspring of those "living in sin" (Abraham–Van der Mark 1973:14–15).

### Industrialization; the Shell Refinery.

In 1918, when Shell established a large oil refinery on the island, dramatic changes occurred. The immigration of thousands of laborers and an increasing number of births caused a rapid population growth. Moreover, the great variety of national and ethnic groups among newcomers resulted in a complex system of social stratification. The majority of the new groups were intended to be nonpermanent residents, to be disposed of whenever it suited the management. They were both socially and physically segregated (Van Soest 1976:242–249). Gradually, however, the number of local men employed by Shell became considerably larger, and by the late 1940s, as the percentage of local workers continued to increase, Shell launched a series of measures offering material rewards to legally married couples (Abraham–Van der Mark 1973:16). A legal wife and children were given medical care and when their husband/father died they received a pension. Moreover, married couples were given the opportunity to buy houses on attrative terms. Later more benefits were added. Indeed, this seems to support June Nash's (1976:8) observation that to service and maintain a male work force, "The family is implicitly recognized as a cheap solution, as revealed by industrial managers' attempts to foster the nuclear family by subsidizing reproductive costs and direct payments to workers for family dependents."

As legal marriage became more prevalent over the years, the percentage of female-headed families decreased, and the illegitimacy rate went down from 52 percent in 1920 to 24 percent in 1950 (Abraham–Van der Mark 1973:20). This was, however, not so much a result of the social benefits offered by Shell as a consequence of the total exclusion of women from the industrialization process. The oil refinery with its highly mechanized production techniques provided no employment for lower class women. Although some females were hired as secretaries, typists, and analysts, the production department proved to be a totally male enterprise. Chaney and Schmink (1976:175) state: "It is widely recognized that the 'technological imperative' carries with it a set of sex-role prescriptions, but numerous examples exist of the operation of these norms in conjunction with economic change. In particular, we have noted that women are considered incapable of handling or understanding complex machinery, and thus often are deprived of access to useful tools. . . ."

This generalization, however, must be seen in the particular historical context of dependent development. A Shell informant stated that the exclusion of women from employment at the production department was not only a matter of complex machinery. Before automation was accomplished in the late fifties, work at the plant was quite heavy, and a good part of it was carried out under

376

conditions of filth and extreme heat. Moreover, it was dangerous. There had been various accidents, some of them fatal. He emphasized that it was assumed that women, "the weaker sex," should be protected from filth, heat, and danger. It is clear that there are certain assumptions about *male* and *female* work that are lived up to or cast aside according to necessity and sometimes in view of the possibility of extracting surplus value.

Training for work at the plant was provided by Shell at its own technical school (to which girls have never been admitted) as well as on the job. Shell has proved to be a firm believer in the separation of the sexes, and even today women are not allowed on the terrain of the refinery. The office and laboratory in which a number of women are working, are completely separated from the refinery. Women were neither employed by a British phosphate company on the island nor by the shipping and construction companies. The activity of companies in the latter sector increased as a result of the general economic prosperity due to the Shell refinery.

Industrialization also brought with it the end of agriculture and crafts in which women had played an important role. Moreover, the traditional female domain of small trade was taken over by males of foreign minority groups that had settled on the island or foreigners who regularly visited the island to provide the market with new supplies. Thus, women were left with only a residue of economic tasks and became a reserve labor force to be used or cast aside in accord with economic needs. More and more articles that used to be homemade and sold by women were replaced by machine-made substitutes. The worker and his family in their capacity as consumers were first discovered by foreign peddlers and then other merchants, who invented the most seductive systems of installments purchase from which they reaped enormous profits. While the earnings of more than 10,000 Shell laborers and employees, as well as many others who participated in the system of production, caused a rise in the general standard of living, there was also a concomitant increase in the cost of living. On the other hand, however, women's access to subsistence opportunities decreased, which, together with the full employment for men, caused an increase in the gap in earnings between men and women. Ideally, women were now to be confined to marriage and children. For those without formal training or education—that is, the large majority—possibilities to earn money were limited to domestic work, selling sweets and cakes and the trade in legal and illegal lottery tickets.

For the least valued female occupations, sleep-in maids and prostitutes, women were brought in from outside the island; black domestics from the British islands, brown prostitutes from Cuba, Santo Domingo, and Columbia. Prostitution was set up as a highly profitable government sponsored enterprise, enabling a number of men of different socioeconomic strata to earn an attractive extra income. The advantage of importing domestics and prostitutes was that when their services were no longer needed, these women had no right whatever to stay on the island and could be disposed of without any problem. Up to today foreign domestics who become pregnant are immediately repatriated.

## Marginalization of women and increase of legal marriage

Blumberg and Garcia (1976) have formulated four "conditions" for the emergence and prevalence, of female-headed families that are ultimately related to the mode of production. Empirically, these conditions focus on: (1) the demand for female labor in the society's major productive activities; (2) the compatibility of women's economic activities with simultaneous child-care responsibilities; (3) the compensation received by women for their participation in production both at an absolute level and in proportion to the compensation of the men of their class; and (4) the level and availability of alternate sources of income aside from the women's own economic compensation, such as welfare, children's earnings, and so forth.

I shall now consider to what extent these conditions obtain in Curaçao. As I try to show in this article, the demand for female labour in this society's major productive activities is quite low. Generally speaking, the close-knit social network of relatives among Curaçao's black population provides facilities for child care, thus freeing some women for economic activities. Writing on Barbardos, Sutton (1977:306) notes: "A job or career for a woman is never spoken of as an alternative to marriage or maternity. Although it is realized that a woman's household and child-care responsibilities might necessitate her withdrawal from work for short periods, the 'dual career' conflict experienced by women in industrial societies is not marked. This reflects not only different expectations and assumptions about a woman's economic and social roles but also the presence of a family and kinship system that acts as a support for women of all ages." This also holds true for Curaçao.

378

After the establishment of the oil refinery, women's access to subsistence opportunities has continuously declined, and their financial resources are considerably lower than those of men of the same class when they do obtain employment. My interviews with 375 families in Curaçao (Abraham–Van der Mark 1973) revealed a direct relationship between female-headed households and poverty. Although most female heads of households in my sample received some financial contribution from a man, nearly all of them had a very hard time making ends meet. Moreover, male support may be withdrawn, especially if the man is not a legal husband. I quote my informant E.S.: "After the birth of the fifth child, it really became too much for him; he left and I have not seen him since."

In many female-headed households the old-age pension of a living-in maternal grandmother was the only income that could be counted on since the earnings of most women were irregular and unpredictable. All incomes in this category were considerably lower than in the male-headed households. Thus, as women's position becomes marginal, their dependence on men's earnings increases. In many cases marriage enabled a woman to obtain a standard of living that she would seldom have acquired if she had been forced to fend for herself. But in order to maintain this standard of living, a woman is dependent on the stability of the marriage. Thus, the imbalance in the economic potential between husband and wife may be an explanation of Curaçao's relatively low divorce rate. As Blumberg suggests, when a woman's own economic possibilities are poor and the likelihood of her finding another man with a stable job is not very great, a woman married to an employed man will try to preserve the marriage.

In the late fifties, as a result of automation and other causes, the prosperity brought by Shell suddenly came to an end. There were large-scale layoffs and a rapidly increasing structural unemployment developed. This has had far-reaching effects for women, whether they were married or not. With or without the presence of a husband, it is taken for granted that earnings of children living in the household are controlled by their mother. A woman's position becomes more stable and autonomous when her children start working. Adult sons who have left their mother's house often feel a lasting obligation to give her financial support, which sometimes leads to tension between mothers and daughters-in-law as they compete for a man's earnings (Abraham–Van der Mark 1973). Today, because of increasing unemployment all of this has become more problematic. The most recent statistics show an overall unemployment figure of 28 percent, but the estimate, for women and those of both sexes fifteen to twenty-years of age are higher (Nationale Advies Raad voor Ontwikkelings-samenwerking 1978). Thus, if children are employed, their earnings have to be shared by a larger number of persons.

In the late 1960s cutbacks at the oil refinery caused severe insecurity and frustration among workers as well as among those who had been laid off. As Shell put out to contract more and more maintenance and repair work, people who had lost their job at the refinery were now performing the same tasks for various companies who had been given the contracts by Shell, but at much lower wages. Escalating labor conflicts and the failure to reach agreement on a collective labor contract resulted in a general strike that was accompanied by severe riots in May 1969, during which a good part of the island's capital was burned down. Women did not actively participate in this strike, which was an outcome of conflicts in an economic sector that exclusively employed males. The impact of these riots has been considerable, such as a new valuation on being black or colored as opposed to being white, a stronger position for the unions, and a number of social welfare measures. However, these welfare measures apply only to members of labor unions, which increases the marginality of the unemployed and those irregularly employed; this is particularly true for women.

### Texas Instruments

Because of a rapidly deteriorating economic situation in the late sixties, a development program, drawn up by the Stanford Research Institute, was recommended for Curaçao in which electronic assembling industries were encouraged to settle on the island. These electronic assembling plants are able to take advantage of a special U.S. regulation that limits the import tariffs on products assembled abroad by American companies to an assessment based on the increased value (Kok 1974:56). A campaign was started to attract this type of industry, and the availability of a large reservoir of cheap female labour was strongly emphasized as one of the attractions. Thus, Curaçao presents a good illustration of how certain types of industry prefer males and others females (see Ramos, 1970:155–156) and at the same time shows that the preference for one sex over the other is not necessarily related to certain stages or the development process.

Four companies were seriously interested; but when they discovered the existence of unions and a minimum wage structure, one of these industries withdrew at the last moment to settle in Jamaica. Of the three corporations that did come to Curaçao, Texas Instruments, Schlumberger, and Rockwell, the latter moved out of Mexico when the ILO rule prohibiting the employment of women in night shifts became operative in that country. Rockwell as well as Schlumberger closed their establishments in Curaçao after only a few years.

Texas Instruments settled in Curaçao in 1968 and exported all of its products. To encourage it to come to Curaçao, it was given several advantages (Kok 1974:57) such as: a ten years' tax holiday; permission to employ women in night shifts; the right to leave Curaçao at will; buildings to be constructed for the company by the Curaçaon government and let at a minimal rent. Although Texas Instruments is definitely an industrial company, it was classified in the lowest minimum-wage category, which is usually accorded only to companies providing services. This implied that in its first year the company paid its workers monthly wages of A.f. (Antillean florin) 175, ($91.62) at that time the same salary as that of a full-time domestic worker. Gradually wages were raised to A.f. (Antillean florin) 320 ($167.54) in 1976. Texas Instruments provided employment for 1,600 women, who were hired for the assembly of semi-conductors. This highly monotonous assembly-line work demands a great deal of accuracy. The women worked in three shifts: 8:00 A.M. to 4:00 P.M., 4:00 P.M. to 12:00 P.M., and 12:00 P.M. to 8:00 A.M. Wages were the same for the three shifts, and a major disadvantage for many of the workers was that assignment to a shift was permanent, so that women in the night shift had to remain in it for years without any hope for change. Although the work was dull, extremely fatiguing on the eyes, and poorly paid, employment was highly valued, both because of the regular income and the many social contacts at work. Headaches and eye infections were not seen as a policy issue of the company but as the personal worries of the women concerned. The importance of the company to the Curaçao economy was minimal (Kok 1974:57). Its contributions to the national production was quite small. It employed only unskilled workers receiving minimum wages, and it offered little stable employment.

The management of Texas Instruments resisted union organization but finally gave in (Verton 1977:90). However, when forced to accede to union demands for higher wages, the management first laid off some workers and then reduced the work force permanently. In 1976, only eight years after its arrival but with the immanent end to its tax holiday, the company closed its doors and left the island.

The six hundred women still employed at that time, nearly all single women who were the sole or main provider for their children and in many cases for other relatives as well, were discharged without any compensation. The union that represented them participated in the negotiations that were aimed at keeping the plant on the island or at least getting compensation for the workers that were fired. However, it was completely powerless because the right to leave Curaçao at will was one of the conditions that the company had set upon its arrival and that had been accepted by the government. Reasons given for the departure were the general slackness in the American electronics industry because of Japanese competition and more particularly the fact that in 1975, France, one of the company's foremost clients, raised the tariffs for semimanufactured articles produced in other countries of the European Economic Community (to which Curaçao belongs as an associate member).

Despite the disadvantages of the firm to the local economy, other governments approached Texas Instruments asking for the relocation of the factory in their countries on conditions that were even more favorable than those which had been met in Curaçao. Amongst these was the Haitain government, which guaranteed female workers for wages that were only 20 percent of those paid in Curaçao as well as the prohibition of unions. The Curaçao plant, however, was not relocated but simply shut down.

A small survey (Cuales 1977) undertaken in 1977 gives a glimpse of the impact of employment by Texas Instruments on the women involved. First, data from the local Foundation for Family Planning showed an increased use of contraceptives by the employed women (Cuales 1977:44–45). Moreover, regular employment provided an impetus for these women to search for still other means for increasing their income (Cuales 1977:53–61). A few women tried to earn extra income by sewing, washing, and ironing, in addition to their full-time jobs at Texas Instruments. But in particular the traditional female domain of petty trade was given new life when these women met a large reservoir of potential clients at work: legal and illegal lottery tickets, foodstuffs of all kinds, clothing, jewelry, and craft products were sold within the factory. Sometimes the sellers even acted as agents for female relatives or friends. An astonishingly large variety of items was sold on credit, with accounts to be settled on payday. Many rotating credit associations were organized as well.

In short, entrepreneurship flourished. This did not, however, affect women's work on the assembly line as the Curaçao plant of Texas Instruments proved to be the second in productivity (output per worker) among the company's plants, a plant in West Germany being the first. After the Curaçao plant was closed down, women decreased their commercial activities or gave them up altogether because they lost the numerous social contacts with potential buyers as well as the money to invest in merchandise.

Interviews with a number of women who had worked at the company showed that their patterns of consumption (Cuales 1977:61), especially for expensive items, had changed. They had purchased refrigerators, stoves, furniture and cars. This may seem incredible considering the low wages, but in all cases these commodities had been bought under a very easy system of installment purchase. However, as a consequence of this installment buying, many women had large debts when they lost their jobs.

### After Texas Instrument

Of the women who were discharged in 1976, only a few have found other employment. Some have become street sweepers; but the majority, at least 50 percent of those employed by the electronic industries, have emigrated to the Netherlands where they benefit from the material security of the welfare state (Verbal communication with Mr. Martina, Office of the Delegate Minister of the Netherlands Antilles, The Hague, 1981).

The majority of the forty-three women who were interviewed in Curaçao in 1977 felt resentment about their sudden dismissal, but said that they would not hesitate to go back to Texas Instruments or any other firm if that were possible. "If Texas or whatever American company comes here tomorrow, I'll be the first one to start working for them. I'd rather start today than tomorrow and I do not want to work for eight years as I did for Texas but for twenty years or more" (Cuales 1977:60). But this does not mean that they would accept any kind of work under any conditions. A rapid change in the evaluation of occupations has taken place since the late sixties. As stated above, working at Texas Instruments and the other electronic assembling industries was highly valued, and while the social valuation on sweeping streets (until the sixties done only by Portuguese men, at that time the underdogs of society) has increased surprisingly in the last few years, domestic work is more and more look down upon and associated with exploitation, lack of personal freedom, and social isolation. Such employment is acceptable only to the younger generation of women if there is no alternative. I quote one of the young streetsweepers: "As a maid in someone's house, you feel as though you are buried; and you are bored to death. Here in Punda [the center of the city], I see people, meet friends; things are happening; there is always excitement." But she is lucky to be one of the sweepers as there is a waiting list of over a hundred women who have applied for this work.

In the seventies female participation in politics, which has always existed, has increased; and the government has passed and enforced certain laws which are aimed at the diminishing of inequality between the sexes. Moreover, women appear to have acquired a new militancy. They are now working in jobs that before were exclusively done by men, such as police, customs officers, and guards, in addition to streetsweepers. The female police, who initially met a lot of resistance and paternalism from the staff, made good progress in their struggle for equality with male officers. This culminated in the issue as to whether they should be armed. The superintendent stated, "The women do not need to be armed. Their most powerful weapon is their feminine charm." This opinion, however, was ridiculed and scorned (Abraham 1974). The number of women working in tourism and in the many shops and boutiques that sell clothing and articles of luxury to shoppers from the United States and Venezuela has increased slightly. Curaçao, as well as Aruba and St. Maarten, boast of being unique in employing women as croupiers in their casinos. It is, however, particularly in casinos that exploitation of women occurs (see Kagie 1981). Then there have always been two ways to social mobility open to a very limited number of women. One is through the patronage system of a political party. Political activity and loyalty may be rewarded by a job, even if one is not qualified for the particular work. However, this may be risky, because today's winner is tomorrow's loser. The other way is selling illegal lottery tickets. A few women have acquired a small fortune in this way. They provide something for which many people on the island have a great passion and for which the demand seems to increase as the economy gets worse. I quote one of these women who has been quite successful: "Yes, I have made it. I am the first black woman who has visited Paris and Rome. I have my house, my wigs, and my golden jewelry. And I have earned everything myself; I have never stolen anything. Of course my trade is illegal, but everybody wants my 'number' (illegal tickets) and even all the policemen come to me to buy them."

But unemployment of women is more than 28 percent and in all the areas mentioned the supply of female labor is many times larger than the number of jobs that are available. Curaçao provides an example of the marginalization of women under capitalism: from slavery up through industrialization we see that women's position is not necessarily based on family demands, for the family structure itself may be determined by the marginal role of women in a particular economic system (Saffioti 1978).

Slaves were excluded from legal marriage until 1863, and stable relationships between the sexes were in no way encouraged. It is in the twentieth century, with active government intervention, a multinational corporation, and the influence of the Roman Catholic Church that legal marriage and the nuclear family with a single wage earner have become increasingly institutionalized. These ideals have been imposed on people from without.

Curaçao has a complex system of stratification based on class, race, ethnicity, and sex. Women's position across the various strata differs enormously and within the strata it differs according to age and other factors. Although women in this society have considerable social power, economic and political power are firmly controlled by men. This is true despite the fact that some women occupy prominent positions and others own and/or control considerable economic resources. Even though social mobility for individuals and groups has increased and a growing percentage of women in the upper and middle strata is joining the labor force, the position of black lower-class women has gone from relative autonomy to increasing dependency.

### References

Abraham–Van der Mark, Eva E. 1973. *Yu'i Mama, Enkele facetten van gezinsstructuur op Curaçao.* Assen: Van Gorcum.

Abraham, J.A. 1974. *Community Consultation Project: Police women in Curaçao,* unpublished paper.

Blumberg, Rae Lesser with Maria Garcia Pilar. 1976. "The Political Economy of the Mother-Child Family: A Cross-societal View." In *Beyond the Nuclear Family Model,* ed. L. Lenero-Otero. London: Sage.

Chaney, Elsa M. and Schmink, Marianne. 1976. "Women and Modernization: Access to Tools." In *Sex and Class in Latin America,* eds. J. Nash and H. Safa pp. 160–183. New York: Praeger.

Cuales, Sonia M. 1977. "Verslag van een leeronderzoek naar de positie van de Curacaose vrouw die bij Texas Instruments heeft gewerkt in de periode 1968–1976." Unpublished report, Leyden.

Hoetink, H. 1958. *Het Patroon van de oude Curacaose Samenleving.* Aruba: De Wit.

Kagie, R. 1981. Traditice, Hanen, en roulette." In *N.R.C./Handelsblad*, May 12th.

Kok, Michiel. 1974. *De economische struktuur van de Nederlandse Antillen* Curaçao: St. Augustinus.

Nash, June, 1976. "A Critique of Social Science Roles in Latin America," In *Sex and Class in Latin America*, eds. J. Nash and H. Safa, pp. 1–21. New York: Praeger.

Nationale Advies Raad voor Ontwikkelingssamenwerking. 1978. *Advies Nederlandse Antillen*. The Hague: Ministerie van Buitenlandse Zaken.

Ramos, Joseph R. 1970. *Labor and Development in Latin America*. New York: Columbia University Press.

Saffioti, Heleieth I.B. 1978. *Women in Class Society*. New York: Monthly Review Press.

Sanday, Peggy R. 1973. "Toward a Theory of the Status of Women," *American Anthropologist* 75:1682–1700.

Schlegel, Alice. 1977. "Toward a Theory of Sexual Stratification," In *Sexual Stratification: A Cross-cultural View*, ed. A. Schlegel. New York: Columbia University Press.

Sutton, Constance and Makiesky-Barrow, Susan. 1977. "Social Inequality and Sexual Status in Barbados." In *Sexual Stratification: A Cross-cultural View*, ed. A. Schegel, pp. 292–326. New York: Columbia University Press.

Van Soest, Jaap. 1976. *Olie als Water, De Curacaose economie in de eerste helft van de twintigste eeuw*. Curaçao: Centraal Historisch Archief.

Verton, Peter. 1977. *Politieke dynamiek en dekolonisatie, de Nederlandse Antillen tussen autonomie en onafhankelijkheid*. Alphen aan de Rijn: Samson.

CHAPTER 16

# The Emergence of Small-Scale Industry in a Taiwanese Rural Community

Hu Tai-Li

## Introduction

Current modes of industrialization in less developed countries resemble, on the surface, processes that took place in Europe and the United States during the nineteenth and early twentieth centuries. However, when examined closely, they reveal characteristics that have never been present before. This paper points out that the small-scale factory in a Taiwanese rural community is geared into the national and international subcontracting system. As will be seen, family owned "auxiliary" factories operating as suppliers of larger export-oriented domestic factories or trading companies are a response to both the limitations of local agricultural production and the demands of the larger international economy.

In addition to broad economic constraints, changing perceptions regarding status and prosperity as well as skills learned by villagers in an urban setting can contribute to generate environments in which factory work is preferred over farming. However, far from being a permanent economic solution, small family-owned factories are constantly at the mercy of supply and demand fluctuations that frequently force owners to seek other means of support or to increase the number of hours they work while at the same time earning smaller wages.

The shift from limited agricultural production to unstable factory work has had a powerful impact upon the lives of rural Taiwanese people who must resort to the bonds of kinship as a way to adjust to a changing world. Such bonds are not impervious to tensions and pressures but they often provide the only solid base for continued survival.

This paper considers these issues to three sections. First I examine the early industrialization and import-substitution periods in Taiwan as a way to provide a context for understanding commonalities and differences vis-a-vis later phases of development. Section two describes in some detail the characteristics of small-scale industrialization in suburban Taichung, an area located in Central Taiwan. An important aspect of this description is an understanding of the part that kinship plays in the formation and sustenance of small-scale factory production in a rural milieu. In the concluding section, I summarize findings and point to the unique character of auxiliary plants in Taiwan.

## 1. Past and Present Processes of Industrialization in Taiwan

Between October of 1976 and March of 1978 I lived in Liu Ts'o, a central Taiwanese village in suburban Taichung with a population of 789 living in an area totaling around 70 hectares. Deceived by its surrounding large area of paddy fields, I assumed in the beginning that it was an agrarian community whose inhabitants subsisted mainly by cultivating the land. It did not take me long to realize, however, that this village, like many others in the island, had been transformed from an agriculture-dominated to an agriculture-sub-ordinated community in recent years. Another phenomenon in Liu Ts'o also attracted my attention. As I visited the farm houses, I often heard the sound of machines. The villagers told me that since 1970, about twenty small-scale factories had emerged in this small town. I did not recall any ethnographic studies on rural Taiwan that described this kind of development in detail. It seemed that, all of a sudden, villagers had built these plants in growing numbers.

I couldn't help thinking of Fei Hsiao-T'ung's and Chang Chih-I's works (Fei 1939 and 1948, Fei and Chang 1945). Fei proposed to revive small-scale rural industry as a strategy for indigenous development. In his opinion, rural China, with its dense population and limited land, could not produce enough agriculturally to support its people, and so he proposed a revival of traditional rural crafts. Although not technologically complex, this type of industry could supplement farm income and solve the problem of cyclical unemployment during agricultural slack seasons. The decline of traditional rural industry was attributed to the intrusion of Western mechanized factory production. After losing supplementary income, more and more petty owners sank to the status of tenants; and farm rents became unbearable.

Fei supported moderate land-to-tiller programs; landlords would be compensated for their confiscated land and persuaded to invest in industry. At the same time, former tenants would become owner-cultivators capable of accumulating capital for reviving rural industry. He held that the ideal and practical type of industry should be complementary to agricultural work, diffused in villages or in centers near villages, and cooperatively owned by workers. In addition the profits should be wisely distributed among the peasants. How far is Liu Ts'o's small-scale industry from Fei's ideal? What are the main characteristics of and conditions for the emergence of Liu Ts'o's factories? How are they related to island-wide industrial development and in turn to the international organization of industry? To answer these questions, let us first examine the historical course that industrialization has followed in Taiwan.

*The Japanese Colonial Period.* During this stage (1895–1945), Taiwan exported agricultural goods (rice, sugar) to Japan in exchange for industrial goods (textiles, fertilizer). The dominant industries were related to food processing, especially sugar refining and preliminary processing of rice and pineapple. After 1931 the Japanese colonial government began to develop some basic industries including cement, chemicals, petroleum refining, pulp and paper, metallurgy, and fertilizer. Transportation and electrification improved. But most factories were built through Japanese investment because political barriers prevented the participation of Taiwanese entrepreneurs.

In 1935 the island had 7,032 factories (Chou 1958); 59 percent of them had fewer than five employees, and only 4.7 percent employed more than thirty persons. In the Taichung area, the more advanced industries were food processing, timber, textiles, and the assembly of sewing machines. Liu Ts'o is located in the Nan T'un district. The local gazeteer records that in 1932 this district had a total of 12 factories, all assembled in the market street. Most of them were food processing factories including rice processing, bamboo processing, soy sauce, peanut oil, incense, paper, and so forth.

A cassava-processing factory was developed in Liu Ts'o village around 1936 as a result of Japanese investment. This factory was situated by the main road that led to the market street of Nan T'un.

Every year when cassava on the nearby Ta-Tu tableland was harvested, the factory hired between thirty and forty laborers in the surrounding villages to do temporary work.

During the agricultural slack season many Liu Ts'o villagers engaged in traditional handicrafts such as the weaving of straw hats, straw mats, and baskets. It was not easy for the small farmer to maintain a basic standard of living, let alone invest in industry. Throughout the Japanese colonial period, the Liu Ts'o residents owned only 4 to 15 percent of the total sixty-five hectares of land in the area; the remaining fields were in absentee landlords' hands.

Generally speaking, industries prior to 1945 were largely developed in cities and market towns and were dependent on locally available raw materials.

*The Import-Substitution Period.* In the 1950s Taiwan experienced an import-substitution phase that was characterized by the heavy emphasis on the replacement of nondurable consumer-goods imports (such as textiles, apparel, wood products, and leather products) by domestic production. The growth of the textile industry was a good example. In the prewar period, Taiwan relied on imports for 90 percent of its textile goods. Since 1951 the government has provided necessary raw cotton to domestic textile firms and restricted the import of finished textile products.

In the agricultural sector, land reform began in the early 1950s. The stable growth of the population, agricultural productivity, and technology in the rural areas enhanced the development of the industrial sector that was highly reliant on surplus rural labor to produce, and local markets to consume, industrial products. Many young villagers flowed into urban factories for industrial training in the 1950s and 1960s.

The statistical record reveals that in 1956 Nan T'un had twenty-six registered plants. Twenty-one of them were food-processing factories. The rest were kiln, textile, and machinery manufacturers. However, in Liu Ts'o industrialization advanced slowly. The cassava-processing factory closed down when Japan returned Taiwan to China in 1945; and between 1945 and 1970, only two small-scale factories appeared in the village. One of them was Chen Tien-Wang's sewing machine assembly plant. It was no surprise that the first industry extending to Liu Ts'o was related to sewing machine manufacture, for Taichung has been the base of Taiwan's sewing machine industry since 1936.

390

One day, forty-two-year-old Chen Tien-Wahng sat in his grocery store tracing his career history:

> After graduating from primary school in 1951, I found a job in Taichung City. I was probably the first one in Liu Ts'o to go to the city and learn industrial skills. In the 1950s there were already many kinds of industries in Taichung, but the factories were few in number.
>
> I was hired by a sewing machine factory and learned how to assemble parts. At that time it was a very profitable industry. The sewing machines we produced were sold in domestic markets. I returned to Liu Ts'o and taught my younger brother and several villagers the skill. But the best years passed. This industry has been declining and the wages seldom rise. At present, I assemble about three sewing machines a day for a bigger machine factory in Taichung city. During my free time I take care of my rice paddy and grocery store.

Another small-scale factory in Liu Ts'o was Liu Fu-Chih's sewing machine painting factory, which was established in 1957. Liu Fu-Chih was an absentee landlord who had a paper factory at Ta-Tu district in Taichung county during the Japanese colonial period. After the Chinese restoration, he moved to Liu Ts'o. The failure of his paper factory forced him to sell 1.5 hectares of land and start a new business. The sewing machine painting factory, which employed about seven workers, was handed down to one of his sons after Liu Fu-Chih died in 1973. Unfortunately, it closed down in 1977.

During the import-substitution period, a young baker opened a cake factory in Taichung in 1959. Some girls in Liu Ts'o were employed in a big textile factory in the nearby market town of Wu-Jih. The Chung-Ho Joint Stock Textile Company with a registered capital of NT$110,000,000 was established in 1955. Its rapid growth was obviously encouraged by the import-substitution policy.

*The Export-Substitution Period.* By the end of the 1950s Taiwan's domestic markets for nondurable consumer goods had been exhausted. This brought about a shift from import-substitution to export-processing meant to solve the problems of small markets and provide employment to agricultural surplus labor.

In 1960 the government enacted a nineteen-point reform program to improve the investment climate, encourage export, and liberalize the administrative controls on industry and trade. The first export-processing zone was established in Kaohsiung in 1965. By 1969 two more export-processing zones were established on the outskirts of Kaohsiung and Taichung. Moreover, the government established

*391*

seventeen industrial districts in the rural areas to promote private investment. Along with the growth of government induced industry, a great number of export-oriented private factories appeared in cities and suburban areas.

In the Nan T'un district, the importance once held by food-processing industries was taken over by machinery, chemical, and metal plants in the 1970s. Some young villagers who were sent to the city to learn industrial skills returned home and established auxiliary processing factories right in or next to their farm houses. At the same time larger-scale factories moved from Taichung city to Nan T'un district. They provided working opportunities for the rural youth. The industrial development of Liu Ts'o during this period is described below.

## 2. The Booming Small-Scale Village Industries

New factories were not established in Liu Ts'o during the 1960s. Only one family invested in a machinery-processing factory which produced auto parts in Taichung city. But then circumstances changed dramatically. Since 1970 approximately twenty small-scale factories have emerged in the village. Thirteen of them are machinery-processing plants. The remaining ones are dedicated to wood product manufacturing, electroplating, vacuum-modeling and sealing, electronics assembly, and hat and bag manufacturing. In addition, four families have established similar kinds of small-scale factories outside the village; and some outsiders have rented Liu Ts'o's houses as factories.

A detailed description of one machinery-processing factory from its establishment through 1980 will serve to acquaint the reader with the general conditions of Liu Ts'o's small-scale industries:

The narrow space between the left-wing room and the yard's wall in Li Chin-I's home was roofed with tiles and made into a machinery-processing factory in 1974. Li Chin-I operated a borer, the only machine in the factory.

Around 1958 Chin-I was persuaded by a neighbor's son to drop out of junior high school and go to Taichung city to learn how to operate machines. Going from one factory to another, he was finally hired by a big plant where he learned the fine skill of operating the boring machine. He was aware that boring machines were rather expensive, but the rewards were also very high. As an employee of this large factory, his monthly payment was steady. He thought that if he owned a boring machine, his income would undoubtedly increase.

An opportunity to achieve this goal came when Chin-I heard that an old boring machine of poor quality would be sold at a low price (NT$35,000). He bought it and left his job in order to concentrate on reconstructing the secondhand machine. However, he was not sure whether he would succeed:

> The reconstruction took ten months. That was the most miserable period in my life. My mother took care of the children. My wife planted rice and mellons on our 0.8 hectare of rented land and was hired to carry heavy loads of straw during agricultural slack seasons. I had no income at all. We lived on loans borrowed from the Farmers' Association and my wife's sister. Two years before we had had a big family split. My older brother, who had accused my wife of causing the family breakup, took an indifferent attitude toward us. He would rather lend money to his son-in-law to establish a hat-manufacturing factory than offer us any help.

It seemed like a miracle when, with his own boring machine, Chin-I's income increased tenfold. He not only paid back all loans but saved a lot of money. He bought a camera and several electronic-controlled airplanes for himself, an electronic watch and motorcycle for his wife, a piano and many toys for his children. In 1979 he purchased a two-storied house.

For the first three years, Chin-I's factory had only one boring machine doing the work delivered to him by four "center" factories in Taichung city and county. These center factories accepted orders from foreign countries and distributed the work to auxiliary plants. After founding, boring, milling, and so forth, the finished parts were collected and assembled in the center factories.

Chin-I was very proud of his skill. He claimed that he was always able to meet the center factories' precision requirements. He worked hard, about ten hours a day. But at his leisure, he often chewed areca nuts while chatting in the village's grocery store or watched television (he loved western films and stage shows) or read the newpaper.

In 1977 Chin-I was thinking of buying a second boring machine. His wife's cousin, a trained machinist was pleased to accept his suggestion that they each invest NT$60,000 dollars to buy a secondhand item. The cousin did the reconstruction work under Chin-I's direction. During the reconstruction period, Chin-I gave him NT$3,000 (1 U.S. dollar = 38 N.T. dollars) per month. Once the machine was in use, 40 percent of the income would belong to Chin-I.

Chin-I then discovered that the available electric power was not sufficient for the operation of two boring machines. By law, unlicesed factories could not apply for electricity destined for industrial use. Chin-I's factory did not get authorization from the Bureau of Industry because Nan T'un district had been officially designated as an area for agricultural production only. Ironically, the same business, registered as a "machinery factory" in the Tax Bureau's record, had to pay an extra tax to the government.

It was all for the better; Chin-I preferred not to apply for industry-use electricity because that required a basic monthly fee no matter how much power was used. In the end he managed to get an additional supply of electricity by furnishing the left-wing bedroom with a larger air conditioner. It was clear that an unlicensed small-scale factory had the advantage of paying lower tax and electricity fees. Nonetheless, it did not have the right to bid for contracts or issue invoices. Chin-I always let the center factories deduct the government's tax from his wages beforehand.

During the same period, Chin-I's older brother bought a milling machine for the factory. This was the result of subtle familial pressures. Chin-I's success was known to all villagers. Therefore, it was a big emotional blow for his older brother when he heard that his younger sibling was planning to recruit an "outsider" for his plant. Forced by public opinion, Chin-I suggested that his older brother buy a milling machine for his only son, A-Shiang, who was employed in the village's wood-product factory. The older brother happily bought the machine with the money he had saved through a mutual-aid grain association.[1]

---

1. A grain association is a mutual-aid credit club. A person who needs money can initiate a grain association and ask relatives and friends to join it. In the first meeting, each participant pays money in the value of 1,000 k.g. grain to the organizer who has the obligation to offer a banquet semiannually, then collects money for the one who wins the bid from the other members. If the bid is 200 k.g. grain, each person only has to pay 800 k.g. grain to the winner. In other words, they get 200 k.g grain as interest. The organizer and the winner would pay 1,000 grain in all subsequent meetings. But there is a recent trend that the monthly-held money association is replacing the grain association, because its organizer does not have to offer banquets and the participants have more chances to meet immediate needs.

The milling machine was much cheaper and easier for a beginner to operate. A-Shiang learned the skill in one week. Although the wages were low when compared to his uncle's, A-Shiang claimed that if he milled five iron pieces a day, in ten days he could earn NT$5,000, that is, a sum equivalent to his monthly salary in the wood-product factory.

A-Shiang worked very hard day and night. Unfortunately his uncle did not find enough work for him to do. Each month he worked about ten days at home and in the remaining days he still had to be employed elsewhere. Before entering the military service in 1979, A-Shiang tried to teach his father how to operate the machine, but his father gave up quite soon. At forty-four years of age, he believed that a farmer's hands could not control a machine.

I was surprised to see that Chin-I's older brother built his own factory adjacent to the right wing of the farm house and bought a new milling machine after his son left home. Who was going to operate it? His oldest son-in-law, who had tired of ship-repair work in southern Taiwan, showed great interest and moved in with his wife and two children.

During my most recent visits to the village (December 1979; February and June, 1980), I was told that both Chin-I's and his older brother's factories were in trouble. Chin-I explained that this was due to the economic depression. He had lost contracts with three center factories and the remaining one could not supply enough work. Besides, the center factories preferred to send work to auxiliary plants with high-quality, computer-controlled boring machines which cost more than NT$2million each. "If I had that much money," reflected Chin-I, "I would rather buy a house whose value remains while machines get old." The condition of his older brother's factory was even worse. His son-in-law worked only a few days a month at very low pay. He was deeply depressed and trying to find another job.

After visiting other two machinery processing factories in Liu Ts'o and one center machine factory in Nan T'un, the problems faced by small-scale rural factories became clearer. Competition for sub-contracting work is fierce and those who invest in machinery soon see the payment for their work lowered by others entering the field. Testimonies from other villagers confirmed this impression. While I was in the field in 1977, a widow with 0.2 hectare of land had told me that two of her sons were working in a machine factory in Taichung city. Two years later, the two brothers rented a house and established their own factory. The younger brother had a lathe; and the older one, Mu-Fa, bought a boring machine. When I interviewed him, he spoke frankly:

I heard that Chin-I earned a lot of money with a boring machine. He is a strange guy. Once I entered his factory, and he stopped working immediately for fear that I might steal his skill. I never went back again.

Two years ago I learned how to operate the boring machine through an introductory book published by the National Technical College and three days training in the Takang Industry, in Nan T'un. The skill is no longer a secret. Any one can learn it in one year.

My boring machine cost NT$300,000. It is jointly owned by four persons: my brother-in-law, two uncles on my mother's side, and myself. On the average, I earn NT$40,000 a month. After paying rent and electricity (about NT$5,000) and my own salary (NT$10,000), the remaining NT$25,000 are divided among the four investors.

It is true that the economy is in depression, but the situation is not that bad. The reason that Chin-I cannot get enough work is that he became used to doing work for high wages. As more people have learned the skill, the center factories naturally deliver the work to those auxiliaries that are willing to accept lower wages. In the past Chin-I earned NT$600 for each bored piece. I only get NT$500. Some people are willing to do it for NT$300. Moreover, no one delivers iron pieces to you unless you have a "popular face" in the field of machinery work. The first son-in-law of Chin-I's older brother is a newcomer, and therefore his machine is always idle.

My younger brother is operating a lathe. He earns about NT$20,000 a month. We are financially separated. I work more than ten hours a day. It's too bad that I have to share the income with the other investors.

The second factory I visited in Liu Ts'o is jointly owned by a family. This family first opened a machine-processing factory in Taichung city in 1962. The head Lee Ta's six sons all worked there. In 1950 the second and third sons were sent out to learn skills while the oldest one stayed at home farming. They talked the father into establishing a machinery-processing factory in Taichung city and taught the other four brothers the skill. In 1978, the family started another factory in the left wing of the farm house. Taichung's factory was managed by the third son who declared himself economically independent from the others. The remaining five sons transferred to the new factory, which has one machine to spray iron filings, two grinding machines, and three lathes (one of which belongs to Lee Ta's nephew). The oldest son is the financial manager of the factory. He says:

The money we earn must be handed over to my father. All the brothers (except the third one) and our wives and children live and eat together. We do not get wages. If anyone needs money, he has to make a request to my father.

We produce small motorcycle parts that are mainly for domestic markets. Export did not begin until 1970. We have maintained stable relations with six middle-scale center factories. No contracts exist between us. As long as our factory does not ask for high wages, it can get an adequate supply of work. We had difficulties only during the oil crisis of 1973–74. Oh yes, Chin-I made a lot of money in the past two or three years, because there was great demand in foreign markets. Now the demand is drastically decreasing. Three years ago the center factories were not capable of buying many expensive boring machines. Since then they have earned money, they have bought machines and hired workers for their own factories. Less work was left for the auxiliary plants.

I also visited the Takang Industry Company, in Nan T'un, which produces high-speed precision lathes. The amount of capital invested was NT$2.4 million. This factory was established in Si T'un district in 1974 and moved to Nan T'un in 1976. The sales manager offered an apt description:

This is a middle-size factory with about one hundred employees and eighty to ninety machines. The workers work eight hours a day, six days a week. On the average they earn less than NT$10,000 each month. When export was expanding, more than 70 percent of our work was done by auxiliary factories. The products were largely exported to the United States and Europe. We received orders from foreign merchants by advertising in magazines and by participating in machinery exhibitions in big cities. During the past prosperous years, our factory added a lot of machines and workers. Recently, the economy has been depressed and we no longer have much surplus work for auxiliary factories. The most important thing is to keep our own machines running and workers employed. We are reserving energy for economic recovery. At present most lathes we produce are sold in domestic markets.

A quality control inspector at the factory explained that there are still some auxiliary factories doing work for Takang. They not only do quality work, and have a good reputation and social relations in the field of "black hands,"—workers who operate machines such as lathes and thus soil their hands from the oil—but are also willing to accept lower wages.

While I lived in Liu Ts'o, I saw three machinery-processing factories appear and then disappear within a short period. They were very small with one or two lathes operated by the families' young men who had a few years' experience working in the city's machinery plants. The capital invested was less than NT$100,000. They all closed down because they were unable to get a continuous supply of work.

Among the surviving machinery-processing factories, the one owned by A-Lao, with about fifteen lathes, is the largest one. A-Lao's oldest son is an experienced machine worker. In 1968 A-Lao sold 0.7 hectare of land. His son persuaded him to establish an auto-part factory in 1971. In addition to A-Lao's four sons, the factory hired some workers in the nearby area. But if it had not been for the financial support provided by a rich person living on Nan T'un street, A-Lao's factory would have been closed in 1977. Now the rich person is the real boss in A-Lao's factory.

Liu Nan-Chuan also established a machinery factory in his farm house in 1978. He has seven sons. Three are married; the oldest son sells vegetables in Nan T'un's market and lives at home. The second one, who serves in the Bureau of Telephone and Telegram, and the third, who is employed in a sewing machine company, have moved away from the family. The fourth, fifth, and seventh sons have had working experience at machinery factories in and outside of Liu Ts'o. It was the sixth son, an electrician, who suggested opening a factory at home.

When asked how they got the necessary supply of electricity for their industrial operations, Liu Nan-Chuan proudly but vaguely replied that the sixth son's friend, an Electricity Company employee, provided help. Their equipment cost approximately NT$200,000. This amount was raised mostly through mutual-aid grain associations.

The factory has a total of ten machines. Liu Nan-Chuan bought four lathes that are operated by the fourth, fifth, and seventh sons along with a hired villager. A portion of the factory was rented out to two nephews who bought two of the lathes and to a neighbor who contributed four of them. The sixth son is the factory's financial manager. All money earned was saved in Liu Nan-Chuan's savings account. The sons understood that their father's savings would be used for their wedding expenses. They obtained pocket money by selling scrap iron. In the beginning they did subcontracted work for A-Lao's factory. Later on they signed one and a half year's contracts with a center factory in southern Tainan city. They had to process three thousand machine parts each month. The finished products were then exported to the Philippines.

As may be seen, under circumstances of great economic instability, fostered in large part by the demands and abrupt fluctuations of the contemporary international economy, all family members have to pool their labor in order to make ends meet. In two small factories,

I discovered that two women worked side by side with their husbands who had taught them how to operate lathes.

Besides machinery production, other sectors of industrial activity have been affected by the internationalization of investments. A few examples will suffice to illustrte this point. Tung-Hsin Wood-Product Company, located in the right yard of the richest Liu lineage of the Japanese period was the largest factory in Liu Ts'o. In 1972 this factory was jointly owned by descendants of this family. Liu Chen-Lei, who had sold 0.36 hectare of land the same year, was elected as the factory's general manager for he held more stock than the others. The total capital investment of two million was partly used to finance the purchase of fifteen machines that employed fifteen to twenty workers under the direct supervision of a hired personnel manager. Employees worked eight hours a day and had only one day off every two weeks. They were often forced to work overtime to meet production deadlines.

Many believed that the factory was not making profits on account of poor management. But a reduction in demand by the foreign market played a part in its demise. After all the smaller stockholders dropped out, the plant finally closed in 1979. The premises were rented to an outsider who changed it into a leather-suit-case–manufacturing factory.

In 1974, A-Nan established a hat-making factory in his father-in-law's farm house in Liu Ts'o. Due to the difficulty of recruiting enough female workers in the village, the factory moved to Nan T'un street in 1976. When I first visited it, the factory employed eight female sewers and one male cutter. The employees usually worked ten hours a day. They got two nights off each week and one day off every two weeks. The monthly salary varied according to the number of hats each worker made. An experienced worker's income was between NT$4,000 and 6,000. A newcomer could only earn a few hundred dollars excluding fees for boarding.

A-Nan's factory was an auxiliary producing mainly for export. Recently, I had the opportunity to visit its center factory: San-Shen Hat-Manufacturing Company. The firm's owner explained that in the Japanese period, his job was to cut straws for a straw hat-manufacturing factory. He saved some money and bought 0.25 hectare of land. In 1970 he built two work premises on the plot and purchased six machines. Luckily, he met a merchant in Taipei city who gave him an order from a foreign customer. That was the beginning of a prosperous exporting period. In 1973 he was able to open a branch office in Taipei city. He entrusted his three sons with all business matters. The oldest son was named general manager and stayed in the Taipei office three days of the week. His daughter-in-law was the factory's accountant. His second son was responsible for the cowboy-hat section; and the third son managed the visor section.

This center factory's products were largely for export to the United States. About 85 percent of the hats manufacture took place in a plant that hired two hundred persons. Each employee worked eight to nine hours a day and got one day off every two weeks. The remaining 15 percent of production was carried out by twenty to thirty auxiliary factories. A-Nan's factory was one of them. When the center factory paid NT$4 (excluding the cost of the material) per hat to A-Nan, he would only give NT$2 to the worker. In general, A-Nan's factory was profitable unless it was short of workers or its products were being rejected for poor quality. But at times of economic depression, the center factory did not have enough work for its auxiliary factories to carry out.

In addition to hiring unmarried females to work at the factory, A-Nan also practiced a kind of "putting-out system"; he provided sewing machines and materials to married women in the farm houses. By doing so he solved the problem of female labor shortage.

The nonmachinery sector in Liu Ts'o is further exemplified by an electroplating factory and a vacuum-modeling and sealing factory managed by two brothers. The older brother learned the skill of electroplating in his brother-in-law's factory in Taichung county. In 1973 his father spent NT$300,000–400,000 collected from several grain associations to buy a whole set of equipment for him. He then hired four or five male workers, who were always threatening to leave. In 1978 the older brother received bad checks (the account was overdrawn) in the amount of NT$20,000 from the center factory. His father was forced to sell land to prevent the factory from closing down.

The second son's vacuum-modeling and sealing factory was also established in 1973. His father bought him one vacuum-modeling machine and two vacuum-sealing machines that cost NT$100,000–150,000. He hired eight female workers: four were relatives residing in Liu Ts'o, three were from a neighboring village, and another one from Liu Ts'o. Its center factory in Taichung city accepted orders from Taipei's export merchants, then delivered work to different kinds of auxiliary factories. The younger brother's factory sealed finished products such as knives into plastic models.

Finally, other nonmachinery factories in Liu Ts'o included an electronic factory supported through the joint investment of Lee Ta's third son and his friends (six of seven females workers employed in that plant were Lee Ta's relatives); one factory for making TV cabinets operated by a married couple; and a one-man bakery.

### 3. Conclusions

As stated above, during the Japanese colonial period Liu Ts'o's economic base consisted of handicrafts and an agriculture-related (cassava-processing) industry made possible by Japanese capital investments. In the 1950s and 1960s, due to the influence of emerging domestic market-oriented, urban-based industries, two auxiliary (sewing machine assembly) factories were established. In the 1970s, the village has dramatically spawned approximately twenty small-scale factories that have not only changed Liu Ts'o's outlook but its structure as well.

In the preceding sections I have described in some detail the conditions under which such factories have emerged. A glimpse of the circumstances of the world system of production that keep them alive or threaten their existence has also been offered. In the following concluding pages, I will focus on some of the structural characteristics of auxiliary plants as a way to sum up the lessons learned from Liu Ts'o's economic development.

First, unlike industrial zones, Liu Ts'o's small-scale industries emerged spontaneously and without government planning. Auxiliaries have been related to the expansion of export-oriented, labor-intensive manufacturing. As land for industrial use and labor became increasingly difficult to obtain in the cities, industrial enterprises began appearing in market towns and eventually in villages that could provide cheaper land and labor as well as convenient transportation and electricity. As a result during the 1970s many small-scale, in-village factories have been established right in the farm houses of Liu Ts'o and other villages of the suburban Nan T'un district.

Second, Liu Ts'o's small-scale industries have emerged from the small-scale farm economy of the post-land reform period. Their establishment mainly depends on farm families' supply of land, capital, labor, and skill. After 1950 agricultural conditions improved. With reduced rents and improved technology, the self-subsistent farmers were able to save some money. Nevertheless, the amount of capital accumulated was restricted by the government's low rice-pricing policy, the norms guiding family land division, and population increase.

As a result of this, during the 1950s and 1960s, agricultural work and income diminished while industries located in the cities began to absorb and then train young workers from rural areas. Nonagricultural wages supplemented, in important ways, the income of farm families. As the export-oriented industries further expanded, trained young villagers returned to the countryside and established small-scale industries in the farm houses. Thus, return migration played a significant part in enabling the emergence of auxiliary plants as economic alternatives. The capital investment in these factories was small, ranging from NT$30,000 to NT$2,000,000. The number of machines bought fluctuated between one and twenty. An idea of how small these factories actually were is given by Table 16–1.

Third, at the bottom of the subcontracting system, Liu Ts'o's small-scale industries are all auxiliary factories producing non-agriculture-allied goods for center plants. These center plants are owned by Taiwanese capitalists. In most cases, the larger center factories get orders by direct contact with foreign import merchants and companies, and the smaller ones often receive them through domestic trading companies which find foreign companies and help them supervising the production and export of the ordered goods assembled in the center factories. The normal procedure is like this: The foreign import merchant or company sends a Letter of Credit obtained from his country's bank to the export trading company or to the center factory in Taiwan. With the Letter of Credit, the producer can apply for loans from the local bank to buy raw material. After the ordered product was shipped for export, the producer is entitled to get the buyer's payment through the bank. Sometimes the producer is willing

Table 16–1. Number of Workers in Liu Ts'o's Factories, 1977

| Number of workers | Number of factories |
|---|---|
| 1 | 2 |
| 2 | 9 |
| 3 | 1 |
| 4 | 1 |
| 5 | 1 |
| 6 | 1 |
| 7 | 1 |
| 8 | 1 |
| 9 | – |
| 10–20 | 3 |

to accept delayed payment so that the foreign import merchant can sell the product first, then pay money with interest. An auxiliary factory can establish relations with several center factories and vice-versa. No contracts exist between them. Thus, their relationship can cease whenever one side decides to terminate it. When center factories do not have enough capital, land, or labor to expand, they can encourage the development of auxiliary factories in order to increase their capacity for production and share investment risks in an unstable economic environment. If the quality of the auxiliary factories' goods do not meet standards, the center factories can refuse to pay.

During periods of economic depression, small-scale auxiliary factories are more vulnerable than center factories. As foreign orders are sharply reduced, center factories may not have enough work for their auxiliaries. Then competition among the latter becomes fierce. Only those willing to accept low wages, those capable of producing high-quality products within strict time limits, and those having good public relations can survive.

Fourth, the male workers' expectation of becoming capitalists and free workers with higher income and social status was an important stimulus to the emergence of Liu Ts'o's industries. I often heard farmers say that "doing work at home provides greater freedom." When they worked in urban factories, they rarely became used to the rigid time schedules and did not like to work overtime. Working in their own factories, they experienced a psychological release. Paradoxically, most of them toil voluntarily for longer hours at home (more than nine hours a day, seven days a week) when they are able to obtain an adequate supply of work. The distinction between capitalists and workers in most small-scale in-village factories in Liu Ts'o is not clear cut; the owners are also workers. But once they are in the position to hire workers, they often demand that workers devote as much time and labor as they possibly can. There are big differences between employer and employee in terms of status, profits, treatment, and degree of freedom. Not surprisingly, everyone wants to establish his own business.

Fifth, Liu Ts'o's small-scale industries are not built on a juridical base. Most of them do not have licenses from the Bureau of Industry. They can neither apply for industry-use electricity nor have the right to bid for contracts and issue invoices. Their workers do not participate in government-sponsored health and accident insurance. They also work overtime, which is against national labor law. When they are in a financial crisis, they find that it is very difficult to get bank loans. On the one hand, the slack enforcement of laws give them certain advantages (such as the chance to exist, lower taxes and electricity fees, etc.); but on the other hand, they are threatened by their marginal financial status, poor management, and lack of institutional regulation.

Sixth, workers in small-scale factories of Liu Ts'o do not engage in agricultural work. Long ago farmers used to plant rice twice a year in addition to a winter crop. But the fields have lain fallow in the winter ever since 1971. It is said that this was due to the high wages of agricultural laborers and the low price of the products. Villagers preferred to be hired outside their own fields in the winter season to boost their wages. Is Liu Ts'o's agricultural labor in shortage or in surplus? During the slack season, one person's labor is enough for taking care of one hectare of family land at present technological levels. As the nonagricultural sector efficiently absorbs many extra members of a single family, the labor surplus problem of the slack season becomes almost nonexistent. But during the busy transplanting and harvesting seasons, Liu Ts'o experiences a definite shortage. Many people must hire laborers to cultivate their land. Agricultural mechanization has partially, but not completely solved this problem. The absence of a self-sufficient agricultural base accentuate the dependence of families on small-scale auxiliary factory production.

According to Fei-Hsiao-T'ung, the ideal type of rural industry should be complementary to agricultural work. But in Liu Ts'o the emergence of small-scale in-village industries has not strengthen workers' vulnerable economic position or resolved the problem of cyclical unemployment. When the youth work full-time in the factories, they are not willing to help in transplanting and harvesting. Older farmers do not want to participate in factory work during their leisure time. Thus, the imagined complementarity between rural industry and farming is negated by Liu Ts'o's experience.

Seventh, all small-scale factories established in Liu Ts'o are family-based enterprises. In two-thirds of the total, the older generation in the family provides capital and facilities, whereas the younger generation contributes labor and skill. The workers in nine of these factories were exclusively family members; three factories were operated by both family members and close kinsmen. Only those factories with more than five workers hired people outside the kin network. It is common to see several brothers or the husband and the wife working together in the family-owned factory. The financial management of factories installed by joint and stem families was often based on the rule of the inclusive family economy. A few Liu

Ts'o factories were jointly owned by divided families or kinsmen. The profits were carefully calculated and distributed among them.

It is probable that the older generation's ideal of maintaining joint families—households comprised of two or more married sons—or stem families—those comprised of one married child—with common residence, eating arrangements, and budget was another stimulus for the establishment of in-village factories. When family input into agricultural work diminished and income became smaller, land ceased to be an effective means of production to unify the young and older generations in the family. The father's agricultural experience ceased to be appreciated by his sons whose industrial training gave them a kind of money-making superiority over their father. Depressed fathers were often thrilled by the idea of establishing factories at home. They managed to get capital to buy machines for their sons who were then obliged to share profits with the investors. Machines, instead of land, became the new means of production thus contributing to a cementing of father-son relations. In 1976–77 Liu Ts'o had twenty-nine (seventeen married and twelve unmarried) males working in family-owned in-village factories. Twenty five of them were born after 1945. Roughly speaking, small-scale industries have reduced the rate of migratory outflow and strengthened social and economic ties among family members.

Finally, in recent years this kind of small-scale rural industrieshave become more and more evident in Taiwan. As manufacturing has pulled out increasing labor and capital from the rural communities, the emergence of small-scale factories in villages such as Liu Ts'o indicates a trend of reversion rather than rampant growth in the cities. In accord with Fei's ideal of rural industry, such factories are decentralized in the village, established with local labor and capital, operated with machines, and producing parts which are later assembled in center factories. The differences are: the government has not given these rural factories encouragement and instruction; the Land Reform is one but not the main contributor to the farm families' capital accumulation for the development of rural industry; as auxiliary factories of the export-oriented center factories, they do not depend on local raw material and the domestic market; even though the villagers own the small-scale factories, the degree of cooperation is low and the profits are not equitably distributed between the center and the auxiliary factories, just as they are not equitably distributed between the capitalists and the hired workers; nor are such industries complementary to agriculture, since the factory workers do not want to be farmers and vice versa.

Although Taiwan's export-oriented economy is not stable and well grounded, the island's unique pattern of economic and sociocultural development has puzzled many scholars who look outside the core of the world capitalist system for supportive evidence of the dependency theory which maintains that reliance on export trade rather than industries producing for internal consumption bolsters urban metropolitan centers at the expense of the rural hinterland (Amsden 1979, Harrell, 1981). The examination of the development of auxiliary industries in a Taiwanese rural area can contribute to the understanding of the local dynamics of Taiwan's industrialization.

## *References*
Amsden, A.H. 1979. "Taiwan's Economic History: A Case of Etatisme and a Challenge to Dependency Theory." *Modern China* 5, no. 3, pp. 341–381.
Chou Hsian-Wen. 1958. "Taiwan's Industrial Economy during the Japanese Period." *Taiwan Bank Quarterly* 8, no. 4.
Fei Hsiao-Tung. 1939. *Peasant Life in China: A Field Study of Country Life in the Yangtze Valley*. London: Routledge and Kegan Paul. 1948. *Rural Reconstruction*. Shanghai.
Fei Hsiao-Tung and Chang Chih-I. 1949. *Earthbound China: A Study of Rural Economy in Yunnan*. London: Routledge and Kegan Paul.
Harrell, Steven. 1981. "Effects of Economic Changes on Two Taiwanese Villages." *Modern China* 7, 1:31–54.
Lin Ching-Yuan. 1973. *Industrialization in Taiwan, 1946–72: Trade and Import-Substitution Policies for Developing Countries*. New York: Praeger.
Nan T'un District Office. 1932. *Gazetteer of Nan T'un*.

# CHAPTER 17

# Women Textile Workers in the Militarization of Southeast Asia

CYNTHIA H. ENLOE

The nineteen-year-old Filipino woman sewing the difficult side seam along the denim cloth of a Levi's blue jeans pant leg in a new industrial zone outside Manilla is systemically related to the Filipino paramilitary policeman on a search-and-destroy mission against Muslim rebels far to the south on the rebellious island on Mindanao. The young member of the new Philippines female proletariat is a reflection of the profound domestic and international contradictions that are prompting the current Marcos regime to expand its military and police forces.*

Militarization of a society is the systematic further curtailing of individuals' control of their own lives by the expansion of the state's coercive institutions and the defining of more and more areas of public policy as matters of "national security." Militarization escalates sanctions against those who try to extend control over their lives. Militarization is pursued by male elites when they are nervous, insecure in their grasp on power. In the Philippines—as in South Korea, Taiwan, Hong Kong, Singapore, Indonesia, Malaysia and Thailand—governmental insecurity stems from a keen awareness that state maintenance rests on nineteen-year-old women factory workers and on the gender ideologies of dexterity, docility, and family obedience that enable foreign and local entrepreneurs to

---

* A somewhat different version of this paper was originally presented at the Conference on Women and Power in The Third World, Duke University, Durham, N. C., March 26–28, 1981.

mobilize them. Patriarchy alone—without police and military rein-forcement—is seen by elites as inadequate to sustain the kind of discipline they need in order to reassure foreign investors that their societies are "good bets" for profitable investments.

Yet at the same time as Southeast Asian textile workers hired by multinationals or their subcontractors increasingly are subjected to police and military control, as well as to the usual capitalist man-agerial control, they can reveal the basic fragility of those awesome patriarchal control systems, based as they are on the contradictions of integration into an international capitalist political economy over which they have insufficient control to insure that societal needs are met.

The challenge for feminists is to appreciate Asian women textile workers' political potential *without blaming the victims* for the fail-ures, suppressions, and reversals that are inevitable, given the growing reliance of governments on coercive force in order to compete in the international political economy.

## *Women Textile Workers in the Evolution of the International Political Economy**

Women were in the vanguard of the first industrial revolution. In England, France, and the United States, textiles led the way in creating a new process of manufacture dependent on capital, tech-nology, and a spatially concentrated labor force. The work force mobilized by the nascent textile industries in these countries was comprised largely of young women, most of whom were recruited off family farms in the rural areas surrounding the newly urbanized factory towns. The famous "Lowell girls" of Lowell, Massachusetts, as well as their counterparts in towns such as Halstead, England, were in the forefront of an industrializing process that would radically

---

* As used in government reports, *Textile workers* and the *textile industry* include (1) the manufacture of cloths and man-made fibers, (2) garments or apparel manufacture, and sometimes (3) footware. But for accurate political analysis, I think women in cloth factories and women in garment factories should not be simply lumped together. The intrafactory divisions of labor are different; the location of factories is different (e.g., cloth manufacturers often locate in small factory towns, and often one company dominates a town; whereas garment makers workshops can be much smaller and usually are clustered together in one or two areas of a large city). Thus, although this paper will include both cloth and garment workers under the *textile* rubric, we need to be conscious of the different problems women workers in each sector face when they try to organize or to act politically.

alter not only local political economies, but the political economy of the international system.[1]

The textile and garment industries have been among those industrial sectors most dependent on female labor (though the move from natural fibers to synthetic, chemically based fibers has been accompanied by a rise in the proportion of male workers in textile manufacturing). For instance, in 1896 women comprised over 87 percent of French clothing workers and 51 percent of French textile workers; in Britain in 1976 women comprised 45.22 of all textile workers and 72.5 percent of all workers in leather, footware and clothing manufacturing; in Canada in 1971, women comprised 90.1 percent of sewing machine operators; in the Soviet Union in 1970 women comprised 85 percent of textile workers and 93 percent of "sewing industry workers"; in Tunisia in 1972 women comprised 74 percent of textile workers; and in Hong Kong in the early 1970s women made up 80 percent of the work force in garment factories.[2]

The women being recruited from the countryside to work for the new textile factories in the Third World in many ways are experiencing some of the same hopes, frustrations and risks that their Western sisters did 150 years ago—removal from their families, regimentation of factory organization, wage payments, female companionship, incentives for literacy, textile dust, job layoffs, crowded boarding houses, tension from piecework payment, loneliness. But a young women sewing a Levi's pant seam in Manila in 1981 is *not* simply a Third World Lowell girl.

Women textile workers live *in history*. Whereas the cotton spinner in Lowell, Massachusetts, and the silk spinners in Halstead, Essex, produced for national markets, Southeast Asian textile workers today are being recruited by foreign corporations as well as by local Asian executives who transfer the produce for sale in an international market. Furthermore, the governments which permit and subsidize these textile firms are themselves in a dependent position internationally. The Philippines, Malaysia, Singapore, and Indonesia in the 1970s and 1980s are ex-colonies of Spain, the United States, Britain, and Holland; they are in debt to the International Monetary Fund, the World Bank, the Asian Development Bank, as well as to private multinational banking consortia. They may try to assert state dominance over resistent adjacent territories (e.g., Mindanao, highland Luzon, East Timor), but they themselves still are client states of great powers in the global interstate military and economic system.

In other words, today's Southeast Asian women textile workers are filling a different function because they are being recruited into industry at a different point in the evolution of the international political economy and in a different part of the structure of that international system. The consequence is that these women are, if possible, even more precariously located than were their Western foresisters. They are meant to serve regimes more insecure than expansionist. The insecurity endemic to these contemporary regimes has meant that they need cheap, docile labor of women to attract globally mobile multinationals but also that they need militarization to keep wages down, docility intact, and thus foreign investors content.

Textiles (cloth manufacture and garment manufacture) today remain Western Europe's largest industry. At the end of the 1970s there were three million textile workers in Western Europe. But it was the industry with the highest proportion of *un*skilled workers, thus especially vulnerable to competition from the Third World, to which multinational corporations and investment capital (i.e., loans, not direct investment, a featured form of Western interventions in the Third World in the 1970s) were migrating in search of cheap labor and higher profits. By 1980, three of every ten pairs of trousers or jeans and six out of ten shirts sold in Europe were being made by Asian women, not European or American women. And the proportions are growing annually.[3] A European industry study late in 1980 showed that in the most expensive textile-producing countries labor was thirty times more costly than in the cheapest countries. Belgium had labor costs of eight dollars an hour, followed by the United States at four dollars an hour and Britain at three dollars. By contrast, hourly wage rates average forty-five cents in South Korea, thirty-six cents in Egypt and twenty-eight cents in Pakistan.[4]

Today women textile workers in the industrialized countries are being encouraged by businessmen, labor leaders, and government officials to see Third World women textile workers as their enemies, as threats to their jobs, as low paid and exploitative as those jobs may be.[5] It is this escalating need to be internationally competitive that is one of the prime incentives for Third World governments to enforce social discipline through increasing militarization if the traditional class and gender social ordering structures and ideologies no longer can contain the growing contradictions and conflicts.

Cloth and garment companies need more than *cheap* labor; they need labor *literacy* and labor *availability*. Furthermore, companies want assurance of political *stability*. This means guarantees that the central government, the companies' protector, has the resources to stay in power; it also means that it can either prevent labor organizing altogether or permit it in such a manner that it remains passive and easily coopted. Governments first in East Asia and now in Southeast Asia have been eager to supply migrating textile capital with precisely these assurances.

During the decade of the 1970s a total one million jobs in the textile industry disappeared in Western Europe.[6] During 1920–1940 textile jobs in Europe fell by 290,000, while Japan and India doubled their textile employment. But Asian countries became serious exporters of cloth and garments only after World War II. Between 1960 and 1969, Hong Kong, still a British colony, quadrupled its employment in textiles. South Korea and Taiwan were only recently liberated from Japanese colonial rule but were quickly absorbed into the U.S. military/economic sphere of influence. In those countries in the 1960s, one out of every three new jobs created was in textiles.[7]

During the 1970s Singapore, Malaysia, Thailand, the Philippines and Mexico entered the competitive international textile trade, thanks to the influx of foreign capital and the advice of international development experts from the World Bank, IMF and the U.S. Agency for International Development. In the late 1970s the governments of Indonesia, Sri Lanka, Bangladesh and Egypt stepped up their industrializing textile efforts. Today Sri Lankan government officials explicitly seek Singapore government advice, on the assumption that the latter's formula for success is as exportable as a pair of Levi's. That formula includes cheap female labor. A recent commentary in *The Wall Street Journal* lauded Sri Lanka's United National Party regime, which came into power in 1977. The American analyst saw as practical and realistic the UNP's promises to denationalize the economy, to encourage private foreign investment through the establishment of free trade zones and tax holidays, and to reduce unemployment by attracting workers to the new, light industrial factories.[8]

The Third World, therefore, is not monolithic. States, entrepreneurs, and women workers are absorbed into the capitalist international political economy at different rates. South Korean women textile workers had lessons to tell Philippine and Singapore women, and they all could pass along caveats to Sri Lankan women now being hired in the newest of Asia's textile factories.

The most recent entry into the interstate rivalry to use young women workers in the international textile trade is China. The post-Mao regime of Deng Hsiao-Ping has welcomed foreign joint-venture capital in textiles and other light industries to help solve the problems of urban unemployment. Although none of the business news stories have pointed out that it is the low pay and abundance of Chinese women workers that is the attraction, every accompanying news photo shows rows of women in the Chinese factories.[9] One might imagine that multinational textile companies setting up joint ventures in China in the 1980s would have to modify their gender ideologies and resultant labor practices in order to comply with the Peking leadership's socialist commitment to women's emancipation. But the admittedly still limited information we have suggests that that is a weak reed of hope to lean on as Japanese, Hong Kong, European and American capital flows into the cloth and garment sectors of China's economy. Even before the current *Four Modernizations* era, women in textile factories found their needs overshadowed by Chinese male enterprise managers' preoccupation with productivity.[10]

The international trade in textiles is one of the most government regulated.[11] That means that the labor force in a textile industry in any country competing in the international market—and increasingly this includes Eastern European socialist countries as well as those in the capitalist world—is one of the sectors of labor most subject both to domestic state regulation and interstate rivalry and bargaining.[12] Since women make up the largest part of the factory workers in the cloth and garment manufacture, women are among the most directly affected by how each state organizes its economy so as to compete and negotiate in the interstate system.[13]

## Women textile workers in the Philippines

The Philippines entered the industrial stage (especially the manufacturing for export) in the 1970s. During the whole time of the Philippines industrial surge the country has been under martial law. Militarization seems *part* of, not just parallel to, this development phase because of the strategy chosen by the Philippine state elite.

The key to the Philippines state strategy—as it had been previously in Taiwan, Hong Kong, South Korea, and Singapore—was the avaiabiliity of internationally attractive labor: a work force that was (1) *available* (not already fully employed in the wage economy), (2) *cheap* (could be recruited and kept on the job for at least four or five years for low rates of pay; low benefits; and low investment in technology, training, and safety) and (3) *docile* (workers would be so obedient to parents and/or managers that they would not protest should the conditions of pay or work prove (intolerable). Cloth, garment, food processing, toys, and microelectronics were the industrial manufacturers most attracted by these conditions.[14]

These conditions were promoted by various Asian forms of patriarchy, though these countries are not all identical culturally: Taiwan, South Korea, and Hong Kong are most influenced by Chinese Confucianism; Malaysia is Islamic and Buddhist; Indonesia is Islamic; the Philippines is largely Catholic. But the conditions also are encouraged by more recent socioeconomic factors, especially the spread of rural landlessness, the pressures on families for more wage income due to soaring inflation, and the government pursuit of English as the chief nonindigenous medium of school instruction.

In *Taiwan* in 1965, 13.2 percent of all employed women were engaged in manufacturing or transport; by mid-1977, 33.9 percent of all employed Taiwanese women were in manufacturing and transport.[15] Among younger workers the figures are even more indicative of industrialization riding on the backs (and "fast hands") of newly proletarianized women: by mid-1977, 65.9 percent of all fifteen to nineteen-year-old Taiwanese women were in the manufacturing and transport sectors, particularly in light industries such as textiles and electronics.[16] In *Singapore* in 1957, only 3.7 percent of employed Malay women and 21 percent of employed Chinese women were working in manufacturing jobs. But by 1978, 55.3 percent of all Singaporean Malay women workers and 36.1 percent of all Chinese women workers were in manufacturing.[17] In *Malaysia* young women are the backbone of the new industrial work force that the Malay-led National Front government is using to fulfill its 1969 promise that it will compensate its Malay constituents for the colonial legacy of economic inequality.

The Philippines government established its first export processing zone in 1969. Like the EPZs in Taiwan, South Korea, and Malaysia, it was designed to attract foreign capital investment. The industries would be light manufacturing; the market would be outside the Philippines; the labor would be mainly young, single, and female. Companies in the Bataan EPZ were a mixture of wholly owned subsidiaries of multinational corporations and joint ventures between local Filipino businessmen and Japanese, American, Hong Kong, and Taiwanese firms. Such joint ventures nurtured a new entrepreneurial bourgeoisie that would be beholden to the regime of President Marcos. "Export-led industrialization" was the formula advised by the World Bank and IMF and by the United States–trained government technocrats in Marcos' Finance Ministry and National Economic Development Authority.

By 1978 industry made up 34.8 percent of the Philippines total output; agriculture, 27.2 percent; services (including tourism, in which women are also a chief part of the proletariat), 38.0 percent.[18] Of all exports in 1980, manufacturers (clothing, electrical equipment and components, processed food, chemicals) amounted to 25.2 percent; coconut products, 24.2 percent; mineral products (e.g., copper) 16.2 percent; and sugar products (once the dominant export product), 13.2 percent. The cumulative external debt, nonetheless, was projected to be $11.7 billion for 1981, and inflation was between 17 and 24 percent annually. Although Japan had become a major trading partner and investor for the Philippines by 1978, twenty-five years after decolonization, the United States still accounted for more than half the total foreign investment in the country and 23 percent of the Philippines total imports. Marcos had made land reform, an end to corruption, and the reduction of the power of the local landed elite the platform on which to launch martial law in 1972. But six years later, the World Bank concluded that 50 percent of the Philippines national income went to less than 20 percent of the population, 5 percent of the national income went to the lowest 20 percent of the population, and income distribution actually had worsened during the years of martial law.[19] The development strategy for which young women workers were being mobilized was producing as many local contradictions as foreign profits.

Textile manufacturing was intended by the World Bank and its Philippines technocratic allies to be the "locomotive" of the country's export drive and thus of its overall socioeconomic development in the 1970s. By 1978, there was an estimated one thousand garment establishments in the Philippines; they employed some 500,200 workers. But, of these, more than half were working outside the industrial sector, in rural based cottage industries; about 200,000 garment workers were in firms located in Metro Manila and the Bataan Export Processing Zone.[20] The rural and the urban workers in the garment industry do not reflect the so-called dual economy that is conventionally portrayed as just the lag between modern and traditional sectors any more than they did in early nineteenth century England. The 300,000 rural pieceworkers are "often times used by TNCs (Transnational Corporations) to undermine the bargaining position of (urban) daily wage workers."[21] This sort of divide and rule among women garment workers is one of the tactics that lessens a regime's dependence on outright coercive force to mobilize yet control the cheap, docile labor force demanded by the multinationals.

Also limiting the need for military and police force to insure the sort of labor condition the Marcos regime has deemed necessary has been the structure of the family and land relationships in the 1970s. Robert Snow has interviewed young women working in the EPZ factories. One woman, whom he calls Nelia, is typical. Nelia came to the zone because she needed a cash income for herself and her family because rural Filipinos have been squeezed economically by the loss of the land and the rise in prices of everyday goods.[22] She also came to the city in the hope of delaying early marriage and childbearing, the common experience of young Filipino women who remain in the rural barrios. Although Nelia finished second in her high school class and thus could speak and write English, she found herself competing with thousands of other women for jobs in the zone. She finally got a job in a factory producing men's suits under contract to a U. S. middleman for sale in the United States. Most of the training she received from the company was learning the company regulations, not learning marketable technical skills she could use when she got laid off this job due to downswings in the international textile market. Of her $20.60 salary per month, about one-fourth went to her family, another 50 percent covered her meals and her bed space in a private boarding house. She was left with about $5.50 a month for transportation (she returned home most weekends), clothing, entertainment, and savings for education.

Levi-Strauss opened its jeans plant in 1972 in the new city adjacent to the old city of Manila, a huge commercial sector filled with modern bank buildings and long, low factory buildings to which thousands of Filipino women and men commute each morning to produce cloth, garments, and electronic components, mostly for export.[23] By 1980 Levi's employed forty-four thousand workers worldwide and derived 35 percent of its profits from its non–U.S. operations. Blue-Bell, maker of Wrangler jeans and Levi's chief competitor, similarly derived 36 percent of its total revenues from non–U.S. sales. In the Philippines, Blue-Bell was both a competitor and a supplier; it owned a controlling share in the denim cloth factory from which Levi's bought its materials for locally marketed jeans (Levi's made its jeans for export, however, from better quality Japanese denim).

Levi's open its plant at the start of Marco's martial law period. The blue jeans produced here are exported to Europe. Levi's now has a big enough market in Europe so that it can afford to transport its goods from Asia rather than continue to hire the better-paid workers in its European plants. In the Philippines 95 percent of

Levi's factory workers are women, mostly in their early twenties and recently arrived from rural areas. Despite being the majority of workers in the jeans factory, women were largely confined on the factory floor to piece-rate sewing jobs; the higher-paid cutters and pressers were Filipino young men.

Rarely do these textile jobs in the World Bank–promoted, multinational-funded and Marcos-protected industries bring with them employment security. These workers are "valuable" only so long as they are cheap—that is, they have little seniority and are single. They are at the whim of the international market. And they have been given few skills that will allow them to survive in different job sectors. The security sought by the Philippine state, therefore, is not the women workers' security. The security sought is *state security.*

### Militarization of Philippine Society

*Militarization* is the process by which, over time, military priorities pervade all sectors of social life. It is one form of state expansion. It occurs when both nonstate social ordering mechanisms,, such as economic dependence or cultural taboos, break down and the state's civil devices for control, such as social security laws or official ideological instruments, cannot fill the breach.

The most obvious indicators of militarization are: (1) the growth in military and police expenditures, (2) the expansion in military and police organizational mandates, (3) the increase in the import of or local production of weapons or transportation and electronic equipments used in military and police operations, (4) the increase in defense and interior ministries' influence in all spheres of policymaking. These are important trends to monitor. But the fundamental process in militarization is more elusive and harder to monitor: to what extent is security *the* criterion for determining public officials' actions? And to what extent is that security presumed to be the *state's* security, not the ordinary citizen's security?[24]

All of the Southeast Asian governments that have made concentrated and deliberate efforts to achieve rapid development through the attraction of foreign investmment in light industries geared for export are closely tied to major European or American nations. Although those Western nation elites are now being pressed by domestic lobbies to impose tariffs and quotas that will reduce the import of Asian textiles, they are also major providers of military and police assistance to countries like the Philippines, Indonesia,

Singapore, and Malaysia. This aid takes the form of sales credits, training, and outright grants. These do not show up on military expenditure charts, though they are crucial components of any trend toward militarization (see Tables 17–1 through 17–4). In 1977 the U. S. Congress prohibited the sale of Amereican made police equipment to foreign countries; but there is indication that the Philippines, for instance, is still receiving U. S. police training and equipment, only they travel now through defense channels.

The significance of such military and police expenditures and imports is not measured by their direct use on women textile workers. In fact, most of the operations of the government's coercive forces since declaration of martial law in 1972 have been focused on New Peoples Army insurgents in the rural areas of Luzon and Samar and on the Muslim rebels on the southern island of Mindanao. But militarization has important implications for women textile workers (and women in general) in the Philippines insofar as it frames all policy decisions in terms of achieving a kind of social order that will sustain an increasingly shaky regime and reassure foreign investors looking for "political stability." Those conditions have been harder and harder for the Marcos regime to sustain, as the formula of industrialization for export via cheap female labor has proved incapable of solving the problems of growing rural landlessness, unemployment, and spiraling inflation. More immediately, expenditures on military and police expansion deprive the Marcos government of resources for those sorts of health, education, and social-security programs that could reduce the risks and double burdens that women take on when they go to work in the EPZ factories. But, as the government buys more military and police equipment overseas (while also starting to produce its own M16 rifles locally, under license from Colt Industries), it will need the foreign currency earnings derived from cheap female labor in the textile and electronics factories all the more. So the contradictions grow more severe. And the government's sense of insecurity grows more acute. And militarization proceeds.

In January, 1981, President Marcos announced the end of martial law. Those opposed to his regime, however, hesitated to see in this as a reversal of the militarizing trend of the past eight years. Marcos still has formidable powers. The Philippines military and police remain among the most influential institutions in political life. A confidential World Bank report predicted the military might attempt a coup d'etat when Marcos retired.[25]

*417*

*Table 17-1.* Comparative Resources, 1980

| | Population (in thousands) | | Public Expenditures—Million U.S.$ | | | Armed Forces* Personnel (in thousands) |
| | | GNP | Military[a] | Education | Health | |
|---|---|---|---|---|---|---|
| Indonesia | 142,187 | 36,840 | 1,174 | 921 | 332 | 247 |
| Malaysia | 13,024 | 12,616 | 637 | 849 | 222 | 64 |
| Philippines | 45,356 | 20,614 | 550 | 360 | 141 | 99 |
| Singapore | 2,308 | 6,448 | 413 | 163 | 99 | 36 |
| South Korea | 37,893 | 33,305 | 2,016 | 904 | 97 | 635 |
| Taiwan | 16,788 | 19,477 | 1,508 | 183 | 39 | 460 |
| Sri Lanka | 14,106 | 3,700 | 26 | 115 | 59 | 13 |

*Source:* Ruth Leger Sivard, *World Military and Social Expenditures*, Leesburg, Va.: World Priorities, 1980, p. 22.
[a] These figures do *not* cover personnel in the police or in internal security operations.

*Table 17-2.* From World Ranking of 140 Countries, by Military Indicators, 1977

| | Military[a] | | | | |
| | Public Expenditures per capita | | Public Expenditures per soldier | | Economic and Social Standing average rank |
| | Rank | U.S.$ | Rank | U.S.$ | |
|---|---|---|---|---|---|
| Indonesia | 96 | 8 | 82 | 4,753 | 107 |
| Malaysia | 51 | 49 | 42 | 9,953 | 58 |
| Philippines | 82 | 12 | 74 | 5,556 | 92 |
| Singapore | 21 | 179 | 38 | 11,472 | 37 |
| South Korea | 49 | 53 | 98 | 3,175 | 69 |
| Taiwan | 33 | 90 | 97 | 3,278 | 62 |
| Sri Lanka | 127 | 2 | 116 | 2,000 | 84 |

*Source:* Ruth Leger Sivard, *World Military and Social Expenditures*, (Leesburg, Va., World Priorities, 1980), p. 26.
[a] These figures do *not* cover police or internal security.

*Table 17-3.* U.S. Police Gear Exports to the Philippines Fiscal Years 1975–77

| | Commercial Sale | | Foreign Military Sale | |
| Weapon | Quantity : | Value | Quantity : | Value |
|---|---|---|---|---|
| Ammunition Manufacturing equipment | | $ 649,525 | | |
| Ammunition Raw Material | | 89,089 | | $ 77,300 |
| Armor Plate | | 82,500 | | |
| Armored Car | 20 : | 2,171,540 | | |
| Armored Vest | 1 : | 130 | | |
| Armored Personnel carrier | | | | 1,889,000 |
| Carbines | | | 55: | 2,000 |
| Chemical Agent Equipment | | 1,606 | | |
| Grenades | | 500 | 49,920 : | 150,000 |
| Rifles M16A1 | 5,728 : | 1,015,290 | | |
| Rifles | 28,818 : | 1,378,025 | 16,645 : | 315,000 |
| Riot Control Agents | 72 : | 47,214 | | |
| Total Value U.S.$ | | | | |
| | | | | 7,814,156 |

*Source:* Delia Miller, "Memorandum on US Military Assistance to the Philippines", Militarism and Disarmament Project, Washington: Institute for Policy Studies, 1979.

Other Southeast Asian states dependent on young female labor for their internationally competitive industrialization also have been militarizing. The Malaysian government, for instance, announced at the beginning of 1981 that both its police and military—each heavily

Table 17-4. U. S. Military Exports to the Philippines

| Year | Total in thousands U.S.$ |
| --- | --- |
| 1972 | 14,908 |
| 1973 | 18,300 |
| 1974 | 21,510 |
| 1975 | 54,823 |
| 1976 | 69,530 |
| 1977 | 99,114 |
| 1978 | 58,593 |
| 1979 (estimated) | 86,250 |
| 1980 (proposed) | 95,700 |

Source: Delia Miller, "Memorandum on U. S. Military Assistance to the Philippines," *Militarism and Disarmament Project*, Institute for Policy Studies, Washington, D. C., October, 1979, p. 6.

Malay in its ethnic compositions—would be expanded in personnel and budgetary allocations. Under the 1976–81 Third Malaysia Plan defense received M$1.5 million; under the Fourth Malaysia Plan defense would jump to M$9.8 million allocation. The Malaysian army grew from 52,500 men in 1978 to 90,000 in 1980 and was scheduled to expand even further; the paramilitary arm of the Malaysian police was expected to grow from 58,000 men in 1981 to 120,000 men in 1985.[26] This growth occurs as U.S., German, Dutch and Japanese firms are being encouraged to set up factories and hire nineteen year old village girls, with the accompanying assurance from the local state elite that they can maintain the social order and "stability" that foreign capitalists need if cheap female labor is to be translated into maximum profits.

## Women Textile Workers as Actors, Not, Just Pawns

Women textile workers have been in the forefront of political activism in every industrializing country. They are employed in labor-intensive factories and are in an economic sector that is given saliency by the government. Their pay and working conditions are exploitative. The government and employers make an alliance in order to suppress any meaningful labor organizing, which, in turn heightens women workers' politicization. In the United States in the 1920s, Lawrence and Paterson mill strikes galvanized women workers. In Russia women textile workers were among the most responsive to Aleksandra Kollontai's and other Bolshevik feminists' call to strike

420

in 1915–17. In Poland in 1980–81, women textile workers comprised the most visible female sector striking under the banner of Solidarity.

In the newly industrializing countries of Asia, it has been extremely difficult for women textile workers to protest. Unions, when allowed at all, are coopted by the companies and the government. Malaysian and Filipino women have reported that when workers in their factories attempted to engage in organized protest, the police were called in.[27] Although the military and police may give their top priority to rural insurgents, their enlarged mandates, manpower, political access, and coercive communications and computer equipment enable them to intervene in labor disputes even more quickly and penetratingly.

Nevertheless, women textile workers in Asia already may be showing that the very conditions that make collective action so difficult are *also* conditions that are generating political protest. In 1977 women workers in the Dong-II Textile Company in Inchon, South Korea, which produces cotton yarn and fabric for export, met to protest exploitation by the management and passivity of the company-controlled union. Women textile workers in the southern provinces became one of the catalysts in the popular protest that eventually shook the entire state, despite (because of?) the fact that South Korea had become one of the most militarized societies in Asia by the late 1970s. Furthermore, these workers were aware that it was an increasingly integrated capitalist international political economy that tightened the link between their labor conditions and South Korea's militarized regime. On January 30, 1980, twenty-one textile workers, including twelve women, seized control of the Asian-American Free Labor Institute in downtown Seoul. The workers charged that this U.S.–funded organization was a tool of the Korean military regime in efforts to pacify the garment workers who were trying to organize a more meaningful, independent union. The military regime of President Chun used troops to oust the workers after his return from the United States where he had been talking to American bankers about increasing investment in South Korean industry.[28]

Whether women textile workers in the Philippines and other Asian countries or the Middle East or Latin America manage to achieve the level of political mobilization experienced by the Dong-II workers will not, therefore, depend solely on the effectiveness of their respective governments' security apparatus. The very growth of these coercive forces and the increasing dependence of civilian regimes on them to resolve deepening contradictions suggest that women workers sewing a blue jeans pant leg or feeding fibers into a spinning machine may be close to the core of the flawed state formulas for development and security. From that strategic vantage point, they may be among the most cognizant of the vulnerability, not the invincability, of their militarized states.

But the women working in the new textile factories in the Philippines or Indonesia are not just part of their countries' domestic politics. Their struggle, as individuals sending paychecks home to parents and as groups protesting poor ventilation, is occuring in and is shaped by the international political economy. To what extent they succeed in organizing will, in turn, affect the international sexual division of labor. The "Lowell girls" in 1830s Massachusetts, the needlewomen in nineteenth century London, and the silk workers in Essex also worked within and helped shape the international political economy of then expanding capital. Today the competition *between* capitalist states is a critical dynamic in the international system. Textiles is one of the most visible arenas in which that competition is occuring. It will be a test of women's international solidarity to resist an alliance with a patriarchal state in that competition and, instead, to create bonds of support among women textile workers throughout the world.

## Notes

1. There is a wealth of splendid feminist historical studies now coming out concerning women in the early industrialization of garments and textiles. Just a sampling includes: Sally Alexander, Anna Davin, Eve Hostettler, "Laboring Women: A Reply to Eric Hobsbawm," *History Workshop Journal*, no. 8 (autumn, 1979):174–182; Judy Lown, "Mill Life and, Peculiar Duties'— Lives of Women and Girls in a nineteenth Century Essex Silk Town" (Paper presented at a conference on "Women, Work and Education," Roehampton College, London, March 13, 1981 c/o Department of Sociology, University of Essex, Colchester; Barbara Taylor, "The Men Are as Bad as Their Masters: Socialism, Feminism, and Sexual Antagonism in the London Tailoring Trade in the Early 1830's," *Feminist Studies* 5, no. 1 (Spring, 1979) 7–40; Mary Lynn McDougall, "Working Class Women During the Industrial Revolution, 1780–1914," pp. 255–279; Theresa McBride, "The Long Road Home: Women's Work and Industrialization," pp. 280–295; in *Becoming Visible in European History,* eds. Renata Bridentahl and Claudia Koonz, (Boston: Houghton Mifflin), 1977, Tamara Hareven, *Amoskeag* (N. Y.: Pantheon, 1979); Thomas Dublin, *Women at Work* (N. Y.: Columbia University Press, 1979); Meredith Tax, *The Rising of Women: Feminist Solidarity and Class Conflict, 1880–1917* (N. Y.: Monthly Review Press, 1980).

In addition, there is a new, provacative film about women in the nineteenth century clothing industry in London: *The Song of the Shirt*, The Film and History Project, London, 1979 (this film is now available through the

Museum of Modern Art in New York). A half-hour radio documentary on women textile workers in nineteenth century Massachusetts is: "Women Who Wove: Women in the 19th century Textile Industry," WGBH, Public Radio,, Boston, July 3, 1980. The Cuban film *Teresa* focuses on the struggle of a Cuban textile worker who, though ten years after the revolution,, faces sexist double standards.

2. Mary Lynn McDougall, "Working Class Women during the Industrial Revolution," in *Becoming Visible: Women in European History,* eds. Renate Budenthal and Claudia Koonz, (Boston: Houghton Mifflin, 1977):268. Esther Breitenbach, "A Comparative Study of the Women's Trade Union Conference and the Scottish Women's Trade Union Conference," *Feminist Review,* no. 7 (Spring, 1981):66; Patricia Connelly, *Last Hired, First Fired: Women and the Canadian Work Force* (Toronto: The Women's Press, 1978):91; Maggie McAndrew and Jo Peers, *The New Soviet Woman—Model or Myth* (London: Change—International Reports: Women and Society, 1981):25; Sophie Ferchiov, "Women's Work and Family Production in Tunesia," *Feminist Issues* 1, no. 2 (Winter, 1981); Janet W. Salaff, *Working Daughters of Hong Kong* (Cambridge: Cambridge University Press, 1981):22.

3. An excellent television documentary is available showing the competition between European and Asian garment workers: "Inside Europe: Shirt off Our Backs," World Series, WGBH Public Television, Boston, Mass., 1980. The renewed use of recently immigrating women *within* Europe and the United States brings the danger of First World—Third World women's alleged "competition" even closer to home. In early 1981 there were, for instance, investigations of the reemergence of sweatshops in the United States garment industry. Paying exploitative wages and avoiding unionization and safety regulations, garment firms and their subcontractors hired Hispanic and Asian women, many of them vulnerable because of illegal alien status (*New York Times*, April 25, 1981; *Wall Street Journal*, May 20, 1981). And in Greenock, Scotland, the mainly female work force at a branch factory of Lees jeans organized a factory sit-in when they were told by the management that the factory was to be moved to Ireland to take advantage of tax breaks and cheaper labor (*Spare Rib*, no. 106, May 1981):16.

4. "Textiles Reel off the Ropes," *Economist*, Dec. 6, 1980, p. 82.

5. "Shirt off our Backs," op. cit.

6. "Textiles Reel off the Ropes," op. cit.

7. "Textiles: Restless Giant," *The Economist,* January 3, 1981, p. 49.

8. Alvin Rabushka, "Sri Lanka's Experiment in Economic Liberalism," *Wall Street Journal*, May 18, 1981.

9. David Bonavia, "China: The Jobless Generation," *Far Eastern Economic Review,* March 6, 1981, p. 30–31.

10. Jeanne L. Wilson (Political Science, Indiana University, Bloomington, Indiana), "The Role and Status of Women Workers in the People's Republic of China: A Case Study of the Hangzhou Textile Industry 1949–1960," (paper prepared for the Annual Meeting of the Midwest Political Science Association, Cincinnati, April 16–18, 1981); Phyllis Andors, *To Be Liberated* (Bloomington, Indiana University Press, 1983) also assess the Chinese government's policies toward women workers from 1960–1980.

11. "French Textiles," *The Economist*, Nov. 15, 1980, p. 76; *Wall Street Journal*, Jan. 30, 1981.

12. In recognition of this essentially *statist* character of the textile industry, the UN Conference on Trade and Development (UNCTAD) issued a major report in April 1981 calling for the thirty-five to forty textile multinationals who effectively control world textile trade to be subject to interstate controls so as to reduce the increasing gap between developed and developing societies (*Guardian* [London], April 9, 1981).

13. The major interstate agreement shaping the textile trade is the MultiFiber Agreement. It is due for renegotiation in 1981 ("Sewing up the Rag Trade," *Economist*, Dec. 6, 1980).

14. There is now a substantial literature on the internationalized electronics industry, its global strategy, its intraindustry structure (it has been controlled largely by U. S. firms centered in California's famed "Silicon Valley," but now more west European and Japanese firms are making gains), and its use of Southeast Asian young women workers; see Linda Lim, *Women Workers in Multinational Corporations*, Occasional Papers in Women's Studies, no. 9, Ann Arbor, Michican: Fall, 1978; Rachel Grossman, "Women's Place in the Integrated Circuit," in special joint issue of *Southeast Asia Chronicle* and *Pacific Research* on "Changing Role of Southeast Asian Women," 1978–79; Robert Snow, "The New International Division of Labor and the U. S. Workforce: The Case of the Electronics Industry," Honolulu: Working Papers of the East-West Cultural Learning Institute, East-West Center, 1980; Susan Green, "Silicon Valley's Women Workers," Honolulu: Working Papers of the East-West Cultural Learning Institute, East-West Center, 1980; A. Sivanadan, "Imperialism and Disorganic Development in the Silicon Age," *Race and Class* 22, no. 2 (1979), pp. 111–126; Barbara Ehrenreich and Anna Fuentes, "Life on the Global Assembly Line," *Ms*, Jan., 1981; Lenny Siegel, "Delicate Bonds: The Global Semiconductor Industry," *Pacific Research*, Jan. 1981. (Pacific Research also puts out a special newsletter critical of the electronics industry: *Global Electronics Information Newsletter.* 867 West Dana Street, Mountain View, CA. 94041); Jane Khoo and Lai An Eng, "Women Electronic Workers in Penang, Malaysia," Women and Development Project, Institute of Development Studies, University of Sussex, England, Feb. 1981.

15. Linda Gail Arrigo, "The International Work Force of Young Women in Taiwan," *Bulletin of Concerned Asian Scholars* 12, no. 2 (April/June 1980), p. 26.

16. Ibid.

17. These differences between Malay and Chinese women in Singapore should alert us to the different political and economic realities women confront within a single state due to *ethnicity.*

18. Walden Bello, "Building on Martial Law," *Multinational Monitor* 2, no. 2, (Feb. 1981), p. 9.

19. Ibid.

20. Elsa P. Jurado, "Some Sources of Social Tension in Philippine Industrialization" (Paper presented in the Asian Regional Conference on Industrial Relations, Tokyo, Japan, March 13–16, 1979), p. 14. Elsa Jurado is on the faculty of the Political Science Department, University of the Philippines.

21. Ibid.

22. Robert Snow, "Multi National Corporations in Asia: The Labor Intensive Factory," *Bulletin of Cocerned Asian Scholars* 11, no. 4, pp. 28–29. See also Sasahara Kyoko, "Marivales: Servitude in the Free Trade Zone," *AMPO* 12, no. 2 (1980), pp. 74–80.

23. I interviewed Filipino managers and workers in Levi's Manila plant in March 1980; see Cynthia Enloe, "Sex and Levis: The International Sexual Division of Labor," Cambridge, Mass., 1980, available from the author; John Brooks, "Annals of Business: A Friendly Product," *New Yorker Magazine*, Nov. 12, 1979; "A Newly Aggressive Blue Bell," *New York Times*, Feb. 17, 1981.

24. I've tried to think about these questions in two books: Enloe, *Police, Military and Ethnicity: Foundations of State Power* (New Brunswick, N. J.: Transaction Books, 1980); Enloe, *Ethnic Soldiers: State Security in Divided Societies* (London: Penguin Books, 1980 and Athens, Ga.: University of Georgia Press, 1980). See also: Michael Klare, "Militarism: The Issues Today," *Bulletin of Peace Proposals* 2, (1978), pp. 121–128; Ulrich Albrecht, "Technology and Militarization of Third World Countries in Theoretical Perspectives," *Bulletin of Peace* Proposals, no. 2, (1977) pp. 124–126.

25. *New York Times*, Jan. 20, Jan. 25, March 22, 1981; "And After Marcos?", *The Asia Record*, Dec., 1980, supplement.

26. K. Das, "Time for the Big Battalions," *Far Eastern Economic Review*, March 6, 1981, pp. 26–27. This general trend is predicted by Jon Halliday in "Capitalism and Socialism in East Asia," *New Left Review*, no. 124, (Nov.–Dec. 1980), pp. 3–24.

27. Noeleen Heyzer, "The Relocation of International Production and Low-Pay Female Employment: The case of Singapore," in *Women in the Capitalist Process*, eds. Kate Young et al. (London, Harvester Press, 1980); Sasahara Kyoko, op. cit., p. 80; Diane Elson and Ruth Pearson," 'Nimble Fingers Make Cheap Workers': An Analysis of Women's Employment in Third World Export Manufacturing," *Feminist Review*, no. 7 (spring 1981), pp. 87–107.

28. "Outcries of the Poor Workers," *ISIS International Bulletin*, no. 10, special issue on "Women and Work," winter, 1978–79, pp. 7–9. Henry Scott Stokes, "Unions are Battered in Seoul Sweatshops," *New York Times*, March 1, 1981. In July 1982, thousands of women workers in the Bataan EPZ went on strike.

CHAPTER 18

# Global Industries and Malay
# Peasants in Peninsular Malaysia

AIHWA ONG

"The absence of class consciousness in the modern sense does not imply
the absence of classes and class conflict." E.J. Hobsbawm (1971:11)

It is often assumed by scholars in African studies[1] that global
industries in the underdeveloped periphery engender a "labor aristocracy" whose political docility is a necessarily condition for capitalist hegemony. Using data from fieldwork in and around free trade
zones (FTZs) in Peninsular Malaysia, I will argue that the capital-
wage labor relationship should not be construed as mechanistic nor
should the social consequences of class formation and political consciousness be predetermined.

The concept of "labor aristocracy," derived from Lenin
(1974[1939]:14) and employed by Giovanni Arrighi (1967) and Samir
Amin (1976[1973]), makes two basic assumptions. (1) Transnational
corporations in Third World countries necessarily generate a "sem-
iproletariat" (or "semiaristocracy") or a labor aristocracy. A gradualist
progression from the peasantry, through unskilled urban masses, to
a "proletariat proper" is identified, the latter owing their emergence
and consolidation to monopoly capital (Arrighi 1967:239, 256). (2)
Workers in multinational industries all enjoy economic security that

Paper presented at the Eightieth Annual Meeting of the American Anthropological
Association, Dec. 2–6, 1981, Los Angeles, in the session "Development, Underdevelopment, and Economic Transformations." This study is based on field research
funded by the National Science Foundation (BNS-787639) and by the International
Development Research Centre, Ottawa.

enable them to sever ties of social obligations with rural households. Thus, their investment in the status quo and identification with bourgeois values automatically ensure their political quiescence(ibid.; Amin1976:214).

I suggest that the labor aristocracy model is rather deterministic, obscuring social reality and the need for closer inspection of surface phenonmena.[2] In this paper differentiation among Malay workers of multinational corporations in Peninsular Malaysia is examined, in relation to the mode of capitalist integration and the role of the state. Secondly, anthropological research reveals that covert resistance and protests by local groups and isolated individuals are not absent below the surface political tranquility.

## The Internationalization of Capital Accumulation

The point of departure for this discussion is the assumption that in the historical development of a global capitalist system, the different parts of the world became structured in relations of dependence and domination.[3] Under colonial imperialism, the encroachments of merchant capital disrupted noncapitalist modes of production and integrated their producers into the world market economy. In recent decades, this process of unequal trade and production relations became even more intensified as industrial capital has sought labor reserves in the periphery.

Rapid capital accumulation in the United States, Europe, and Japan since the 1950s has required access to labor markets abroad as the latent, relatively surplus population traditionally provided by the agricultural sector becomes used up (Braverman 1974:384). The initial mechanism in this international movement of labor was to import workers from neighbouring less-developed regions; for example, Mexican immigrant workers in the United States and guest workers from the Mediterranean periphery drawn to West Germany and France (Castles 1972).

Technological change in the early 1960s increased the possibility of exporting industries from the central capitalist economics instead of importing workers. The microchip revolution greatly facilitated capital mobility so that massive transfers of labor-intensive industries to the peripheral regions became feasible and profitable. Multinational corporations, by distributing their production activities all over the world, impose a vertical integration that cuts across national, political, and ethnic lines, incorporating peoples of economically less-developed countries in a new international division of labor (Amin, 1976; Braverman 1974: 251–289; Frobel et al. 1979). The large-scale export of unskilled occupations to the periphery has brought about changes in the capital-wage labor relationship.

The electronics industry best exemplifies the process whereby technological change and "a *changing* product bring about new and different process of labor, a new occupational distribution of the employed population, and thus a changed working class" (Braverman 1978:253). In the electronics industry, technological research and automated production of some components are retained at the metropolitan center while the labor-intensive processes are exported to the periphery, where Third World laborers, especially rural women, become the ideal reservoir for the manual assembly of microcomponents.

Market considerations and production costs are usually the main factors for overseas processing carried out by subsidiaries of multinational corporations. The Japanese electronics industry, for instance, following the 1974 Arab oil embargo and labor shortage at home, made massive investments in southeast Asia (Kenji 1977:41). Malaysia became a popular locale for such labor-intensive industries because of her good infrastructural facilities and relatively well educated population. By late 1970s there were 138 electronics firms in the country, mainly Japanese owned, which employed 47,000 workers, overwhelmingly female. Manufacturing has become, in this agrarian economy, the largest generator of new jobs (30 percent of the total) for women (*Malaysian Digest* Jan. 31, 1981, p. 7). Over 50 percent of these industrial workers were Malay, most of them newly arrived from the countryside. Furthermore, the state played a major role in ensuring these laborers for the transnational industries.

## The Role of the State and the Modern Corporation

Malaysia is a neocolonial economy[4] that exports most of the world's supplies of rubber, tin, palm oil, and tropical timber. Over half of her thirteen million popultion are Malays, primarily smallholders engaged in the production of rice, rubber, and other cash crops. The descendants of Chinese and Indian immigrants are dominant in plantation agriculture, tin mining, commerce, tertiary services, and the urban professions. In recent years government projects and extension of credit have helped generated a small Malay middle class in towns. Besides, an export-oriented industrialization program was introduced in the early 1970s to help restructure the existing ethnic division of labor by bringing more Malays into the industrial work force.[5]

The Malay-dominated smallholder sector of the economy has been declining in the past two decades. High population growth, land fragmentation under Islamic rules of inheritance, land concentration by the upperclass peasantry and salariat, and dominance by merchant and usury capital have increased impoverishment among Malay peasants (Fisk 1962, Swift 1968). The dislocated peasant economy thus released an increasing surplus of near landless, under-employed and unemployed people to the towns. Labor-intensive, export-oriented industrialization, by absorbing Malay migrants into previously Chinese- and Indian-dominated blue-collar occupations, was seen as a solution to the threat of economic and political unrest. There are currently fifty-nine industrial estates in the country, of which nine are free trade zones. In these zones, industries set up by foreign investors can apply for "pioneer" status, which qualifies them for tax relief for up to ten years, minimal customs fees for import and export of materials, and free transfers of capital and profits[6] (FIDA 1978: 9–17).

Besides lowering tariff barriers to the entry of capital, the state has tightened up its labor laws to ensure a politically controlled labor force, which the foreign companies consider a necessary condition for profit-maximization. This assurance is spelled out in a government investment brochure. Investment policies, it is explained, were formulated to favor the needs of the labor-intensive, export-oriented industries—"Adequate legislation in industrial relations ensures the maintenance of industrial peace and harmony, thereby guaranteeing the smooth operation of production without undue disruptions" (FIDA 1978:11). In practice, this labor legislation, both by omission and by implementation, has facilitated the multinational corporations in their selective use of the local population as a labor reserve to be attracted and discharged according to world market conditions.

Government labor laws neglected to set a legal minimum to the wage rate in the country nor were attempts made to equalize the wage levels of male and female workers. Thus, the large-scale entry of labor-intensive industries such as garment manufacturing, food processing, but especially electronics assembly greatly increased the absorption of rural Malay women into the industrial labor force. In 1970, there were not more than one thousand Malay migrant women employed in manufacturing; by 1976 it was estimated that over sixty thousand of them were found in various manufacturing companies

(Jamilah Ariffin 1981). They represented a fairly well-educated labor pool, which was often overqualified for the mass semiskilled factory occupations. About 50 percent of these workers had at least lower secondary education, and many had aspired to become typists, secretaries, trainee nurses, or teachers. Failing to gain entry into white-collar positions, these women migrants, who included illiterates as well as graduates from primary and secondary schools, were absorbed into the factories as semiskilled operators, with little or no prospects for job promotion (Jamilah Ariffin 1981, Munster 1980).[7]

The state also encouraged transnational corporations to locate factories in the countryside so that Malay peasant women could become industrial workers without leaving their *kampong* ("villages").[8] As part of this attempt at rural industrialization a small FTZ was set up in Kuala Langat, a coastal district in Selangor where I did fieldwork. In this region of plantations and Malay villages producing coconut, coffee, rubber, and oil palm, three Japanese companies installed electronics and micromachine factories in the mid-1970s. By 1979 there were approximately two thousand employees in these factories, the majority of them young Malay women recruited from the local villages and other agricultural districts. The operators were usually aged between sixteen and twenty-five, not yet married, and living at home with their parents. They commuted to the FTZ daily in buses or on bicycles. Their wages were between $3.10 and $4.55 per day, which was about two dollars less than wages earned by their counterparts in urban FTZs (e.g., in Sungai Way). Nevertheless, these meagre earnings came to form regular supplementary incomes to their village households, many of which depended on nonagricultural earnings in addition to cash crop production.

Maximum production output was extracted from these rural women by the factories, which employed them as "instruments of labor". Quickly exhausted operators were replaced by the next crop of school leavers. By keeping the wages low, the factories motivated the operators to work overtime on a regular basis, to take on more unpleasant tasks (which exposed them to fumes and acids), or to work at an increased pace in order to earn special cash allowances (see also Grossman 1979:11). Freshly recruited workers were routinely assigned to the production processes[9] that required continual use of microscopes. Thus most workers, by the end of a couple of years, suffered from eye strain and deterioration of their eyesight. A few continued in the same section by wearing glasses; others were transfered to nonmicroscope work sections although many had to resign because their physical capacity for the work had literally been used up.[10]

The industrial firms not only exploited the workers in this manner, but they also attempted to limit their employment to the early stage of their adult life, a strategy that ensured fresh labor capable of sustained intensive work at low wages.[11] In one factory new workers were employed on six month contracts so that they could be released or rehired at the same low wage rates. Government legislation for the protection of pregnant female workers has had the unintended effect of reinforcing factory policy to discourage married women from applying, although employed workers who got married could stay on. Married workers were given advice on family planning and provided with free contraceptives by the factory clinic.

The rapid exhaustion of the operators also resulted in most of them leaving of their own accord after three to four years of factory employment, although an increasing number remained working, even after marriage. Operators leaving the factories have not acquired any skills which would equip them for any but the same dead-end jobs.[12] The lack of legislative protection for women in the labor market and their low wages discouraged them from staying on longer in industrial employment. This weak structural integration of the women in the industrial sector, a situation fostered by corporate employment strategy, has been used by male supremacists and capitalists to justify the low wages of operators in multinational corporations.

The higher turnover of the female workers is also a mechanism for disrupting union formation. Malaysian labor laws allowed union formation in the so-called pioneer industries but only by workers who have been employed for three consecutive years. In practice, this regulation has not come into effect because the government registrar has refused to register any union set up by electronics workers (Lim 1978), who represented the majority of women in industries. Even unionized workers in male-dominated industries were severely restricted by the "industrial relations law," which forbade work to rule over dismissals by the management and prohibited strikes once a dispute has been brought before the industrial court (FIDA, 1978:11). Thus, between 1963 and 1973, the time lost in strikes declined from over 305,000 days to 40,000 days (a reduction to one-eighth) while the workers involved in these strikes had increased fourfold, from 17,200 to 64,000 (Hassan & Sundram 1980).

In the Kuala Langat FTZ, two factories had set up a company union and a "consultative committee" to monitor and control workers' grievances. Following repeated rejections of their proposals, the workers lost confidence in their representatives. In the third factory, regular management-parents' meetings took the place of any pretense at union-type activities set up by the management. The state labor laws, in thus delivering women to the industries without any legal defence of their employment situation, facilitated the creation of an unending flow of cheap female labor at the disposal of industrial capitalism.

## Differentiation of the Industrial Workers

The massive investments by transnational corporation in Malaysia have thus produced an increasingly heterogeneous industrial labor force that may be differentiated according to ethnicity, skill grades, security of employment, and sex. Capital-intensive industries such as metal and rubber goods production, vehicular assembly, lumber mills, and sea port services employed a small but growing proportion of skilled Malay male workers. These formed the core of a permanent Malay working class, largely resident in towns. Because they enjoyed a relative degree of employment security, they could ensure their own long-term reproduction without depending on social relations with their home villages.

A significant majority of workers in the multinational industries were, however, temporarily employed, poorly paid, semiskilled women. Thousands of these workers lived in crowded rooming houses in the periphery of the urban FTZs, trying to make ends meet on their low wages as well as to remit monthly sums of money to village families (Jamilah Ariffin 1980). This industrial preference for rural female labor also benefitted the state, because women could be relied upon to accept poorly paid "supplementary" employment on the one hand and on the other their daily domestic activities ensured the cheap provision of the labor force required for the economic development of the country.

Foreign industries in Malaysia, then, have generated two opposing but related processes of labor differentiation among Malay migrants.[13] A gradual process of proletarianization has occurred among Malay male migrants employed as skilled industrial workers who earned sufficient incomes to keep their families in towns. However, more recent male migrants have only managed to become casual laborers in the informal sector or merely swelled the urban population of the stagnant unemployed.[14] On the other hand, the great increase in the employment of rural women for a short phase of their life cycle has rapidly expanded a "floating" labor reserve army in the countryside. It is doubtful whether this ever-replenished labor pool would ever be employed as labor-intensive industries continue to convert more processes to full automation. The Japanese director of an electronics firm explained that "the time will come when in Malaysia we cannot rely on manual labor."[15]

For the present, the semiskilled workers have not been integrated into an industrial work force capable of maintaining itself; they relied on the home villages or urban informal sector for social security and reproduction (see Munster 1980). Operating from the smallholder economy, peasant households regularly send grown children for short- and long-term cash employment in the towns and FTZs. Wage employment is part of peasant adaptations to noneconomical holdings, so that wage earnings form an alternative or supplement to cash cropping. This process of "peasantization of wage employment" (Leys 1971:316) in Kuala Langat meant that families with daughters employed in factories received from 10 percent to 75 percent of monthly income in wages. A random survey of 242 village households revealed that 50 percent of the directly productive women, and 39 percent of the men were earning wages in the industrial sector.

Wherever the female workers sought employment, most of their families remained in the *kampong*, still the social and political focus of Malay life. Services provided by rural households in raising children, housework, and caring for the unemployed, sick, and aged ensured the daily maintenance of the workers and the reproduction of the next generation. Interhousehold relations shared resources, credit, and services. This mutual assistance enabled families to survive crises that involved extraordinary expenses or the loss of a household wage earner. Long-term social security for individuals and families was thus provided by reciprocal relations maintained between village households and between migrants and the village community. This rural safety net ensured protection against unexpected contingencies such as the sudden layoffs of industrial workers,[16] and thus enabled them to perpetuate themselves in the interstices between industrial capitalism and small-scale peasant agriculture.

In this symbiosis of the Malay peasant economy and the FTZ industrialization, the semiskilled workers of the multinational corporations cannot be considered a working class, much less a labor aristocracy. In the objective sense of *class*, these workers were mainly of poor peasant background, employed as the lowest category of exploited factor labor. Nevertheless, the limited and contingent nature of their employment means that they properly constitute a labor reserve army. Women released from factory employment, for instance, became part of the population of casual workers in the urban milieu, picking up earnings as shop assistants, seamstresses, food vendors, petrol pump attendants, and prostitutes.[17] Others married skilled industrial workers and became incorporated into the nascent Malay proletariat. In Kuala Langat, former factory women married peasants and rural laborers and remained part of the village communities.

The fluid composition and heterogeneity of this labor reserve were also reflected in their lack of a specific class consciousness. However, the absence of collective labor organization did not mean that the women workers were passive victims of exploitation. Consciousness of exploitation in the experience of labor was fragmented into local groups and individuals who undertook isolated acts of protests. Alternately, the experience of not being treated like "human beings" made for a universal sense of injustice. This at once narrow and global social consciousness, common in preindustrial societies, often went beyond any consciousness of "classness" (Hobsbawm 1971:10). One operator described the traumatic change from self-directed work in the village to the external discipline of the assembly line:

> "The workers want fair treatment. . . . we have to work three shifts and when the night shift comes round we feel sort of drowsy and yet have to use the microscopes. With our wages so low we feel as though we have been tricked or forced into work. . . . sometimes the manager puts a lot of pressure on our production as if he does not think of us as human beings too. . . . thus from time to time we must protest"[18]

With no collective means to channel their grievances and restrained by Malay cultural prohibitions against expressions of anger and dissatisfaction, the women workers resorted to oblique cultural strategies of protest.

Malay girls are socialized to be submissive and loyal, in accordance with village notions of female modesty. Females are considered especially vulnerable to spirit possession and other supernatural dangers, a belief which operates as a sanction against self-assertion on the part of young unmarried women (Ackerman 1979:13). Malay operators, in an unconscious inversion of its function, found in spirit possession (*kena hantu*) a mode of indirect retaliation on the shop floor. Since the large-scale employment of Malay women in industries from the late 1960s, local newspapers have reported mass hysteria

434

outbreaks among Malay operators (*Asiaweek*, Aug. 4, 1978). The incidents usually began with one (or more) victim suddenly crying and screaming, running around and struggling fiercely with anyone coming to her aid. The seizure was soon transmitted to nearby Malay workers who joined in a mass hysteria so that sometimes the entire work section or factory floor had to be closed down. The management then was compelled to give the afflicted workers medical leave for a few days (Lim 1978:32–33; Grossman 1979:16). In her study of spirit possession among Malay factory women, Ackerman (1979) points out that the victims were usually not considered responsible for their affliction and were not punished. In effect, the enactment of this ritualized rebellion by the operators did not directly confront the real cause of their distress and instead, by operating as a safety valve, tended to reinforce existing unequal relations.

In the Kuala Langat FTZ, spirit possession episodes were very common soon after the first factory opened in 1975. By the end of the year, a local *imam* had to be called in to cleanse ritually the factory premises. Thereafter, spirit-possession incidents among workers were reduced to once every few weeks and involved small numbers of victims. Most of the afflicted workers were from the microscope sections (mounting and pin insertion); they usually reported seeing spirits in the microscopes or in the locker rooms (where they sought refuge from the work bench). Spirit-possession episodes have become so routine that coworkers gained experience in dealing with the victims and limiting work disruption.

In another factory the management was less tolerant; it was a widely known but unwritten rule that any worker with two past episodes of hysteria was to be dismissed "for security reasons." When the village elders protested, pointing out that the spirits in the factory were responsible for their daughters' seizures, the manager agreed but explained that the hysterical workers might hurt themselves on the machines, risking electrocution.

Operators often attempted to seek relief from the mind-deadening work by asking permission to go to the locker room; alternately, they sought permission to go to the prayer room, where as Muslims they could perform the obligatory worship five times a day. Factory foremen, who were usually Chinese and Indian men, sometimes refused them permission if their requests were too frequent or else monitored their movements once they left the work bench. Operators thus found particular foremen to be too zealous about enforcing work discipline and too insistent in pressing for high production targets.

Village men sometimes performed acts of violence on behalf of women workers when their oblique strategies of resistance failed. Operators reported their grievances about certain hard-driving foremen to their village families. *Kampong* youths then ganged up on the blacklisted foremen, attacking them with sticks as they left the factory in the evening. A few such incidents had occurred since 1976, involving attacks on one Chinese, one Indian, and two Malay foremen (all originally from outside the district), who were so badly beatened up that they had to be hospitalized and sutured. Rural youths, resentful that they were not qualified for the positions of factory foremen, had warned all the male supervisory staff in the FTZ against mistreating the operators.

The workers themselves, in their daily life, made covert protests by damaging the components that they had painstakingly assembled. In one transistor factory, where about five million components were assembled each month, sometimes tens of thousands of transistors had to be rejected because of defects found. Occasionally, workers delibertely stalled the machines so that production was slowed down. A Malay technician reported that he was aware of these subversive acts but said that it was impossible to trace the workers responsible for them. Besides, he felt that their aggression was legitimate because there was too much discipline enforced at work, and the operators had no one to listen to their complaints.[19] There appeared, then, to be a growing political consciousness[20] among industrial workers, which, however ineffective, has identified the points of conflicting interests with the management.

In summary then, metropolitan capital in its latest stage of accumulation has engendered a multiplicity of working classes from the disintegrating Malay peasant society. This process has thus far involved the peasantization of wage employment rather than the proletarianization of peasants. Casual laborers, peddlers, car attendants, waitresses, paupers were as much a product of the transnational corporations as were unskilled operators and skilled industrial workers; these have not yet coalesced into a working class. If we take *class* to be "a self-defining historical formation, which men and women make out of their own experience of struggle" (Thompson 1978:46), then we need to go beyond convenient rubrics like *labor aristocracy* and analyse the details of classes "in the making."

## Notes

1. Lenin considered the "labour aristocracy" as "the principal *social* (not military) *prop of the bourgeoisie.* They are the real *agents of the bourgeoisie in the labour movement. . . .*" (1974 [1939]:14). Franz Fanon applied this model to the workers in colonial territories. He remarked that "the proletariat is the nucleus of the colonized population which has been most pampered by the colonial regime. The embryonic proletariat of the towns is in a comparatively privileged position . . . representing that fraction of the colonised nation which is necessary and irreplaceable if the colonial machinery is to run smoothly . . ." (1963:108–109). This theme was picked up by Peter Worsley, who argued that "urban workers in large scale industries . . . are unrevolutionary" (1967:160–163).

2. See Colin Leys (1971) for his criticism of the "deterministic model" substituting itself for reality in neocolonial Africa. Gregory McLennan (1981) comments that the paradigm was not an explanatory tool but rather a social and ideological phenonmenon itself in need of closer description.

3. See Bukharin 1973 (1929), Banaji 1973, Wallerstein 1974, Amin 1976(1972).

4. In the early 1970s, over 60 percent of the country's wealth was controlled by foreign interests (Government Press 1976: 183).

5. Following racial riots in May 1969, the Malaysian government formulated a New Economic Policy (NEP) that aimed at the "progressive transformation of the country's racially-compartmentalized economic system into one in which the composition of Malaysian society is *visibly* reflected in its countryside and towns, farms and factories, shops and offices" (Government Printing Press 1976:9—italics added). Since then the percentage of Malays employed in manufacturing (in the lower ranks of occupations) has increased from 29 percent in 1970 to 38 percent in 1978 (*New Straits Times,* Mar. 20, 1979).

6. These pioneer industries are also guaranteed against nationalization; they are encouraged to have joint ownership with Malaysians, but this proposal is not usually compulsory.

7. A Japanese engineer at the Kuala Langat FTZ explained to me that "the highly educated person is very hard to control; there is a very low resignation rate for standard six graduates."

8. See Susan Ackerman (1979) for her study of industrial conflict in rural factories located in Malacca.

9. For a detailed presentation of my findings, see my *Women and Industries: Malay Peasants in Coastal Selangor 1975–80,* Ph.D. thesis, Columbia Univeristy. 1982.

10. The basic production processes in an electronics factory in 1979–1980 included selecting out pellets, pin insertion, mounting, bonding, moulding, quality control and packaging. The first four processes required continual use of the microscope for intricate assembling of parts of components. The average number of mountings an operator was expected to do was 2,500 per day, although some operators could assemble 4,600 components. In the bonding section, workers processed between 3,200 to 6,000 components daily (i.e., in each eight hour shift).

11. An in-factory survey found that on the average, young unmarried women (aged 16 to 24 years) in the bonding and mounting sections, could assemble 1,400 more components per day than married women, aged 25–28. (These sections had more workers than other processes.). The factory supervisor commented, "It is very clear that married ladies cannot handle microscopes [sic] jobs".

12. The Japanese director of a factory commented succinctly, "Fresh female labor, after some training, is highly efficient."

13. A worker in the Sungai Way FTZ told a reporter, "If I could get an office job I would *belah* ["split"] from this place. There's no future here. There are thousands of us and only a few promotions" (*New Straits Times*, August 31, 1979).

14. See Bravermann (1978:391–392) for an analysis of such trends in the working class under monopoly capitalism.

15. Unemployment among youths 15–19 years was 19 percent in the towns, and 17 percent in the countryside, according to government figures for 1976. The majority of these unemployed youths were Malays, with at least lower secondary education (Government Press 1976:141). D.J. Blake notes that since the 1960s, the average length of unemployment seemed to have increased among these youthful educated people; the expectations raised by their education might have contributed to their long periods of job hunting (1975). Most Malay youths and increasingly young women from all over the peninsula migrate to the Klang valley and Penang in search of work. The unsuccessful ones live in poverty, pick up cash by guarding and washing cars, although some become absorbed into the drug culture (*New Straits Times* Oct. 10, 1977).

16. He went on to say that in general, material wastage was higher when manpower was used than in automation. Machines were better at quality control than human beings and took up less space and time. He complained that the costs of taking back defective components was very high. "With automation, manpower is changed from assembling to tending machines." In his factory, this process had already begun, with full automation planned for the end of 1979. The existing 900 operators could be retained because production would be expanded.

17. In the 1974–75 recession, thousands of electronics workers in Singapore and Malaysia were suddenly laid off (Lim 1978:230). After being retrenched, some Malay women did not return to their villages but sought to make a living as prostitutes.

18. "Pekerja kehendakan keadilan . . . kita ni mempunya tiga *shift* jadi bila tiba *midnight shift* tu kan kita rasa macam mengantukkan jadi kita kena pakai *microscope*, dah tu gaji kita rendah kita rasa jadi macam seolah macam dipaksa. . . . (*manager*) kandang kadang dia terlampau sangat kan menderih kita bekerja sedangkan dia tak fikir bahawa kita ni pun manusia bukannya apakan jadi ada kalanya kita mesti membatahkan. . . ." Operators in the Kuala Langat FTZ had to work eight-hour shifts, doing three shifts in turn. They had two fifteen minute breaks and a half hour for lunch. They were at the bottom of a work hierarchy that included male supervisors, foremen, technicians, female charge hands and line leaders. Many operators, unused to the air conditioning, suffered from persistent colds and chest pains.

19. "There is a great deal of discipline . . . but when there is too much discipline, it is not good because the operators, due to their small wages, frequently rebel; they often damage the machines in ways that are not apparent. . . . Sometimes they damage the products. . . . Such actions were carried out by individual operators, on their own. I feel that it is indeed proper that they do this because their wages are small and so we cannot blame them. Blaming operator is nothing . . . if they have problems they will not tell anyone, because (foremen, supervisors) will not listen to their complaints. . . . I don't know why—because they do not have a union." (*Discipline* mestilah banyak . . . tapi kalau banyak *discipline* pun kurang baik, sebab itu *operator* tu kadang kadang kan dia gaji kechil, dia selalu melawan, dia merosak-rosakkan *machine* selalu kan dengan cara yang tidak ketara. . . . Kadang kadang merosakkan *product* ke, itu semua. Jadi itu terpulang kepada *individual operator* lah, masing masing. Saya rasa memang patut mereka buat bagitu sebab gaji mereka pun kechil jadi kita tak boleh *blame* dia. *Blaming operator is nothing* sebab . . . jadi kalau dia ada masaalah mereka tak akan memberi tahu sesiapa. Sebab tak akan mendengar cakap cakap dia . . tak tahu . . . sebab tak ada [*union*].

20. This needs to be documented and analysed further than I have done here to reveal the great variations in social consciousness, given the enduring social stratificatory system in Malay society. As Joan Vincent cautions in her study of peasantization in colonial eastern Uganda, "Only further, more detailed, analysis of household economies and family histories can account for the multiplicity of forms that political protest took in Teso, its processual nature and, above all, its continuities and discontinuities" (1978:12).

# References

Ackerman, Susan E. 1979. "Industrial Conflict in Malaysia: A Case Study of Rural Malay Female Workers." Unpublished MS.

Amin, Samir. 1976 (1973). *Unequal Development: An Essay on the Social Formation of Peripheral Capitalism,* New York: Monthly Review Press.

Arrighi, Giovanni. 1976. "International Corporations, Labor Aristocracies and Economic Development in Tropical Africa." In *Imperialism and Underdevelopment,* ed. R.I. Rhodes.

Banaji, J. 1973. "Backward Capitalism, Primitive Accumulation and Modes of Production." *Journal of Contemporary Asia* 3 no. 4, pp. 393–414.

Blake, D. J. 1975. "Unemployment: The West Malaysia Example." In *Readings in Malaysian Economic Development.* Kuala Lumpur: Oxford University Press, 1975.

Braverman, Harry. 1974. *Labor and Monopoly Capital: The Degradation of Work in the Twentieth Century,* New York: Monthly Review Press.

Bukharin, N. 1973 (1929). *Imperialism and World Economy.* New York: Monthly Review Press.

Castles, S and Kosack, G. 1972. "The Function of Labour Immigration in Western European Capitalism." *New Left Review* 73.

Fanon, Franz. 1963 (1961). *The Wretched of the Earth.* New York: Grove Press.

FIDA (Federal Industrial Development Authority, Malaysia). 1978. *Malaysia: Your Profit Centre in Asia.* Kuala Lumpur.

Fisk, E.K. 1963. "Features of the Rural Economy." In *The Political Economy of Independent Malaya,* E.H. Silcock and E.K. Fisk. Berkeley: University of California Press.

Fröbel, F.; Heinrichs, J. and Kreye, O. 1980 (1977). *The New International Division of Labour: Structural Unemployment in Industrialized Countries and Industrialization in Developing Countries.* London: Cambridge University Press.

Government Press, Malaysia. 1976. *Third Malaysia Plan, 1976–1980.* Kuala Lumpur.

440

Grossman, Rachel. 1979. "Women's Place in the Integrated Circuit." *Southeast Asia Chronicle,* no. 66.

Hassan, O.R. and Sundaram, J.K.. 1980. "Wage Trends in Peninsular Malaysia Manufacturing, 1963–1973." Paper presented at the 6th. Convention of the Malaysian Economic Association, Penang, May 1980.

Hobsbawm, E.J. 1971. "Class Consciousness in History." In *Aspects of History and Class Consciousness,* ed. I. Meszaros. London: Routledge & K. Paul.

Jamilah Ariffin. 1980. "The Position of Women Workers in the Manufacturing Industries in Malaysia." Paper presented at the Consumers' Association of Penang Seminar, Nov. 1980.

Lenin, V.I. 1974 (1939). *Imperialism, the Highest Stage of Capitalism: A Popular Outline.* New York: International.

Leys, Colin. 1971. "Politics in Kenya: The Development of Peasant Society." *British Journal of Political Science.* 1:301–337.

Lim, Linda Y.C. 1978. "Women Workers in Multinational Corporations: The Case of the Electronics Industry in Malaysia and Singapore." *Michigan Occasional Paper,* no. 9.

McLennan, Gregor. 1981. "'The Labour Aristocracy' and 'Incorporation': Notes on Some Terms in the Social History of the Working Class." *Social History.* 6:1.

Munster, Anne-Marie. 1980. "Export of Industries and Changing Structures of the International Labour Market." Paper presented at the Consumers' Association of Penang Seminar, Nov. 1980.

Nakano Kenji. 1977. "Japan's Overseas Investment Patterns and FTZs." In *AMPO* special issue, *Free Trade Zones and Industrialization of Asia.* Tokyo.

Ong Aihwa. 1982. *Women and Industry: Malay Peasants in Coastal Selangor, 1975–80.* Ph.D. thesis, Columbia University.

S. Husin Ali. 1975. *Malay Peasant Society and Leadership.* Kuala Lumpur: Oxford University Press.

Swift, Michael. 1976. "Economic Concentration and Malay Peasant Society." In *Social Organization,* ed. Maurice Freedman. London: Cass.

Thompson, E.P. 1978. *The Poverty of Theory and Other Essays.* New York: Monthly Review Press.

Worsley, Peter. 1964. *The Third World.* University of Chicago Press.

Vincent, Joan. 1978. "Political Consciousness and Struggle among an African Peasantry." Paper presented at the IUEAS meeting, Lucknow, 1978.

# Index

*443*